AN
AFRICAN
HISTORY
OF
AFRICA

AN
AFRICAN
HISTORY
OF
AFRICA

From the Dawn of Humanity
to Independence

ZEINAB BADAWI

President of SOAS University of London

I

WH Allen, an imprint of Ebury Publishing
20 Vauxhall Bridge Road
London SW1V 2SA

WH Allen is part of the Penguin Random House group of companies
whose addresses can be found at global.penguinrandomhouse.com

Penguin
Random House
UK

Copyright © Zeinab Badawi 2024
Maps © Helen Stirling

Zeinab Badawi has asserted her right to be identified as the author of this
Work in accordance with the Copyright, Designs and Patents Act 1988

First published by WH Allen in 2024

www.penguin.co.uk

A CIP catalogue record for this book is available from the British Library

Hardback ISBN 9780753560129
Trade Paperback ISBN 9780753560136

Typeset in 13.5/16 pt Garamond MT Std by Jouve (UK), Milton Keynes
Printed and bound in Great Britain by Clays Ltd, Elcograf S.p.A.

The authorised representative in the EEA is Penguin Random House Ireland,
Morrison Chambers, 32 Nassau Street, Dublin D02 YH68

Penguin Random House is committed to a sustainable future
for our business, our readers and our planet. This book is made
from Forest Stewardship Council® certified paper.

MIX
Paper | Supporting
responsible forestry
FSC® C018179

For my mother Asia Malik and my father M.K. Badawi

Africa Today

Mediterranean Sea

Morocco
Tunisia
Algeria
Libya
Egypt

*Western Sahara

Cabo Verde
Mauritania
Mali
Niger
Chad
Sudan
Eritrea
Djibouti

Red Sea

Senegal
Gambia
Guinea-Bissau
Guinea
Burkina Faso
Sierra Leone
Côte d'Ivoire
Liberia
Nigeria
Central African Republic
South Sudan
Ethiopia
Somalia

Ghana Togo
Benin
Cameroon
Uganda
Kenya

Equatorial Guinea
Gabon
Democratic Rep. of Congo
Rwanda
Burundi
Tanzania

São Tomé and Príncipe
Congo

Seychelles

Comoros

Angola
Zambia
Malawi

Mauritius
Réunion

Namibia
Zimbabwe
Mozambique
Botswana
Madagascar

Atlantic Ocean

Lesotho
Eswatini
South Africa

Indian Ocean

0   1000 miles
0   2000 km

* Non-self-governing territory

Contents

CONTENTS

Introduction

Everyone is originally from Africa, and this book is therefore for everyone.

Africa is the birthplace of humankind itself, yet little of its ancient and modern history is widely known. It has an extraordinary past: engrossing narratives of warrior queens, kings, chiefs, priests and priestesses; of mighty civilisations blooming on the banks of rivers or in the shade of sacred mountains; of lavish buildings hewn out of rock, exquisite libraries bursting with discovery, bustling caravan routes and market squares thick with the voices of traders, travellers, farmers and entertainers.

But for many, the history of Africa begins only a few centuries ago, with the arrival of the Europeans. It has been dominated by the subjects of slavery, imperialism and colonialism, and written mostly by Western historians, missionaries and explorers. And while these are of critical importance, Africa's history is more than that.

I wanted to write this book because it is the kind of work I wish I had been able to find and read myself many years ago. As a person born under the African sun, I had long been aware of the continent's rich history. But it was a fragmented knowledge, and I searched in vain for an accessible and relatively comprehensive history of Africa, highlighting key chapters in its story – and told by Africans themselves.

At last, I had the opportunity to embark on such a project myself, and it is one that has engaged me for the best part of a decade. Over a period of about seven years I visited more than 30 African countries, and travelled across these nations in pursuit of a first-hand experience of Africa's history from the perspective of Africans. This book draws on my conversations and the interviews I conducted with dozens of people, ranging from academics to ordinary engaged citizens, who enlightened me about their culture, history and the amazing sites I visited. Some of these were off the beaten track, such as the ancient ruins of Eritrea, or Chinguetti in Mauritania, while some were tricky or risky to get to, such as Timbuktu in Mali, or the Hausa parts of northern Nigeria. I used just about every means of transport known to humankind, from modern sleek 4x4 vehicles, to riding on camelback and donkey carts. I was awestruck by the beauty of the continent: the natural wonders such as the Falls of the Zambezi River in Zimbabwe, or the vast territory of Katanga in the Congo and the Virunga Mountains of Rwanda.

I wish to introduce the history of Africa to all readers who want to dispel the myopia of a post-imperial education and especially to young students with an African background seeking to learn more about their history. Most people would struggle to name an African king beyond Tutankhamun, and few of them would even be able to give the years of his reign. One former African president told me he was better able to list the names of English medieval kings than those in Africa. This is not an academic book, nor is it about 'contested history' – setting one narrative against another in a confrontational framework. Nor does it seek to make comparisons between civilisations. I aim to provide a counter-balance to the many negative perceptions of the continent and its people, improve our collective understanding of its history by ventilating African scholarship that has been occluded, and in this way reveal a different and more honest history of Africa.

This book is an overview of the continent from the beginning of humanity to the modern era. It is by no means comprehensive, and there is plenty of history that I could not include. As much as possible, the focus is on pre-colonial history rather than on what occurred in the twentieth century, since contemporary history and current events have received more attention and coverage. I have selected personalities who helped shape the continent because I believe history is most easily understood when it is seared into the imagination. The figures examined are predominantly rulers, since sources drawn from African oral tradition consist largely of the lives and deeds of leaders. To those who will admonish me for omitting certain individuals, I apologise in advance. I could not do justice to everyone in a single book. I have strived to cover all regions of Africa and emphasised the significant role that women play.

We begin with the origins of humankind: what makes us unique, and how human societies and culture developed. I celebrate our common and shared beginnings. In chapter 2 we move to ancient Egypt, the best-known aspect of Africa's history, for a comprehensive overview. Less famous are the histories of ancient Sudan, Ethiopia and Eritrea – civilisations that gave rise to magnificent monuments and which are the focus of chapters 3, 4 and 5. In chapters 6 and 7, I explore the early story of North Africa and the strong impact the region had on the three major monotheistic religions. The fabulously wealthy Mansa Musa, the fourteenth-century king of the Mali Empire, is the centrepiece of chapter 8, in which we will also examine the kingdoms of West Africa. The lesser-known Indian Ocean trade in enslaved Africans that lasted a thousand years is the topic of chapter 9, while in chapter 10 we look at Benin, whose bronzes have been the focus of efforts to repatriate looted and stolen African artwork, 90 per cent of which is found outside of the continent. The southern kingdoms of Africa are the focus of the following chapter, including Great Zimbabwe, a civilisation that Europeans refused to believe was built by Africans. The Asante people, and in particular Queen Mother Yaa Asantewaa, are the subject of chapters 12 and 13. In chapter 14 we revisit the tragic topic of slavery, this time examining the impact of the transatlantic trade on Africans and their continent. European invasions and occupation underscore chapters 15, 16 and 17, but the protagonists are always African, including King Shaka Zulu, Queen Njinga and the heroic communities who resisted European rule and fought for liberation. Finally, the Epilogue reflects on the future of the continent, and how it is being shaped by Africa's youth.

I fervently hope that you will emerge with a stronger and deeper knowledge of Africa's history and be encouraged to learn more about the subjects I have covered.

In my research for this book I was privileged to meet some of Africa's best academics. Their passion, rigour and brilliance, even in resource-starved university departments, are remarkable and merit a much wider audience. Every single academic I met was extremely generous with their time, even when the perils of traffic and a packed schedule meant I was sometimes late for appointments. So keen were they to be heard that they were to a man and woman gracious about my tardiness and indeed I often had to tear myself away from them to reach my next destination.

I also relied greatly on the work of a unique project called the *General History of Africa*, the *GHA*, which is one of the continent's best-kept secrets: Africa's history, written largely by African scholars. The project was begun in the early 1960s, during the period of rapid decolonisation in Africa. Several of the newly independent African leaders decided that, after decolonising their countries, they also wanted to decolonise their history, so they approached UNESCO (the UN's Educational, Scientific and Cultural Organization) to help them implement the project. UNESCO formed a special committee and identified the continent's leading historians, anthropologists, archaeologists and experts in other fields. In total, UNESCO gathered around 350 scholars – mostly African – to undertake this work. They compiled 11 volumes with more to come, starting from the origins of humankind and evolution, and continuing to contemporary eras. They used written records, including those that had been overlooked; as well as archaeology, art, song, poetry, oral storytelling, traditions, dance, craft and archaeobotany. Using the *GHA* as my inspiration and compass, my sources and references are predominantly African and non-European, in contrast to the many histories of Africa written by Western authors.

I was struck by the words of the late Kenyan palaeoanthropologist Dr Richard Leakey, who was a good friend, and is sadly missed by many, including me. He told me that it was imperative to challenge the prejudices some people hold 'in their thinking about Africa. It will probably take time to break that down; but break it down we must, and we do so – not with fairy tales but with facts.' So this book is my attempt to do just that.

I

Our Family and Other Hominins

As the young museum attendant diligently unlocked the door I was full of excitement. I was about to meet a superstar – albeit one who had been dead for millions of years. With great reverence and awe I gently stroked her hand with the tip of a finger and felt as though I had made contact with a long-lost relative. This was Lucy, or Dinkenesh, as she is known in Ethiopia – part of the lineage that eventually led to us: *Homo sapiens sapiens*, Latin for 'wise and thinking man'.

Africa is where it all began for us modern humans. We should be united by our shared beginning in a way that enables us to look beyond race, to a time when such differences did not exist. When one examines the long history of humankind, it becomes apparent that racial differentiation is a relatively recent occurrence; genetics present us with facts that are at odds with the cultural construct of racism. There may be new genetic interpretations in the future, but current thinking indicates that characteristics of the 'white race' emerged between 8,000 and 12,000 years ago, well after many genetic divisions in

Africa itself. Unfortunately, as the late Kenyan palaeoanthropologist Dr Richard Leakey described, some are still reluctant 'to embrace fully the idea that humans, whether blue-eyed Europeans or pale-skinned Asians, originated in Africa'.[1]

Dr Leakey and his equally illustrious parents, Louis and Mary Leakey, were making ground-breaking fossil discoveries at a time in the twentieth century when there was still ongoing research in the field aimed at disproving the theory that we all came out of Africa and were thus originally black. The discovery of a complete ancient skull in China in 1929, dubbed 'Peking Man', for example, led the Beijing authorities to fund research by Chinese palaeontologists aimed at showing that *Homo sapiens* first evolved in Asia, or that Peking Man was an ancestor of modern East Asian people. Such efforts persisted into the twenty-first century.

That we are all part of the original African diaspora is no longer disputed scientifically. New paleontological discoveries are still being made and the vast majority of the pieces in this fragmented and ever-developing jigsaw puzzle are missing, but even if there is still debate about precisely where it happened within the continent, Africa is certainly where the human story began. We are an African animal, an African species who colonised the world, at different times and in different ways. No human being on earth can deny that Africa is their first home.

About 2 to 3 million years ago there was a big freeze that killed the majority of animal life on land and sea. Africa was the region least affected by the Ice Age and life continued to flourish there. As wet, warm grasslands spread across the continent, these habitats created the perfect conditions for the evolution of the great apes: gorillas, chimpanzees and later the hominins or hominids (creatures between ape and human), from which we modern humans finally appeared. These primates gingerly came down from the trees to inhabit the ground and placed their safety in their wits rather than their strength.

It was the Victorian biologist Charles Darwin who first made the observation, in his 1871 book *The Descent of Man*, that since the African gorilla and chimpanzee are most like us in terms of their anatomy, and because they only existed in Africa, then humans must have originated there. Although Darwin's reasoning may not meet today's scientific standards, he had advanced a ground-breaking theory that creationists and many religious conservatives found abhorrent.

Gorillas are now only found in a few places in Africa, mainly in the Great Lakes region. More than a third of the 1,000 surviving mountain gorillas live under protection in the wild forests of the Virunga National Park. The mountains, a chain of volcanoes, span parts of Rwanda, the Democratic Republic of the Congo (DRC) and Uganda. I set off to see these endangered creatures in northern Rwanda, a mission that involved a long hike starting at dawn, through masses of thick vegetation glistening with morning dew. My exertions paid off when I eventually spotted the gorillas through the foliage. A couple of adult gorillas, including one majestic silverback, lay indolently on the ground – seemingly revelling in the early morning sunshine, while a pair of young gorillas tumbled down from a mound and played together on the muddy earth. It was remarkable to see how similar they are to humans. They live in family groups and their movements, antics and expressions are so like ours. In fact, data shows that humans and gorillas differ in only 1.75 per cent of their DNA, far less than previously assumed. (Chimpanzees – our closest relatives – differ only 1.37 per cent from our genomes.)

Once Charles Darwin had advanced his theory that humans originated in Africa, other scientists began to try to piece together the evolutionary chain from gorillas and chimpanzees to humans by studying extinct species of hominins and looking at bipedalism in particular. Bipedalism, which occurred about 6 million years ago, meant a primate's hands could remain free. About 3 million years later, this led to hominins being able to use their intelligence to make tools or hunt with weapons, assisted by their ability to rotate the wrist, a feature unique to apes and humans. Habitual bipedalism, the ability to walk permanently on two legs, is a defining characteristic of what makes us human. One theory, propounded by early twentieth-century experts such as the Australian palaeoanthropologist Raymond Dart, posits that walking on two legs developed because, as the climate changed, there was less woodland and more grassland, making bipedalism a more efficient way of moving around. There was a long intermediate stage, during which bipedal hominins still had a divergent big toe for climbing up trees to escape predators on the ground and could swing from branch to branch with their rotating wrists.

Once hominins became upright around 4.4 million years ago, anatomical changes to the hands, shoulders, elbows, pelvis and spine took place. As the evolutionary chain developed, they began to look more like humans today.

Our Ancestral Trail

Toumai, 7 million years ago

Scientists wanted to establish the date at which our human line diverged from other primates, and the breakthrough came in 2001. After a decade of digging through the sand dunes in the Sahara of northern Chad, a Franco–Chadian team of palaeontologists were rewarded for their efforts. They found fossilised bones, a partial skull and a mandible, ascribed to an ape-man who they dubbed Toumai, meaning 'hope of life' in the local Daza language. Some experts believe Toumai, known as *Sahelanthropus tchadensis*, was from a species of primate that was a common ancestor to both humans and chimpanzees. Molecular evidence suggests that Toumai lived close to the gorilla/chimpanzee–human divergence approximately 7 million years ago, but it is not known if he or she was at times bipedal. This was nevertheless the point at which the evolutionary process that made us fully upright began.

Lucy or Dinkenesh, 3.2 million years ago

Let us fast forward another 4 million years to one of the most iconic discoveries: Lucy, a celebrity in the world of palaeontology. She was a member of a species known as *Australopithecus afarensis*, and was named after the Beatles song 'Lucy in the Sky with Diamonds', which was playing on the camp radio when she was discovered in Harar in eastern Ethiopia in 1974. Lucy is known as Dinkenesh in Ethiopia, meaning 'you are marvellous' in the Amharic language, and it is how I refer to her.

There is a model of what Dinkenesh would have looked like at the National Museum of Ethiopia in the capital Addis Ababa. The real skeleton of Dinkenesh is under lock and key in a climatically controlled room, where the temperature is maintained at an optimum level for the preservation of her remains. An impressive 40 per cent of her skeleton was found, and its constituent parts are kept in carefully identified and classified pieces placed in special padded drawers. It was wonderful to see and touch Dinkenesh's bones under the supervision of Professor Yohannes Haile-Selassie, a leading Ethiopian palaeontologist. He described her as 'the icon of palaeoanthropology', adding that experts like him are still learning a lot from her.

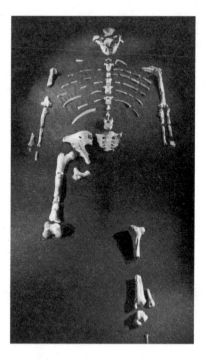

The skeleton of Dinkenesh

Yohannes proceeded to tell me how Dinkenesh lived 3.2 million years ago. A reconstruction of her head shows that its lower half points forward, unlike the flat faces of modern humans, and that her brain was no bigger than that of an ape. Her jaw was relatively small but her teeth were large. An adult, she stood about a metre tall and weighed just under 30kg. She regularly walked on two legs, freeing up her arms, which were relatively longer than ours. Dinkenesh would have used her hands to make simple tools like sharpened twigs in order to fish, dig out termites or kill small animals. Fossilised turtle and crocodile eggs were found near where she died, and support the theory that she foraged for food, possibly by raiding reptile nests. Still, Dinkenesh would mainly have enjoyed a plant- and fruit-based diet.

Dinkenesh probably slept in trees for safety. One theory holds that she may have died by falling from a tree – ironically, peril lay in her refuge. Despite her superstar status in hominin history, modern humans are not direct descendants of Dinkenesh. But she is still part of the lineage that eventually led to us.

Taung Child, 2.8 million years ago

The first evidence of a 'hominin' was discovered much earlier. Professor Raymond Dart found the Taung Child in a limestone formation at Taung near Kimberley, in South Africa's Northern Cape province in 1924. Taung Child lived about 2.8 million years ago and is from a species of hominins called *Australopithecus africanus*. I went along to the University of the Witwatersrand in Johannesburg, where he is kept. The prominent South African palaeoanthropologist Professor Francis Thackeray pointed out the braincase of the skull and the front of the face and lower jaw, and explained that for decades it was thought that our hominin ancestors were voracious predators, or 'killer apes'. Some nearby eggshells were accordingly interpreted as the child's lunch, but showing me the cracks in the Taung Child's skull and eye-sockets, he told me that in the 1990s scientists like him began to notice that the damage looked similar to that of modern monkeys killed by eagles. It seems that the Taung Child was not at home in his cave, but in the lair of a huge bird of prey, probably an ancient eagle, which killed him and dragged him there. It is a window into a time when our forebears were both predator and prey. Taung Child was the first hominin to be found in Africa, and he appeared much more archaic than other remains found elsewhere at the time. He provided the first hint that Charles Darwin may have been correct about humans originating in Africa.

Mrs Ples, 2.5 million years ago

Some 20 years after the discovery of the Taung Child, South African palaeontologists Robert Broom and John T. Robinson uncovered a pre-human skull in the caves of Sterkfontein, north of Johannesburg, in 1947. She was called Mrs Ples as a snappier alternative to the initial scientific name, *Plesianthropus transvaalensis*. After 2 million years of peaceful entombment, Mrs Ples's head was blown up by the dynamite of a lime mining operation. Scientists have pieced it back together, and it is now almost complete. Mrs Ples, like Dinkenesh, had a small brain, similar in size to those of chimpanzees, and about a third of ours, but she walked on two legs. She was a significant find; her skull proved for the first time that walking upright had evolved well before any significant growth in brain size. Experts can gauge whether a hominin walked on two legs from a hole at the back of the skull called the 'foramen magnum' through which the vertebrae and spinal cord enter. Mrs Ples had such a hole and it pointed downwards, indicating she had been bipedal.

Different kinds of hominins co-existed in Africa and scientists are constantly trying to work out how various types such as the Taung Child, Mrs Ples and Dinkenesh are related, but what we do know is that as various lines died out, just one, the '*Homo* genus', led directly to us modern humans. This is where the detective work shifts eastwards on the continent.

Zinj, 1.75 million years ago

The East African Rift Valley, a huge split in the earth's crust that spans Tanzania, Kenya and Ethiopia, is rich in the remains of hominins impeccably preserved in its soil and rock. As I went down the Olduvai Gorge in northern Tanzania and picked my way through the dust and rocks, I gazed at the layers of sediment, made up of clay, sandstone and con-glomerates, formed over thousands of millennia. In 1959 the English-born Kenyan palaeoanthropologist Mary Leakey came across an exceptionally complete skull in the Olduvai Gorge, along with stone tools. The specimen became known as *Zinjanthropus boisei* (Zinj), and was given the species name *Paranthropus boisei*. Previously it had been thought that such pre-humans lived 500,000 years ago but, to the surprise of contemporary scientists, Zinj could be dated to 1.75 million years ago, and his teeth suggested he was a grazer.

I was relieved to see there was a plaque at the spot where Zinj had been discovered, acknowledging Mary Leakey's pioneering discovery. She was a feisty and formidable woman who had received only sporadic teaching but showed an exceptional talent for archaeology and excavation. She mar-ried a Cambridge archaeologist and anthropologist, Louis Leakey, and they moved to East Africa in the late 1930s and established a site at Olduvai Gorge. As a woman working in a field dominated by men, much of the credit for Mary's earlier contributions went to Louis.

Homo habilis, 1.7 million years ago

In 1961, Mary and Louis Leakey's diligent efforts paid off with another major find in Olduvai: a partial skull and a lower jaw dating from 1.7 million years ago – making the specimen a bit younger than Zinj. The plot thickened: the skull was much more similar to our own than *Australopithecus* or *Paran-thropus*. It had a large brain chamber, and so this hominin would have enjoyed using its hands in a more sophisticated manner with fingers that could hold and manipulate objects, such as stones and tools for cutting meat off the bone. He was named *Homo habilis*, Latin for 'dextrous man'.

Turkana Boy or *Homo erectus*, 1.5 million years ago

In 1984, a team working under Louis and Mary's son, Richard Leakey, made a startling discovery that filled a huge gap in our knowledge of human evolution. They found remains in the Turkana Basin in northern Kenya that provided stunning evidence of the group that would eventually lead to us. This was Turkana Boy or *Homo erectus*, meaning 'upright man'. He lived 1.5 million years ago and, unlike other lines such as *Homo habilis* that died out, *Homo erectus* survived and evolved. Turkana Boy was prepubescent – probably about 12 years old. His skeleton is the most complete of any hominin found so far. He stood a metre and a half tall.

Most experts believe that *Homo erectus* acquired the knowledge of how to start a fire by rubbing together flintstones, so his ribcage (and therefore guts) as well as his teeth were smaller due to eating softer, cooked food, which enabled his brain to grow more quickly as protein intake increased. At around the same time, language, probably involving the extensive use of tongue clicking, developed. Turkana Boy is likely to have communicated in this way. *Homo erectus*'s brain grew ever larger, until around 400,000 years ago this hominin became the archaic *Homo sapiens*. Two hundred thousand years later, *Homo erectus* had fully developed into *Homo sapiens*, anatomically the same as us. *Homo sapiens sapiens*, the modern human, was fully formed genetically about 100,000 years ago.

The First Migrants, 90,000 Years Ago

Around 90,000 years ago, *Homo sapiens sapiens* had spread over the whole of Africa. The number of people on the continent at this time probably numbered 1 million, and they lived in small communities of around 150.

Then disaster struck. Parts of Africa started drying out, and food and water became scarce. Our ancestors, suddenly in competition for scant resources, needed to find a way to survive. Earlier hominins, notably *Homo erectus*, had migrated out of Africa 2 million years earlier, but it was only between 90,000 and 60,000 years ago that many desperate *Homo sapiens sapiens* sought their fortunes away from the continent and left. There is nothing new about the phenomenon of human migration.

The first groups arrived in the Arabian Peninsula, from where further pioneers journeyed to Europe and Asia. There, they encountered other descendants of *Homo erectus* – *Homo neanderthalensis* and *Homo heidelbergensis* in Europe, and in Asia the Denisovan groups, *Homo floresiensis*, *Homo longi*, *Homo luzonensis*, and very probably other species of archaic humans too. At this time, we were only one provincially African constituent of a dizzying farrago of humanity. We co-existed with our genetic cousins for millennia, sharing not only the landscape but also, more intimately, our genes by mating with them. To this day, Eurasians have residual vestiges of Neanderthal DNA, and Asians, Pacific peoples and Native Americans carry traces of other hominins. It is still not properly understood why we are the only branch to have survived, but it is likely that our superior cognitive abilities and the changing environment played their part, so that other archaic humans were bred into extinction.

Until 8,000 to 12,000 years ago, all humans were dark-skinned. Pale complexions, fair hair and light-coloured irises only evolved as humans migrated beyond Africa and adapted to different climates, which over time led to the varied racial characteristics we see today. Our lineage, *Homo*, and our place in it, is the subject of much study, conjecture and disagreement. There is growing evidence that archaic humans

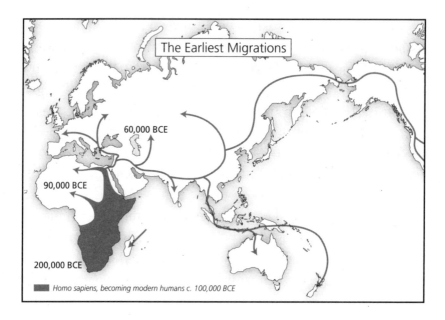

originated in different parts of Africa. However, what we can say with absolute certainty is that 99 per cent of our evolutionary history occurred on the continent. Everyone today is either African or the descendant of an African migrant.

Early Humans

Homo sapiens sapiens very quickly engaged in characteristically human activities, such as making art for the sake of art. In the Sahara Desert of northern Mauritania, I clambered up a rocky path to admire the artistic endeavours in the caves of the Agrour Amogjar mountains. The images, 5,000 years old, were fascinating: a giraffe, an elephant, a gazelle and a man with his arms outstretched and women with exaggerated hips, a sign of fertility, no doubt. Higher up I could see a drawing of the sun – rays beaming – and four circles that are believed to depict the seasons.

I was treated to a crash course in prehistoric art by the ebullient director of the National Centre for Prehistoric, Anthropological and Historical Research (CNRPAH) in Algiers, Dr Slimane Hachi. He said that Algeria, Africa's largest country, has so much rock art that it is the 'biggest open-air museum in the world!' We sat together looking at marvellous pictures of rock art at Tassili n'Ajjer, from around 10,000 years ago, depicting landscapes and wildlife such as buffaloes, giraffes and elephants. The outsized human figures have heads drawn as circles. As human development progressed, Saharan rock art came to depict farmers, shepherds, ox-drivers and sheep – tokens of a long-lost world marooned in oceans of sand.

The oldest rock painting found so far in Africa dates back to 26,000–28,000 years ago. Located in Namibia, it comprises seven stone slabs. Depicted on the brown-grey quartzite are a number of animals painted in white, ochre and charcoal pigment. But rock and cave paintings are far from the first of *sapiens'* artworks. The ability to conceptualise the future and the past is part of what makes us human. Experts such as Dr Hachi cannot be sure when early humans started to acquire the necessary faculties of imagination and abstraction, but perhaps the oldest evidence for an object representing symbolic thought is a smooth piece of stone about 4 centimetres long dating back between 75,000 and 100,000 years, found in the Blombos Cave 300 kilometres east of Cape Town and now kept at a museum in Johannesburg. When I held it in my hand under the watchful eye of the curator, it looked like an unremarkable, small red stone. The curator pointed out the cross-hatched pattern resulting in a diamond shape with three parallel lines deliberately scraped through it. Found elsewhere in the Blombos Cave was a large seashell with remnants of powdered ochre mixed with fluids to make pigments and paint for body or facial decoration. It is estimated to be 100,000 years old, which would surely qualify as the world's oldest surviving make-up kit. Clearly, early humans were like us: creating art, talking, telling stories and jokes, singing, making music and dancing, with their own belief systems and spirituality. Such is the human condition, in Africa and everywhere in the world, then as now.

The Hadzabe

To gain an insight into our social and cultural origins, experts can learn a great deal from a unique community of hunter-gatherers known as the Hadzabe or Hadza, who are based in the Rift Valley in Tanzania on the edge of the Serengeti plains. They are the last remaining people to hunt big game as our ancestors did. Early humans were hunter-gatherers, fishing in brooks with bone hooks and vine lines, foraging in the undergrowth for fruit, honey and nuts, and stalking prey with spears on the plains. If resources were exhausted in one area, the next was exploited. This was our lifestyle for 99 per cent of our history.

I was keen to meet the Hadzabe, having read about them in a study by the brilliant Tanzanian professor Audax Mabulla, director of the Tanzania National Museum. I travelled to Lake Eyasi, less than 100 kilometres from the Ngorongoro crater, to visit them. The Ngorongoro crater is the world's most complete volcanic crater. *Homo sapiens sapiens* and our ancestors have lived in its ecosystem for more than 3 million years. The area in which the Hadzabe live is made up of wide expanses of green land sculpted by volcanic eruptions. The final part of my journey in the bush could only be made on foot, through thick vegetation. My guide and interpreter, David Maragu, walking ahead of me, helpfully pushed aside the lush greenery obstructing our way and created a clear path for us.

After a while, there appeared several small huts made of branches and foliage nestling among the trees. In the clearing, a group of about a dozen men, with baboon fur tails wrapped around their heads, sat crouched on the ground, a fire smouldering beside them. They were singing while one man played melodiously on a simple string instrument placed under his chin. Behind them I could see tall baobab trees, and on their branches dangled the skulls and bone fragments of animals they had hunted down.

As Professor Mabulla explained, the Hadzabe, who number about a thousand in total, live in small autonomous groups. Now only about a quarter maintain their traditional way of life, foraging and hunting full time. They have hunting dogs, do not keep livestock nor grow food, and they follow patterns of animal migration, moving to new grounds every few weeks, building temporary huts for shelter. Even though the Hadzabe have been offered permanent shelter by successive Tanzanian governments, many prefer to live as our ancestors did; indeed, their rejection of the trappings of modernity and their deep connection with nature provide a salutary lesson for us all as we grapple with the damage inflicted on the environment by human activity and pursuit of material wealth.

Life is intensely communal; at night they all sleep together, but by day the women and children stay in a different part of the compound. I noticed that the children in this 25-strong community were raised collectively by all the women. This practice, called alloparenting by anthropologists, is not unusual in Africa. Among the Kung of Botswana, for instance, each child is looked after by many adults and older children also contribute to the care of younger ones. One study of the Efe people of the Democratic Republic of the Congo found that infants had an average of 14 alloparents a day by the time they were 18 weeks old. It is a system that is consistent with how paleoanthropologists believe early humans and hunter-gatherers ordered their societies, and which some psychiatrists today believe can reduce stress and pressure on mothers and lead to less anxiety for children. The concept of the nuclear family is a recent invention, which broke with evolutionary history and is not one with which the Hadzabe identify. Although the Hadzabe practise serial monogamy, each relationship may last only for a short time, so in reality a woman may not be certain of her child's paternity.

It is an egalitarian society in which everything is shared. The women and children forage for tuber roots, gather wild plants, collect berries and kill small animals such as mice and birds. Honey collection, however, falls to the men. The Hadzabe do not store food; if they kill a big animal, it is eaten within five days. No part of the beast goes to waste. At dawn, boys accompany the men into the bush to watch them hunt and learn from their skills. Before I set off on a hunting expedition with the Hadzabe, one of them instructed me on how to pull a bow. I failed miserably and was put to shame by a three-year-old, who fired his arrow further than I. The hunters wear baboon skins to make them look and smell like an animal so they can get nearer to their prey. They sharpen their arrows, which are dipped in poison extracted from plants or beetles, making them more deadly. If an animal is not killed instantly, it will be debilitated by the poison and once it eventually dies the Hadzabe can track its location from the vultures circling overhead. On that day we returned to base empty handed.

The women's foraging proved more productive, as it is a much more reliable source of food than the men's hunting – and it was ever thus! On our return, the men used climbing pegs hammered into the trunks to ascend the baobab trees and collect the hard-shelled fruit. Later that evening the community enjoyed a cooked meal of baobab fruit and root vegetables – a vegan delight.

Amid much jocularity, we all sat around a fire at dusk, chatting through my interpreter, who had helped me build a rapport with the Hadzabe. They speak Hadzane, which has no real connection with any other African language, though it bears some similarities to the click languages of the Khoisan people of Eastern, Central and Southern Africa, a small group which is occasionally classified within the Niger-Congo family.[2]

The Hadzabe believe their ancestors painted the rock art in the Lake Eyasi Basin. These artworks show fine-line paintings of wild animals, stylised human figures and red-coloured abstract designs of concentric circles or dots and lines. There are images of baobab fruits and berries and of humans holding bows and arrows aimed at animals. Some of the rock art may have been made by shamans or medicine men, who ate mood-altering plants and experienced out-of-body hallucinations. For our ancestors, medicinal plants were important, just as they are for Africans today. The Hadzabe peel and boil the bark of mondoko and use it as a compress; for chest congestion they boil the bark of morongodako and drink the infusion. However, as Professor Mabulla explained, in the past, if a person did not respond to treatment and was too sick or weak to migrate with the others, then the community would have no choice but to leave him or her and let nature take its course.

African Religions

We cannot be sure what kind of belief systems early humans had, but the Hadzabe to this day believe in a cosmology that is the sun, stars and moon; they have no religious hierarchy nor elaborate burial practices. Like the Hadzabe, archaic hunter-gatherer societies buried their dead in rock shelters, possibly with grave goods, and other species such as Neanderthals did this too.

There are many indigenous spiritual systems in Africa, reflecting the diversity of its people, but there are also many similarities. I should say that, although I use it as a convenient shorthand, there is a terminological problem with the phrase 'African religions'. The word 'religion' incorporates so much of the Abrahamic traditions that it colours and obscures our understanding of African spiritual ideas and beliefs. Descriptions of African belief systems were established by Western academics, theologians and missionaries, and were influenced by their own religious perspectives. As the late Kenyan academic John Mbiti wrote: 'These earlier descriptions left us with terms which are inadequate, derogatory and prejudicial'.[3]

For example, the English anthropologist E.B. Tylor described African religious practices in his 1871 book *Primitive Culture* as 'animism', having invented the term from the Latin word *anima*, meaning breath or soul. He wrote that 'primitive people' believe every object has its own soul, giving rise to countless spirits in the universe, who would then be worshipped in a kind of polytheism, placing African spirituality at the bottom rung of religious evolution. The term 'animism' is still in popular use today even though it has long been abandoned by African academics as a misrepresentation of the spiritual beliefs it denotes. Only around the middle of the twentieth century did serious and more sympathetic approaches to African traditional beliefs arise, and Mbiti has contributed much to our knowledge about the subject.[4] According to him most African languages do not even have a word for religion and there are no sacred scriptures. Existing African religions such as Vodun, Vodu, Orisha and Inkice are open to constant innovations, but discussions about monotheism or polytheism are not relevant. These African beliefs all share common features such as the idea of a force that is at once transcendent and immanent. This is present everywhere in creation, in the trees, plants, the wind and other aspects of nature, hence the misnomer 'animism'.

The idea that Africans practise 'ancestor worship' has also proved remarkably enduring in Western views of African traditions, though it is one rejected by African academics. The English scholar Herbert Spencer first used the term 'ancestor worship' in his 1885 book *The Principles of Sociology* to describe the relationship between 'savage' people, as he put it, and the spirits of the dead. In reality, most African traditional beliefs hold that ancestors exist in another world and can be invoked to intervene in present affairs. There are 'holy people' in the community – spiritual entities who are intercessors between those on earth and those who have departed. There is a deep connection between the living and those in the afterlife; the dead still form part of the family, and are offered prayers and sacrifices so that 'good' emanates from them back to earth. It is a very practical spirituality. There is no idea of a hell awaiting sinners, nor a paradise awaiting believers. The pursuit of a moral life is not encouraged in order to secure a happy existence in the next world; it is the present life that matters. In this way, traditional African religions are often less about the individual and more about community. Many readers are familiar with the southern African word *ubuntu* in the Nguni language, which means 'humanity to others' or 'I am what I am, because of who we all are', which captures the essence of Africa's indigenous beliefs.

Zimbabwean culture expert, Pathisa Nyathi, took me to meet a community in the Matobo Hills in Matabeleland, who were engaged in a ceremony to summon the spirits of the ancestors. I was transfixed by a group of four men and a woman as they sat on the ground ululating loudly and clapping their hands as they invoked the names of their ancestors, demanding they look after their progeny. Pathisa explained that African spiritual beliefs are not doctrinal, and that the idea of conversion in African religions is alien, which means that throughout history there have been no religious wars stemming from conflicts between African belief systems. I found it a sobering and remarkable insight. In a world where religion has so often been an exacerbating factor in conflict, we could all learn from the way adherents of traditional African beliefs, such as the Hadzabe, lead their lives.

Human Development

Cattle

Although we have lived as hunter-gatherers for nearly all of our existence, it is during the last 1 per cent – the past 12,000 years – that we have experienced the most dramatic transformation. Some 8,000 to 10,000 years ago the climate of Africa was very wet; lifestyles were closely bound up with water over a vast area including the then much smaller Sahara Desert and larger equatorial forest.

Between 7000 and 5000 BCE humans became pastoralists and farmers. We began to communicate and cooperate with one another, and form ties beyond those based merely on kinship. By 7000 BCE, coastal inhabitants began to exploit the abundant fish and shellfish of the lagoons and estuaries. Groups of people dependent on fish settled beside the oceans, seas, lakes and rivers, and became receptive to the notion of collective food production. They continued to hunt animals such as giraffes, antelopes and buffaloes, but they also began to protect and breed the wild animals that were of most use to them, such as wild goats, sheep and, later, cattle, gradually domesticating these species. Early pastoralists used animals more often for milk than meat, and the Maasai still have much in common with their lifestyle. The Maasai take their name from their language, Maa. They live in northern Tanzania and southern Kenya, and fossil remains of domesticated animals prove that pastoralists have long inhabited the region.

I visited one Maasai settlement on the Serengeti in northern Tanzania. A collection of around 30 straw huts housed many extended families. As I descended from my car to shake hands with several of the community waiting to greet me, I was instantly impressed by their elegant appearance: tall and slender women in deep red robes, with beautifully sculpted shaved heads and elaborate beaded jewellery around their long necks, their earrings hanging from elongated earlobes. Nearby I could see a young boy running ahead of his seemingly well-tended flock of sheep who obligingly followed his lead – the responsibility of herding livestock falls to Maasai boys and their faithful dogs. The Maasai are nomadic, moving around with their animals looking for fresh pasture. Outside the compound was a fence of acacia thorns built to keep out the wild animals which roam the Serengeti. The huts, which are constructed by the women, are made of mud, sticks, grass and cow dung bound together with cow urine.

Kinama Marite, a local Maasai guide, who spoke English with style and animation, told me that cattle are everything to the Maasai: 'No cattle, no milk, no meat equals no Maasai people.' They obtain all their basic needs from their cattle: food, milk, hide and dung for building materials. Traditionally, Maasai fighters would drink the blood of cows to fortify themselves, and Kinama said he had done so on numerous occasions himself, joking that it was a good hang-over cure. Pastoralist communities all over Africa, not just the Maasai, have to make the most of their environmental resources, and this has led to an exceptional capacity for survival and adaptation as well as a highly developed system of solidarity.

Crops

Also around 7000 BCE, inland communities began to build settlements and farm on land that was commonly owned. At first, they grew crops such as millet, wheat and sorghum. When such crops could not grow successfully in the wild without human cultivation, it meant they had become domesticated and this is how farming developed. Archaeological evidence from stone tools indicates that by about 1000 BCE there was a substantial agricultural base in most parts of the continent.

The farming family I spent the day with in the Matobo Hills in southern Zimbabwe was a tightly knit bunch and as smallholders their methods differ little from their ancestors. Charles Dube, his two friendly but shy wives Kukhanya and Sibongile and his mother Cezanne grow a variety of crops including maize and green beans, and sell their surplus at market. Farming is something of a family affair; it was a Sunday, and with no school the children were helping out. Farming is labour intensive and the Dubes still rely on rain-fed agriculture, which leaves them vulnerable to the caprices of the weather: too much water and the crops are washed away, too little and there is drought. This means they cannot scale up their production. Their farming equipment is very basic but many centuries ago these same iron tools had a transformative impact on farming in Africa.

Iron, a dense and abundant metal, is stronger and more versatile than copper or bronze. Iron ore was found across much of Africa and had to be extracted from the ground and smelted in furnaces at high temperatures (1,200°C) before it could be fashioned into anything handy. The discovery of smelting around 2500 BCE enabled the development of hardier tools: axes and hoes for farming, cooking pots also used for storing and carrying food, and weaponry. Ironmaking knowledge and skills were kept within families and were prized assets that brought reverence and honour. In some communities a good blacksmith was believed to possess a spirit who would issue instructions about where to find a source of iron and how to smelt it. The earliest and most successful African civilisations were those that were adept at ironmaking, including the ancient Egyptians and the Nok culture of the Jos plateau in West Africa.

So between 7,000 and 5,000 years ago two distinct types of African community developed: the cattle-dependent nomadic pastoralists and the more settled farmers who built permanent shelters using materials such as mud, stone and reeds; of course, many also hunted, gathered, foraged and fished at the same time. The fact that land was seldom privately owned meant that Africa did not go through upheavals involving revolts by peasants against a landowning elite, as with feudal Europe, in which serfs toiled for overlords who had been granted land in exchange for loyalty to a king. For a much longer period than any other continent, Africa evolved outside the confines of private or state ownership of land.

However, the absence of a large landowning class did not mean African societies were egalitarian. There were rich elites who owned domestic animals. As people began living together, chiefs emerged to answer the need for organised groups of men to herd their cattle and carry out raids on their behalf. These elites prospered and accumulated wealth, and, in order to protect it, formed armies and made strategic alliances by marrying women from other groups. To preserve their status, the chiefs set up a hereditary system of rule. In return for their people's loyalty, labour and service, the chiefs would protect those in their care. Owning cattle was and still is a huge factor in determining power and wealth in many parts of Africa.

Once ironwork was established, food production, gathering, preparation and storage became more efficient and people across Africa were left with more spare time for other activities. They began to provide services and make goods and ornaments for barter, establishing a new economic system in which they ceased to grow food themselves and instead acquired it from farmers, creating commercial and trade networks. In some regions of Africa, farming communities developed sophisticated methods of agriculture and irrigation, which led to more varied and advanced lifestyles. Urban centres and then kingdoms and empires emerged across the continent, populated by vibrant and resourceful citizens, and ruled by colourful and charismatic kings and queens, whose soldiers fought in battles in which the victor took all the spoils. Yet we do not know as much about these very early cultures as we do about one glittering civilisation that is often not even recognised as African.

2

Gift of the Nile

No other civilisation in Africa has captured the popular imagination more than that of ancient Egypt. The pyramids, temples, mummified remains, sarcophagi, artefacts, treasures and the boy king Tutankhamun are known the world over, and libraries of books have been written about them. It is the only part of African history that is taught widely in schools: I, for one, remember how it delighted and engrossed me as a pupil in London.

The fifth-century BCE Greek historian Herodotus devoted a whole volume of his *Histories* to Egypt, describing it as 'the gift of the Nile'. The Romans were deeply engaged by its art, and centuries later Renaissance artists in Europe made use of hieroglyphic symbols and other aspects of Egyptian culture.

Emperor Napoleon Bonaparte's campaign in Egypt (1798 to 1801), during which he was accompanied by archaeologists, drove breakthroughs in scholarship. The discovery of the Rosetta Stone by members of his expedition generated much excitement and effectively triggered the discipline of Egyptology.

Architectural styles in Europe and North America also drew on Egyptian influences. In London, the 1812 Egyptian Hall in Piccadilly was the first building in England to include Egyptian motifs, such as sun discs, papyrus columns and sloping side walls. Obelisks, including the Washington Monument in the USA sprouted across the world, pyramids were built as memorials for the dead in cemeteries, and London's Highgate Cemetery boasts an Egyptian Avenue. After the expansion of the British colonial presence in Egypt in the late nineteenth century, the country attracted more European tourists, who took advantage of its accessibility compared to other parts of Africa.

In 1922, interest in Egypt skyrocketed after the discovery of Tutankhamun's tomb, teeming with thousands of artefacts, jewels and furniture. Objects and art in the Egyptian style were soon being mass produced in Europe and North America, including jewellery, clothing, cosmetics, pictures and sculptures. The Egyptians themselves capitalised on the appetite for all things Egyptian and produced goods for international and domestic markets; they still do so today, as any tourist in the country knows. The popular 1937 novel by British author Agatha Christie, *Death on the Nile*, was inspired by her own numerous trips to Egypt.

Egyptomania reached the upper echelons of the art world in Paris in the nineteenth and twentieth centuries. The renowned French sculptor Auguste Rodin drew on Egyptian sculptures and reliefs, as did the Italian Alberto Giacometti, whose *Head of Isabel* of *c.* 1937 bears a striking resemblance to the bust of the Egyptian queen Nefertiti. Ancient Egypt had become associated with exoticism, wealth and luxury for Europeans, but across the Atlantic it had a special significance for the descendants of enslaved Africans, who were struggling for recognition as equal citizens.

African American artists such as Rodin's protégé, Meta Vaux Warrick Fuller, availed themselves of the lustre of Egypt not only artistically, but politically. Fuller's 1921 *Ethiopia* statue depicts a black woman emerging from a mummy wrapping to symbolise the rebirth of black people. Fuller wrote: 'Here was a group who had once made history and now after a long sleep was awaking, gradually unwinding the bandage of its mummied past and looking out on life again, expectant but unafraid and with it at least a graceful gesture.' The intellectuals and artists of what became known as the Harlem Renaissance, spanning the 1920s and 1930s, claimed ancient Egypt as an African civilisation and used its culture to express messages of emancipation and black pride. Fuller said: 'the most brilliant period, perhaps of Egyptian history is the period of the negro kings'.[1] Such sentiment is still widely spread both in the African diaspora and on the continent itself, resulting in heated controversy.

Many people, including in Egypt itself, see ancient Egyptian history as somehow different and set apart from the rest of the continent. Implicit in this thought is the idea that such a great civilisation could not have emerged from within 'black Africa' and that somehow forces from outside the continent were responsible for shaping its origins and development.

One major furore occurred in early 2023 over the casting of a black British actress, Adele James, as Cleopatra in a Netflix docudrama series, produced by African American Jada Pinkett Smith. The Egyptian Ministry of Tourism and Antiquities lambasted what it described as the drama-documentary's inaccuracy of the 'historical and scientific facts' about Cleopatra's ethnicity – Cleopatra was of Greek-Macedonian ancestry. Adele James responded to the backlash on Egyptian social media by saying: 'It really speaks to the degree to which some people in Egypt potentially would prefer to distance themselves from the rest of Africa.'

The prominent Egyptian comedian and commentator Bassem Youssef waded into the row in an interview on American television: 'The problem for me is not about colour . . . we have a diverse population in Egypt. This is about the falsification of history by the Afrocentric movement, which started in the last century to teach African Americans about their rich history of the kingdoms of West Africa, but they cannot claim that it was their ancestors who built ancient Egypt, this is an appropriation of my culture.'

A similar controversy broke out in February 2023 involving the African American comedian Kevin Hart, with calls in Egypt for his show to be cancelled there over his alleged support for putting 'Afrocentrism' at the heart of ancient Egyptian history, and indeed in the end Kevin Hart pulled out.

It would be oversimplistic to extrapolate from the reaction in Egypt that racism is at the heart of such objections; as Bassem Youssef explained, the matter has less to do with race and more to do with the erasure of Egyptians from their own history in popular culture and teachings. Nevertheless, such discussions are not new and remind me of conversations I have had with Africans involved in UNESCO's *General History of Africa* (*GHA*), about the ethnicity of ancient Egyptians. The late Senegalese academic Cheikh Anta Diop, who contributed to the chapters about ancient Egypt in the *GHA*, caused a massive stir in the 1970s when he stated categorically that the ancient Egyptians were not only African but were 'negro'. His opinions were disowned by several contributors to the *GHA*.

The identity of the ancient Egyptians generates much emotion because they built such a spectacular civilisation, and so people of African descent are naturally keen to ensure it is seen as part of their heritage. After all, when Mesopotamia and ancient Egypt were evolving as civilisations with cities, extensive agriculture and writing, the world was still dominated by migratory hunter-gatherers.

The Egyptians were the first people in Africa to be conquered by the Arabs in the 640s CE, and most now identify as Arabs, complicating, for some, any straightforward identification as African. In my view, the point is not to define ancient Egypt as being African or not on the basis of the race of its inhabitants; it is about the need to challenge our definitions, and perhaps our stereotypes, of Africans. There is more racial and ethnic diversity in Africa than in any other continent on earth, and it is impossible – and needless – to reduce 'Africanness' to race. Egypt had from the very beginning close links with the cultures surrounding it, both in Africa and in western Asia. But its location on the African continent ensures that ultimately it is, was, and will always be African.

Ancient Egyptian Culture and Society

The first archaeological evidence for human settlement along the River Nile is from 7000 BCE, but the area was probably inhabited long before then. More migrants arrived from other parts of Africa around 3000 BCE, attracted by the riverine climate as the Sahara became drier. These groups converged on the narrow strip of land in the Nile Valley and settled along the river's fertile banks. It was a simple existence: people hunted, raised livestock and farmed. They used mud from the banks to build basic houses, and as their civilisation progressed, they graduated to making mudbricks by mixing the mud with straw and water.

The mighty Nile was at the heart of life. The river is

composed of the Blue Nile, with its source to the southeast in the highlands of Ethiopia, and the longer White Nile, which originates in the Congo Basin and the Rwenzori mountains. The two rivers meet in the Sudanese capital Khartoum and from there flow as one river, meandering through Sudan and into Egypt. I have managed twice over the years to visit Khartoum at the right time to witness the extraordinary phenomenon when the waters of the two Niles remain separate at the confluence: it is as though a straight line has been drawn between them, on one side the light grey of the White Nile, on the other the blueish-green hue of the Blue Nile. They derive their colours from the sediments they carry, with the Blue Nile providing the rich fertile mud on which Egypt's agricultural development has depended for millennia. Modern-day tensions between Egypt and Ethiopia, where 85 per cent of the Blue Nile flows, are centred on the Grand Ethiopian Renaissance Dam, which opened in 2020 and uses the Blue Nile to provide hydroelectric power, leading to anxiety among Egyptians that this will reduce their own water capacity.

Ancient Egyptians were almost entirely reliant on the Nile for their livelihoods. They tamed it through a system of dykes and basins, drained its swamps and diverted its water through canals. The river flooded so severely every year that the population of the Nile Valley had to learn to control the floodwater to avoid seeing their villages and crops washed away. The floods covered such a huge area that moving away from the Nile was not a viable option, and therefore the Egyptians developed 'nilometers' to calculate water levels so that dykes and canals could be prepared accordingly. Too much water would be destructive; too little meant there was not enough for crops. An extensive system of year-round irrigation ensured the right amount of water could be raised from canals or from deep pits dug down to the water table.

Irrigation freed Egyptians from the rainfed subsistence farming of Africans elsewhere on the continent, and consequently they ate well, using cereal crops for bread and beer, enjoying vegetables such as broad beans, onions, leeks, lettuce, cucumber and chickpeas, and savouring dates, figs, sycamore nuts and grapes. Honey was extracted from beehives, oil from sesame seeds and fish from the Nile. Poultry, goat and sheep were kept in enclosures. A surplus of food, which could be stored in warehouses, meant citizens could pursue other activities, such as making pottery, furniture and luxury items. The goods produced by these skilled artisans were bought and sold through a barter system. The Egyptians did not have a currency, using instead a non-tradeable unit of measure called a 'deben', which was a small token of copper. It could be used as a measurement but could not itself be exchanged, so a beautiful piece of dyed material could be worth 20 debens whereas a bale of hay would be worth far fewer.

Traders transported their goods along the Nile all year round except at the first of the river's six cataracts, in Aswan – the other five are upstream in modern-day Sudan. These cataracts are waterfalls gushing over rock formations that jut out dramatically from the riverbed, forcing the water to accelerate as it flows around them. When the waters are not high enough, boats can easily run aground and become wrecked; at such a time the Nile is unnavigable, forcing people to use arduous and scorching overland routes through the desert.

The large-scale collaborations needed to manage the Nile necessitated better communication, organisation and unity. A way of recording information was needed, slowly developing into a writing system for representing words and numerals. The ancient Egyptians wrote with reed brushes and pens on papyrus and also inscribed pottery and stones. Papyrus is a reed that grows naturally and abundantly in Nilotic marshes. It was used for a variety of purposes – baskets, seals, ropes, clothing, footwear, wicks for oil lamps, boats, and it may even have been eaten at one time; but most importantly, it was used from about 3000 BCE to make paper (the English word 'paper' is derived from papyrus).

Egyptian writing used pictograms (one symbol or picture per word) and also syllabograms (one per syllable), as well as what we would call 'letters', deriving their symbols from their rich African environment. Last used organically in the fourth century CE, Egyptian hieroglyphs were little understood until after the discovery of the Rosetta Stone. A grey granite stone over a metre tall, the Rosetta Stone was inscribed with three versions of a decree issued in Memphis in 196 BCE – in hieroglyphs, Demotic and in Classical Greek. Napoleon's soldiers took ink prints of the stone and disseminated copies to French scholars. It did not unlock the mysteries of Egyptian hieroglyphics, but was central to decipherment efforts, allowing scholars to isolate Egyptian names and work out alphabetic sounds, but other bilingual texts were also significant. Around ten years after the Rosetta Stone was found, the hieroglyphics could be interpreted. Ancient Egyptians could at last be understood, but the cracking of the code by Europeans also served to put them centre stage in the study of ancient Egypt.

Along with writing, the ancient Egyptians were one of the first civilisations to use calendars. They also used the moon to measure the passing of a month and developed a science of astronomy to study celestial bodies and judge the seasons. They calculated a year of 365 days, which they divided into 12 months of 30 days with 5 spare days left over, subsequently refining this into the more correct 365 and one-third of a day.

The collaborative nature of these early communities led to greater centralisation and then to political structures known as 'nomes'. These coalitions eventually formed two kingdoms: one to the north, one to the south, and later they gave rise to the great pharaonic dynasties, which were lines of hereditary rulers. The third-century BCE Egyptian priest and historian Manetho put together a timeline of the pharaohs of Egypt, which, along with information from monuments, tablets and scrolls, tells us with a fair degree of certainty that there were 31 dynasties of pharaohs between 3000 and 330 BCE, when Egypt was conquered by Alexander the Great. These are spread across three periods: the Old (or Archaic), Middle and New Kingdoms.

The Old Kingdom, c. 3000–2200 BCE

The founder of the first dynasty of the Old Kingdom was Narmer, who came from Upper Egypt (the southern part of the country; Lower Egypt is the north). I went to the Egyptian Museum in Cairo to meet Ahmed Samir, its engaging curator, to find out more about Egypt's first pharaohs and to see the Narmer Palette, a beautifully carved piece that is more than 60 centimetres high, made of smooth greyish-green siltstone. It depicts King Narmer twice, once sporting a crown, walking towards the decapitated bodies of his foes, and then grasping an enemy by the hair, with his arm raised as if he were about to smite him.

For Ahmed Samir, Narmer's ethnicity was not particularly relevant to our discussions, as his view was that Egypt's population has long been mixed. For him, Narmer is significant because he was the first king to unify north and south Egypt under one government of 'viziers' or officials. The

The Narmer Palette

word 'pharaoh' derives from this earliest period and comes from the old Egyptian *per-ao*, meaning 'Great House' of the prince. Narmer established his capital at Memphis, which was a meeting point for people from Upper and Lower Egypt and is situated about 25 kilometres from modern-day Cairo. Today, there is little to see of this great city. Egyptian and ancient Greek historians record various stories about Narmer. According to the first-century Greek historian Diodorus Siculus, Narmer introduced the worship of the gods and the practice of sacrifice and enjoyed a luxurious lifestyle. Manetho records that Narmer reigned for 62 years and was, rather unregally, mauled to death by a hippopotamus.

The most striking monument at Memphis is the first pyramid built by a pharaoh. Zoser was part of the third dynasty of the Old Kingdom and relied heavily on his right-hand man, a brilliant and visionary individual called Imhotep. The ancient Egyptians had a sophisticated administrative system, in which a class of scribes or learned men could be engineers, doctors, architects, tax collectors, generals in the army and priests in the temples. Imhotep was the equivalent of a head of government or a chancellor, and he was also the architect of the step pyramid at Saqqara, built about 2780 BCE. Imhotep introduced the use of limestone for construction instead of the customary mudbrick. The step pyramid is made up of six 'mastabas' or steps stacked on top of one another. It lacks the smooth sides of later 'complete' pyramids. Little is known about Imhotep. An inscription with his name was found at the site, illustrating his importance at court. It accords him a variety of titles, including 'chief of the sculptors and chief of the seers'. Imhotep was one of the few commoners to be accorded divine status after his death.

Around a century and a half later, the ambitious Snefru, pharaoh for more than 50 years at the start of the fourth dynasty, sought to outdo his predecessors by building a different kind of pyramid. He presided over the construction of the 'bent' and 'red' pyramids. The bent pyramid has an impressive double slope with smooth sides, while the adjacent red pyramid derives its name from the red limestone of its masonry. The full triangular pyramid was finally accomplished at Giza (just outside modern-day Cairo) by Snefru's son Khufu. He built the first and biggest of the three Great Pyramids of Giza, which stands nearly 150 metres high and is 230 metres at its widest. It is composed of 2.5 million stones, with each weighing 2.5 tons. It is an astounding feat of architecture, logistics and engineering, which must have appeared unimaginably impressive to people at the time.

Khufu's son Khafre (2575–c. 2465 BCE) built the second of the pyramids of Giza. It appears taller than Khufu's because Khafre built it on higher ground. The third pyramid is considerably smaller and was constructed around 2490 BCE by the pharaoh Menkaure, who was probably Khafre's son. These pyramids are an emblem of the prosperity of this period of the Old Kingdom. Adjacent to the pyramids is the Sphinx, an enormous 20-metre-high limestone statue depicting a lion's body and a human face. It bears no inscription so experts are not certain whether it was built by Khufu or Khafre.

In total there are well over 100 pyramids in Egypt, but the Great Pyramids at Giza are the ones that have induced wonder for millennia, ranking among the most magnificent of human achievements. They are so overwhelming in size that as I gazed up at them I felt like a mere speck caught up in the grand sweep of history. Going inside the pyramids I could smell the damp and dank air of the distant past, and once I made my way through the narrow stone passageways into the inner burial chamber, the sound of traffic gave way to a reverential silence.

The question of whether the Giza pyramids were built by enslaved labour has stimulated debate for centuries. However, most Egyptian experts, such as the high-profile archaeologist Dr Zahi Hawass, insist they were constructed by Egyptians rather than imported enslaved people. He was keen to emphasise that ancient Egypt was not a society where slavery was common and that the huge slabs of stone were unlikely to have been put in place by men in chains, lashed by vicious overseers, but by workers doing highly prized service to their gods, especially Ma'at – the goddess of truth and right. Farmers would also have provided a pool of paid labour when they were idle during the Nile floods. Moreover, Dr Hawass told me that the names on the tombs of pyramid builders found in Giza indicated they were Egyptian because enslaved people would never have been buried near the pyramids themselves. Additionally, pyramid building was seen as a national endeavour, one that projected the prestige of

Egypt and therefore did not require an enslaved workforce. However, it is possible that some Egyptians may have felt impelled to sell their services to pay off debts and that foreigners or captives were used as forced labour.

Much of what we know about the ancient Egyptians comes from their religious beliefs and burial practices. Like other traditional African spiritual systems, they believed earth and heaven were filled with countless spirits, which lived in animals, plants and objects. They saw divine forces in the sun, moon, stars, sky and the Nile floods. When a pharaoh died, his body was purified and embalmed. The custom of mummification was based on the Egyptians' belief in the afterlife and so the preservation of the body was critical for the survival of the soul.

Consequently, the ancient Egyptians built up a detailed knowledge of anatomy and developed surgical techniques. The pharaoh's organs were removed and placed in vessels known as 'canopic jars'. The brain would be drawn out through the nose with a hooked implement, the intestines through an incision in the side of the body. The heart was either left intact or removed, preserved and put back in the body, since it was believed to be the seat of intelligence. There is some evidence that later dynasties left the brain untouched. The Egyptians worked out that the chemical natron, naturally occurring in certain areas of the country, could be used as a preservative, so the body would be soaked in natron for 70 days, then wrapped in linen bandages, placed in a coffin, and finally in a sarcophagus.

During the third and fourth dynasties of the Old Kingdom, political unity was fully consummated. This was a period of great stability during which Egyptian pharaohs developed their distinctive religious dogma, whereby the ruler was regarded as not merely human, but a god. The falcon-headed Horus was god of the sky and kingship. Their main god was Amun-Ra, meaning the 'hidden one', a fusion of Amun the ram-headed god and the sun god Ra. His wife was the sky goddess Mut and their son the moon god Khonsu. Osiris was the god of the afterlife, and this concept played a prominent part in the belief systems of the living. The Ka, a guardian spirit which inhabited each person at birth, remained with them throughout life and passed before them to the afterworld. Funerary furniture was for the use of the Ka. On the walls and sarcophagi of the pyramids at Saqqara there were carved texts containing spells to protect the pharaoh's remains, resurrect his dead body and help him reach the heavens.

There is evidence the ancient Egyptians had their own concept of citizen and human rights, notwithstanding their social hierarchy. The *Westcar Papyrus*, an ancient text that described life in the court of King Khufu and his sons, explicitly expressed the idea that all humans are equal: 'Do not use violence on men . . . they were born from the eyes of [the god] Ra, they are his issue.' The pharaoh ruled with the goddess Ma'at, and so would have to govern with truth and right.

While the pyramids were all about the afterlife, royal residences and the homes of the elite were impressive, composed of buildings that resembled small towns, with palace complexes that had multiple halls, kitchens, bathrooms and bedrooms (the rich would sleep on beds with mattresses stuffed with wool and feathers). There would be villas – usually single storey with flat roofs, central courtyards and a series of connecting rooms – for officials and their families to live in, as well as more modest staff quarters. The Egyptians built their homes with small windows placed high so as to avoid direct sunlight and to allow hot air to escape. Stone was occasionally used for column bases and windows. I saw a home built and decorated in the style of a nobleman's house at a visitor attraction – the Pharaonic Village in Cairo – and quite honestly even by today's standards it would be classed as lavish accommodation!

The Old Kingdom came to an end in the sixth dynasty with the reign of Pharaoh Pepi II. He had become king when he was six and died at a very ripe old age. But as Pepi II grew older, his powers declined. Provincial rulers and princes exploited the power vacuum at the centre, carrying out destructive raids on one another's territories. The sage Ipu-wer, who witnessed the carnage, wrote: 'All is ruin. A man smites his brother . . . plague is throughout the land. Blood is everywhere. A few lawless men have ventured to despoil the land of kingship.' Pepi II's death resulted in a collapse of pharaonic rule and a long period of anarchy.

The Middle Kingdom, c. *2030–1650 BCE*

Around 2055 BCE, a man emerged who restored Egypt's pharaonic glory and began the first dynasty of the Middle Kingdom. Like Narmer before him, Mentuhotep II hailed from southern Egypt, rather than its Mediterranean coast. He was the ruler of Thebes (modern-day Luxor), which was then a relatively unimportant city about 650 kilometres south of Memphis. With a powerful and disciplined army, Mentuhotep reunited the two lands of the north and south of Egypt, which had split apart during the interregnum. He re-established a strong centralised government, set out a functioning administration and made major contributions to architecture and the development of religion. Egypt's population would then have numbered about 2 million, when there would have been about 10 million people in the whole of Europe.

Mentuhotep began the temple complex at Karnak, near Luxor today, a huge site of temples, obelisks and walkways that was enlarged, destroyed and restored over a period of 1,500 years. At this point, Karnak became the most important place of worship in ancient Egypt, and it is a glorious destination. At the entrance on both sides of the walkway there are statues of the god Amun-Ra, bearing the head of a ram, but with the shoulders, paws, claws and tail of a lion. Built to look like a thicket of papyrus, with flowers opening at the top, Karnak is dotted with massive columns dedicated to various pharaohs. While the shrine at Karnak was built for the worship of the three main deities of Thebes – Amun-Ra, Mut and their son Khonsu – Mentuhotep was also a proponent of the underworld god Osiris, a local Theban deity with a strong connection to the River Nile. The cult of Osiris had offered even the humblest of his followers the prospect of eternal life. At death, a person faced judgement by a tribunal of 42 divine judges. If they had lived in accordance with the precepts of the goddess Ma'at, the person was welcomed into the kingdom of Osiris. If found guilty, they would be thrown to a fierce animal who would devour them, denying them eternal life.

During the Middle Kingdom's flourishing, the pharaohs established a standing army for the purposes of maintaining security, keeping the country united and warding off invasions. Mentuhotep's successors were largely preoccupied with holding their kingdom together and their achievements were limited by this constant claim on their attention. The Middle Kingdom came to an end when a series of listless and short-lived pharaohs once again lost control to regional leaders. Crop failures may also have played a part by creating food shortages, destabilising central authority. The twelfth dynasty – the last of the Middle Kingdom – produced no heirs, so from about 1800 BCE there followed a period of 150 years during which the Egyptians were for the first time invaded and ruled by foreigners, the Hyksos, who were originally from western Asia and had settled in the northeastern region of the Nile Delta. The Hyksos were organised and well-equipped. They introduced the horse and chariot to ancient Egypt as well as more advanced weaponry; up until then the Egyptians had relied on shields and bows and arrows as their main form of defence.

The New Kingdom, 1520–1075 BCE

After a century of fragmentation and subjugation, the Egyptians beat back the Hyksos under the command of Ahmose, who was a local leader from Thebes. Ahmose I re-established Egyptian rule and began the New Kingdom under the eighteenth dynasty. This heralded the start of a golden age for ancient Egypt, during which it became and remained prosperous and powerful for five centuries. The army was expanded, further professionalised and divided into two corps – infantry and charioteers. Egypt built an empire, conquering territory in what would today constitute parts of Syria, Lebanon and Israel. This was a point in world history known as the Bronze Age, when a sophisticated civilisation had emerged in China, when the Middle East was dominated by advanced states, and when much of Europe was made up of hamlets and small villages. In Salisbury, in southern England, the last of the Stonehenge monuments was being built.

The New Kingdom gives us the celebrity pharaohs, such as Tutankhamun, Hatshepsut and Ramesses the Great. My guide at the Valley of the Kings was archaeologist Yasser Abdelrazik. We sat on a ledge outside the tomb of Thutmose III as he imparted his knowledge with infectious enthusiasm. He said the large sprawling area, spanning several thousand kilometres, served as the burial site of the pharaohs for some 500 years. Early on during the New Kingdom the pharaohs gave up using pyramids as tombs and moved to the practice of cutting burial chambers out of natural rock in the Valley of the Kings. The workers who excavated and decorated the royal tombs were given the title 'Servants of the Place of Truth'. Together Yasser and I climbed up the steep metal steps into the tomb of Thutmose III – of whom more later – and admired the walls decorated with scenes of legendary battles and images of Egyptian mythology.

Queen Hatshepsut, c. 1507–1458 BCE

It was rare to be a female ruler in dynastic Egypt. Precedents were few: in the Old Kingdom, Nitokris took the throne during an interregnum, Sebeknefru was briefly queen at the end of the twelfth dynasty and Tauosre was considered a usurper. Royal women wielded influence and the mothers, wives, sisters and daughters of kings received honours. In ancient Egypt, women enjoyed freedom and had equal rights of property ownership. However, Hatshepsut was distinctive. She was not prepared to wait around for the son of another wife to become pharaoh. More than that, she wanted the ultimate power of the throne.

Hatshepsut had married her half-brother, Thutmose II. Royal incest was not a taboo for the ancient Egyptians – after all, the god Osiris had married his sister Isis, and the king was a god. Incestuous marriages were a way of concentrating power and wealth, and keeping it within the royal family. A pharaoh could marry his sister or daughter, and polygamy was acceptable, though most ordinary men had just one wife and marriage between siblings would not have been possible for commoners.

Hatshepsut had only one child, a daughter Neferure with Thutmose II. On the latter's death, his son by Iset, a secondary wife, was to be king, but this child Thutmose III was only an infant and so Hatshepsut, who was both his stepmother and blood aunt, was made regent. She was well practised in what it took to be a pharaoh, having observed her father on the throne and having ruled alongside her brother-husband Thutmose II, and so she adroitly manoeuvred herself into a position of supreme power.

From 1473 BCE, Hatshepsut was effectively pharaoh for nearly two decades, fortifying her hold on the throne through religion, claiming that she was a daughter of the god Amun-Ra. Carved on her monuments is an inscription from Amun to bolster this claim: 'Welcome my sweet daughter, my favourite, the King of Upper and Lower Egypt, Maatkaare, Hatshepsut. Thou art the Pharaoh, taking possession of the Two Lands'. Maatkaare, meaning 'truth is the soul of the Sun God', was a name Hatshepsut gave herself. Egyptian society would have baulked at a female pharaoh, so Hatshepsut was sometimes depicted sporting a full beard or even with a male body in royal statues, busts and engravings. Since iconographic traditions were based around male power, this might have been a way to mollify concerns about her gender.

Hatshepsut also set about burnishing her credentials by becoming one of the most prolific builders in ancient Egypt. The pharaohs were not self-effacing types, and the significance of the height and grandeur of monuments would be lost neither on subjects nor rivals. Hatshepsut excelled at

The sphinx of Hatshepsut

this. She commissioned hundreds of construction projects throughout the country. Her masterpiece was a mortuary temple in a complex at Deir el-Bahri near the Valley of the Kings.

Hatshepsut's massive building programme was both an exercise in self-promotion and evidence of how much wealth was accumulated during her reign. She presided over a peaceful period during which her shrewd economic management swelled the royal coffers. She sponsored trade expeditions to develop economic relations, and sent Egyptian merchant fleets gliding down the Red Sea towards what we would now call the Horn of Africa. About a decade into her reign she dispatched a fleet of five ships to Punt and brought back myrrh trees to plant in Egypt. Incidentally, she is credited with being the first to use finely ground burned frankincense to produce black kohl for eyeliner. The Egyptians also sought gold from other parts of Africa. They were one of the earliest civilisations to value the metal, believing the flesh of the gods was made of gold, their bones of silver and hair of lapis lazuli.

Hatshepsut probably died of natural causes after a long and successful reign. Popular myth, however, states she was murdered by Thutmose III (1479–1425 BCE) once he had come of age, but according to archaeologist Dr Zahi Hawass this is unlikely. He has written a book about Hatshepsut and told me that a CT scan on her mummified remains by Egyptian experts shows that she was obese and diabetic when she died in her mid-fifties from cancer – probably bone cancer. Hatshepsut's obelisk at Karnak, tipped with gold, towers above all the rest. She was the first queen to be buried in the Valley of the Kings – the cemetery of the pharaohs of the New Kingdom.

At the beginning of the reign of her successor Thutmose III, some of Hatshepsut's statues and monuments were damaged or destroyed, and her name and image chiselled off stone walls. Some historians attribute this to the vengeance of Thutmose III; others are not so certain that he was behind the destruction. However this attempt at erasure has not diminished Hatshepsut's place as one of the most accomplished and successful pharaohs during this illustrious period of ancient Egyptian history.

Thutmose III, c. 1481–1425 BCE

Thutmose III married Hatshepsut's daughter Neferure. No other reign is as well documented as his, and he is sometimes referred to as Thutmose the Great. The walls of his tomb at the Valley of the Kings are covered with depictions of his battles. Dr Zahi Hawass describes him as the Napoleon Bonaparte of the ancient world, such was his military prowess.

Unlike his mother-in-law, he was a soldier-pharaoh who

carried out about 14 campaigns in western Asia and south into modern-day Sudan. Egypt sought to conquer to protect its borders but also to attain the riches of those it defeated, and Thutmose often took young vanquished princes to Egypt to acculturate them; having ensured their enduring loyalty he would send them back home to rule. Thutmose III also had an interest in nature, taking plant specimens back to Egypt to grow and establishing a zoo at Karnak.

Tutankhamun, c. 1341–1323 BCE

Tutankhamun ascended the throne when he was about nine years old in 1332 BCE and is believed to be the son of Akhenaten, who had also ruled as pharaoh. Akhenaten had overturned Egyptian tradition by claiming the sun god Aten as the sole state deity, destroying statues of the popular god Amun-Ra, which gained him a reputation as being something of a heretic; some claim that he was the world's first monotheist. A few years after Akhenaten's death, Tutankhamun became pharaoh, an event that brought much relief to the kingdom, with the young king's advisers seizing the chance to revert to Egypt's previous religious traditions. When he was nine, Tutankhamun married Ankhesenamun, a daughter of Akhenaten and his wife Nefertiti, so his wife was his half-sister. Little is known about Tutankhamun's stepmother Queen Nefertiti, although she has come to symbolise the feminine beauty of ancient Egypt. Her almond eyes, high cheekbones, long neck and elegant profile are captured in a famous bust, and she may have ruled for a year or two after her husband's death under the name Djeser-ka-re or Neferneferuaten.

Tutankhamun had a disorder that prevented him from

GIFT OF THE NILE

walking with ease, and he died when he was around 18 years old. I descended with anticipation into his burial chamber. The main wall was richly painted, depicting Tutankhamun with several gods and goddesses. Encased in a glass coffin-like display cabinet were his mummified remains, covered by a simple white sheet with only his skull exposed. There lay the superstar boy pharaoh, who is perhaps the only African king whose name is known the world over.

The magnificent quartzite sarcophagus that contained his golden coffin is also exhibited in the surprisingly small chamber, which was crammed with nearly 6,000 objects for him to use in the afterlife. Most of his grave goods are in the Egyptian Museum in Cairo. The curator there, Ahmed Samir, had shown me Tutankhamun's iconic 11-kilogram solid-gold death mask, fashioned to look like Tutankhamun so that his soul could recognise his body and facilitate his resurrection. Other possessions on display included his jewellery, hunting knives, gloves that he would have used when riding his chariot, and a rather unglamorous large pair of linen underpants. Why was Tutankhamun's tomb found intact? Unlike other tombs in the Valley of the Kings, that of Tutankhamun's lay in a low position in the valley and had been covered by centuries of limestone and chippings from the tomb of another pharaoh. This meant its entrance was hidden, protecting it from the pillage and plunder that befell other tombs.

The lavish goods found in Tutankhamun's tomb in 1922 gave rise to a global fascination with him, despite his minor role in Egypt's history. The death mask made his face instantly recognisable during an era of mass media when photographs could be published all over the world in newspapers and journals. Given Tutankhamun's relatively meagre impact on Egypt, I can hardly fathom how much more spectacular the contents of the tombs of more important pharaohs must have been. Just imagine!

The pharaohs who succeeded Tutankhamun are more distinguished examples of pharaonic rule. The nineteenth dynasty of the New Kingdom was a line of warrior kings and under them Egypt reached the zenith of its power. The Nile Delta was wide open to attack from across the Mediterranean and for many years Egypt had waged intermittent war on the Syrians and Hittites. A stele in Tanis in the Delta area describes these pirates as coming in 'their war-ships from the midst of the sea and none were able to stand before them'. King Seti I and his son Ramesses II made it their life's work to beat back these seafaring warriors and recover Egypt's prestige.

Ramesses the Great, c. 1303–1213 BCE

Ramesses II, also known as Ramesses the Great, built some of the finest monuments of ancient Egypt, and his name was carved on more stone surfaces than any other pharaoh. Sometimes he had the name of his predecessors chiselled out and substituted his own. The temple of Luxor was begun by Thutmose III, enlarged by Amenhotep III (1390–1352 BCE) and the colonnade was built by Horemhab (1323–1295 BCE). Ramesses II added the First Pylon (the great gate), flanked by two colossal statues of himself and two of the highest obelisks, one of which now stands in Paris. The complex sits in the centre of modern Luxor, cars whizzing by, with the minarets of modern mosques competing for attention with the remaining obelisk. Ramesses also added the Hypostyle Hall at the temple of Karnak, which has 134 gigantic columns distributed in 16 rows. It is a magnificent and extensive

Ramesses the Great

site, and when I walked through the complex in the late afternoon I marvelled at how the rays of the sun darted playfully between the columns, adding to the temple's allure.

Ramesses II's appetite for huge building projects was matched by his sexual abundance; a libidinous fellow, he had about 50 wives and concubines and more than a hundred children, perhaps as many as 160. By the age of 15 he was already a father of seven!

Outside of the bedroom, Ramesses II was renowned as a courageous, unflappable and effective commander; his military campaign against the Hittites in Asia Minor resulted in an advantageous peace agreement for the Egyptians. A famous battle that took place at Kadesh on the Orontes River around 1274 BCE is described on the walls of his temples at Abu Simbel, Derr, Abydos and Karnak. After one of his armies was decimated by Hittite charioteers, Ramesses regrouped his forces and managed to seize a dramatic and improbable victory from the jaws of defeat. Riding his chariot, he pronounced: 'I shall go for them like the pounce of a falcon, killing, slaughtering and felling them to the ground.' The record of the battle is the earliest known example of a written description of tactics and formations in warfare. The peace treaty in the twenty-first year of his reign is believed to be the first such treaty ever put in writing in the history of the world. To consolidate the truce, Ramesses (perhaps unsurprisingly, given his romantic career) chose to marry the eldest daughter of the Hittite king Hattusilis. The match heralded one of the high points of ancient Egypt: newfound peace abroad, guaranteed by a vigorous army that deterred invasion and reinforced domestic prosperity. Ramesses the Great indeed.

According to the priest Manetho, Ramesses reigned for some 67 years, during which time he built at Abu Simbel in the far south of Egypt two of the most colossal rock-cut temples: one to himself as the god Amun-Ra, and the other to his favourite wife Nefertari as Hathor – the cow goddess of fertility, abundance and music. He was given to saying 'the sun will not appear before my beloved Nefertari does'. Her tomb at the Valley of the Queens is one of the most visited and admired today.

After Ramesses' death, military struggles with various peoples of the eastern Mediterranean resumed. From the long perspective of history, this marked the beginning of the end of pharaonic dynastic rule in ancient Egypt.

At that time, an important part of the population of the Delta hailed from what is now Libya. As the climate of North Africa became drier, these people were forced to move eastward, closer to the munificent Nile. While Seti I and Ramesses II had constructed a series of fortifications to keep them out, Rameses III gave these Libyans permission to settle in the western Delta. They were valued as cattle breeders, supplying the Egyptians with livestock that they could take as tribute or seize during raids. From the nineteenth dynasty onwards, the Libyans became a powerful military resource for the Egyptians. They were recognisable from the feathers in their headdresses, but their bodies were also branded with red hot iron to identify them. They proved effective soldiers, especially as charioteers. By the late twenty-first dynasty their numbers had grown so much within the army that when Egypt became divided once more, the Libyans seized control in 1085 BCE and ruled Egypt for 200 years, so the twenty-second to twenty-fourth dynasties of the New Kingdom were of Libyan descent.

The Libyans did not adhere to the same religious beliefs as the Egyptians and neither protected nor respected their places of worship. They were pushed out by the Kushites who originated downstream in what is now Sudan. The Kushites, who are the subject of the following chapter, had similar customs to the ancient Egyptians, and they governed Egypt for the best part of a century as its twenty-fifth dynasty. The next dominant force in Egypt was the Persians, and like the Libyans they were openly contemptuous of Egyptian deities, mocking the locals for worshipping gods in the shape of animals. They conquered Egypt in 530 BCE, and the country was now headed by Persian kings.

A return to rule by Egyptian pharaohs was brief, and the country became divided and weak. The kings of the last few dynasties maintained their power until the second Persian conquest in 341 BCE, at which time the history of Egypt as an independent power came to an end. Egypt had a great strategic significance owing to its geographical position. It was accessible from the south through the Nile

Valley, across the Mediterranean Sea from western Asia and Europe, and to the east from the Red Sea. This strengthened its civilisation, not only through facilitating lucrative trade but also a profitable interchange of cultures and ideas. However, its geography ultimately made it vulnerable to foreign invasion.

Alexander the Great, 356–323 BCE

Alexander the Great, son of King Philip II of Macedon, swept through areas as distant as Greece and India, conquering all before him, but he chose a strategically placed small fishing village on the Mediterranean coast of Africa, in Egypt, to build a new capital, Alexandria. When Alexander defeated the Persians in Egypt in 330 BCE he was welcomed by a people deeply resentful of two centuries of Persian rule. They saw Alexander as their liberator. He acknowledged their culture and embraced their religious beliefs, even presenting himself, according to ancient Egyptian tradition, as the son of the god Amun-Ra. To do so, he compelled an already exhausted army to make a gruelling six-month march across the desert to the temple of Amun-Ra at Siwa near the modern-day Libyan border. He knew that the gains in citizen morale and personal prestige made the journey indispensable. Alexander died at the age of 32 in Babylon, present-day Iraq, either from a fever or poison. Posterity will always remember him from busts and images, showing his face tilting to the right as though he were overseeing his many kingdoms, his hair curly and messy to reflect the dust and wind of battle, with an expressionless gaze, as if looking towards eternity. Within a century, the city he had founded was the most populous in the world, and today a statue of

Alexander on horseback brandishing a sword stands prominently in the city's centre.

Ptolemaic Rule, 323–30 BCE

After Alexander's death in 323 BCE, three dynasties founded by his generals controlled his empire: the Antigonids in Macedonia, the Seleucids in Asia and the Ptolemies in Egypt. His general Ptolemy became the first ruler of a dynasty that ruled Egypt for three centuries. Its kings went further than Alexander in practising Egyptian traditions. Indeed, Ptolemy, like a pharaoh, married his sister and began building a library at Alexandria. However, it was under his successor Ptolemy II, known as Ptolemy Lagis, that Alexandria became one of the main cultural and intellectual centres of the ancient world. Ptolemy II was not only a king and military ruler, he was also a historian, documenting the conquests of Alexander the Great. He spent lavishly on a 'House of Wisdom', a marvellous collection of books that made Alexandria irresistible to some of the greatest thinkers of the day, whether they specialised in science, law or the arts and humanities. The mathematician Archimedes (of 'Eureka' fame) was among those who studied there, and the polymath Eratosthenes was one of an illustrious line of head librarians until his death in the third century BCE. This gave Alexandria – a city in Africa – a unique status in the history of knowledge: for two centuries the Great Library there was the intellectual hub of the Mediterranean world. However, most of it was probably burned down in the last century BCE by Julius Caesar's forces; certainly its importance dwindled to the extent that it did not survive.

Although the Ptolemies were Greeks from Macedonia, by the end of their dynastic rule they had firmly asserted Egypt's status as an African civilisation. They built their monuments not in the Mediterranean metropolis of Alexandria, but in the south, deeper within the continent of Africa and in a pharaonic style. Their most important temples do not attract as many visitors as the Valley of the Kings and pyramids but warrant the effort. I journeyed north of Aswan to Kom Ombo. The site there combines two temples, with an open-air courtyard and imposing facade of columns, built for the worship of Sobek the crocodile god and Horus. Not far away at Edfu is a temple complex begun under Ptolemy III, which consists of traditional Egyptian elements from the New Kingdom along with Greek influences, and includes the well-preserved temple at Dendera. One new death ritual emerged during the Ptolemaic era: the use of gold in the mummification process. Several mummies were discovered within a collection of tombs just north of Cairo in late 2022. These had been fitted with golden tongues, toenails, fingernails and eye coverings. Egyptian archaeologists working for the Ministry of Antiquities believe the golden tongues were meant to allow the dead to converse with Osiris, the god of the afterlife, so that they could journey through the world of darkness.

The reputation and riches of Egypt, augmented – at least at first – by the shrewd management of the Ptolemies, drew the envy of Rome, giving rise to one of the most celebrated episodes in ancient history.

Cleopatra, 69–30 BCE

Cleopatra's name is a magical one. It conjures up beauty and romance, an image of a great seductress who cast her spell over two illustrious Romans (Julius Caesar and Mark Antony), before dying by suicide by clutching an asp to her bosom. Much of what we know about her is derived from Roman historians such as Plutarch, who, writing nearly 200 years after her death, demonised her as sexually depraved and an arch manipulator. His accounts provided a source for Shakespeare's play *Antony and Cleopatra*, and the 1963 epic film starring Elizabeth Taylor. I wondered how this perception might tally with an Egyptian academic's view of her. Dr Bahia Shaheen is a historian at Alexandria University and during a delightful walk around the city she put me straight, keenly telling me of Cleopatra's brilliance, which she said verged on genius. Cleopatra was a shrewd and gifted politician who succeeded in turning around the fortunes of Egypt after her father's reign severely depleted the royal coffers.

Cleopatra VII, a Ptolemaic princess, was only about 17 years old when she and her brother Ptolemy XIII succeeded their father in 51 BCE. They inherited an atmosphere of mounting acrimony and instability at the heart of government. Around that time, Julius Caesar, consul of the Roman Republic, was in Egypt; he had gone there in pursuit of the Roman general Pompey, who had fled to Alexandria after Caesar defeated him in the civil war. Cleopatra, sensing Caesar could be an asset in her rivalry with Ptolemy XIII, visited him to plead her case. It is a great story, but there is no real evidence that she was wrapped in a carpet and smuggled in to see him. Cleopatra remained for nearly a year with Caesar, who was more than twice her age, bearing him a son, Caesarion. Upon Caesar's return to Rome, Cleopatra joined him there and stayed for about two years. After Caesar was assassinated in 44 BCE, Cleopatra returned to Egypt, where she became the prime suspect in her brother's killing. With Caesar gone, Cleopatra needed to protect her throne, so she turned to the Roman general Mark Antony in what became her second celebrated political and romantic alliance. Cleopatra had three children with him: twins Alexander Helios and Cleopatra Selene, and a son, Ptolemy Philadelphos. Only her daughter survived to adulthood, becoming the wife of the North African king Juba II.

After Caesar's death, another civil war broke out in Rome between Mark Antony and Caesar's nephew and appointed heir, Octavian. In 31 BCE at the naval Battle of Actium (part of modern-day Greece) Octavian's forces prevailed. Mark Antony and Cleopatra escaped back to Egypt where Mark Antony died by his own hand, stabbing himself in the stomach. Cleopatra, now 39 years old, spent the next few days trying to seek a deal with Octavian. He refused, so she also took her own life, probably by taking poison rather than the more evocative but less reliable means of clasping an asp to her bosom. Her son with Julius Caesar did not escape death either; he was murdered by Octavian.

Cleopatra had an eventful life, but the attention given to her appearance has overwhelmed some of the more astonishing facts about her. The Roman historian Cassius Dio, who lived two centuries after Cleopatra, described her as an 'exceptionally beautiful woman who possessed a most charming voice', but Dr Shaheen says that statues, busts, coins and temple reliefs that depict Cleopatra show her to be not particularly attractive. From these we can see she had a disproportionately prominent nose, strong chin and deep-set eyes, but there are no contemporaneous accounts, so it is difficult to know what she looked like for certain.

Medieval Islamic writings describe Cleopatra as a virtuous scholar and a talented linguist who spoke around ten languages fluently; she was the only member of her Greek-speaking dynasty who could speak and read ancient Egyptian. She studied geography, history, astronomy, philosophy, mathematics and science, and enjoyed surrounding herself with intellectuals. These are the accounts that inform Dr Shaheen's view of Cleopatra, and stand in fulsome contrast with her exoticisation as a devious femme fatale in the Roman sources and in her contemporary reception in the modern West, where she has come to exemplify Western ideas of the luxurious and libidinous Orient. As a former student of Latin and Roman history at school, I now see how Cleopatra might have been the victim of Roman propaganda; after my time with Dr Shaheen I will not regard her in the same light ever again!

Cleopatra's death ended Ptolemaic and pharaonic rule in Egypt. In 30 BCE, Octavian took the title Augustus Caesar, Emperor of Rome, at the same time styling himself as pharaoh of Egypt. Augustus turned Egypt into an imperial province and used it as his own private estate, supplying Rome with grain. He and his successors did little to develop the country. Roman and later Byzantine rule in Egypt continued until it was conquered by the Arabs in 640 CE. As we will see in chapter 7, the near universal adoption of Islam and the Arabic language that the conquest brought formed the Egypt we know today: a leading Arab nation.

Let's turn back now to the words of Herodotus, who said that Egypt is the gift of the Nile. Egyptian archaeologist Dr Zahi Hawass believes that Egypt was, more accurately speaking, 'the gift of the Egyptians'. In his view, Egypt became a towering civilisation for other reasons, including, first, the influence of Ma'at, the goddess of justice and truth, was critical in ensuring that the rights of citizens were upheld by their leaders; and, second, the building of the pyramids was seen as a nationwide project, and this helped to unite all Egyptians in a common endeavour.

Ancient Egypt was a great chapter in Africa's history. Egypt's civilisation originated and endured there, and most of its impressive monuments were built 1,000 kilometres from the Mediterranean Sea, firmly within the continent – as African as the majestic River Nile itself.

3

The Kingdom of Kush

Kush was an ancient kingdom in what is today northern Sudan. Although it lasted for 3,000 years, many people have never heard of it. A leading Sudanese archaeologist Dr Shadia Taha, whose expertise informs and inspires much of this chapter, holds that the history of ancient Sudan has been obscured by Egypto-centric scholars. Most of the archaeologists who went to work in Sudan were Egyptologists, who saw ancient Sudan as a colony or 'offshoot' of Egyptian culture that always copied Egypt and was just 'a recipient of knowledge from there'. Dr Taha believes that 'both countries influenced each other . . . ancient Sudan was an advanced civilisation [that in its earliest form] predated ancient Greece and Rome . . . but has never received the credit it deserves'.

The US-trained archaeologist George Reisner epitomised the kind of Egypto-centricity Dr Taha describes: upon seeing some of the ruins of ancient Sudan in 1918 he wrote, 'The native negroid race had never developed either its trade or any industry worthy of mention, and owed their cultural position to the Egyptian immigrants and to the imported Egyptian civilisation.'[1] Such views began to be challenged with the construction of the Aswan High Dam in Egypt in the 1960s. This civil project necessitated the displacement and relocation of tens of thousands of people in both southern Egypt and northern Sudan, triggering fears that Sudan's undiscovered heritage would be lost forever and stimulating interest in its ancient past. While progress has since been made, Sudan is a huge country that is still underexplored and insufficiently researched. The punishing heat of the Sudanese desert means progress has been painfully slow; archaeological digs are only possible a few months a year. Furthermore, archaeology, as is the case across most of Africa, has received far less government funding over the decades than science, technology and medicine.

This part of Africa's story is very special to me since Kush is the region of Sudan from where my family hails, and so, as I stitched together the magical threads of the lives of Kushites long gone and visited the relics of their civilisation, I experienced a frisson of wonder that a country which today is synonymous with misrule, conflict and underdevelopment has a great history. It is that same instability and lack of investment which has, by contrast with Egypt, stymied tourism in Sudan for so long. To this day, the paucity of guests in their country makes the Sudanese extraordinarily hospitable to those who do visit.

The Kushites' achievements were impressive: treasures and objects have been found including exquisitely decorated ceramic pottery, dating as early as 8000 BCE, which, according to Dr Taha, predate any pottery found in Egypt by some 3,000 years. The Kushites also built 1,000 pyramids; 250 are still standing or have kept part of their superstructure. Their richly decorated interiors contained the treasures, furniture and personal belongings of the deceased king or queen, though these have long been plundered or removed for display in museums, with only the wall paintings remaining. The best-preserved collection of pyramids is at Al Begrawiya, around 250 kilometres north of Khartoum. There, in the vast expanse of the Sudanese Sahara Desert, dozens of pyramids loom upwards seemingly in the middle of nowhere. The change in climate over the centuries has since rendered the Kushites' region – once blessed with lakes, grasslands and choruses of birdsong – into a relentless ocean of sand.

I find the link between the old and new in Sudan endlessly fascinating. That some customs last even to the present day shows that history cannot simply be consigned to the past. My visit one afternoon to a mudbrick house in a small settlement in the quiet town of El Kurru, nestling at the foothills of the ancient mountain of Jebel Barkal, in northern Sudan, proved this point. The women welcomed me warmly, dressed in multicoloured Sudanese saris – the *tobe*. They took me around their home and showed me the earthenware water urns called *zeers*, their *angareb* or beds made of wooden posts with rope mattresses, ostrich feather fans and ceramic incense burners. These are some of the same objects the Kushites used. The women's eyes were made up with black kohl liner like the Kushite women I had spotted in temple reliefs, they wore gold bangles, put henna on their hands and they sported similar plaited hairstyles. One elderly woman bore facial scars, which also existed in the Kushite era, though scarification has now practically disappeared in northern Sudan.

Like many Sudanese today, ordinary Kushites were farmers who kept livestock and grew plentiful crops in the floodplains of the Nile. The Kushites did not fish there; in fact, they considered eating fish an abomination, perhaps because of its smell and tendency to grow putrid in the heat. This age-old abhorrence still influences modern-day Sudanese, whose fish consumption is one of the lowest in the world; on average it is just over 1 kilogram per person per year compared to nearly 25 kilograms in Egypt. One of my brothers has never eaten fish all his life and we joke that it must be his genetic memory at play.

The First Kingdom of Kush, Kerma, c. *2500–1450 BCE*

I wanted to learn more about the origins of Kush and so I sought out the expertise of both Dr Shadia Taha and archaeologist Dr Abdelrahman Ali, General Director of the Sudanese National Corporation for Antiquities and Museums. By 2500 BCE, one of the earliest city settlements in Africa and the world had established itself in Kerma (modern-day Karima), about 350 kilometres north of Khartoum. The region was accessible through the Nile southwards to Ethiopia and northwards to Egypt and the wider Mediterranean, and it was also well-connected to desert trade routes both west to Libya and southwest to sub-Saharan Africa. Its strategic position helped it become a major centre for intra-African trade.

Although the Kushites had to rely on oxen and donkeys for transportation of goods, for the camel had not yet been introduced, I gained an idea of how gruelling these desert routes must have been when I came across a camel train during a trip to Dongola in northern Sudan. The temperature must have been at least 40°C, though the climate would have been cooler in ancient times. The exhausted camel driver said his journey from western Sudan to Egypt would take about 45 days. After a short excursion on one of his camels, I wished him good luck, bade him farewell, and made a hasty and grateful retreat to the air-conditioning of my vehicle.

The city at Kerma would have been populated by people living in mudbrick homes such as the one I had visited at El Kurru. These were built around 'dafufas', which are huge, striking edifices constructed of the same material. The dafufas are large and imposing, dominating the flat expanse of desert under the baking heat, and alongside them are the clear archaeological remains of a large and sprawling urban settlement.

Of the two still standing, the western dafufa has three storeys and is 18 metres tall; it is believed to have been the residence of the native ruler of Kush. The eastern one is a funerary chapel surrounded by a cemetery of mound graves. About 30,000 graves discovered there give us a valuable insight into the Kerma civilisation. Traditional Kerma graves are marked by a dome-shaped earthen tumulus, ringed by

The western dafufa at Karima, Sudan

black stones and studded with white pebbles. Inside the grave, bodies were placed on the right-hand side of a bed with a wooden headrest, along with a pair of sandals and pottery for use in the afterlife – an ostrich feather was a dashing final touch. Such treatment was probably not for the masses, only for local princes and their families. I remember my late father telling me that as a little boy growing up in the far north of Sudan in the 1930s, he had memories of people leaving pots and pans in the graves of newly deceased relatives.

The settlement at Kerma, which united many communities in northern Sudan, was contemporary with the first dynasties of the Egyptian Old Kingdom, and the two traded together from the start through the Nile, with Kerma supplying Egypt with goods from the African interior, including gold, ebony, ivory, animal skins and ostrich feathers, in return for grain, linen and wood. Between 1780 to 1580 BCE, Kerma's vibrant tradition of craftsmanship produced fine objects

A traditional Kerma grave

such as delicate pottery, stoneware, jewellery and bronze mirrors. In their similarity to contemporaneous Egyptian artefacts, they demonstrate that these civilisations learned from each other, having developed from a common origin in prehistoric times. Recent research by Sudanese academics suggests that expertise in enamelling pottery and dyeing fabric first emerged in Kush before reaching Egypt. The columns of the dafufas are believed to have been decorated in a blue glazed ceramic coating, which would have looked rather splendid.

While trade flowed up and down the Nile, the Kushites had similar religious practices to the Egyptians, worshipping gods such as Osiris and Isis, calling the latter 'Mistress of Kush'. In addition to these, they had their own unique deity: the lion-god Apedemak, the god of war, for whom they built great temples. The Kushite kings were also fervent worshippers of the ram-headed god, Amun-Ra, and his power was universal. They frequently dedicated their womenfolk to his service in temples. Amun may have been a local deity of Egyptian Thebes, but Dr Taha cites evidence that the Kushites had independently considered the ram to be sacred. The Kushites (and Egyptians) believed Amun-Ra resided inside the holy mountain at Jebel Barkal, near Karima, about 350 kilometres north of the capital Khartoum, and for centuries its kings were buried at the site. The mountain still has special significance for the local population, now all Muslim: several women I encountered just outside Karima said they enjoyed regular excursions to the mountain, with one of them telling me she felt intense spiritual relief whenever she went there. Its temples are considered sacred.

Relations between Kerma and Egypt could by turns be hostile or friendly – as the remains of defensive forts in southern Egypt attest. Each raided the other, with the balance of power swinging back and forth. As mentioned, five of the River Nile's six cataracts are in modern-day Sudan, only one is in Egypt. This gave the Kushites an excellent natural defence against attacks by boats from the north. Herodotus, writing in the fifth century BCE, noted when describing a journey in northern Sudan: 'sharp rocks, some showing above water, and many just awash, make the river impracticable for boats'.

However, by 1550 BCE, ancient Egypt had entered its golden age. Queen Hatshepsut had expanded trading links so much that she coveted the Kushites' control of trans-African trade. Hatshepsut's successor, Thutmose III, sent an army up the Nile past the first two cataracts and defeated the people of Kerma in 1525 BCE. In about 1450 BCE, the rulers of Kerma decided to relocate their power base further south to Napata on the west bank of the River Nile, between its third and fourth cataracts (about 400 kilometres north of modern-day Khartoum), perhaps better to protect themselves from the Egyptians. Dr Shadia Taha believes their move was mostly motivated by economic and religious reasons: Napata was an excellent location for trans-Saharan trade and they were now closer to their sacred mountain of Jebel Barkal.

By the end of the first millennium BCE Egypt's power was in decline. Engulfed by its internal rivalries, Egypt paid little attention to its southern neighbour, meaning the kingdom at Napata could develop free of external interference. A few centuries later, in the eighth century BCE, the Kushites would reach the height of their power during a period of history often seen as the beginning of Western classical antiquity, when ancient Greece was founding colonies in the east Mediterranean and Rome was still a quiet backwater in southern Europe.

The Second Kingdom of Kush, Napata, c. 1450–580 BCE

Kashta the Pious, r. 760–747 BCE

The kings of Kush are among the figures in African history who fascinate me the most. Naturally I *would* say that, since this is also the history of my forebears, but I believe they are some of the most charismatic rulers of ancient Africa.

Alara was Kush's first named king. Little is known about him, though he is believed to have had a long reign. Alara's successor Kashta, probably pronounced Kushto, was a formidable leader. It is not certain how he became king of Kush, but he was most likely Alara's younger brother. Around 750 BCE Kashta became so dismayed by the decadence of Egypt that he believed it was his duty to save it from further ruin. He owned the gold mines that had helped Egypt flourish in its heyday and he controlled major trade routes along the Nile and overland. Like the Egyptian system, trade was based on barter rather than coinage.

Kashta's main place of worship was at the temple by the mountain of Jebel Barkal. The Egyptians had been the first to identify it as a holy site and by the time of Tutankhamun in the 1300s BCE there was a shrine there to the god Amun Ra, which was expanded into a temple, probably by Kashta's predecessor Alara. The Kushites depicted the god Amun Ra most frequently as a ram-headed human figure, holding a divine staff in one hand. In the other he held an 'ankh', a T-shaped cross with a loop above the horizontal bar; it was the symbol of life. His image was crowned with a sun-disc with tall feathers behind it. The Kushites held Thebes, home of Amun Ra, in high regard. They were indignant at the religious degeneration that a century of Libyan rule had wrought.

Libyan princes had found little resistance when they moved into Lower Egypt in the mid-tenth century BCE and established the twenty-second dynasty. They worshipped Egyptian gods and intermarried with the locals but for the most part kept to themselves, speaking their own language and living outside Egyptian settlements. The religious centre Thebes particularly had fallen into neglect. Taxes were imposed by royal representatives from Lower Egypt and buildings were left unrepaired, provoking outrage. Although Upper Egypt in the south was not occupied by the Libyans, their writ extended there. Around 832 BCE, the people of Thebes rebelled against the Libyan kings in Tanis and the revolt spread across the south. Libyan monuments and buildings were destroyed, and the Libyans retaliated by brutally suppressing the scribes and administrators of Thebes, arresting and burning the ringleaders alive. A stalemate ensued; for another century Thebes remained defiant, weakening Libyan rule.

This vacuum of power and erosion of traditions coincided with an ascendant Kushite kingdom, prompting King Kashta to act. Judging by his subsequent deeds it is possible that he did not seek to assert Kushite hegemony over the Egyptians, but rather saw himself as the true and pious guardian of their best interests, capable of returning Egypt to its righteous path and high religious standing.

The stage was set but, naturally, a redoubtable army would need to be assembled for, though weakened, Egypt would still mount a vigorous defence. Kashta rose to the challenge. The Kushite army laid great stress on training and expertise, and its cavalry and archers were some of the most skilled in the ancient world. The Egyptians sometimes referred to Kush as *Ta Sety*, 'Land of the Bow', and during Egyptian periods of dominance they conscripted Kush's best archers into their army. Their quivers were made of leather and their arrows of cane or smooth wooden shafts headed by metal, tipped with stone and dipped in poison. A special technique, now known as the Mongolian release, enabled greater power and accuracy. Using stone rings, the Kushite archers pulled back the bowstring with their thumbs, rather than with their fingers. Herodotus described Kushite soldiers: 'clad in panther and lion skin, carrying long bows . . . besides this they had javelins, and at the tip was an antelope horn, made sharp like a lance, they also had knotted clubs. When they were going into battle they smeared one half of their body with chalk and the other with red ochre'.

Kashta's two sons, Piankhi and Shabaqo, were his military commanders, and their mother Queen Pebatjma and sisters Amenirdis and Pejstater joined them in their campaign into Egypt – as was common practice for royal households. The people of Thebes mostly welcomed the army from the south as liberators, and the city was soon taken. Kashta asked the high priestess of the great temple of Amun at Thebes, an Egyptian princess called Shepenwepet, to take charge of his eldest daughter Princess Amenirdis, to treat her as though she were her own child and train her as a priestess. Amenirdis became the indispensable protectress of Kushite interests in Thebes, gathering vital intelligence for her father; through her, Kashta managed to maintain control of the city – she was his eyes and ears and could warn him of any impending challenges to his authority.

Unlike in many ancient societies, Kushite women had a powerful role to play in politics. Although they did not ascend to the throne, the female line of descent was of paramount significance. The succession in Kush differed from that in Egypt, where it was usual for a son to succeed his father.

In Kush, a king could be chosen from the deceased king's brothers, sons, cousins or nephews, depending partly on who his mother was. Queens in Kush could reign as equals with their husbands or sons; a ruling female coregent would be accorded the title *Kandake* (probably pronounced 'Kanda-key', and likely meaning 'queen' or 'queen mother' in the Kushite language). Greek and Roman writers would later mistake it for a personal name, which eventually gave rise to 'Candice'. The name 'Candassa' is still used in parts of Sudan, and during the country's popular uprising in April 2019, during which President Omar al-Bashir was removed from power, the female protesters who predominantly led the demonstrations were described as 'Kandakas'.

Female members of the royal family such as Princess Amenirdis were fashion conscious. She would have worn elaborate jewellery, like the fine gold rings, earrings, colourful beaded necklaces of ostrich eggshell, oversized bangles and ankle bracelets that I saw on display at the Sudan National Museum in Khartoum. Amenirdis would have kept her nails long and her hair closely cropped, perhaps with a topknot for special effect, and stained with henna, as is still the practice today. Unlike their Egyptian counterparts, Kushite women were usually depicted in temple reliefs as plump, with ample bottoms – markers of prosperity. Amenirdis, however, was expected to maintain a slim figure, like her Egyptian mentor Shepenwepet.

After gaining control of Thebes, Kashta assumed the trappings and style of a pharaoh and became 'Lord of the Two Lands', but the campaign into Egypt brought personal tragedy. His wife and his daughter Pejstater died during the mission, and they were buried at Abydos in Egypt. Three years after he had begun his invasion of Egypt, Kashta himself died. He was laid to rest in his homeland at El Kurru. His body had been mummified in the Egyptian manner, covered in gold foil and then placed in an elaborate wooden coffin inlaid with coloured glass and lapis lazuli. Kashta's body lay in an extended position, perpendicular to the River Nile, so that he faced east in the direction of sunrise.

As a dead king, Kashta would need a full store of grave goods for the afterlife, and so pottery, personal ornaments, furniture and jewellery were buried with him. Earlier Kushite burials placed the tomb outside their pyramid to one side, but Kashta's was placed on the floor of his pyramid. Kushite pyramids differ from those in Egypt: they are much smaller, steeper, and made of red sandstone, not granite. According to Dr Taha, this was due to the fact that pyramid burial in ancient Sudan was not just for the elite but for whoever could afford it, hence pyramids were smaller in size and more numerous. Although his territorial gains in his 13-year reign were relatively modest, Kashta established a crucial foothold for the Kushites in Egypt. His son Piankhi took his father's conquest further.

Piankhi the Conqueror, r. 747–c. 716 BCE

Piankhi, also known as Piye, was crowned king at the temple of Amun in Jebel Barkal. We know more about Piankhi thanks to the stele of Piankhi/Piye, a massive slab of dark grey granite measuring 1.80 by 1.84 metres, 0.43 metres thick and weighing about 2,300 kilograms, found at the temple of Amun in the nineteenth century. It is covered with 159 lines of text written in Egyptian hieroglyphics and is known as the 'Victory Stele'. It recounts how Piankhi defeated Egypt and ruled by establishing loyal princedoms. Although likely a form of propaganda, it is by far our best source for these events. It begins with Piankhi's words:

Hear of what I did, more than the ancestors. I am a king, divine emanation, living image of Atum, who came forth from the womb, adorned as a ruler, of whom those greater than he were afraid; whose father knew, and whose mother recognised that he would rule in the egg, the Good God, beloved of the gods, achieving with his hands.

Piankhi believed he was born a divine being, and that he had been commanded by the gods to act on their behalf for the greater good, and to uphold their values and virtue by defeating the unrighteous. He was a religious zealot with a touch of the megalomaniac about him, but not one who craved the use of unnecessary force.

The kings of Kush were polygamous. Piankhi's main wife was Tabiry, who was most likely the daughter of Alara and his queen Kasaqa – and therefore his cousin. Tabiry's funerary stele at El Kurru called her the 'First Great Wife of his Majesty'. Piankhi had four other wives, including another cousin, Abar, and possibly his sister, Pejstater. As in ancient Egypt, incestuous marriage within royal circles was common practice.

Piankhi's father, Kashta, had left an army presence in Upper Egypt and forged alliances with several Libyan rulers in the region. After becoming king, Piankhi took about four years to organise his troops and prepare for a big offensive north into Lower Egypt.

In the early 740s BCE his soldiers first advanced through Kush by land, and then sailed downstream to Thebes. In keeping with his deep religious beliefs, Piankhi, for whom this was a holy war, told his men that on their arrival at Thebes they should first wash themselves in the River Nile and worship at the temple of Amun, to fortify themselves and seek his protection so that one 'soldier alone could take a thousand men'. Accordingly, they bathed, dressed in fine linen and unstrung their bows, loosened their arrows and worshipped at the temple of Amun, sprinkling themselves with the water of the altars. They called on Amun to 'Give us the way, that we may fight in the shadow of thy sword'. Then they declared their allegiance to Piankhi by lying 'on their bellies' face down, crying out:

> It is thy name which imbues us with might, and thy counsel is the mooring post of thy army, thy bread is in our bellies, on every march, thy beer quenches our thirst.
>
> It is thy valour that giveth us might and there is strength at the remembrance of thy name; for no army prevails whose commander is a coward. Thou art a victorious king.

The Kushite army swept north and smashed through a languishing and fragmented Lower Egypt. When Piankhi heard the news of his army's victory, he was nevertheless displeased that one important prince, Tefnakht, had escaped further north, as recorded on the Victory Stele: 'His Majesty was enraged thereat like a panther . . . "I swear as Ra loves me! I will myself go northward so that I may destroy that which he has done, that I may make him turn back from fighting for ever . . . I shall make the Northland taste the taste of my fingers."'

Piankhi set sail to Egypt himself and took personal charge of the army. When he arrived at Thebes he met his sister Amenirdis and left his daughters, the princesses Mutirdis and another called Shepenwepet – just a child – in his sister's charge. Indeed, Shepenwepet became a divine worshipper and stayed at the temple at Thebes for 50 years. This was a position that accorded the holder a high status. They would be allocated property, cattle and geese, and provided daily with food such as bread, beer, milk and cakes. The death of a high priestess merited burial inscriptions praising her religious devotion and dedication.

Piankhi and his army set up camp on the southwest of Hermopolis – an important and influential city in the Delta – and lay siege to it. They surrounded the city walls with an embankment and built a tower from which archers could attack. The defences were soon overcome. A triumphant Piankhi entered the city and searched through all the rooms of the palace to see what he could take as booty. Whether out of piety or disdain he spurned the royal wives and daughters offered to him. When he entered the stables at the palace and saw that the horses had been left to starve, he became furious with Tefnakht, the defeated prince of Hermopolis: 'I swear that as Ra loves me, as my nostrils are rejuvenated with life, it is more grievous in my heart that the horses have suffered hunger; than any other evil deed that thou hast done in the prosecution of thy desire.' The Kushites not only appreciated the value of horses as the most efficient means of overland transport but believed they had inherent value, prizing the best specimens.

At the top of the stele, Piankhi can be seen with his back turned to the god Amun. He is receiving a ruler of Hermopolis with his wife and three other Libyan kings as well as several princes, from whom he is demanding loyalty and allegiance. The stele states:

He to whom I say 'You are a chief' he shall be a chief.

He to whom I say 'You are not a chief' he shall not be a chief.

He to whom I say 'Make an appearance as king', he shall make an appearance.

He to whom I say 'Do not make an appearance as king', he shall not make an appearance.

Piankhi then turned his attention to Memphis: 'I will take it like a flood of water as I have been commanded by Amun.' He ordered an assault on Memphis harbour in a fierce battle that lasted a day. It seems he himself assumed command, urging his men to go 'forward against it! Mount the walls! Penetrate the houses over the wall.'

The Kushite army delivered a decisive outcome: 'a multitude of people were slain therein or brought as living captives'. But the devout Piankhi ensured the temples were untouched amid the carnage. Once news of the defeat of Memphis became known, all the towns and villages in Lower Egypt capitulated: 'Then came the kings and princes of the Northland, all the chiefs, who wore the feather, every vizier, and every king's friends from the west, the east and the isles in the midst, to behold the beauty of his majesty.'

They offered Piankhi the treasures from their state coffers and their finest horses. He accepted and demanded their allegiance: 'Every one of them if he conceals his horses and hides his obligation shall dieth the death of his father'. After Piankhi's military campaign had concluded, he filled his ships with the treasures he had amassed and headed south to Kush, understandably 'with glad heart'. He would never go back to Egypt.

On his return to Napata, Piankhi assumed the throne-name Usermaetre. He brought with him architects and sculptors from Egypt and used the fine timber he had been given from the defeated Egyptian rulers to extend and enhance the Great Temple at Jebel Barkal to new levels of magnificence. At the entrance to Piankhi's temple were two red granite lions whose eyes were inlaid with jewels. Ten granite rams lined the avenue leading to the temple, and huge black granite falcons were among the statues that adorned the temple forecourt. The complex would have astonished contemporary onlookers. Unfortunately, the ravages of time meant that when I visited the site I was confronted only with the vestiges of columns on either side of the avenue, but its scale was nevertheless apparent, and through computer-generated images we can appreciate its former splendour.

At his death around 716 BCE, Piankhi was buried at El Kurru in a tomb that is believed to have been surmounted by a pyramid. His body was taken into a subterranean burial chamber, approached by a staircase cut into the rock. As I walked around Piankhi's pyramid, I felt a deep satisfaction that I could take the very same path as my ancestors when they buried their king. Piankhi's pyramid was raised over the burial chamber, entirely surrounded by an enclosure. It has lost a fair deal of its structure and in parts is missing some of its sandstone bricks. Like other Kushite kings Piankhi was not only fond of horses in life but wanted to take his best ones with him on his death; his four favourite horses were slaughtered, decorated with silver collars, plumes and beads, and entombed to serve their master forever. Piankhi's tomb was plundered: only its foundations remain, its treasures stolen. Mere fragments of furniture were found: a fine bronze stand, amulets with his name on them and bits of gold foil and lapis lazuli.

Shabaka the Builder, r. c. 716–702 BCE

Piankhi's younger brother Shabaka inherited a delicate situation. Egypt was proving difficult to subdue fully and he needed to find a way to consolidate Kushite authority. The Kushites had found a nation fractured into separate seats of power: the religious centre of Thebes (the most important, and brought under complete control by Kashta and Piankhi); Tanis, seat of the Libyans; and thirdly the Delta city of Leontopolis. Some rulers in the Delta remained loyal to the Kushites, while others soon rebelled.

To assert his presence in Egypt, Shabaka set up residence at Memphis, assumed the pharaoh throne-name of Nefer-kare and installed his son Haremakhet as high priest of Amun at the temple of Thebes. At the palace in Memphis, Shabaka lived in style with his wives, who included Queen Qalhata, believed to be Piankhi's daughter, and Tabakenamun – probably a sister-wife, though she might have been the daughter of a Libyan king, Mesbat. Shabaka had several children.

The energetic Shabaka had inherited the military talent of his father Kashta and won over some of the rebellious northern areas in successful campaigns. But he was a pragmatist too and was therefore content to forge alliances with those Libyan princes and chiefs in the Delta with whom he felt he could co-exist.

Shabaka is believed to have been a just ruler. Herodotus wrote of the characteristic combination of clemency and practicality that led Shabaka to introduce an ancient form of community service:

> When an Egyptian committed a crime it was not the custom of Shabaka to punish him with death; but instead of the death penalty he compelled the offender, according to the seriousness of the offence, to raise the level of the soil in the neighbourhood of his native town. In this way the cities came to stand very high indeed.

Through these dykes, towns were protected from the flood waters of the Nile. The Kushites were not remembered for using enslaved labour in building their monuments and Herodotus' account suggests they used convicts to help construct their cities.

Egypt entered a new period of prosperity under Kushite rule. Shabaka struck up trading links with Phoenicia, in modern-day Lebanon, importing cedar wood for his major building works in Egypt. He moved his capital to Thebes, where many of his most prestigious projects were based. He built an embalming house and a new treasury, and expanded the temple there, including the addition of a new main gate with huge images of himself carved out – an imposing projection of power.

However, in establishing ties with western Asian allies such as Phoenicia, Shabaka had also unwittingly made himself and his successors vulnerable to a dangerous rival: King Sennacherib of Assyria (based to the east of Egypt in Asia, between the Tigris and Euphrates rivers) who had succeeded his father Sargon in 705 BCE. While Shabaka and Sargon had enjoyed relatively good relations, Sennacherib was more ambitious and coveted Egypt. He resented the encroachment of the Kushites in areas he regarded as being in his sphere of influence.

Shabaka's alliance with Judah (the West Bank of the River Jordan) set the rivalry into motion. King Hezekiah of Judah felt his kingdom was under threat from the Assyrians and sent envoys to Shabaka, who agreed to offer him protection. Preoccupied with the confusion that had ensued upon his succession, Sennacherib decided to bide his time: he was not yet in a position to take on the Kushites and Egypt.

Shabaka spent most of his life in Egypt rather than Kush, but when he died in 702 BCE, his body was returned to his homeland for burial near Jebel Barkal. Shabaka had paved the way for the Kushites to become even bigger players on the world stage, but this brought his successors into direct confrontation with one of the most powerful armies in the ancient world.

Shebitqo the Global Player, r. *c.* 702–690 BCE

Shabaka's son Shebitqo was crowned as the new pharaoh in Memphis around 702 BCE, followed by a second coronation in the traditional Kushite capital Napata. By now King Sennacherib was asserting himself militarily. In 700 BCE, he ransacked the city of Babylon, took tens of thousands of people captive and destroyed the fields of anyone who rebelled against him. His ruthless Assyrian army pillaged its way throughout western Asia. City after city succumbed. Shebitqo was immediately drawn into the conflicts. He prepared an army to intervene in western Asia to help Egypt's allies. King Hezekiah of Judah again appealed to Kush to fend off the Assyrian advance.

Sennacherib sent personal envoys with a message for Hezekiah, which they proclaimed in Hebrew outside the walls of Jerusalem: 'Tell Hezekiah that the king of Assyria has a message for him. You have no one to depend on; no strategy, no strength of your own. You may be depending on Egypt for chariots and horsemen, but Egypt is a splintered reed that you would try to use for a staff. It will pierce your hand if you lean on it.' The Assyrians added for good measure that their message was for all the people of Jerusalem. It was unsubtle: 'Like you they will have to eat their own dung and drink their own urine . . . Hear the message of the Great King, the King of Assyria. These are the King's words.'[2]

The Kushite–Egyptian army, made up of the forces of Lower Egypt and Shebitqo's own Kushite troops, went into western Asia beyond Ashdod and established their headquarters at Gaza. A fierce battle ensued as two vast intercontinental armies met. Had Shebitqo lost, the path would have lain open for the Assyrians to attack Egypt. But Shebitqo's men prevailed. Jerusalem remained in Hezekiah's hands, and Kushite influence in the southeast Mediterranean burgeoned. At the temple of Osiris in Karnak, on the outer walls of the building, there is a scene of Amun offering Shebitqo a sword, around which are inscriptions of his success fighting foreign forces – a tantalising allusion to other battles.

When Shebitqo died in 690 BCE the kingdom passed peacefully to Taharqo, probably his brother. It was up to Taharqo to enhance the superpower status of this African dynasty.

Taharqo the Soldier-King, r. 690–664 BCE

Taharqo was crowned at Memphis amid delight and festivity in 690 BCE. Taharqo, his head wife Tekahatamani and his heir apparent, Prince Ushanukhuru, headed a royal household of considerable prestige and wealth. Following the practice of Kashta, Piankhi and Shabaka, Taharqo sent his daughter, Amenirdis II, to the temple of Amun at Memphis to train as a priestess. The Egyptian princess Shepenwepet had died, so Piankhi's sister, Amenirdis I, reigned at the temple with Piankhi's daughter Shepenwepet II as her designated successor. Now that the Kushites were a presence in Asia, Taharqo moved his palace further north to Tanis in the Delta, positioning himself closer to the Mediterranean Sea.

The early years of Taharqo's reign brought further peace and prosperity to Egypt. In his sixth year there was a bountiful harvest, and an inscription on a stele found in Kawa in northern Sudan quotes him: 'I heaped up the harvest into granaries, incalculable was the amount of Upper and Lower Egyptian grain and the various other cereals native to the land'. Taharqo converted enhanced political influence into stronger trade links with western Asia and obtained cedar wood and juniper from Phoenicia and Byblos, in modern-day Lebanon. This provided raw material for buildings throughout Egypt and Kush, such as the temple to the goddess Mut in Thebes and a new temple at Kawa in Kush. Taharqo favoured elegant designs, with entrances that had colonnaded porticoes.

One of my favourite buildings is a temple at Jebel Barkal. From a distance, the mountain of Jebel Barkal is an imposing 100-metre-tall outcrop of sandstone rock in the middle of a plain. As I drew nearer to it, I began to make out the remains of a temple carved inside it. Once I descended the dimly lit steps into the dark chamber, I was unexpectedly confronted by faintly decorated walls, the remnants of their colourings clearly evident, with patches of red, blue and yellow. On one wall is the image of King Taharqo making an offering of gold necklaces to Amun-Ra. On his head is a tight-fitting crown, possibly made of metal, with twin serpents representing the lands of Kush and Egypt. He is dressed in what we would describe today as a kilt, and on his feet are multicoloured leather sandals with a high curving strap. We know what the Kushite kings looked like from such portraits, as well as from dark granite statues from the eighth and seventh centuries BCE, which depict strong muscular physiques and features that have more than a passing resemblance to contemporary northern Sudanese.

While Kushite confidence steadily grew, Assyria was in turmoil. In 681 BCE Sennacherib was likely murdered by two of his sons as he made a sacrifice in a temple at Nineveh, possibly because they objected to his anointing a younger brother, Esarhaddon, as his successor. A crisis of succession ensued until Esarhaddon emerged as king. In an example of how determined and murderous he was Esarhaddon executed his brothers and their sons. Esarhaddon reasserted Assyrian power on the coast, and once local rulers in Tyre

Granite statues of the Kushite kings

and along the coast of Palestine had yielded, he turned his attention to the big prize: Egypt.

Taharqo was ready and met the might and fury of the invading force with a robust defence. Eventually, Esarhaddon and his Assyrians were forced to retreat. Taharqo consolidated his victory by providing support to rulers in cities that had been conquered by the Assyrians. Phoenicia, an important trading hub, closed its ports to Assyrian trade. But while Taharqo had succeeded in beating back the Assyrians, Esarhaddon's humiliation flamed up into a red-hot desire for revenge. He returned to Assyria to prepare for a major new offensive against Taharqo.

The following year, 671 BCE, Esarhaddon set off again

from Assyria, marching west through the Fertile Crescent, Phoenicia, Philistia and the Sinai Peninsula at the head of a vast army. His blustering claims that he was without equal among all kings and more powerful than Taharqo seemed truer than ever. The scene was set for a second encounter between the two rivals.

At Ishkhupri on the Egyptian coast, Taharqo was waiting. There ensued a ferocious engagement between the two armies, three battles fought without interruption over the course of 15 days in July. At length, the Kushites were routed, and Memphis fell to the Assyrians. Taharqo withdrew, probably wounded from the battlefield, and headed south to Thebes. As Esarhaddon entered Memphis, the remaining forces inside the city put up a brave resistance, fighting street by street. Kushite and Egyptian blood ran and congealed in the dust of the gutters of the royal city. Fatalities were immense. Esarhaddon recorded his victory over Taharqo and its macabre aftermath thus:

> Memphis, his royal city, in half a day with mines, tunnels, assault ladders I destroyed it, tore down its walls and burnt it down . . . I defeated and killed them with my weapons . . .
> In the city square their corpses were heaped upon one another, I erected piles of their heads . . . I entered his plundered palace. There I found his wives, his sons and daughters who like him had skins as dark as pitch.

Esarhaddon, astonished at the amount of wealth the Kushites had accumulated, gleefully looted the treasures and military equipment of Memphis. Taharqo had not expected to be defeated by the Assyrians, or he would not have left his chief wife Queen Tekahatamani and Crown Prince Ushanukhuru at Memphis and so vulnerable to attack. It is not certain what fate befell them, but it is believed that at least the queen was dispatched to Assyria. In shock along with the rest of Kush and Egypt, Taharqo, the great soldier-king, retreated to Thebes with the remnants of his army.

However, Esarhaddon had not fully conquered Egypt. He had only succeeded in pushing Taharqo out of Memphis and the Delta. He installed Assyrian officials to rule in his name, leaving them in position so long as they accepted his sovereignty. To the local population the Assyrians were a foreign conquering force and they quickly became restless. Taharqo spent some time recovering in Thebes and set about restoring his army to full strength. Esarhaddon had overstretched himself and while he had been out of Assyria on his military campaigns there had been a major rebellion against him, which he had to return to deal with. Taharqo seized his chance and moved back to Memphis. With his army refreshed he regained control of the city. The rulers and princes whom the Assyrians had installed scattered into the open country.

News of Taharqo's re-emergence reached Esarhaddon. He had managed to put down the insurrection against him in Assyria, and in 669 BCE he set off to make war with Taharqo for the third time. But Esarhaddon was struck down by illness and died en route to Egypt. He was succeeded by his son Assurbanipal, who immediately turned his attention to his father's incomplete mission. He resolved to quell Egypt and defeat the Kushites once and for all.

The seesaw in the balance of power between the Assyrians and Taharqo had by now left many rulers in western Asia sceptical of the latter, and so they failed to rally to his support. They threw in their lot with Assurbanipal, supplying him with armies that swelled his own substantial troop numbers. Despite the overwhelming size of the Assyrian forces, Taharqo was not deterred. When he heard of the advance of the Assyrian army in Memphis, he called up his soldiers, but they were no match for the Assyrians and their allies. A defeated Taharqo once again retreated to his stronghold in Thebes. Assurbanipal reinstated the princes and rulers of the Delta whom his father Esarhaddon had appointed.

Taharqo died soon after, probably in Thebes, and was buried at Nuri, about 20 kilometres from El Kurru, at the base of Jebel Barkal in Kush. Taharqo had chosen Nuri as his burial site, which henceforth became the royal cemetery, and he allocated himself the highest point for his tomb. His pyramid is the largest of those standing today.

Taharqo may not in the end have been able to ward off the Assyrian invasion of Memphis and the Delta, but his military prowess was considerable and his impact on the region indisputable. Without Taharqo's formidable opposition, it seems likely that the Assyrians would have conquered the lands of western Asia with greater ease, gone into all of Egypt and perhaps Kush itself. Taharqo kept the Assyrians at bay and tempered their influence. His name, appearing as Tirharka, is mentioned twice in the Bible, in recognition of his standing and as the protector of King Hezekiah. In Hebrew he is described as the 'King of Cush', in Greek as 'King of Ethiopia' (not to be confused with modern-day Ethiopia).

After the death of Taharqo, the succession was not certain because so many of his potential heirs had been killed, and his remaining sons may have been too young to rule. Eventually the crown passed to Tantamani, son of Taharqo's sister Qalhata.

Tantamani the Restorer, r. 664–653 BCE

Unlike his predecessor, Tantamani became king at what could hardly be described as an auspicious time. Part of his kingdom was in the hands of the Assyrians and their proxies. Tantamani was probably living in Thebes at the time of his accession, but he was crowned at Napata in Kush. A few months after his coronation, Tantamani had a dream, as the Dream Stele relates:

> His Majesty beheld a dream in the night – two snakes, one to his right, the other to his left, and when he awoke His Majesty found them no more. He said, 'Explain these things to me on the moment . . .' and lo they [his advisers] told him that this meant that he already ruled southern or Upper Egypt and now had to 'seize the northlands . . . and the two crowns will be put upon thy head, for there is given unto thee, the earth in all its width and breadth and there will not be another can compete with thee in power'.

Tantamani's resolve to recapture Memphis is recorded: 'Verily it was true what I dreamt . . . a boon it is for him who acts after God's heart, a plague for him who does not know it'. Tantamani set off north. In the Delta, the rulers who owed their position to the Assyrians tried to fend off the Kushite attack, but Tantamani's forces defeated them: 'there was a great slaughter amongst them, there is no knowing the number of the dead'. He recaptured Memphis from the Assyrians, and the death of the principal king of the Delta led to a Kushite reassertion of control over both Upper and Lower Egypt. However, Tantamani's success was short-lived: in 663 BCE Assurbanipal, outraged by the Kushites' re-emergence, marched his army back to Egypt and wrought revenge.

Assurbanipal conquered Thebes, which had escaped plunder and destruction in the earlier confrontations between the Assyrians and Kushites. He destroyed it. The greatest treasures at the temple of Amun, restored to magnificence by Piankhi and his successors, were looted and removed by the

Assyrians in what must rank as one of the biggest catastrophes of the ancient world. Taharqo's son Nesishutefnut was probably captured by the Assyrians in Thebes. Nevertheless, Upper Egypt was a distant land for the Assyrians, and after their destruction of Thebes they did not contest its government. They withdrew from Thebes, leaving Tantamani free to return.

Tantamani therefore was still pharaoh as far as the people of Upper Egypt were concerned. Monthuemat, an important Egyptian official married to the granddaughter of Piankhi, continued to administer Thebes on the Kushites' behalf.

In the Delta, closer to Egypt's Mediterranean coast, it was a different matter. There, the Assyrians reappointed their allies in the region, with one assuming the name Psamtik I as king. So Egypt was effectively being governed by two pharaohs: Tantamani, a Kushite, in the south and Psamtik in the north. In time, Psamtik I gained the upper hand and all of Egypt came under his influence. Despite his heroic efforts at restoration, Tantamani had lost Egypt after barely a decade in power. With his prestige and that of his kingdom badly damaged, he returned to Kush where he ruled as king until his death in 653 BCE.

Fifty years later, Psamtik II was on the throne of Egypt and Aspelta was king of Kush. Psamtik, perhaps still fearful of this kingdom to the south, invaded Kush. His army reached Napata, the Kushite capital. Aspelta withdrew further south to the ancient site of Meroe near the modern-day city of Shendi.

Dr Shadia Taha disputes the conventional view that the Kushites relocated to Meroe to put greater distance between themselves and Egypt. She says it is possible that feuding within the royal family precipitated the departure of a branch to Meroe, but it is more likely that they moved in pursuit of greener pastures to support better their growing population, and to take advantage of Meroe's large deposits of iron ore and acacia forests, which provided raw materials for their manufactured goods.

While the Kushite kings would never again try to conquer Egypt, they would rule Kush for another thousand years. Psamtik II and subsequent Egyptian pharaohs tried to erase the memory of Kushite rule in Egypt. For instance, at the Osirian temple of Taharqo at Karnak, Taharqo's name was removed and replaced by that of Psamtik II. Kushite monuments also slumber under the sand, waiting to be excavated; contributing to the relative obscurity of Kushite kings both in antiquity and in our modern era.

The Third Kingdom of Kush, Meroe, c. 590 BCE–fourth century CE

The ancient city of Meroe, not to be confused with the modern city of Meroe, is about 200 kilometres north of Khartoum and is now known as Al Begrawiya. It has the best-preserved remains of the Kushite civilisation so I was naturally curious to see it. After a long drive through the desert from Khartoum, with dwellings diminishing in number and the sandy landscape looming endlessly, I arrived at the site: on the horizon, set against reddish-brown hills, dozens of pyramids suddenly appeared, some lacking their proud pinnacle, others with tips rather incongruously restored by concrete. To the west lay the Royal City, with its ruins showing evidence of a palace, library and temples, each with carvings on their walls and pillars. A bathhouse with large, elaborate stone seats was further evidence of the level

The pyramids at Meroe

of sophistication this society enjoyed. The attendant gener-
ously unlocked the door of the bathhouse and allowed me to
sit on one of the seats, giving full rein to my imagination of
how a Kushite woman might indulge in a steam bath and
massage while enjoying a good gossip with her fellow bath-
ers. To supply water to the city and to expand their agriculture,
the Kushites built reservoirs and tanks, and developed a type
of waterwheel that improved irrigation.

Meroe prospered and served as a focal point for commerce, using riverine and overland routes to connect with
territories in northern and southern Africa, as well as east
across the Red Sea coast. Trade was brisk and extended
even to India and China. Iron ore and acacia wood were
used to make furniture and tools, which were exported.
The smelting of metals such as iron was a huge industry,
and numerous furnaces have been found in Meroe, leading

to its description as 'the Birmingham of Africa' (that city being at the heart of the nineteenth-century Industrial Revolution in England).

The Kushites sent envoys to Rome and West Asia, and enjoyed cultural exchanges with other civilisations, as evident from their architecture at the site of Musawwarat, near the Royal City. The temple there has columns built in the Greek style, and the complex also bears inscriptions in Latin, one of which is believed to have been made by a third-century Roman official, wishing 'Good fortune to the Lady Queen' of Kush. A larger-than-life bronze head of the first Roman emperor Augustus with its distinctive piercing eyes and dated about 25 BCE, on display at the British Museum in London, was found at the Meroe site and was probably looted by the Kushites from Roman Egypt.

At Meroe, power was more decentralised than it had been in Napata and the role of royal women or Kandakas became even more significant. For example, the Meroitic queen Amanishakheto, who ruled at the end of the first century BCE, is depicted on the walls of a temple as a woman of ample proportions, weapon-handed, towering over her fair-skinned enemies. As I stood by Amanishakheto's pyramid and tomb at Meroe, I felt frustration that they, along with many others, had been desecrated and plundered over the centuries. The pyramid's tip was destroyed and its priceless storehouse of fine jewels and personal belongings were looted by Italian soldier turned treasure hunter, Giuseppe Ferlini, in the 1830s.

Amanirenas, another renowned Kushite queen, was a soldier who lost an eye fighting alongside her son against the Romans in 30 BCE. Kushite queens not only fought but could also lead their men into battle. Amanirenas kept the Romans, who now governed Egypt, away from her kingdom, signing a peace treaty with them in 22 BCE.

The Kushites spoke their own language, and their writing system differed from the Egyptian one. 'Meroitic hieroglyphics', as they are known, cannot be understood; experts have an idea of how words might have sounded but not their meaning. Until we can decipher the script, inscriptions on Kushite monuments remain a mystery, so it was with a degree of exasperation that I peered at a column with Meroitic writing, hoping that soon some archaeological discovery will help unlock their secrets.

Little is known of the last age of the Kushite kingdom at Meroe, but it seems that again tensions within the ruling family and environmental degradation, such as overgrazing by cattle and soil erosion, played a part in its decline. Moreover, trade caravans began to find different and easier routes through the Nile Valley and across the Red Sea. By the fourth century CE, the emergence of Aksum, a powerful new kingdom based further south in Africa on the Red Sea coast, had begun to encroach on Meroe's status as a trade centre. Meroe fragmented into small kingdoms until it completely collapsed in about the sixth century CE and the sun set on a magnificent era in Sudan's ancient history.

The veteran Swiss archaeologist Charles Bonnet, whose work in Sudan spans more than five decades, believes that much has yet to be discovered and excavated there. He said in 2017: 'We have here [in Sudan] an extraordinary history of the world; maybe after some years we will have Sudanology as strong as Egyptology.'³ Few people today realise that a substantial number of Egypt's monuments were built by the Kushite kings. When I visited Karnak in Egypt, I gazed up at a tall stone pillar, the only one remaining of ten built by Taharqo that still stands at its original height, and I sat by the edge of the sacred lake, a large rectangular basin that receives its water from the Nile. Its construction predated the Kushites, but it owes its present form and shape to Taharqo. It was a quiet spot to reflect and ask myself why the accomplishments of the ancient Sudanese during this period have been forgotten. In my opinion, the answer has a great deal to do with the fact that Egypt's twenty-fifth dynasty is described by Egyptian and Western academics as 'Nubian', which can obscure the Sudanese origins of these Kushite pharaohs and serve to 'Egyptianise' them. Referring to these kings as 'Nubian' could imply they hailed from Egypt, which also has a Nubian population. The Kushites were ancient Sudanese – though of course modern Sudan encompasses not only Kush, but the history of many other peoples besides. Archaeologists and historians in Sudan generally do not refer to them as Nubian; indeed, the term was not even in existence at the time of the Kushites.

Additionally, the Sudanese themselves have not been as diligent as the Egyptians in promoting their heroic ancient past. Conversations with many ordinary Sudanese revealed that very few had more than a superficial grasp of their history. When I asked my elderly mother, an educated woman, what she knew about the Kushite period, she struggled to tell me anything other than what the pyramids looked like. We need more research into and accounts – accessible and easy to understand – of this splendid chapter of Africa's story. I hope this one can be a start.

4

Ezana of Aksum and the Rise of a Christian Kingdom

As Meroe's star waned, that of Aksum's rose. Its fame spread far and wide. The third-century Persian mystic and historian Mani was so impressed by what he learned about Aksum that he described it as 'one of the four greatest civilisations of the ancient world', along with Babylon (or Persia), Rome and China. Another illustrious African kingdom then, that like Kush has fallen into the footnotes of global history.

The kingdom of Aksum, which lasted a thousand years, was located on the northern edge of the highland zone of the Red Sea. At its peak between the third and sixth centuries it covered a large expanse of territory that today includes Ethiopia and Eritrea, and its influence extended further into eastern Africa and even beyond into Arabia. At around the same time, most of western and central Europe was under Roman rule. From the late fifth century, with the fall of Rome, Germanic groups such as the Ostrogoths and Vandals began to take over parts of Europe, so that the continent fell into what is described in European history as the Dark Ages, from 500 to 1000 CE. Practical and cultural knowledge from Classical antiquity dissipated and was lost, and living standards radically declined across Europe.

Meanwhile, the Aksumites had their own written script, coinage, and were building castles, monuments, churches and monasteries. Their kingdom was the second in the world after Armenia to adopt Christianity as its official religion, many centuries before Christianity had even reached other parts of Africa south of the Sahara. While most of their region – what became known as the Horn of Africa – became Islamised, Ethiopia retained Christianity as its state religion until 1975.

Today there is a city in northern Ethiopia called Aksum, and as befitting its lofty historical status it is situated 2,100 metres above sea level. The air is thin, and it took me a while to acclimatise as I wandered along its wide streets. Shopkeepers in their tidy stores seemed to be doing a brisk business. As I passed two churches within close proximity of each other, I thought of the twin pillars on which the ancient kingdom of Aksum had thrived and prospered: trade and religion.

Pre-Aksumite Civilisation

Even before Aksum became rich and powerful from international trade, commerce had been established as the lifeblood of the region. This part of Africa enjoyed extensive economic ties with the ancient Egyptians dating back 3,500 years. The Egyptians named it the Land of Punt (meaning 'land of the gods') and it likely comprised parts of what are today Eritrea, Ethiopia, eastern Sudan and Somalia.

In the first millennium BCE, a large group of traders,

settlers and farmers in search of fertile land boarded their boats and sailed from Saba (modern-day Yemen) across the sparkling swells of the Red Sea to Punt. It would not have been a long and difficult journey – at its closest point the Arabian Peninsula lies less than 20 kilometres from the Red Sea coast of Africa. The Sabaeans and locals exchanged ideas and skills, and shared knowledge about methods of cattle management. New irrigation techniques were developed, which boosted crop yields. The region's climate, rainfall patterns and rich soil made it ideal for farming and herding livestock, so in addition to trade the people had a secure agricultural base on which to build their civilisation and prosper further.

Over time this community established a port at Adulis (locals call it Azuli today) about 55 kilometres south of the modern Eritrean port of Massawa. Adulis became one of the most important port-cities in the ancient world. Today, it is an uninhabited wasteland, silent, dusty and deserted, save for the odd passerby.

The ruins there attest to its amazing past: the remains of houses, distributed between narrow winding alleys, with rooms that would have been adorned with art, indicate that its ancient inhabitants enjoyed a very comfortable lifestyle. Much of Adulis remains to be excavated but Eritrean archaeologists are gradually uncovering its former glory. Exquisite glassware, beautiful pottery, bronze lamps and other fine objects provide a tantalising glimpse into a little-known civilisation. One of the most striking finds is a small sphinx dating from about the 800s BCE, discovered in an area further west from Adulis called Adi Gramaten. It is made of limestone, and a Sabaean inscription under it refers to the sacrificial stone that accompanied it. The figure displays the head of a woman and the body of a lion, and its style confirms connections with Kush and Egypt.

The sphinx found in Adi Gramaten

The mountainous region of southern Eritrea, where Adulis lay, encompasses the site of Qohaito. Rock art found there shows the area was inhabited for some 7,000 years. The mist that bathed the tops of the mountains on the morning I set off to visit Qohaito heightened my expectations of what I might see. I was taken aback by the sheer number of archaeological remains I found there. These are spread over a wide area and include the temple of Mariam Wakiro, which has four columns, square pillars, and a mass of fallen stones as well as the clear ruins of walls. The local Eritrean guide Sulaiman Umar who took me on a tour of the site was visibly excited to show me around, for visitors are rare. He stamped his feet on the ground, telling me that beneath us lay perhaps up to 30 more sites yet to be excavated. Eritrea, which gained its independence from Ethiopia in 1991, is internationally isolated and a lack of public funds means excavation work has not yet begun in earnest. So, our knowledge of its ancient history is scant, but the various societies that lived both inland at Qohaito and closer to the sea at Adulis must have had dealings with one another, although they were probably distinct communities. In time, inhabitants of both Qohaito and Adulis interacted with the Sabaeans who had arrived in their midst.

The best-preserved remains of the fusion of local and Sabaean culture are found at Yeha, in northern Ethiopia, about 16 kilometres outside the modern city of Aksum. Comprising a palace and temple, the site is believed to have been built about 500 BCE, although the region was settled long before that. Yeha was probably the first urban centre in a short-lived kingdom bearing the name Damat, or D'mt, and would have been a commercial hub, given it was not far from the port of Adulis. The inhabitants of Yeha included priests, soldiers and farmers as well as artisans, and tools made of iron have been excavated, suggesting they had developed small-scale industries.

As the years went by, the Sabaean language of the settlers mixed with the local tongue and gave rise to a new dialect, Ge'ez, which gradually supplanted others and evolved into the modern Amharic and Tigrinya languages of today. The first examples of a specific Ethiopic script, similar but distinct from Sabaean, date from the late third or early fourth centuries CE, making it one of the oldest written languages in Africa. It was this early civilisation that laid the foundations for Aksum in the first century CE.

Aksum, first to tenth centuries

The rise of the kingdom of Aksum was gradual. Initially a principality, over time it became the capital of a feudal kingdom that established its power over segmentary states in northern Ethiopia. Sometimes a new king would have to flex his muscles in a show of strength to maintain his authority. The state had its centre at Aksum and beyond lay its vassal kingdoms, whose rulers swore allegiance to the Aksumite king. In order to secure a degree of autonomy they had to pay him substantial annual tributes, which greatly swelled his state coffers.

Like the Kushites before them, the kings of Aksum grew rich and powerful from their control of the Red Sea trade between Africa, India, Asia and Arabia, and their grip on crucial overland and maritime routes in the ancient world was made possible by their military might, which they exploited in full to maximise the advantages of their strategic position. The Aksumites held sway over the critical Bab el-Mandeb Strait, connecting the Red Sea to the Persian Gulf and India, and traded through the Malacca Strait, a gateway to southeast and eastern Asia.

Aksumite sites have yielded large quantities of archaeological material such as terracotta vessels (mostly red but some black), decorated in animal motifs, reflecting the high level of artistry in Aksum. The Aksumites also imported goods, artefacts and wine from the Mediterranean and China, and from across the Indian Ocean, including wine goblets with hints of turquoise, vessels for oil, glassware, gold ornaments and fine jewellery. The king received the lion's share of trade revenues, but the ruins of residences indicate there was a large upper class, and tombs and monuments point readily to the considerable wealth of these elites. Trade was brisk, plentiful and profitable and the Aksumites patrolled both sides of the Red Sea to ward off attacks by pirates who tried to seize ships laden with valuable imports or exports such as salt, gold, ivory, frankincense and myrrh – the Egyptians needed copious amounts of incense to burn in their temples.

The port at Adulis was a significant centre for the ivory trade, and the Greeks mentioned it as a commercial hub for rhino horn and tortoiseshell too. Ivory was especially valued by the Aksumites, and they had learned how to capture and tame elephants, which they also used in the royal court, in warfare and as an efficient means of transportation.

To facilitate their international trade the Aksumite rulers developed coins. Aksum was one of the first places in Africa to mint its own gold, silver, bronze and copper coins under King Endybis in the second half of the third century. These coins circulated far beyond the borders of Aksum – some were discovered in India, providing further evidence of the kingdom's extensive geographic networks. The coins preserve the names of some 20 kings.

As I scrutinised a collection of ancient coins at the Archaeological Museum of Aksum with archaeologist Yalem Tesfay, I struggled to distinguish one king from another. They all looked very similar, represented usually in profile with large almond-shaped eyes and noses that fell straight from the forehead. Endybis is depicted sporting a simple headcloth, while subsequent rulers were given a crown in more grandiose style, and from the late fourth century the king is shown

Coins depicting Endybis. Crescent moons are visible at the tops of the coins

carrying a sceptre or fly whisk. Several thousand coins have been found in and around Aksum with Greek writing and then later the Ethiopic Ge'ez script, and featured various symbols such as a disc and a crescent (before they became Christians the Aksumites worshipped the moon god Almaqah, whose symbol was the crescent). The coins also bore the names of kings such as Ousanas (also known as Ella Amida), Wazeba and Ezana – of whom more later. The first recorded king of Aksum is Za Hakala, who ruled around 100 CE.

Little if anything is known about Za Hakala (or Zoscales), but he is given a mixed review in a first-century Greek text, *Periplus of the Erythraean Sea*, which was a trading guide, possibly written by an Egyptian merchant: 'These places from the Calf-Eaters to the other Berber country are governed by Zoscales, who is miserly in his ways and always striving for more, but otherwise upright and acquainted with Greek literature.'

However, there is an altogether more romantic tale of the Aksumite kingdom's origins.

The Queen of Sheba, hypothetically c. *tenth century* BCE

The story of the Queen of Sheba founding the Aksumite kingdom owes at least as much to tradition as it does to historical fact. According to Ethiopian sources, the Queen of Sheba travelled from Aksum to the kingdom of Judah to visit King Solomon. He was renowned for his great wisdom and she wanted to seek and test his advice on a number of significant issues. Indeed, the Torah and the Old Testament describe her as arriving in Jerusalem with 'a very great retinue, with camels bearing spices, very great amounts of gold and precious stones'. The Ethiopian account of Sheba and Solomon is set out in the *Kebra Nagast*: the book of the 'Glory of the Kings'.

The *Kebra Nagast* is a compilation of legends, folklore and traditions relating the heroic deeds and victories of Aksum's kings and queens. It was written in the Ethiopic language Ge'ez in the thirteenth century, possibly by monks, and plays a central role in Ethiopian culture to this day.

Descendants of Ethiopia's last emperor, Haile Selassie, who view themselves as the living embodiment of a great imperial past, are particularly attached to the *Kebra Nagast*. I discovered this first-hand from Haile Selassie's eldest granddaughter Princess Mariam Sena in Addis Ababa. Dressed in elegant traditional Ethiopian robes made of spun cotton, spectacles perched on the end of her nose, and sitting in an elegant room surrounded by family pictures of the emperor and her late father (Haile Selassie's eldest son, the crown prince), she told me she firmly believes the story of Sheba and Solomon is grounded in history and that it provides the foundational basis for Ethiopia's identity and culture as well as its Christian traditions. Princess Mariam views the Queen of Sheba as a strong role model and inspiration for women in Ethiopia today, and is certain that she is descended from her.

The account is one familiar to many Ethiopians: the Queen of Sheba visited King Solomon in Jerusalem, specifically to gain his guidance on how to govern – for, according to the *Kebra Nagast*, women in Aksum could inherit and rule and enjoy equal status with men. The two monarchs fell in love and on her return to her homeland Sheba gave birth to Solomon's son, Menelik. The *Kebra Nagast* also states that Sheba was converted to Judaism by Solomon. When Menelik was old enough, Sheba sent him to Jerusalem to seek his father's blessing. On his departure from Jerusalem, Menelik surreptitiously took the sacred Ark of the Covenant back to Aksum for safekeeping. This contained the Ten Commandments handed to the prophet Moses by God.

According to Ethiopian tradition, the sacred Ark of the Covenant is kept in a small, simple outbuilding of the Church of St Mary of Zion in Aksum and is watched over by a lone monk who lives there and rarely ventures out, guarding this precious and sacred treasure of Christian Ethiopians. When I stood outside the plain white building, white doves fluttering in the forecourt, it was incredible to think that inside was a mysterious individual performing this most holy of duties. Both custodian and hallowed object are hidden from view. Even the patriarch of the Ethiopian Orthodox Church, Abune Mathias, has never seen the Ark of the Covenant. Dressed in black robes, with a matching headdress, three crucifixes on long silver chains around his neck and sporting a full grey beard, he told me he had no doubt the Ark of the Covenant was indeed kept at Aksum and that some of his predecessors had seen it. Replicas of it are used in churches all over Ethiopia and these are shielded from public gaze by a sheet called a *tabot*. The assumed presence of the sacred Ark of the Covenant helped to make Aksum a religious hub in Christendom and attracted early Christians from across continents. The *Kebra Nagast* records that Menelik is the first king of Aksum.

The Queen of Sheba herself continues to fuel controversy. Some historians doubt her existence, others suggest that Sheba was actually from the ancient land of Saba in southern Arabia, today's Yemen, or that she was ruler of both southern Arabia and Aksum. Not far from the modern city of Aksum is the site of Dungur, a sprawling collection of ruins, tidily stacked and clearly showing a series of rooms and corridors, which locals will tell you are the remains of Sheba's palace. The 40-room mansion at Dungur would have had several upper storeys and a basement. Built of timber and stone, its doors and window frames were wooden. The ruins include bathrooms and the remnants of large ovens in kitchens, a hint at the lavish feasts that would have been held there. However, the palace is believed to date from the seventh century, so the dates do not tally with when the Queen of Sheba is believed to have existed, hundreds of years earlier. It is more likely to have been the home of a noble Aksumite family.

The story of the Queen of Sheba and the Ark of the Covenant are embedded in the Ethiopian national psyche. Even when historical fact and archaeological evidence contradict such beliefs, tradition has a powerful role to play in augmenting, explaining and preserving the past, as well as articulating present identities.

King Ezana, r. c. 320–360

Aksum's most significant king was Ezana. This may seem like an ill-deserved accolade since his rule, even by the standards of most Aksumite kings, was particularly absolute and autocratic. He relied greatly on administrative personnel to run his domains and one hopes they were more benevolent than their sovereign. Ezana was both ruthless and brave and for a powerful king showed little regard for his own personal safety, leading his men into battle. Ezana claimed the title 'King of Kings' and carried out successful military campaigns against neighbouring communities such as the Afar to the east. He held sway over the Horn of Africa and parts of southern Arabia. Ezana meted out severe punishments to those who opposed him and exacted substantial tributes from people he defeated. He had a large labour force and army, and his fighting ranks were augmented by enslaved men captured from neighbouring populations. Ezana's military expeditions included one to the Kushite kingdom at Meroe. Current Ethiopian historians such as

Dr Teklehaimanot Gebreselassie Engida support the conventional view that Ezana defeated the Kushites at Meroe. However, the Sudanese archaeologist Dr Shadia Taha believes his dominance over them was less a reflection of his strength and more the result of a decline in Kushite power brought about by internal factors. In any case, Aksumite power eclipsed that of the Kushite kingdom.

Dr Engida told me that Ezana was originally a pagan and practised human sacrifice to appease his gods – a fate that befell some unfortunate individuals whom he had conquered in battle. Much of what we know about him is from the Ezana Stone, a large slab of grey stone with inscriptions written in Ge'ez, Sabaean and Greek. The first writings on the stone relate to Ezana's pagan beliefs, and record that 'a dozen oxen were offered up at a single sacrifice'. They list victories and describe him as the 'King of the Aksumites ... king of kings ... son of the invincible god Ares'. One inscription, giving particular thanks to Ares, states: 'On behalf of the favour of the one who begot me, the invincible Ares, I erected to him statues, one gold, one silver and three brass for good.'

The stone states of Ezana: 'I am the son of Ella Amida'. King Ella Amida was a contemporary of Constantine the Great of Byzantium – the Eastern Roman Empire. In the early fourth century, Constantine had moved his capital from Rome to Constantinople, modern-day Istanbul. The court of Aksum was on friendly terms with the Byzantines and the two kingdoms enjoyed a good number of commercial and cultural links. Ella Amida and his son Ezana would have studied and spoken Greek, which at the time was the lingua franca of the eastern Mediterranean. During Ella Amida's reign a significant event took place that would subsequently transform Ezana and change the course of Aksumite history.

Two Syrian Christian brothers from Tyre were captured on

the Red Sea coast, probably on their way to India, and taken to the court of Aksum. One brother, Aedesius, became a royal cup bearer. The other, Frumentius, also known as Frumentatos, so impressed the king with his knowledge and demeanour that he appointed him counsellor and tutor to the royal children. When King Ella Amida died, the queen asked Frumentius to remain at court to assist the young Ezana – still a boy – as he governed. Frumentius took the opportunity to imbue Ezana with Christian teachings. Initially Ezana tried to integrate this new religion's thinking with his old traditional beliefs.

At some stage during Ezana's reign, Frumentius went to Alexandria in Egypt to meet the patriarch there, Athanasius I, who was a hugely influential theological thinker, a venerated figure seen as a pillar of Christianity. Frumentius asked Patriarch Athanasius to nominate a bishop for the Christians living in Aksum. In an enormous demonstration of confidence, Athanasius decided there was none better suited to the role than Frumentius himself and so he was duly appointed bishop of Aksum.

Upon his return to Aksum, Frumentius, suitably aggrandised, baptised Ezana and the royal family. Ezana had by now been on the throne for some years, and his conversion was therefore a rather protracted affair. Did Ezana have a change of heart and mend his former ruthless ways? Well, after his conversion, there are no records of human sacrifices being carried out on his command, and newly minted coins bore statements such as 'may it please the people', 'by the Grace of God', and 'mercy, peace, joy and salvation to the people'. Henceforth iconography on the centre of coins included the symbol of the cross.

Later inscriptions attributed to Ezana suggest that despite his long-simmering conversion, he eventually drew considerable strength from the Christian God:

Coins depicting Ezana, including the symbol of the cross

I am not able to tell the full measure of His favour, because my mouth and my mind are not able to tell all the gracious things which He has done for me: that He made me strong and powerful and He gave me a great name through His son in whom I believe and He made me leader of all my kingdom because of faith in Christ, by His will and the power of Christ; because He himself led me, and in Him I believe, and He Himself became my leader ... Christ is with us, I am the son of Christ, the father, the son and the Holy Ghost who saved me, who guides me.

Nevertheless, Ezana remained a strong and authoritarian ruler and did not jettison his sense of self-importance. When he died an enormous stele was erected in his memory. This is one of the distinctive narrow stelae that were built from solid stone and marked the tombs of the rulers of Aksum, which lay beneath them. The largest ones are intricately carved with details modelled on the architectural features of Aksumite palaces. Several are found in a site just outside the city of Aksum, in a rather unprepossessing field. Some lie broken on the ground, but of those still standing, Ezana's is the tallest,

Ezana's stele

reflecting his desire to be remembered in majestic style for posterity. Ethiopians today still mark their graves with a small marble monument, which resembles a stele.

Following Ezana's conversion, Christianity flourished in Aksum, partly because it was embraced by the elite. Dr Gebre-selassie told me that there is no real evidence of resistance to Christianity, nor proof that people were forced to adopt it. Christianity may have remained the religion of the city of Aksum while people in other parts retained their traditional pagan beliefs, worshipping several gods. In any case, the 'Nine Saints', monks that hailed from different parts of the Byzantine Empire, were instrumental in expanding Christianity among the general population. They sailed to Aksum in the mid-400s to escape persecution following disagreements over

Christian teachings. The nine embarked on proselytising missions, first along Red Sea coastal communities and then further inland, translating the Bible and many Christian texts into Ge'ez. Indeed, one priest showed me with reverential care a bible written in Ge'ez that he told me was 1,000 years old: delicate and fragile parchments of paper held a tightly packed script in heavy dark ink, on pages that were loosely bound and which I feared were threatening to come apart.

The Nine Saints also founded churches and monasteries such as Abba Pantaleon near Aksum, introducing monasticism to the region, and there is still a strong cult of worship of the Nine in the Ethiopian Orthodox Church today. As Dr Gebreselassie pointed out, Aksum's early adoption of Christianity gave it a strong identity. Its religious alliance with Alexandria, a key city in the ancient world, also helped nurture its reputation as an important civilisation in Africa.

Kaleb, r. c. 514–540

After Aksum had been established as a great Christian kingdom, it was Ezana's great-great-grandson, Kaleb, who sustained Aksum's reputation as a religious power. By the early sixth century, with its official religion and hierarchical civil structure, Aksum enjoyed a long period of prosperity and prestige. Under Kaleb, the kingdom also continued to be a strong military force, with a loyal and disciplined army.

King Kaleb was referred to as a 'Christian brother' by the Byzantine emperor Justin I, who viewed him as a strong, dependable ally. So when news arrived that the Jews of southern Arabia were engaged in clashes with Christians there, and that a number of Christians had been massacred, Justin urged Kaleb to go to southern Arabia to end the bloodshed. Needing little prompting, King Kaleb set off with his army across the Red Sea to the Arabian Peninsula. He would have made a splendid sight. An account by a Byzantine diplomat describes Kaleb as wearing a costume of linen and gold adorned with jewels and beads, and riding on a golden chariot pulled by four elephants.

In 525, after a protracted military engagement, Kaleb succeeded in defeating the Jewish leader Dhu Nawas, annexing southern Arabia into his kingdom, with a Christian viceroy appointed to rule on his behalf. After his victory, Kaleb, who was an enthusiastic builder, established a great cathedral at Sana'a, the modern-day capital of Yemen. Upon his victorious return to Aksum, Kaleb, according to one historical account, gave up his throne and spent the rest of his life in a monastery, while another states that he reigned in Aksum for a further 17 years. As a result of his protection of Christians, Kaleb was later canonised as a defender of the faith – the first Ethiopian to be recognised by both the Greek and Roman Catholic churches as a saint.

His son and successor Gebre Meskel burnished his father's pious credentials and became the patron of Abba Yared, a sixth-century Ethiopian priest and saint credited with writing many religious songs and chants that are still in use today in the Ethiopian Church, as I witnessed, including this hymn to the Virgin Mary: 'What should we call you, oh full of grace? You are the gate of salvation, you are the portal of light, you are the daughter of the palace . . . Your son is the sun of righteousness. His Apostles are your stars; the lamps of your First-Born'.[1]

King Kaleb's military success in southern Arabia was one of the most striking examples of Aksumite power, but it was by no means the earliest. In the late second and early third centuries, King Gadara and his son had already invaded southern Arabia and conquered coastal parts of the land of the Sabaeans, a clear example of Africans occupying and controlling territory outside the continent. Moreover, the early fourth-century king Azbah had waged wars in southern Arabia and conquered more coastal parts of Saba and large regions in Africa – from Egypt to the 'land of incense' in Somalia.

Aksum's towering reputation rested on military might, trading power and religious legitimacy. But its foundations would be severely shaken by the shifting tectonic plates of history as another religion swept through the continent.

5

The Cross and the Crescent

No empire lasts forever, and in time the political power that had once swelled Aksum with prosperity and prestige drained away inexorably. Nevertheless, as we shall explore, one Christian kingdom that followed in its wake gave rise to another impressive chapter in Africa's history and left an indelible mark on Christianity in Ethiopia. At the same time, the power of Christian kings was being challenged by the rise and spread of Islam in East Africa, and the creation of powerful sultanates.

Today, Africa is pretty evenly split between its Muslim and Christian communities, with about 15 per cent accounting for those who adhere to traditional African religions. It would be wrong, however, to use the rivalries between Muslims and Christians described in this chapter as evidence that conflict is inevitable between the two; the competition between them was not based purely on religious grounds. Muslims and Christians all over Africa have co-existed peacefully and indeed intermarriage was and still is not unusual.

The three Abrahamic religions, Judaism, Christianity and Islam, have historic roots in this region and until the last century all three communities lived in Ethiopia. The last of the Jews of Ethiopia, known as the Beit (or Beta) Israel community or Falasha, were airlifted en masse to Israel in the 1970s. People may have practised different religions, but they were ethnically alike, enjoyed similar cultures and spoke the same languages.

Aksum began to decline for several reasons. In 543, a Christian general called Abraha, who had accompanied King Kaleb on his mission to defeat the Jews of southern Arabia, had been left there as his viceroy. But he soon rebelled, weakening the Aksumite kingdom's hold in southern Arabia. Later in the seventh century, northern parts of the kingdom became unstable after an invasion by the warlike Bedja people, who inhabited a vast area of East Africa and still exist in Sudan and Eritrea. Earlier in the century, the Byzantine Empire had lost territories to the Persians, diminishing its position as a strong Christian ally to Aksum, and the growing dominance of Muslim Arabs in North and East Africa further eroded Byzantine influence. Unable to use Red Sea routes, the Byzantines were forced to rely on overland trade routes to India and Africa, substantially reducing Aksum's trade with Byzantium, its major economic partner. The port of Adulis also saw its status as a trade hub wane: Jeddah on the Arabian side of the Red Sea had long been a rival port and by the early eighth century the pendulum had swung in Jeddah's favour.

All these factors had a devastating effect on the Aksumite treasury. Depleted revenues meant Aksumite kings could no longer afford to pay their soldiers generous salaries, resulting in desertion and dwindling army ranks. The kings could not maintain complex administrative structures nor provide their subjects with the kind of amenities they had come to expect, eroding their legitimacy in the eyes of their citizens.

Environmental factors also had a part to play in Aksum's eventual fall: the northern regions of Aksum were affected by the cutting down of trees for timber, which led to drier land, soil erosion and an ensuing decline in arable and cattle farming. In search of more fertile land, the Aksumites moved the kingdom's capital further south into the central highlands away from the coast. This, possibly combined with some endemic diseases, dealt a further blow to the once pulsating port city of Adulis, leaving it a shadow of its former self.

In the early 600s a new monotheistic religion, Islam, emerged, with Mohammed, a merchant from Mecca in modern-day Saudi Arabia, as its prophet. In about 614, a group of his followers fled persecution from the pagan Qurayshi community in Mecca. They crossed the Red Sea and sought refuge at the court of the Christian Aksumite king Armah, who was renowned for his morals and justice. They arrived at Massawa in modern-day Eritrea and the spot where they landed and prayed is today marked by a small mosque, Masjid al-Sahaba, or Mosque of the Companions, proudly displaying a plaque claiming to be the first Muslim shrine in the world. As I climbed up the four steps to stand gratefully in the shade of the shrine and look out across the calm Red Sea, I could feel the historical significance of the site.

These Muslim fugitives – ten men and five women – presented themselves to King Armah, who welcomed them. A member of the party read the chapter in the Qoran about the Virgin Mary to the king, whereupon Armah observed that Islam was a monotheistic religion with similarities to Christianity and granted them the right to remain in Aksum. As the imam in a local mosque in Asmara related to me, Armah refused to accede to the pagan chiefs of Mecca when they sent word demanding the refugees' return. Some eventually went back to Medina in Arabia when it was safe to do so, but several remained in Aksum and were buried in the Muslim cemetery by the mosque in Negash in northern Ethiopia. Their simple rectangular graves are ringed by a stone frame with a jagged thin piece of flint as a headstone, according to a custom still practised by Muslims today.

Bilal, 580–640

Muslim Ethiopians derive considerable pride from the fact that one of Islam's first converts, Bilal ibn Rabah, was from the kingdom of Aksum. His father or grandfather may have moved to Hijaz in Arabia, and he may have been born there. In any case, Bilal, who was enslaved, was mistreated and tortured for his Muslim beliefs in Mecca by his pagan master. Upon seeing Bilal's plight, Abu Bakr, a relative and follower of the Prophet Mohammed, bought him his freedom and took him under his wing. Owing to his sonorous and powerful voice, Bilal was chosen to call Muslims to prayer. He was a member of the Prophet's inner circle, in charge of his daily schedule and finances, and took part in early Muslim campaigns. Bilal died of the plague in Syria in 640, eight years after the death of the Prophet Mohammed, and is highly venerated by Muslims today not only as the first convert from Africa but also as the first muezzin – the man who calls the faithful to prayer.

Although the initial encounter between the Christian Aksumite king Armah and his Muslim guests was amicable, relations between the two communities subsequently hardened. More Arabs arrived in Africa and spread their religion along the edge of the Red Sea and across the north of the continent. The rivalry was not only based on religion, but competition for resources, propelled by the desire for control and power.

To stall the advance of Arab influence, in 702 the Aksumites made a series of attacks on parts of the Arabian Peninsula that they did not control, including the coastal town of Jeddah, which they succeeded in occupying for a short time. They also attacked the city of Hijaz and made incursions on the Arabian coast, provoking retaliation from the Muslim Arabs, who in the eighth century had taken the Dahlak Islands on the Red Sea. These islands were part of the Aksumite Empire, and the Arabs used them as a base to launch attacks on Aksum.

The 200 or so Dahlak Islands are in Eritrea and permission to visit is rarely granted; I was very lucky to be allowed to do so. Largely arid and flat, few of the islands are inhabited since freshwater is scarce. As I disembarked on Dahlak Kebir, the largest of the islands, I came across a group of children playing with a skipping rope, donkeys standing idly by awaiting their next assignment, a goat scratching its side along the exterior of a flimsy home, with women inside cutting up fish and cooking them in large vats. Despite the stark and desolate nature of the settlement, I was greeted by representatives of the local Afar people, who account for most of the islands' population. Several men were standing by a huge, covered pit, which they explained was a cistern storing rainwater. The Dahlak Islands are like stepping stones in the Red Sea. Centuries earlier, they were an ideal location for Arabs hoping to establish themselves in the region, and the local inhabitants became among the first in Africa to embrace Islam.

The Arabs crushed the Aksumite navy and to ensure that the port of Adulis would never regain its former status they destroyed it once and for all. They built a new port in Massawa, through which they managed the vital Red Sea trade. Aksum was now isolated and deprived of the source of its vitality.

The Arabs not only used trade routes to move goods, but also to spread their religion, especially in the eastern part of the Horn of Africa among communities such as the Somalis. Islam took hold relatively easily, as it was not a centralised religion and did not have a complex hierarchical or religious clergy. Believers were able to worship Allah directly without the intercession of a priest. However, if it was the Muslims who had put the Aksumite kings under pressure, it was a Jewish community that dealt the decisive blow, obliterating the Aksumite kingdom.

Queen Yodit, c. tenth century

By the tenth century, Aksum had been in a state of decay for many decades. According to the *Kebra Nagast*, which glorified Christian rule, Aksum was destroyed by a Jewish queen: Judith, or Yodit in Amharic. There had been Jews living in this part of Africa well before Christians, but as Christianity took hold, Jews became victims of prejudice and withdrew to areas that were less accessible to their foes. Many Jews converted to Christianity, but some had kept their faith. The impact of Judaism on Christianity in Ethiopia extends to this day. For instance, the Ethiopian Orthodox Church forbids the eating of pork and enjoins the circumcision of boys, and until recently it recognised the Jewish Sabbath on Saturday as a holy day along with Sunday.

Yodit was probably the daughter of a Jewish chief called Gideon of the Agaw people, who were Judaic both in culture and basic religious beliefs. Some historians believe that Yodit is a composite figure representing several individuals who may have existed over two or three centuries, for example Tirda Gabaz, the last queen of Aksum, or Ga'wa, a sixteenth-century queen. Whatever her provenance, the Ethiopian Orthodox Church believes Yodit was a Jewish woman of high birth, described as a queen, who lay waste to Aksum and destroyed churches, holy artefacts and books in revenge for the harsh treatment of Jews.

The Arab historian Ibn Hawkal wrote around 977 that the 'land of the Abyssinians had been governed for many years by a woman. It is she who killed the Emperor of Abyssinia [Ethiopia] . . . and she still holds sway over her own country and the neighbouring regions'. The memory of her still provokes hatred among Ethiopians. The patriarch of the Orthodox Church, Abune Mathias, spoke about her with great regret, shaking his head in disbelief at the terrible damage she had wrought on the Church. As befitting some-body of near mythical status, popular culture states that Yodit may have died in a whirlwind – a more mundane manner of death would certainly not suffice. Her burial stele lies in a field in Aksum, her name and grave forever connected to the great kingdom she destroyed.

King Lalibela, c. 1162–1221

Ethiopia is often seen only as a conflict-ridden country, blighted in its recent past by a famine, which triggered a wave of humanitarian initiatives in the West such as Live Aid. And certainly its people have suffered in the modern era. Yet Ethiopia can lay claim to having one of the proudest and longest recorded histories in Africa. My mother speaks fondly of her Ethiopian grandmother, who was taken to Sudan as an orphaned child by an Egyptian merchant. And so this is another African nation in which I can claim some roots.

After the fall of Aksum, the weakened descendants of its kings kept a tenuous grip on their throne. Then, in the first half of the 1100s, a group of army officers from a place southeast of Aksum, known as Agew, seized power and replaced them with military leaders. They founded a new capital in the highlands at Adefa and established the Zagwe dynasty. The Zagwes based their lineage and right to rule on the 'Maiden of Sheba'. They claimed that when Sheba visited Solomon, she was accompanied by a handmaiden who was also impregnated by Solomon and that the Zagwes were descendants of that child.

The Zagwes developed a centralised and organised system of tax collection for the royal treasury, boosted their religious credentials by building monasteries and promoted ties with Egypt and Palestine, guaranteeing passage for their pilgrims to Jerusalem. Merchants enjoyed better security and protection, facilitating the restoration of stronger trade links with Arabs across the Red Sea. Initially, relations between the Zagwe kings and Muslim communities in the highlands were relatively cordial. The Christian Zagwes relied on Muslim agents to facilitate trade in Muslim areas. However, tensions emerged, due mostly to their commercial rivalry, and skirmishes broke out between the two. During this period the Muslims had yet to form potent sultanates, so the clashes were fairly minor and the Zagwe dynasty succeeded in maintaining its dominance.

The most famous of the Zagwe kings was Lalibela. According to legend, he was marked out for greatness when a swarm of bees surrounded him at his birth around 1162. This was an omen that he would one day be a strong and prosperous king. The name Lalibela means 'bees obey him' in the local language. Lalibela received a religious education and was deeply pious. What we know about him owes much to the *Kebra Nagast* and the *Gadla Lalibela* (or Acts of Lalibela), which dates to the fourteenth century and relates his life through a collection of documentation and oral tradition.

Lalibela's older half-brother Harbe was on the throne and lived in fear that he would be deposed if the prophecy about Lalibela came true. So he asked his sister (half-sister to Lalibela) to poison Lalibela. She agreed and gave a deacon a gift of beer to take to Lalibela, who was probably in his teens. Little did the hapless deacon know that the ale had been laced with poison. Upon receiving it, Lalibela asked the priest to drink the beer first. The deacon and a dog who happened to be there both drank from the vessel and died. Overcome with guilt, Lalibela himself drank the remnants of the beer and collapsed. The *Gadla Lalibela*, which is chronological in its account but short of dates, since it was not contemporaneous with Lalibela's life, states that the Angel Gabriel carried Lalibela to heaven and that God then showed him ten rock-hewn churches and told him that it was his duty to create them.

After three days and three nights, Lalibela returned to earth but, confronted by the hostile family that had wished him dead, he fled to the desert where he came across a woman whom he decided to marry. But false reports that Lalibela was plotting to take the throne reached his half-brother Harbe, and so the king summoned him to his presence. Lalibela, perhaps rather foolishly, appeared at court only to be arrested and flogged; miraculously he was protected by angels and, to Harbe's astonishment, emerged completely unmarked from his whipping. Lalibela again fled to the desert and subsequently set off to Jerusalem to make a pilgrimage.

Meanwhile, Harbe had a dream in which Jesus Christ condemned him for his cruel treatment of his brother and told him that he should abandon the throne in Lalibela's favour once the latter returned. Upon Lalibela's arrival home, a repentant and transformed Harbe stepped down as sovereign and proclaimed his brother as king.

Lalibela took the throne and is believed to have reigned for 40 years. Under him the Zagwe kingdom prospered, and its people enjoyed a good standard of living. There was peace and stability, and the religious serenity that emanated from their king bestowed a spiritual calm on his subjects.

Lalibela's chief legacy is the remarkable series of churches hewn out of solid rock in a mountainous region about 650 kilometres from Addis Ababa, which continue to excite wonder and disbelief. Pilgrims and visitors flock in their droves to the city that today bears his name. It is a vibrant place bustling with life. With the help of a fluent local guide (who had also escorted both presidents Clinton and George W. Bush around the site), I spent an incredible day visiting the churches. There are 11 and they represent an extraordinary achievement of engineering, all dug out of the basalt rock by hand. Ten are said to have been built by Lalibela – as he had been instructed by divine command. The eleventh, St George, was built by his wife after his death.

The biggest of the churches is Biete Medhane Alem and is the largest single rock-hewn church in the world. Ethiopian Christians believe the churches were built entirely during the reign of Lalibela with the help of angels, and that Lalibela paid the workers all the wages they demanded for the exacting labour. Again, myth and reality at times diverge. Given the extent of the complex and different architectural styles of the churches, it is more likely that they were constructed over a longer period – perhaps ending in the reign of Lalibela.

The Church of Saint George at Lalibela

Each church was hewn from a monolithic rock, which was then further carved to form doorways, windows, columns, floors and roofs, using basic tools such as hammers and chisels. The churches have extensive drainage systems and passages, some leading to hermits' caves. The best preserved is St Mary, which has a staircase cut out of the rock in a spiral that goes to a loft. Its highly decorated interior of religious frescoes, murals and engravings on the plastered walls features images of the Virgin Mary and Jesus Christ, with light brown skin and soft afros. The churches at Lalibela still attract the faithful in their hundreds of thousands every year. I noticed in the corner of one church a man fast asleep, perhaps wearied by his journey, and in the courtyard of another, a pile of skeletons of pilgrims long dead, who may have been sick and wanted to make the pilgrimage to

Lalibela before death claimed them. It was, and still is, considered a blessing to die at Lalibela.

King Lalibela built Golgotha, a church named after the spot where Jesus was crucified in Jerusalem, intending it to be an alternative to the holy places of that city. Hermits and pilgrims unable to reach Jerusalem could instead make a substitute pilgrimage to Lalibela. They would make long journeys on foot across the rough terrain of Lalibela's kingdom to the churches. One hermit whom I encountered, brushing aside his long grey dreadlocks, obligingly showed me the callouses on his feet, acquired from walking for three days from his home to Lalibela. The churches are still active places of worship and are open every day for services – Ethiopia's religious heritage is still central to its current worship.

When King Lalibela died after a short illness, he was laid to rest in Golgotha. Inside the church there is a series of life-size relief carvings of the 12 apostles and a modern colourful depiction of the king, by a curtain, behind which his tomb lies hidden from public display. Lalibela was canonised after his death and the capital city Adefa was renamed Lalibela in his honour. Lalibela's spiritual legacy has left a strong mark on Christianity in Ethiopia. Locals told me how immensely proud they are of the churches. One may have to look down at these magnificent edifices and descend to enter them, but to see them is an experience that lifts the spirit – regardless of the faith you profess.

The Restoration

After Lalibela's demise, the Zagwe dynasty survived for barely half a century. In 1270, the Zagwes were overthrown by Yekuno Amlak, a nobleman belonging to an Aksumite family from the central highlands of Amhara that claimed its lineage from Solomon. With the help of the Muslim sultanate of Shoa, he succeeded in gathering enough support to defeat the Zagwes. The Zagwe king Yitbarek was murdered and Amlak restored the Solomonic dynasty – the ancient line of Aksumite kings that according to tradition had begun with Menelik I. The royal court became a peripatetic one: king, household, courtiers and army moved around the kingdom so that Yekuno Amlak could maintain contact with his subjects across his vast domains to secure their loyalty. Visibility yielded greater legitimacy. Yekuno Amlak's seizure of power laid the foundations for modern Ethiopia, and indeed the Solomonids remained on the throne until the fall of Emperor Haile Selassie. He was toppled by the military in 1975 and was suffocated to death with a pillow while being held in captivity.

Once the Solomonic dynasty was restored, the aforementioned *Kebra Nagast* was begun in the early fourteenth century. It was an intellectual exercise to consolidate the Solomonic kings' divine right to rule by praising them and glorifying their actions. Although it may have been Solomonic propaganda, it provides an invaluable record of the kings and emperors that governed Ethiopia.

Relations between the Muslims and Yekuno Amlak (and his successors) were rocky. The Christian kings had to contend with the growing strength of the Muslim communities. These were made up of local converts, Arabs and a mixture of the two through intermarriage. They moved gradually into the interior from coastal areas and began establishing mosques and religious schools. By the twelfth century there were sufficient Muslim communities for a sultanate to be formed, known as the sultanate of Shoa.

Ahmed Gragn the Left-handed, c. *1506–43*

The sultanate of Shoa, which held sway over much of southern Muslim Aksum, initially enjoyed commercial ties with Christians and the Zagwe kingdom. The Shoans sold silk clothes and other manufactured goods such as swords to the Christians in exchange for gold, ivory and incense. At the end of the late 1200s, the Shoan dynasty, which was dominated by a hereditary aristocracy that claimed Arab origins, experienced fratricidal struggles; its last sultan was deposed and murdered by another sultan, who then established the sultanate of Ifat.

In the 1300s a rivalry developed between Muslim communities over the control of trade. The rulers of Ifat sensed it was in their best interests to retreat from the coast and head deeper into the highlands, but this exposed them to Christians there and led to violent clashes. The Muslims of Ifat were unable to overcome these attacks and eventually withdrew further east where they founded a new sultanate called Adal in the 1400s, and began to build up a new centre of power.

In the early 1500s one prominent Muslim leader emerged: Imam Ahmed ibn Ibrahim al-Ghazi, also known as Ahmed Gragn, meaning Ahmed the Left-handed – for obvious reasons. I turned to historian Dr Ahmed Zekaria, the chief curator at the Institute of Ethiopian Studies Museum, for his perspective. Ahmed Gragn was born in northwestern Somalia – then part of the Adal sultanate, which was under the nominal sovereignty of the Christian Solomonic dynasty. By the 1500s the Solomonic Empire encompassed modern-day Ethiopia, Eritrea, Djibouti and Somalia. There was an exploitative feudal system of farming under hereditary governorships, which led to resentment among Christian farmers. Additionally, the Solomonids' Muslim subjects felt increasingly alienated, and so the Solomonic grip on power was slipping.

Ahmed Gragn was both an imam and a general who excelled on the battlefield. He had a deep suspicion of Ethiopian Christians and resented their suzerainty. Outraged by an attack on Adal by a Christian general, he launched a jihad on the Solomonic king Lebna Dengel in 1529. Ahmed Gragn used modern fighting techniques and firearms he had acquired from the Muslim Ottomans. He even recruited Ottoman troops to fight on his behalf. The Red Sea area had become a flashpoint between the Ottoman Empire with its capital in Constantinople and the seafaring Portuguese kingdom, and so the war between Christians and Muslims in this part of Africa became a proxy war for these two rival powers. The Christian king Lebna Dengel appealed to his fellow Christian Portuguese king, John III, to intervene and help him repel Gragn's efficient fighting machine, but to no avail. Two years later, Lebna Dengel was defeated, though there were heavy losses on both sides. Ahmed Gragn's men looted the stone churches of Lalibela; churches and monasteries were ransacked and destroyed. Ahmed Gragn himself, though fierce in battle, did not condone wanton destruction and pillage, and regretted the excessive actions of his men, according to Dr Zekaria. Lebna Dengel died a fugitive in 1540 and was succeeded by Gelawdewos.

In 1541, Gelawdewos and the Portuguese raised an army under the command of Cristóvão da Gama, son of the famous explorer Vasco da Gama, who landed with his men at the port of Massawa. A year later, the two armies confronted one another at Amba Alagi and Lake Ashenge. One contemporary Portuguese source, Miguel de Castanhoso, records the Portuguese army's first sighting of Ahmed Gragn: 'While his camp was being pitched, the King of Zeila [Imam Ahmed] ascended a hill with several horse and some foot [soldiers] to examine us: he halted on the top with three hundred horse and three large banners, two white with red moons, and one red with a white moon, which always accompanied him, and [by] which he was recognised.'[1]

The two armies engaged in battle in April 1542. The Portuguese had the advantage of muskets and cannons which they fired at Ahmed Gragn's forces. Gragn was wounded by a bullet and beat a retreat. A courageous commander and not one for quitting, he soon recovered and with reinforced numbers renewed his attack on the Portuguese. However, a gunpowder explosion startled the horses of Ahmed Gragn's army; disoriented, his soldiers deserted the battlefield.

Castanhoso described the mayhem: 'the King was carried on men's shoulders in a bed, accompanied by horsemen, and they fled in no order'.[2]

That might have been the end of the story for Ahmed Gragn. The Portuguese intention was to make the most of their advantage and finish him off, but luck was on his side. Ten days of heavy rain marking the start of the wet season made it impossible for the Portuguese to engage for a third time with Gragn and they set up camp awaiting more clement weather. This provided Gragn with an opportunity to strengthen and refresh his forces. He wanted to obtain superior firepower to beat the Portuguese-led army, so called for help from his Muslim neighbours in Arabia across the Red Sea, and they duly obliged, supplying him with 2,000 musketeers and nearly 1,000 Ottoman soldiers. Once the rains had subsided the imam launched an attack on Cristóvão da Gama's men. It was a bloodbath. Gama's troops were almost completely wiped out and Gama himself was captured with around ten of his men. He was offered the chance to live so long as he converted to Islam. He refused and was promptly executed.

Despite this major setback, King Gelawdewos would not accept defeat. He gathered the remnants of the Portuguese forces and their supplies, and along with his army engaged again in battle with Ahmed Gragn. By then Imam Ahmed had been in a state of constant warfare for a decade. In 1543 at the Battle of Wayna Daga near Lake Tana, Gelawdewos's forces got the better of him. A Portuguese musketeer intent on avenging Cristóvão da Gama's death shot Ahmed Gragn, who was mortally wounded. Ahmed Gragn's severed head was put on grisly display by his enemies. He had succeeded in bringing nearly all of the Solomonic kingdom under his control. A hero to Somalis to this day, he is remembered mostly as a ruthless conqueror by Ethiopian Christians.

Gragn's defeated forces along with his wife retreated east to Harar. Gelawdewos had secured his kingdom but at great cost to life. Christian Ethiopia survived and within a decade Gelawdewos had restored an administrative system and re-established the tributary status of the Muslim sultanates. After Gragn's death, his successor Imam Nur took steps to protect Harar and built the city walls that still remain. These were designed to ward off attacks from the Oromos, a powerful pastoralist community, many of whom were neither Christian nor Muslim, and who had no central authority. In time, the Muslims of Harar built alliances with the local Oromos and Harar became an independent state in 1647.

There followed a long period of calm. Harar flourished and became a melting pot of trade networks. A visit to the bustling market within the five gates of the city walls transported me back through time. I made my way to the home of a descendant of the Emir of Harar, who though long deprived of the riches that his illustrious ancestors would have enjoyed, still commands respect in the community. Sitting on the veranda on Persian-style rugs, his back to the wall, this slim, rather enigmatic individual read verses from the Koran, flanked by a handful of acolytes. Speaking to me in Arabic, he explained that he was still vested with religious authority on account of his lineage, and the men half sitting and half lying beside him nodded vigorously in agreement.

Harar was briefly occupied by the Egyptians between 1875 and 1885 before it was incorporated into greater Ethiopia by the Emperor Menelik II in 1886. In the end, Harar, the stronghold of the Muslims in Ethiopia, fell under the control of a Christian emperor, but its status as the pre-eminent centre of Ethiopian Islam was assured. Harar is still Ethiopia's paramount Muslim city, boasting some 80 mosques within the old city walls. The graves of some of the most celebrated Muslims of Ethiopia are found there, such as the tenth-century tomb of Sheikh Abadir, a leading Islamic thinker.

Lalibela and Ahmed Gragn illustrate how both Christian kings and Muslim rulers defined an important episode in the history of this part of Africa. Nevertheless, Ethiopia's state identity remained Christian despite its large number of Muslims. Islam came early to this part of East Africa, yet it was to the north of the continent that the religion and Arab culture, spread by vast conquering Arab armies, had the most potent impact.

6

Ifrikiya and the Amazigh

Today, North Africa is regarded as part of the Arab world and is seen as somehow separate from the rest of what is referred to as sub-Saharan Africa. The mother tongue of most people living in Egypt, Libya, Morocco, Tunisia and Algeria is Arabic, as it is for large populations in Mauritania and Sudan, where Arabic is also the official language.

The Arabisation and Islamisation of northern Africa, which forms part of my own heritage, is a fascinating and crucial aspect of African history that I will turn to in the next chapter. However, the region's pre-Islamic and pre-Arab past has often been obscured, so first I want to throw light on its earlier populations and some of the intriguing and dynamic personalities who shaped this part of the continent.

North Africa has for centuries been a melting pot. Its native population mixed with Africans south of the Sahara, as well as with Asians, Arabs and Europeans through trade, migration and conquest. That melange is evident today in the population, culture and architecture of the region. Among the best-known ethnic groups of North Africa are the Berbers. They call themselves the Amazigh, meaning 'free people' or 'noblemen', and I will use the two terms interchangeably. They are found predominantly in the Maghreb states of North Africa: Algeria, Morocco, Tunisia and Libya, and their history is rich and compelling.

Ibero-Maurusians

Twenty thousand years ago, verdure, humidity and abundance reigned in North Africa, where rock and sand is now king. Based on local Saharan cave art, we can tell that North African settlements were among the earliest of humankind. North Africa's early inhabitants, known as the Ibero-Maurusians, probably originated from East and central Africa, and they had relatively fair complexions and Mediterranean-like features, similar to Iberians from across the straits of southern Spain. We know a little about them from their burial practices: skeletons found in prehistoric caves in Morocco showed they might have deliberately removed some of their front teeth, although we do not know why. They were tall, with long limbs and low foreheads. The Ibero-Maurusians were hunter-gatherers who developed relatively sophisticated tools. One discovery in a necropolis in Morocco of about 180 skeletons showed evidence of trepanation, a hole drilled into the skull, which may qualify as the first example of a neurological intervention by humans, or might have had some ritual significance.

The Capsians

Around 7000 BCE a new people emerged around Capsa (now Gafsa) in modern-day Tunisia and they became known as the

Capsians. Cave paintings depict dark and fair-skinned people so the Capsians were most likely a mix of central Africans and other races from western Asia and southern Europe. The Capsians settled on hilltops near water, where as well as hunting they farmed and kept livestock. We know they were artistic because they decorated ostrich eggs and sculpted and engraved stones. The Capsians who lived inland are not believed to have displaced the coastal Ibero-Maurusians, and the two cultures probably overlapped for some time. They ate enormous quantities of land snails and built large structures formed from thousands of snail shells – a unique form of prehistoric shelter, hence Capsians are sometimes referred to as the *escargotières* (from the French word *escargot*, meaning snail). Today, land snails are still consumed throughout North Africa even though many Muslims elsewhere prefer not to eat them.

The Capsian culture came to an end around 4000 BCE and that is approximately when the Amazigh or Berbers emerged. It is possible that they were a mix of the Capsians and Ibero-Maurusians. In any case, by 2000 BCE they had established themselves as the main population of North Africa. The Amazigh speak an Afro–Asiatic language that was not written down until the second century BCE.

The climate had become increasingly dry over the millennia, and as the Sahara Desert expanded around 1000 BCE, the Amazigh became relatively cut off from the rest of the continent. Yet they were not totally isolated. They could communicate and trade with other parts of Africa, moving from oasis to oasis through the desert. Indeed, the Amazigh were dominant players in trans-Saharan trade, particularly in salt, which was a highly valued product, both for consumption and the preserving of meat and fish. Nevertheless, the difficulties of travelling across the searing heat of the Sahara meant that it was easier for the Amazigh to interact and mix with western Asia and southern Europe. Today, the distance between Tangier in Morocco to the Spanish mainland is less than 15 kilometres; it was about 7 kilometres away 3,000 years ago, when the sea level was lower. This proximity to people outside Africa had profound effects on the ethnic and the sociocultural make-up of the Amazigh.

Today, the Berbers live mainly in the mountainous and desert areas of Morocco. To find out more about them I teamed up with the prominent Moroccan Berber historian Nouhi al-Ouafi, who agreed to take me to a community who proudly proclaim their Berber heritage, living near the Atlas Mountains outside Marrakesh. We journeyed along the mountain road south to the settlement of Ait Ben Haddou, near Ouarzazate, which dates to the twelfth century. As we approached I saw dark sandstone towers with small windows at the base of the Atlas. We made our way to the home of a local Berber with roots in Ait Ben Haddou for generations. Mohammed spoke little Arabic so we communicated via Professor al-Ouafi, sitting on low stools in his courtyard, sipping sweet tea. Mohammed told me that Berbers like him maintain their distinct identity: many do not regard themselves as Arabs but as the original inhabitants of this part of Africa, something Professor al-Ouafi confirmed. Mohammed's compound included pens for his livestock; he and his family are fairly self-sufficient, their animals providing them with food and wool for clothing. The Berbers are expert weavers of woollen products, such as carpets and rugs bearing colourful geometric designs. I learned that Berber men (and the Tuareg nomads, who have common roots with them and live mostly in southern Algeria, Niger and Mauritania) wear veils called *nila*, after the desert plant that provides the veils' rich deep-blue colour. Professor al-Ouafi explained that the veils protect the face from both the sun and sand of the Sahara.

Although the Berbers can rightly claim to be among the first recorded inhabitants of North Africa, over the centuries they have been exposed to various outside influences. The Phoenicians had the greatest impact on Amazigh culture towards the end of the first millennium. Originating from what is now Lebanon, these intrepid maritime people sailed to North Africa in search of silver, copper and tin. Many remained in North Africa and amalgamated with the locals, giving rise to a new culture known as the Punic civilisation.

The only example of a Punic city to have survived is the little-known Kerkouane, dating from the late fourth century BCE. Kerkouane is about 100 kilometres east of Tunis and was constructed from local stone, transported from quarries across long distances. It was once a sophisticated port-city, with spacious homes and private bathrooms equipped with lead water pipes. It is believed there were about 2,000 inhabitants in Kerkouane, mostly middle-class people such as artisans and tradesmen, and clearly they enjoyed a high standard of living. There were smaller buildings for shops, and the streets were wide and straight. Town squares were clearly discernible, as were the remains of a temple, and just over a kilometre away lay a necropolis. In 1929 a local teacher stumbled across the site and proceeded to sell the vast cache of treasures in the tombs to collectors: ceramics, jewellery and other objects. Soon other looters descended on the site and flogged their wares on the black market before the authorities got wind of what was going on. Luckily one precious and possibly unique find was saved from theft: in Kerkouane Museum I saw on display a sarcophagus painted red, whose cover was in the shape of a woman, engraved with the face of the goddess Ishtar, the protector of the dead.

Phoenicians also laid down roots in the ancient city of Hippo in northeastern Algeria, today's Annaba. Algeria teems with historic sites across its vast territory. Travelling around is not easy; the tourism sector is not as well-developed as in Morocco and Tunisia, and a vicious civil war between militants and the authorities in the 1990s has left a legacy of security concerns in the country. After the six-hour drive east from Algiers, I arrived at Annaba, a modern, rather unprepossessing city that encircles the remains of historic Hippo, its once proud pillars damaged or fallen, the remnants of stone walls hinting at the buildings that previously stood there. A port was built at Hippo around 800 BCE, when the town would have been by the shores of the Mediterranean Sea. About 600 years later, in the third century BCE, a Berber king called Gaia, adopted Hippo as his capital and gave it royal status as Hippo Regius.

Hippo and Kerkouane were just two of many Punic settlements. The wealthiest and grandest was Carthage, and Gaia was its ally. Initially established in the ninth century BCE, Carthage became a great trading centre and dominated the western Mediterranean from the sixth to fourth centuries BCE. The Carthaginians took land from the Amazigh communities and held territory roughly equivalent to modern-day Tunisia. They controlled the North African coast from Tripolitania in western Libya to the Atlantic, and held colonies in the Balearic Islands, Corsica, Malta, Sardinia and Sicily. Carthage was a staging post to the silver mines in Spain and its people were skilled builders of boats designed to carry heavy cargo, which facilitated their trade and brought them many riches.

Queen Elyssa or Dido, hypothetically c. ninth century BCE

Carthage is traditionally held to have been founded by Queen Dido, or Elyssa, as she is known in North Africa. Although some experts doubt her existence, for many Tunisians she is a real figure. In the *Aeneid*, the Roman poet Virgil sets out the story of Dido, written from the perspective of the establishment of Rome: the Trojan warrior Aeneas, fleeing his conquered homeland, meets Dido in Carthage on his way to Italy, where he will eventually found Rome. Love blossoms but soon wilts and, maddened by her abandonment, Dido curses Aeneas and his people and takes her own life. Virgil's Dido, though a sympathetic figure, is presented as the harbinger of Rome's gruelling wars with Carthage, which would dominate Roman history for two centuries.

Tunisian archaeologist Leïla Lajimi Sebaï, president of the Friends of Carthage Society, met me amid the ruins of Carthage to discuss Dido, and with great enthusiasm related how Dido was for her an extraordinary and pioneering woman, and how Virgil in her view had completely misrepresented her story, casting her as the victim of a broken heart in order to 'Romanise' her life. Leïla said that Dido had actually killed herself because she did not want to marry a Berber leader. The details of Dido's story do not matter as much as the fact that Leïla and many other academics on the African continent are challenging well-established Western perceptions of a history that has overlooked their perspectives.

In any case, undoubtedly by the third century BCE Carthage had captured the attention of Rome, which covetously eyed its wealth and prestige. This rivalry culminated in a series of military confrontations known as the Punic Wars.

The Punic Wars and Hannibal, c. 247–181 BCE

The First Punic War broke out in 264 BCE when Rome made a land grab for Sicily and took it from the Carthaginian leader Hamilcar. The Second Punic War in 218 BCE gave rise to one of the most famous military campaigns of all time. It was started by the Carthaginian general Hannibal, son of Hamilcar, who from his enclave in southern Spain mobilised his 90,000-strong army and 37 elephants and marched over the Alps. Although Hannibal came very close to taking Rome, in the end he failed to do so, but not without leaving a lasting impression on the history books. Pursued by the Romans, he returned to Carthage and then fled to Asia Minor, to a region that today corresponds to northern Türkiye, where he took his own life.

Leïla described how for Tunisians, Hannibal is a real hero of Carthage, who fought in a war for 20 years and endeavoured to rebuild Carthage after it had been weakened by the First Punic War. She said unfortunately his efforts suffered a setback because there were too many traitors among the local population, who backed Rome. The rivalries between the North Africans themselves was a feature of the Punic Wars that I had not properly appreciated, given the Roman lens through which I had been schooled. Despite his failures, Hannibal's destructive campaign on Roman lands and his near military success engendered among Romans a massive and lasting fear of Carthage.

In 204 BCE, the Roman army, led by the general Scipio, landed close to the port of Utica, near Carthage. Utica had been established as a trading post by the Phoenicians before they built Carthage, and it possessed a harbour and its own merchant fleet. Over the next three years the Romans scored military successes over the Carthaginians, further eroding their power and leaving them without any colonies.

By 149 BCE, the Romans had decided to finish off the Carthaginians and so they mounted a huge offensive in the Third Punic War. Crucially they had the support of a powerful Amazigh king called Massinissa, who was instrumental in their campaign against Carthage.

The Punic Wars and Massinissa, c. 238–148 BCE

When I was taught about the Punic Wars and the resulting destruction of the great city of Carthage, few of us, if any, learned about the actions and role of the North Africans themselves, such as Massinissa, who was a crucial player in the wars. Indeed, if he had not eventually sided with the Romans, what might the impact have been on the destiny of Carthage and Roman efforts to subdue North Africa? There is also a tendency to talk of Roman rule in North Africa during this period in a way that overshadows local history, yet despite the Roman presence in North Africa, Massinissa maintained the Berber identity and culture of his people.

Massinissa, son of Gaia of Hippo Regius, was born around 238 BCE. He was from the Numidian people of the kingdom of Massyli, who were based north of Cirta in Algeria. Upon Gaia's death in 207 BCE, Massinissa returned from overseas only to find that succession to the throne was in dispute between various members of his family and a distant kinsman by the name of Mazetullus. So Massinissa waged a guerrilla war from the mountains and eventually regained his father's kingdom. Massinissa had studied in Carthage, where he learned Latin and Greek, and much of what we know about him comes from Greek and Latin sources. The Roman

An eighteenth-century engraving of Massinissa

writer and historian Livy (59 BCE–17 CE), writing decades later, described him as 'by far the greatest of all the kings of his time . . . his valour is conspicuous'. Massinissa was fearless, unscrupulous and a master diplomat, qualities that made him an invaluable ally for the Romans.

Massinissa was also an accomplished military strategist. In the run up to the First Punic War he fought on behalf of Carthage, but later transferred his loyalty to Rome out of political expediency. During the Second Punic War, at the request of the Roman general Scipio, Massinissa joined forces with him against Hannibal, having calculated that backing the Romans would better enable the realisation of his ambitions to become the dominant power in North Africa. Massinissa's gamble paid off: strengthened and emboldened, he succeeded in uniting his kingdom with those of rival Berber kingdoms such as Mauri and Masaesyli to make one realm called Numidia, which comprised what is now a large swathe of Algeria and parts of Libya, Tunisia and Morocco. Massinissa ruled Numidia in an efficient and able manner. His army and navy were formidable and his treasury well-stocked.

After the Second Punic War and the defeat of Hannibal, Massinissa saw that Carthage, though still prosperous, was substantially weakened. Accordingly, he became more assertive in his dealings with the city. The Carthaginians had signed a treaty with Rome that it would not enter into any wars without Rome's permission and Massinissa exploited this reduction in Carthaginian power. He built a strong agrarian base in his kingdom to rival Carthage's status as a supplier of agricultural goods to Rome, and he also cunningly played on Roman suspicion of Carthage.

In 170 BCE Massinissa sent one of his sons, Gulussa, as a delegate to Rome. Livy writes how Gulussa warned the Senate 'to beware the treachery of the Carthaginians, for they have adopted a plan to prepare a large fleet ostensibly for the Romans and against the Macedonians; when this fleet should be ready and equipped, the Carthaginians would be free to decide for themselves who should be considered an enemy or an ally'. Massinissa wanted to imply that the Carthaginians were rebuilding their navy despite an agreement not to do so and that they might use this new fleet against Rome.

Capitalising on Roman anxiety, in 162 BCE Massinissa seized more and more fertile territory from Carthage – with the tacit support of Rome. Carthage objected to this land acquisition and requested mediation. The senator Cato the Elder went to North Africa to investigate and unsurprisingly declared in Massinissa's favour. Moreover, on his return to the Senate, Cato briefed senators about the situation and advised that Carthage be properly brought to heel, uttering the famous phrase '*Delenda est Carthago*' meaning 'Carthage must be destroyed'. So a Roman fleet was dispatched and landed again at the Punic port of Utica. It took three years for the Romans to defeat the Carthaginians, three years of desperate siege. Carthage was indeed destroyed and burned down. Nearly all its inhabitants were slaughtered, and tens of thousands were enslaved. A hundred years later, the Romans rebuilt a new city of Carthage on the site, so the ruins that I wandered around under the shade of the palm trees overhead were almost entirely of the Roman city and not those of the great Punic settlement that had so captured my imagination as a schoolgirl.

The port-city of Utica became the capital of the North African province of the Roman Empire, which the Romans called 'Ifrikiya'. Eventually the whole continent became known as Ifrikiya, or Africa. Much as I love the word Africa, I cannot help but wonder if the name granted to the province of a European empire in some way presaged what was to follow centuries later: that the continent of Africa would have many of the names of its countries, cities and natural heritage sites imposed by outsiders from Europe and Arabia. Today, while Utica is no longer on the coast, its ancient bay silted up, there are still remnants of this ancient town that was so central to the Romans' victory during the Punic Wars.

Once Carthage was destroyed the pendulum of power swung even more decisively in Massinissa's favour. The Romans recognised Massinissa as a powerful king, which deterred them from making an enemy of him. He was more useful as a friend than a foe. I headed to Massinissa's capital Cirta to meet one of Algeria's foremost experts on the Numidians, Dr Keltoum Kitouni Daho, director of the Cirta Museum. Dressed in a long black cloak and a white headscarf, she argued that Massinissa must be regarded as an African patriot, despite his alliance with the Romans, stating that Massinissa maintained an independent stance, and that he was known to frequently state that 'Africa belongs to the Africans. I lay claim the lands of my fathers and ancestors', and 'the land belongs to those who serve it'. Massinissa was a great unifier of the main communities of North Africa and encouraged the spread of Numidian culture and civilisation through the arts. Dr Kitouni Daho believes that had he lived longer, Massinissa would have expanded his territory further across Africa.

Massinissa chose a lofty site on top of an impressive gorge to build Cirta, which was fortified and protected by valleys and thus was a strategic location for a royal city. It is still one of Algeria's most stunning cities. As the North African travel writer Muhammad al-Abdara wrote of Cirta in the thirteenth century, 'the valley surrounds the mountain like the [brace-let] surrounds the wrist'. It was a city of many buildings, monuments and palaces filled with decorative paintings.

There are few if any residential remains that can tell us how the Numidians lived but it is believed that life at Massinissa's court was lavish and luxurious. Greek musicians would have performed at feasts where tables were laden with golden baskets and silver tableware. Despite being a key Roman ally, Massinissa probably interacted more with Greek rather than Roman culture. Massinissa's Numidian civilisation would have had written knowledge of four languages: Greek, Latin, their Tamazight language written in a local Libyan script, and Punic, which descended from Phoenician. Some charming ancient graffiti inscribed on a stone at the forum in Timgad in Algeria (founded much later around 100 CE), which I read, states in Latin: '*Venari, Levari, Ludari, Viderai, est vivari*' , which can be translated as 'Hunting, consoling, playing and laughing – this is life'. It was an inscription, I thought, which would resonate with many in the modern era, though perhaps with the exception of hunting.

The Numidians were renowned for their light and high-quality cavalry, which earned them a reputation as an effective fighting force. The Roman historian Livy described them as 'by far the best horsemen in Africa', able to ride in masterly fashion over any kind of terrain. They rode bareback, with little or no body protection, controlling their horses with simple rope necks. Their horses were small and agile in war, which greatly contributed to the success of Massinissa's own military campaigns and those he conducted on behalf of his Roman ally. Armed with spears and swords, the horsemen could be deployed for reconnaissance and in battle they carried out rapid attacks on their enemies.

Coins show Massinissa as handsome with a fine elaborate hairstyle and masculine features. Indeed, Massinissa was physically strong with great stamina, able to operate on little food, and a skilled equestrian who could mount his horse unaided into his eighties.

Greek and Latin sources portray Massinissa in a favourable light. A popular king with his own people, the dynasty of Numidian kings that he founded lasted 200 years. He was an African hero whose fame exceeded the confines of Africa and to whom the Greeks erected several statues at Delos. After a full and active life, Massinissa died at the age of about 90 in 148 BCE and he was laid to rest in his pyramid-style mausoleum against a mountainous green backdrop just outside Cirta. At the time of his death, he had more than 40 children – the youngest, a son, Methimannus, was just four years old. The Numidians worshipped the forces of nature represented by gods of fertility and preservation, among others. It seems the gods of fertility had certainly worked their magic on Massinissa.

A contemporary Greek historian Polybius (*c.* 200–118 BCE) wrote about his death:

Massinissa, the king of the Numidians in Africa, one of the best and most fortunate men of our time, reigned over more than 60 [*sic*] years, enjoying excellent health and attaining a great age for he lived till 90 . . . Owing to the affectionate terms they were all on [in his realms] he kept his kingdom during his whole life free from all plots and from any taint of domestic discord. But his greatest and most godlike achievement was this: while Numidia had previously been a barren country thought to be naturally incapable of producing crops. He first and alone proved that it was as capable as any other country of bearing all kinds of crops . . . It is only proper and just to say this tribute to his memory on his death.

Massinissa was succeeded by Micipsa (r. 148–118 BCE) – one of the more level-headed of his many sons, who initially shared the throne with his brothers Mastanabal and Gulussa. Mastanabal handled the day-to-day administrative running of the kingdom and was an excellent sportsman. In fact, when Massinissa was still alive in 164 BCE, Mastanabal had participated in the Olympic Games and won a gold medal for his horsemanship. However, both Mastanabal and Gulussa succumbed to disease and died, leaving Micipsa the sole king. Micipsa was mild mannered and lacked his father's ambition to expand the kingdom. He ruled for 30 years in what was a period of stability and peace for the Numidian kingdom.

Jugurtha, c. *160–104 BCE*

On Micipsa's death in 118 BCE, his nephew Jugurtha, who was the son – possibly illegitimate – of Mastanabal and therefore Massinissa's grandson, shared the throne with Micipsa's two sons Hiempsal and Adherbal. Like his father Massinissa, Micipsa had also decided to divide the Numidian kingdom. Jugurtha was popular, and the Romans had urged Micipsa to adopt him as his heir. Micipsa agreed and put all three candidates on the throne. But Jugurtha wanted to rule alone. He was both courageous and ruthless, a combination which proved lethal for his younger coregents. He had Hiempsal killed, after which he defeated Adherbal in battle. During this period of struggle for dominance, several Roman traders also lost their lives, which enraged the Romans and contributed to the outbreak of the Jugurthine Wars in 112 BCE.

After the destruction of Carthage, the Romans had become increasingly assertive in North Africa. Perhaps Jugurtha saw himself in the mould of an African freedom fighter, using the heat and harsh terrain to wipe out the external influence of Rome on African soil. In any case, he came to a sticky end. He was betrayed by his own father-in-law and was taken to Rome, where he was paraded through the streets, thrown into prison and left to starve to death.

After the ignominious defeat of Jugurtha, the Numidians were weakened – though not entirely cowed. Decades later, around 46 BCE, King Juba I was on the throne. He made one final attempt to challenge the Romans, but he was no match for the formidable general Julius Caesar, who defeated Juba and his forces in battle. Accounts vary about what happened to Juba I; he either retreated into the desert where he was stabbed to death, or he died by suicide. Juba's defeat was significant for it marked the decisive point when the Numidian kings relinquished their autonomy to Rome. At the Museum of Hippo Regius, a bronze statue, now a green hue, stands tall on a plinth, and depicts the toga and armour worn by a Roman soldier. It was commissioned by Julius Caesar to mark his victory. As I stood looking at it I thought wryly of how here in Algeria it was more of a poignant symbol of defeat.

Juba II, c. 50 BCE–23 CE

Juba's young son, who bore his name, was taken to Rome and educated there under the guardianship of Octavia, sister to Octavian, who later became the emperor Augustus. This was a common Roman practice – they sought to integrate the offspring of defeated kings into Roman ways. Juba II married Cleopatra Selene, the daughter of the Roman general Mark Antony and Cleopatra of Egypt, and it seemed to be a happy match. They had two children, Ptolemy and Drusilla.

On his return to North Africa, Juba II built Caesarea – named in Julius Caesar's honour. Now called Cherchell, it is in the Algerian province of Tipasa, about 90 kilometres west of Algiers, on the Mediterranean coast. Algerian archaeologist Redha Hakim, based in Tipasa, talked me through the remains of the city: the amphitheatre, forum and baths with cold, warm and hot rooms that are well preserved to this day. At the local museum, I saw a bronze bust depicting Juba II as a young man with curly hair wearing a crown of ribbon in Roman style, gazing as though deep in thought.

Juba II ruled over land from eastern Algeria to Morocco. In Volubilis, in modern-day northwest Morocco, he established his capital. Today, it is one of the most impressive and extensive ancient sites in North Africa. Set in a beautiful green landscape, the old city's well-preserved civic buildings and magnificent triumphal arch enchanted me at first sight. Close up, I could admire the splendid mosaics depicting the seasons, Venus and the myth of Orpheus, giving me a clear impression of how magnificent this rich and fertile royal city was. The population of Volubilis, which at its peak reached 20,000, came from a multitude of backgrounds including local North Africans, Romans, Greeks, Spaniards and Arabs.

Given his upbringing, Juba II was naturally heavily influenced by Roman culture, but this did not mean he ignored his Numidian roots, as Moroccan archaeologist and historian

The site at Volubilis

Dr Mustafa Atki told me when I met him at Volubilis. For example, Juba II learned how to write in the local Libyan language and some of the coins issued during his reign had the stamp of an elephant, a symbol of Africa. Under Juba II, the Numidian kingdom was regarded by the Romans as being in loyal hands and so Juba was allowed to increase his wealth to extraordinary proportions. He made a fortune selling purple togas to Rome; Volubilis became a centre for dyeing fabrics and Morocco to this day remains a leader in natural dyes (henna for orange, mint for green, saffron for yellow). The Phoenicians had provided the ancient Greeks with purple dye long before, so it is highly likely that the Numidians had inherited the skill of extracting purple dye from shellfish from them. In addition to dyeing, the Numidians excelled at making leather goods. One of the more curious jobs that locals had to carry out was to empty urine from public latrines and take it to the tanneries where it was used to cure leather. In fact, the Romans taxed these urine collections, providing them with a steady flow of income. Urine, after all, was never in short supply.

Juba II was a cultured and respected monarch. He wrote many books about geography and history, including one about ancient Egypt. After 50 years as king, he died in 23 CE and was laid to rest in a mausoleum where his queen Cleopatra Selene was also buried. Built in stone in North African style, the tomb, which has a 60-metre circumference and once stood 40 metres high, has a circular appearance with a square base, topped by a cone or pyramid. In death, as in life, Juba II did not forsake his African heritage.

Juba II's successor was his son Ptolemy. The emperor Caligula was jealous of the wealthy and glamorous young man, the progeny of a North African dynasty – and the grandson of Cleopatra and Mark Antony. Caligula hatched a treacherous plan and invited him to Rome. Unaware that he was falling into a trap, Ptolemy agreed to visit him. He presented himself in great royal splendour, further stoking Caligula's envy. The unfortunate youth was assassinated on Caligula's orders before he could even make a mark on his North African throne.

Thereafter, Rome tightened its grip on North Africa, incorporating the lands that Ptolemy was due to inherit and building new cities across its province of Ifrikiya. This was one of the richest regions of the Roman Empire and covered a large expanse of fertile territory. Its proximity to Rome meant it could develop into a breadbasket of the empire as well as provide a supply of enslaved people, gold, ivory, ostrich plumes and olive oil. The Romans managed their North African lands through a network of rulers who could be Roman, Punic or Amazigh, and there was intermarriage between all these communities.

Today in Algeria, Tunisia, Morocco and Libya, there are extensive and spectacular ruins from this period, including the little-visited amazing sites of Leptis Magna, 100 kilometres from the Libyan capital Tripoli, and its 16,000-seat amphitheatre and baths. Leptis Magna was first settled by Phoenician traders and then expanded in the first century during the reign of Nero. The city was the birthplace of Septimius Severus, who became Roman emperor in 193 CE and died of pneumonia in York, northern England, in 211, where he had been engaged in battle with Caledonian tribes. Timgad in eastern Algeria and Tipasa in the north are also areas that have yet to be fully excavated, but Timgad already boasts a well-preserved amphitheatre and a temple to Jupiter. However, it would be misleading to refer to these simply as 'Roman' ruins: the city planning may have been Roman, but the architectural style bears Numidian traces and the cities were built on Numidian land from local materials by local workmen using local tools. So they are better described as Numidio-Roman.

A group of young boys I encountered at Tipasa told me they were proud of their history and they knew the site dated to the Roman era. I could see that locals enjoyed spending the day there: families picnicking, children playing football amid the ruins, women wearing the hijab enjoying the warm afternoon air. I thought how incongruous these ruins looked, an ancient Roman background for contemporary Algerians with Arab and Muslim heritage. For despite their lasting impact on the landscape in terms of European culture, language and religion, the Romans left a very light footprint in North Africa; rather, it was the arrivals from the east who heralded radical, lasting change in the region.

7

Islam and the Dynasties of North Africa

A large proportion of today's North Africans refer to themselves as Arabs, and the most populous Arab country by far is an African nation: Egypt. However, the North African dynasties, which lasted for 700 years from the eleventh century, and which at various times ruled Sicily, Malta, Corsica and large parts of Portugal and Spain, can more accurately be described as Amazigh/Berber or of mixed Berber and Arab heritage.

Nor should these dynamic rulers be referred to as Moors; now archaic, the word is derived from the Latin *Maurus*, denoting an inhabitant of the Roman province of Mauretania in North Africa. Early Europeans in the Middle Ages described the Muslim inhabitants of North Africa as Moors, regardless of whether they were of Arab or Berber descent, and in time this came to apply to those living in Europe too. The people of the region have never described themselves as Moors. The term was used by William Shakespeare in his

1603 play *Othello*, the fictitious story of a North African military commander who marries the Venetian Desdemona, only to murder her when he is overcome with rage and jealousy. In the West, Othello's fame has eclipsed that of his historical compatriots, such as Yusuf ibn Tashfin of the Almoravids and Yusuf Yaqub al-Mansour, the third Almohad ruler. The amazing monuments built by these North African dynasties are a testament to how sophisticated their cultures were. There is hardly a city in Morocco that does not boast a settlement of grandeur and power – the vestiges of Islamic dynasties buried under the sand, who once ruled over vast domains in Africa and beyond.

But before we get to these Islamic dynasties, it is important to understand the history of the Jewish and Christian communities established in northern Africa prior to the Arab arrival and the spread of Islam in the seventh century. These retained sizeable populations. Jews in the region numbered some 500,000 until 1945 and Coptic Christians, who lived mostly in Egypt, still form at least 10 per cent of the current Egyptian population.

The Jews of Northern Africa

The Jews in what are today Morocco and Tunisia most likely fled conflict in Jerusalem immediately after the destruction of the first Jewish temple by the Babylonians in 587 BCE, and later in 70 CE after the second temple was destroyed by the Romans. It is possible that some had made their way to North Africa much earlier. Many settled in southern Morocco and adopted local ways. They became 'Berberised', while some Berbers adopted the Jewish faith and became 'Judaised'.

This was explained to me by Serge Berdugo, president of the Jewish Community of Morocco, as we sat in the pretty leafy garden of the Jewish Museum in a quiet part of Casablanca. He related how the cult of holy men revered by Jewish communities in Morocco is essentially derived from Berber tradition, highlighting the cross-fertilisation of cultures that occurred. The Jewish Museum where we met is unique in the Arab world. Its display of religious artefacts, Hebrew texts, photographs of long-bearded rabbis, beautiful silver bangles and garments made of heavy velvet with braid trimmings bears witness to how the Jews of Morocco thrived and grew wealthy. The director of the Jewish Museum, a Moroccan Muslim woman, was proud to preside over this part of her country's history and told me that in her view it was separate from the later catastrophic and enduring conflict between the Arab world, Israel and the Palestinians. Nevertheless, there have been tragic aspects of Jewish history in North Africa. For example, up to 6,000 Jews were massacred in 1033 in the city of Fes during a power struggle between rival Berbers.

In the Jewish quarter in the old town of Marrakesh, the synagogue welcomes visitors of all faiths and the rabbi there was hospitable when I dropped by, telling me that generations of his family had lived in the city and that as far as he was concerned he was Moroccan. The current number of Jews in the country is only about 2,500 and they are well integrated into Moroccan society – most speak Arabic at home. King Mohammed VI, in the tradition of his regal predecessors, appoints an adviser to the royal court drawn from Morocco's Jewish community.

The histories of North Africa and Judaism are closely linked. If you embark on a special River Nile excursion in Cairo, you can witness a re-enactment of the Old Testament story of the prophet Moses, revered by the three monotheistic religions. As a baby Moses was found in the bulrushes on the banks of the Nile. He had been hidden there by his mother to save his life following the Egyptian pharaoh's decree that every Hebrew male be drowned. Moses was found by the pharaoh's daughter and brought up in the palace as a member of the royal family. The Jewish and Christian traditions hold that somehow Moses learned of his Hebrew origins, and after around 40 years in Egypt and a stay in the wilderness, he led his people out of Egypt to Mount Sinai where he received the Ten Commandments from God.

Interestingly, Moses married a Kushite woman, from what is now Sudan, much to the dismay of his brother Aaron and sister Miriam. The Book of Numbers 12:1 in the Torah sets out the story of Moses' wife, a Kushite, with the implication that she is black:

> And Miriam and Aaron spoke against Moses because of the Cushite woman whom he had married, for he had married a Cushite woman. And they said Hath the Lord indeed spoken only by Moses? Hath he not spoken also by us? And the Lord heard it ... And the Lord came down in the pillar of the cloud and stood in the door of the tabernacle and called Aaron and Miriam and they both came forth ... And the anger of the Lord was kindled against them; and he departed.

God was evidently angry with Aaron and Miriam for criticising Moses' choice of wife, and ironically God's punishment was to turn Miriam 'leprous, white as snow'.

Notwithstanding the exodus from Egypt by Moses and his people, Jews again settled in Egypt under Ptolemaic rule from around 300 BCE, particularly in Alexandria, a cosmopolitan, multiethnic city composed of native Egyptians, Greeks, Jews and Romans. Many more flocked to Alexandria after the sacking of Jerusalem by the Romans in the first century, making it an important centre for Judaism.

The Christians of Northern Africa

From an early period in its history, Alexandria was also a bastion of Christianity. Mark the Evangelist, one of the most important Christian figures, established the Coptic Church in the city in *c.* 43 CE and became its first bishop. The Christian Church in Egypt adopted the Coptic language so that even the humblest who could not speak Greek could understand its liturgy, and it spread across Egypt.

Keen to get a sense of the Coptic community today, I went to Cairo to meet Father Basilios Sobhy of the Church of the Virgin Mary in the district of Zeitoun. He explained how Coptic devolved from the ancient Egyptian Pharaonic language and is still used in church services today. As he spoke to me, worshippers crowded around images of the Virgin Mary.

Many Muslims in Egypt, particularly in the south, venerate the Virgin Mary. This attachment to her may have its roots in the worship of Isis, the wife of the god Osiris, during Egypt's Pharaonic period. But Mary (or Maryam, as Muslims call her) is also the most revered woman in Islam and has an entire Koranic chapter dedicated to her as the Virgin Mother of the prophet Jesus (Issa, in Arabic).

The path of early Christians in Egypt was not smooth; they were heavily persecuted by the Romans, who considered them members of a new and disturbing 'cult', mainly because they refused to worship Roman gods. Mark the Evangelist was murdered about 68 CE in Alexandria and for about 300 years Christians in Egypt endured unimaginable suffering, living in fear of Roman soldiers taking them away to be tortured, crucified on stage or killed for entertainment. The emperor Constantine converted to Christianity in the early 300s and the persecution was officially ended by the Edict of Milan in 313. A few years later Christianity became the official religion of the Roman Empire.

St Augustine, 354–430

There were also Christians in the Maghreb states of North Africa. One, St Augustine of Hippo, remains among the religion's foremost thinkers. He was born in 354 in what is today eastern Algeria. His mother was Christian, and his father may have been a pagan Berber. Before becoming Christian at about the age of 32, Augustine had a long-time lover whom he never married and with whom he had an illegitimate son, Adeodatus. Augustine's mother, Monica, judged his lover unworthy of being his wife and tried to arrange a more suitable match for him – much to his dismay. He wrote in his *Confessions*, 'My mistress being torn from my side as an impediment to my marriage, my heart, which cleaved to her was racked and wounded and bleeding.'[1]

When his son died, a grief-stricken Augustine became a committed Christian and entered the clergy at Hippo, where he rose to be appointed bishop. In 430 the Vandals – a collection of Germanic tribes from northern Europe under King Gaiseric – took control of key sites in North Africa, including Hippo. They laid siege to the town and for 18 months the people endured starvation and disease. Many lost their lives. St Augustine, by then in his seventies, did not survive the siege, dying in 430. The Vandals sacked the city soon afterwards, but left Augustine's places of worship intact.

At the turn of the fourteenth century, Augustine was canonised and today is regarded by both Roman Catholics and Protestants as an African saint and perhaps the greatest Christian thinker after St Paul. Augustine was a vociferous critic of slavery. He helped formulate the doctrine of original sin and his theory of 'just war' is still influential in discussions about the morality of conflict. He was a representative of a global and diverse Christianity, but has often been portrayed as a white European in Western art.

The St Augustine Basilica, which opened in Hippo in 1900, was built on a hill overlooking the Mediterranean. A large monument with several domes and gorgeous stained-glass windows, it stands in lush gardens. Inside the church, the presiding priest at the time of my visit was Father Ambrose Tshibandu, from the Democratic Republic of the Congo. With great fervour he relayed how proud he was as an African that the great Christian St Augustine should also hail from the continent. As I departed the basilica, I reflected on what I had seen: here was an immaculately preserved edifice to the memory of one of Christianity's foremost thinkers, hosted, maintained and protected deep in the heart of Muslim Algeria under the supervision of an African priest.

Islam in Egypt

When the Arabs arrived in northern Africa, they entered Egypt, then part of the Byzantine Empire, invading it in December 639 CE with a somewhat modest army under the command of a brilliant Arab general called Amr ibn al-As. He was the military governor of Palestine and hailed from the same Qurayshi community as the Prophet Mohammed, who had died a few years earlier in 632. Egypt's Byzantine general, Cyrus of Alexandria, after a series of battles and sieges, was forced to recognise the Arab army's superiority and surrendered. However, the Byzantine emperor Heraclius refused to accept defeat and mounted a rearguard action to save Alexandria – but he was ill and died before he could even prepare his forces. After the exhausted Byzantine defenders of Alexandria made one futile attempt to ward off the Arabs, Amr ibn al-As attacked Alexandria and the city fell in September 642 – and with it Byzantine rule of Egypt collapsed. Judging that, as a coastal city, Alexandria was too vulnerable to attack from across the Mediterranean, Amr ibn al As established a more secure inland capital, Fustat, which today constitutes the old part of Cairo. A wise move indeed, for in 645 the Byzantine navy briefly reoccupied Alexandria. The Arabs reconquered it only with great difficulty and bloodshed.

After the defeat of Egypt, the local Christian Copts forged alliances with the Arab conquerors and were given their religious freedom along with the Jews, as 'ahl al-kitāb' ('people of the book'). This concept, well described in Islam, recognises and respects fellow monotheists who share similar prophets and religious roots. Acceptance of the Arabs was facilitated by Jewish and Coptic resentment of the Byzantines' ruthless and punitive methods of collecting taxes. Coptic Christians had also suffered religious discrimination under the Byzantine Orthodox Church, so the locals offered little resistance to the Arabs – indeed, some even welcomed them. Over time many Egyptians converted to Islam and Arabic supplanted Coptic as the national language in the first quarter of the eighth century. Coptic survived as the lingua franca in the countryside for

200 more years. The Islamisation and Arabisation of Egypt were also consolidated by the steady influx of Arab Bedouins who mixed with local communities.

In 644 Amr ibn al-As was relieved of his duties as provincial governor of Egypt by the Islamic caliphate in Medina due to fears that he was becoming too powerful. He had refused to devolve fiscal administration to another official, stating that under such an arrangement he would be 'holding the cow by the horns while someone else would be milking it'[2] and Abd Allah ibn Sa'd, the governor of Upper Egypt, was put in sole charge of the region.

The Nubians of Northern Sudan

In 652 Abd Allah ibn Sa'd looked southwards from Egypt to what is now Sudan and launched an expedition against the area's inhabitants, known as the 'Nobatae', who may have come from further west in the sixth century. The Greek thinker Eratosthenes in the third century BCE wrote about the 'Novfiat' and later the name occurred in a Latinised form as 'Nobatae', which may have then given rise to the word 'Nubian'. However, the ultimate derivation of 'Nubian' is not certain; it may have come from the ancient Egyptian word *nubu*, meaning gold, as there was much gold in northern Sudan; or from the Coptic *notbt*, meaning to plait, a common hairstyle in the region. In any case, I will refer to riverine northern Sudan as Nubia. This was divided into three kingdoms: Nobatia with its capital at Faras, Makuria centred on Old Dongola, and Alwa, stretching east to the border with Aksum with its capital at Soba on the Blue Nile.

The Nubian Christians had embraced Christianity centuries before the arrival of the Arabs in Egypt, but we know little about their Christian kings. I found it both tantalising and frustrating when I visited the upper floors of Sudan's National Museum in Khartoum to admire the frescoes dating back to Nubia's Christian heritage. These colourful but faded frescoes would have been displayed on the walls of the cathedrals, churches and monasteries built by the kings of Nubia. In these splendid portraits, monarchs, some on horseback, with dark skin, large eyes and aquiline features, are dressed in elaborate robes of luxurious cloth. Their tombs have yet to be discovered and so these frescoes provide a unique glimpse into their identity and world. With a great-grandmother who was born in modern Dongola, as well as other family roots in the region, I have a particular attachment to this chapter of Sudanese history.

Ancient Nubia was an important civilisation and trade hub for centuries, and the Nubians had forged close ties with Egypt. So, when the Arabs invaded Egypt, the Nubians carried out skirmishes against them, compelled to defend their fellow Christians. This provoked the rulers of Medina in Arabia into invading Nubia. However, just like the Kushites before them, the Nubians were a force to be reckoned with. They had continued the archery and equestrianism of the Kushites; mounted Nubian archers were famous for firing their arrows into the eyes of their enemies, blinding them. In the face of such ferocious resistance, the Arabs decided it would be prudent to negotiate. At this time, the people of central and northern Nubia were united under King Qalidurut, who in the early 650s signed a nonaggression pact on equal terms with the Arabs called the 'Bakt Treaty' – an Arabisation of the Latin word *pactum*, or pact in English. This was in part a trade agreement, which remarkably persisted for about five centuries. The Nubians had succeeded in maintaining their independence, their Mediterranean trading links and their Christian faith.

However, as Egypt became increasingly Arabised and Islamised, the Nubians' interaction and trade ties with Egypt meant they too came under such influences. The tide of Islamisation that swept across northern Sudan came not only from the north of the continent but also from the east across the Red Sea, and it gained momentum from the 1200s when many Arabs arrived in search of grazing land for cattle, natural resources, minerals and precious metals such as gold. By the thirteenth and fourteenth centuries, the number of Arabs migrating from Arabia increased from a steady trickle to significant flows, aided by the fact that Christian Nubia had become fragmented. Nubia's Christian heritage further unravelled when in 1323 Kanz al-Dawla, who was king of Dongola, converted to Islam. The migration of the Arabs and the mutual acculturation that followed gradually eclipsed Christianity over the centuries. Yet residual Christian practices persist. For instance, older members of my family, including my late father, like many other northern Sudanese, were taken to the banks of the River Nile as newborns to have water sprinkled on their foreheads in a custom that is an echo of Christian baptism. Similarly, a bride and groom visit the Nile to dip their feet in its waters as a token of good luck. The mingling of Arabs who settled in northern Sudan with the locals has given rise to the unique Sudanese culture of today: a fusion of African and Arab, which is reflected in the appearance, language, religious and cultural traditions of the people. My family's mother tongue has for generations been Arabic, the lingua franca for all Sudanese, though one great-grandmother could speak Nubian.

Islam in Sudan has always had a strong Sufi element. Sufis, in addition to following Islamic law closely, embrace direct, personal contact with Allah through mystic revelation, which may be achieved by various means – by entering a trance, for example.

The Maghreb States of North Africa

By contrast with Sudan, Islam spread suddenly and at times even violently in the Maghreb states of North Africa. In 643 Amr ibn al-As, the conqueror of Egypt, marched on Cyrenaica in modern-day Libya, which was then part of the province of Egypt. He seized it with little resistance. A year later he took Tripoli. In 647 Abd Allah ibn Sa'd, by then governor of Egypt, led a two-year expedition into Byzacena (in what is Tunisia today) with an army of 20,000 horsemen, carrying out raids across the region, but he left two years later before completing his mission: that task fell to another brilliant Arab general.

In 679 Ukba ibn Nafi, the nephew of Amr ibn al-As, was appointed commander of the Arab forces in North Africa. He had inherited his uncle's military skills, overcoming the last Byzantine strongholds and proclaiming Byzacena an Islamic province, which he called Ifrikiya, the name the Romans had given to their North African province eight centuries earlier. He established a capital city in what is today the north of Tunisia and named it Kairouan, meaning camp or arsenal, bringing with him several early followers of the Prophet Mohammed.

However, Ukba ibn Nafi's strategy to quell North Africa and convert it to Islam was a lengthy undertaking. For the next few decades, the Arabs had to deal with disparate communities of Berbers. Some were subjugated, while others resisted or entered into tenuous alliances with them. During this period the Berber population in the towns and on coastal plains were Christian, some mountain inhabitants had adopted Judaism, and the Berbers in the interior had remained largely pagan. The fourteenth-century North African-born historian Ibn Khaldun wrote that the Berbers, their spirit unsubdued by Arab hegemony, 'reverted 40 times' – meaning that every time they converted to Islam, they would simply revert to their original faith as soon as the Arab armies were expelled or withdrew.

Kusayla, early 600s–688

One figure who was instrumental in facilitating the Arab conquest of North Africa was a powerful Berber leader, Kusayla. A recent convert to Islam, he may have previously been a Christian. In 678 he rallied to the Arab cause, supplying Ukba ibn Nafi with thousands of soldiers who, along with Ukba's 15,000 horsemen, notched up significant military victories over the Berbers across North Africa. But Ukba ibn Nafi, the masterful tactician, made one grave and serious miscalculation. Having invaded Kusayla's stronghold Tlemcen in northern Algeria, he allowed his men to go on the rampage and loot the region. Kusayla, furious with Ukba at this betrayal, hatched a plan for revenge. By this time Ukba's Arab troops had become worn out by their long North African campaign, and were desperate to go home. Perhaps carried away by the reputation for invincibility that he had gained, Ukba released many from service back to Arabia. Ukba ibn Nafi was left with a contingent of 5,000 Arab fighters alongside Kusayla's more numerous Berber forces. As they all marched through Kusayla's vast homeland,

Kusayla and his men abandoned Ukba's camp and made their way to the Atlas Mountains, and once there appealed to the Christian Berbers who had taken refuge from the Arabs to join forces with them. They agreed and, in August 683, 50,000 Christian and Muslim Berber fighters combined to confront Ukba ibn Nafi. Outnumbered ten to one, Ukba nevertheless put up a fight, throwing himself into enemy ranks and dying on the battlefield. His body was never found. Kusayla, a man of pure Berber stock, having obliterated Ukba's army, proclaimed himself victor and governor of the whole of Ifrikiya. His success, however, was short-lived, as five years later, in 688, the Arabs attacked North Africa once more. In a heavy and bloody battle, east of Timgad in the Aurès Mountains, Kusayla died with many of his men, and Arab hegemony was restored. However, that did not mean that Berber resistance was over.

Queen Kahina, late 600s–702

A new Arab governor was appointed in Ifrikiya called Hassan ibn al-Nu'man. He encountered bitter opposition from another Berber ruler who refused to accept Arab domination. A fearless, fearsome and charismatic Berber queen, Kahina had observed with growing alarm the machinations of Kusayla and the Arab advance in North Africa. Kahina's father, chief of the Djawara community, may have been killed while fighting the Arabs (perhaps with Kusayla), and she was determined to continue the resistance. Much of what we know about her comes from the writings of the Arab chronicler Ibn Khaldun many centuries later.

Kahina's real name was Dahiya (or a variant of this) bint Tatit. Kahina, meaning 'sorceress' in Arabic and 'priestess' in

Hebrew, was the name given to her by the Arabs, who depicted her as a woman possessed by demons.

Kusayla's death had left a power vacuum, and although the Berbers formed different – sometimes competing – communities they could unite in the face of foreign invasion. Kahina succeeded in persuading the Djawara council of chiefs that despite her gender she had the courage and vision to lead the resistance against the Arabs. News of her bravery and wisdom spread and other Berber tribes rallied behind her. Kahina was tall and beautiful, and her ability to win over doubters was fuelled by rumours of her supernatural powers. She was believed to be able to rouse her troops by speaking to the spirits of the ancestors, who would assist in seeing off the enemy. She personally recruited young men of fighting age from towns and rural areas, craftsmen and peasants who responded with enthusiasm to her call for action and demands to confront their adversaries. She became queen of the Berbers and her position was invested with formal authority and legitimacy.

In 696 on the banks of the Meskiana River, Kahina rode into battle at the head of her army, her long flowing hair tied in a headdress, spear in hand. Kahina proved a formidable opponent during her first clash with the Arabs; her forces killed hundreds and chased survivors back to the coast. Hundreds more were left wounded on the battlefield, in a defeat the Arabs named 'the river of disaster'. Dozens were taken prisoner and Kahina insisted they should not be mistreated. Ibn Khaldun records her saying, satisfied with her achievement: 'They run like grasshoppers that came from the desert to damage our land.'[3]

Kahina decided not to march on the Arab capital Kairouan and withdrew to the mountains. Processions of maidens dressed in silks and fine jewellery and groups of musicians

A statue of Queen Kahina in Khenchela, Algeria

proclaimed her accomplishments as she made her way home to the Aurès, on paths strewn with flowers. Kahina was firm in her belief that the Arabs were interested mostly in plunder, so she decided the best course of action would be to deter them from seizing her land by destroying it. With this plan in mind, she addressed her followers thus:

> Yes, we can fight them to the death but others will come, who will step over our dead bodies to conquer the whole land. They want gold and silver and our palaces and houses. There is not a palm grove, not an oasis, not a spring, not a flower of the valley that did not see me grow to seize the moment when you accepted me and chose me to carry your flame. All the wealth that was given to us we need to sacrifice today to save our land. Yes: the forests, the villages, the farms, our livelihoods, everything needs to be reduced to

ashes, the day the invader comes. Use your axes to cut down the orchards and fields, light fires to burn the buildings, tear down the fortifications, destroy the dams so that the enemy soldier will tire and find nowhere to take refuge. He will see that our land is arid and simply full of smoking debris. So, he will never come back again.

Despite protestations, Kahina persisted with her scorched earth policy and ravaged the region. Admiration turned to resentment. Her actions enraged local Berber communities, farmers, townspeople and merchants and caused division in the ranks of her followers. Many fled the region in a mass exodus to the coast, depriving her of support, while others sided with the Arabs and encouraged them to re-engage in battle with Kahina.

Hassan ibn al-Nu'man, smarting from the disastrous defeat of 696, had vowed revenge on Kahina. 'It will be her head or mine,' he said. He gathered a huge army in 701 and marched back into the Aurès region. Kahina was confronted by an Arab onslaught whose numbers had been swelled by large groups of Berbers now opposed to her rule.

Kahina knew that her weak and demoralised army was no match and she acknowledged defeat. Given a choice of converting to Islam or face slaughter, she ordered her two sons to accept Islam so that their lives could be spared, but she herself remained defiant and refused. She was beheaded and her head was displayed publicly as a trophy. The demise of Kahina, who had prophesied her own death at the hands of the Arabs, spelled the end of Berber resistance. Her burial place has never been found though she may have been killed near a well, and today there is one in Aurès that bears her name, 'Bir al-Kahina'.

Despite her defeat, Kahina is regarded as a heroine, a feminist icon, and a symbol of pride and dignity right across

North Africa – in particular for the Amazigh people. And she is honoured by many on the continent, who see her as an example of strong African female leadership, a woman who sacrificed herself in the cause of independence. As I walked along the green fields at the base of the Aurès Mountains, small blooms trodden underfoot, surveying the part of eastern Algeria where a great African queen once held sway, I thought surely her name should be as well-known as other great 'warrior-queens' of history, such as Boudicca (or Boadicea) of the Iceni people in Britain who fought the Romans in the first century; or Zenobia, the third-century queen of Palmyra in modern-day Syria, another woman who made a stand against subjugation.

Kahina's resistance was based on a rejection of the Arabs' religion, culture and hegemony, but at times even when the Berbers accepted Islam, they would revolt against their Arab overlords, as Kusayla did. Their opposition was not aimed against ordinary Muslim Arabs but only their ruling class. However, other Berbers seized the chance to join Arab armies and even became Arab commanders, so that they could participate in conquest and enjoy a share of the spoils. Kahina's own sons, once converted to Islam, may have even commanded Arab armies in North Africa.

During the first half of the eighth century, the Arabs succeeded in converting swathes of the urban and rural population of North Africa, using such policies as offering liberty, upon conversion, to Berber prisoners of war, especially those from ruling families. In 704 another Arab general, Musa ibn Nusayr, was sent to North Africa to try decisively to end all Berber opposition. After a series of fierce military campaigns across the region, he completed the Arab dominion of the whole of North Africa in 711. The conquest had taken them seven decades.

The Idrissites, c. *788–985*

Towards the end of the 700s a holy man from Mecca called Moulay Idriss took refuge in the old town of Volubilis – the former capital of King Juba II, in modern-day northern Morocco. He had been experiencing problems in Mecca over his adherence to the minority Shia sect of Islam. Moulay Idriss so impressed the Berbers with his piety that they made him their leader. He had children with a local Berber woman called Kenza and gave his name to a new dynasty, the Idrissites. He established the Moroccan city of Fes, which developed rapidly into a bustling urban settlement.

In 803 Moulay Idriss was succeeded by his son Moulay Idriss II. He expanded the state, moved his capital to Fes in about 807, and set about making it into a centre of enlightenment. Upon his death he was succeeded by his son Mohammed, who turned to his grandmother Kenza for advice on how to rule. She recommended that he divide the kingdom between himself and his ten brothers. The arrangement did not work well and weakened the Idrissite dynasty, though they retained some of their power and continued to rule in a decentralised manner for a century more. At some stage, the Idrissites decided to spread the teachings of Sunnism rather than disseminate their own Shia beliefs. Broadly speaking, Sunnis (who today constitute about 90 per cent of global Muslims) focus on following the Prophet's example, with no intercessor being necessary between the believer and Allah; whereas Shias emphasise the lineage of the Prophet's family through a series of imams and rely on a 'clergy' such as ayatollahs to guide them in their faith. The sectarian division occurred during the internecine conflict that ensued immediately after the Prophet's death in 634.

Under the Idrissites, Fes gained a reputation for learning, with a university which by some measures is the oldest one in continuous existence, dating back to the ninth century. Fes is perhaps my favourite city in Morocco. I love the narrow, winding alleys of the main market. I like to admire the mosaics in the mosques with their subtle patterns, the water basins in the courtyards where worshippers perform their ablutions before prayers, and fountains from which a parched passerby can quench their thirst. By the ninth century, North Africa, with fine towns such as Fes and Kairouan, was very much an important part of the Islamic world.

The Fatimids, 909–1171

From Kabylie in central Algeria a powerful new Arab dynasty emerged: the Fatimids, named after Fatima, the daughter of the Prophet Mohammed. They claimed to be descendants of Hussain, the son of Fatima, and her husband Ali, whom they saw as the Prophet's spiritual successor. The Fatimids were unusual in that they followed the minority Shia sect. They conquered North Africa around 909 and a year later their leader Abdullah al-Mahdi declared a caliphate in modern-day Tunisia with a capital, Mahdia, just south of Kairouan. The Fatimids chose this spot on a rocky peninsula as their capital for its proximity to the sea, as they were concerned about attacks from opponents living inland. Abdullah ordered the construction of an impregnable walled city, which still stands today.

The few Fatimids and Arabs were primarily the ruling class. However, they established their system of government on the social and political structures that predated their arrival. The Berbers were the merchant class, builders and craftsmen, and their acceptance of Fatimid rule was fundamental to the Fatimids' hold on power.

Once secure in this part of North Africa, the Fatimids set their sights on Egypt. They had a strong and disciplined army and in 969 they conquered Egypt and built a new capital city, Cairo. They governed the country for 200 years and established its famous mosque, Al-Azhar. It is somewhat ironic that although Al-Azhar has for hundreds of years been the seat of Islamic learning for the mainstream Sunni form of Islam, it was in fact founded by a minority Shia dynasty. Fatimid rule brought great prosperity to Egypt. Trade flourished, the Fatimid dinar became a unit of international currency, the cotton and linen industry thrived, and key pieces of infrastructure such as dams were repaired.

Ensconced in Cairo, the Fatimids' hold on their dominions elsewhere came under challenge. When they relocated to Egypt, the Fatimids had left the day-to-day running of government in Mahdia to the Sanhaja Berbers, also known as the Zirids, named after their patriarch Ziri ibn Manad. They were Shias like the Fatimids. However, in the first half of the eleventh century, the Zirid emir al-Mu'izz ibn Badis renounced the Shia sect and declared his affiliation with the majority Berber Sunnis.

The Fatimids were enraged by his actions and sent tens of thousands of fighters from Upper Egypt to attack the rebellious Zirids. The walled city of Mahdia along the Tunisian coast was impenetrable, but the rest of the region was vulnerable and fell into decline as a result of the conflict.

The Fatimids had become increasingly dependent on an army made up of enslaved Nubians and Turkish horsemen, the latter known as Mamluks (which means 'slaves'). Their loyalty was secure provided they were properly remunerated. The Fatimids relied heavily on taxation of peasants for their income, which was managed by Berbers on their behalf, but it was a corrupt system and the officials pocketed much of the proceeds from taxation themselves. This depleted state coffers and once the Fatimid rulers could no longer pay their army well, their troops became discontent and disloyal.

When the last Fatimid caliph died in 1171, Salah al-Din, also known as Saladin, a Sunni Muslim Kurdish commander who had fought the Christians in the Third Crusade, became ruler of Egypt. He founded the Ayyubid dynasty and relied on the Mamluks for defence, which greatly boosted their standing and prestige. They became so powerful that in 1250 they assassinated the Ayyubid sultan and established the Mamluk dynasty, which ruled Egypt for two and a half centuries until 1517, when the Ottomans defeated them and Egypt became part of the Ottoman Empire. The Ottomans had seized Constantinople in 1453 and their empire stretched from northern Africa to western Asia and southeastern Europe.

The Berber Amazigh Dynasties: The Almoravids 1050–1147

Around 1050, as Fatimid power in Egypt was waning, the Almoravids, the first of three powerful Berber dynasties, came to the fore in what is today Morocco. The Almoravids, who emerged from a coalition of Berber communities living in the western Sahara, founded the city of Marrakesh in 1060 and established a thriving city within its walls.

In 1075, the Almoravid ruler was Yusuf ibn Tashfin, a forceful and charismatic man who regarded himself as a warrior for Islam. He assumed a role as a teacher of Sunni Islam and practised what he preached by leading an exemplary religious life. Under him, the Almoravids seized control of much of Morocco and built an empire. His power extended far and wide, and included territory in modern-day Spain, Algeria, Libya, Mali, Mauritania and Senegal. The Almoravid capital Marrakesh was endowed with numerous mosques and religious schools. It became the cultural and trading centre of their empire – a meeting point for caravan routes – and the Almoravids grew rich, especially by trading salt for gold.

They had so much gold that the Almoravid gold coin was the most trusted currency in the whole of the Mediterranean during this period of history. When Yusuf ibn Tashfin died around 1106 he was succeeded by his son Ali. The first 20 years of Ali's rule saw Marrakesh expand economically and grow as an artistic and literary hub, drawing poets from Spain, who burnished its literary credentials. But the austere lifestyle of his father did not appeal to Ali. He preferred a more sumptuous way of living and successive Almoravid rulers, following his example, became decadent and lacking in discipline. The Almoravids relied on relatives and client rulers to exercise power, so their system of local government was relatively weak. They were accused of oppression and injustice by their subjects, sapping their authority and strength. By 1147 a new dynasty came to dominate the region: the Almohads.

The Almohads, 1147–1269

The Almohads, who hailed from the Atlas Mountains of southern Morocco, rejected the orthodoxy of the Almoravids, adhering instead to Sufism. Faith was important to them, and they viewed themselves as the 'chosen ones'. The

Almohads wanted to make an emphatic religious statement to underscore their piety, and so they built the great Koutoubia Mosque of Marrakesh, which took its name from the Arabic word for books, *kutub*, since there was originally a book market nearby. Still in use today, it is the oldest, most complete and important monumental legacy of the Almohad era. I was struck by the vast scale and elegant simplicity of its arched interior.

The Almohads were great builders, responsible for monuments such as the Great Mosques in Algeria and in Seville. They established a new capital on the site of Rabat, Morocco's current capital city. In addition, they were major patrons of writers and artists, devoting vast resources to science, medicine, mathematics, astronomy and philosophy, and inviting prominent thinkers such as the Andalusian Arab polymath Ibn Rushd (or Averroes) to their court. In this way they helped stimulate new thinking, which later influenced European

The Koutoubia Mosque of Marrakesh

intellectuals. *The School of Athens* fresco by the Renaissance artist Raphael depicts Ibn Rushd alongside luminaries of the Western tradition such as Plato and Aristotle, reflecting his contribution to philosophy. He was described by Dante as 'the commentator', so respected were his opinions. Ibn Rushd's book on medicine – *Kitab al-Kulliyyat*, meaning 'Book of All' in Arabic, which consisted of seven volumes looking at various aspects of medicine, for example anatomy, pathology and physiology – was translated into Latin and used in Europe until the eighteenth century. Walking around the old Almohad fortress in Rabat, and its gardens, I felt delighted that visitors like me can enjoy the same mosaic of flowers that the old sultans did.

The Almohads ruled through an efficient civil service and established coherent taxation systems. Yusuf Yaqub al-Mansour, the third Almohad ruler, in power from 1184 to 1199, was an accomplished man, credited with writing beautiful Arabic prose. He faced such serious opposition from former Almoravid officials and their allies that he was forced to march into modern-day Tunis in 1186 with an army of 20,000 horsemen. In Spain in 1195, he decisively defeated the Christian Castilians, earning the title 'al-Mansour Billah', meaning 'the victor through God'. Falling ill during his Spanish campaign, al-Mansour returned home to die in 1199.

By 1250, the power of the Almohads had drained away. Different regions were now controlled by various powers, of whom the most significant were the Merinids, a nomadic Berber community, who encouraged the cult of holy men. Almohad Spain was also disintegrating. The Almohads had overstretched themselves; keeping so vast an empire intact was no easy task. Facing constant rebellions across different territories, they crumbled. Even the great city of Fes was lost to the Merinids in 1248, and the last Almohad king was deposed by the Merinids in 1269.

The Merinids, 1269–1465

The most famous Merinid king was Abu el-Hassan, who ruled in the late thirteenth century. He was called the Black Sultan, because his mother was from what is today Ethiopia and so he had a dark complexion.

The Black Sultan ruled his empire with resolution and vigour. Under the Merinids, the city of Fes was restored as a capital city and regained its former standing as a centre of learning, culture and craftsmanship. By 1337 Abu el-Hassan exerted great control over trans-Saharan trade after crushing rival rulers in North Africa, and the land under his control was as extensive as the Almohad Empire's had been. Flush from his victories, he embarked on a building programme, expanding the royal Merinid cemetery for example. Yet the wheel of fate soon turned again.

After a failed military campaign that left him shipwrecked and without supporters, Abu el-Hassan was forced to abdicate from power in 1351. He finished his days in the High Atlas Mountains, gazing across the crags and valleys that were once his, brooding on his lost empire. His body was transferred and buried in the royal necropolis he founded at Chellah, which was a former Roman town. The tomb of the Black Sultan is surprisingly bare, just a raised stone burial mound, but the guide to the necropolis explained that there would have been a small pyramid mounted on it, which is now kept by the entrance. Besides the Black Sultan's tomb, I noticed a much smaller one and was told that this might have been the tomb of his son Abu Hisham, who had died in infancy.

The Merinid dynasty, which ended in 1465, was the last of the great Berber dynasties that ruled over North Africa and parts of southern Europe. Thereafter North Africa's history diverged. The parts that constitute Algeria and Tunisia became part of the Ottoman Empire from the 1500s. Morocco took a different path. In the mid-sixteenth century, the Arab Beni Saad, a nomad clan, took control of Marrakesh and Fes. Its most famous ruler was Ahmed al-Mansour, who reigned from about 1578 to 1603. Like the Fatimids, the Saadians claimed descent from the daughter of the Prophet Mohammed, but unlike them they were Sunnis, not Shias. Ahmed al-Mansour developed trade with England, which was then ruled by the Tudor queen, Elizabeth I, daughter of King Henry VIII. He sold sugar to England in return for firearms and obtained goods through violent means, sending military expeditions across the Sahara Desert in search of enslaved people, salt and gold from the Songhay Empire – which we will explore in the next chapter.

By the sixteenth century, the acquisition of treasure through force was a feature of what became known as the Barbary states of Algiers, Tunis, Morocco and Tripoli, which correspond roughly to the Maghreb today. They were so powerful that they extracted annual payments from European kingdoms. The Barbary pirates who raided the Mediterranean coast all the way to Cornwall in southwest England, in search of lucre, were particularly abhorred. They would abduct Europeans from the ships of nations that had not made tributary payments, and exchange them for ransom. The first war of the newly independent United States was against the Barbary states in 1801–5; no longer benefiting from the annual fee paid by England, American merchant ships were being attacked by pirates, so President Jefferson ordered his navy to attack any Barbary ship in an effort to see off the pirates. US victory in the Second Barbary War of 1815 ended all tribute payments from America. By the nineteenth century, the power of the

Barbary states had waned and in 1830, taking advantage of a weakened Ottoman Empire, the French captured Algeria and by the early twentieth century had established protectorates in Tunisia and Morocco. The Saadian dynasty survived colonial rule in Morocco and one of its descendants Mohammed VI is on the throne today.

Islam was and is central to the identity of many North African Berbers, yet even as many gradually adopted the Arabic language, they still maintained a distinct culture. Today, around 40 per cent of the population of Morocco and 30 per cent of Algerians are Berber, and there are small but sizeable minorities in Tunisia and Libya as well as millions of people of mixed heritage. The Berber language is still often spoken within these communities. The Tuareg, who are similar in culture to the Berbers, are found in Mauritania, Niger and Mali. In the end, the conquering Arabs assimilated just as much as the people they had defeated. They did not extinguish the culture that predated their arrival but built on it. The Arabs also took Islam further west across the Sahara, and one Muslim king in West Africa gained a place in the annals of history for one of the most famous pilgrimages to Mecca ever made.

8

Mansa Musa and the Kingdoms
of West Africa

It is a persistent myth that, south of the Sahara, Africa
somehow existed beyond the 'known world' and was cut off
from the global economy. As Islam spread to the west of
Africa, connections across the Sahara enriched communities in both the north and west of the continent. Culture
and ideas flowed with the exchange of goods. The kingdoms that emerged in West Africa were sophisticated and
fully exploited the advantages of trans-Saharan trade, so
much so that Mansa Musa I, the fourteenth-century king of
the Mali Empire, has a credible claim to being the richest
individual to have ever lived. Estimates of his wealth put it
at the equivalent of US$400 billion today. As this chapter
will show, three of the great West African empires – Ghana,
Mali and Songhay – were integrated in international trade
and financial systems.

The Ghana Empire, c. 600–1235

The Ghana Empire, which confusingly has no territorial overlap with the modern nation of Ghana, was the first major empire of West Africa. This kingdom existed between the seventh and thirteenth centuries, though it may have begun as early as the fifth century. The name 'Ghana' may have derived from the Arabic word for forest: *ghaba*.

The empire covered territory in modern-day Mali, Mauritania and Senegal, and its main inhabitants were the Soninke, which was also the name of their language. They called their kingdom Wagadou. The Soninke, who practised their own traditional beliefs, occupied the western Sahel, which gave them a strategic position halfway between the gold fields of the upper Senegal River and the desert of North Africa.

The modern-day Soninke community I met live in Nouakchott, the capital of the little-visited country of Mauritania. The city, which lies on the Atlantic coast, is quiet and rather stark, save for its beaches, full of brightly coloured fishing canoes. I dropped by a Soninke cultural centre to watch a dance performance. In the audience sat dozens of women. Dressed in colourful robes with headscarves, they seemed to be dripping in gold: necklaces, bangles, heavy gold earrings hung low, and even golden hoops were laced through their plaited hair.

The Ghana kingdom was most likely united under Dinga Cisse, a leader considered by his subjects to have semi-divine status, who established a capital at Koumbi Saleh about 1,000 kilometres south from Nouakchott. Most of its people were fishermen, farmers and herdsmen.

The kingdom was based at first on a partially matriarchal system, so when a king died he would not be succeeded by his own son but by his sister's. Local chiefs kept their position but had to be loyal to the king, whom they were obliged to send food and goods. It was common for the king to keep scions of important families as hostages in his royal court, to maintain their loyalty. There was no standing army; Ghana was mostly a peaceful and commerce-based kingdom. But young men would receive military training and served as a defence force, and were deployed in raids. Horses were used as a means of transport and for ceremonial purposes, when they would be dressed in white and attired in red for warfare. Captives from defeated states were sold as enslaved people to Muslim traders, though this did not constitute a big proportion of Ghana's trade. More enslaved people went to North Africa from the region of Lake Chad, further east.

Tenkamenin, r. 1037–75

Tenkamenin, who reigned from 1037 to 1075, was known as 'the people's king'. He was a just and magnanimous ruler who rode on horseback to be among his subjects and listen to their concerns. His officials managed the gold trade in a shrewd and careful manner, from the capital Koumbi Saleh.

In the eleventh century, the Arab-Andalusian geographer Abu Ubayd Abdallah al-Bakri acquired information from Arabic-speaking merchants of North Africa about Koumbi Saleh, which was divided into two – one part occupied by the Soninke and the king, and the other by Muslims, mostly Berbers. He described Koumbi Saleh in his 1057 book *Road and Kingdoms* as:

> two separate towns, situated on a plain, a little distance apart: one which is inhabited by Muslims and is large and possesses 12 mosques, in one of which they assemble for Friday prayers. There are salaried imams and muezzins, as well as jurists and

scholars. The king's royal town is 10 kilometres away, and the area between the two is covered with the stone and wooden houses of the Soninke. The king has a palace and a number of domed dwellings all surrounded with an enclosure like a city wall. Around the king's town are domed buildings and groves and thickets where the sorcerers of these people, men in charge of the religious cult, live. In them too are their idols and tombs of their kings. The king adorns himself with ornaments around the neck and arms. On his head he wears gold embroidered caps covered with turbans of finest cotton. He gives audience to the people for the redressing of grievances in a hut around which are placed ten horses covered in golden cloth. Behind him stand ten slaves carrying shields and swords mounted with gold. On his right are the sons of vassal kings, their hair plaited with gold and wearing costly garments. On the ground around him are seated his ministers, whilst the governor of the city sits before him. On guard at the door are dogs of fine pedigree, wearing collars adorned with gold and silver.[1]

The majority of the inhabitants of Koumbi Saleh were not Muslim. They worshipped a god called Bida, or Wagadou Bida, who was represented by a black snake. When people converted to Islam, they would move to the Muslim quarters of the town. The Soninke king maintained his traditional beliefs but had good relations with the Muslims. Their literary skills made them useful for running his administration and their financial nous helped in managing the taxation system on goods passing through his empire.

However, over time a rivalry grew between the Soninke and the Muslim Berbers based at Awdaghust, a prosperous and large town in modern-day Mauritania. By the middle of the eleventh century, the rulers of Ghana had gained the upper hand and incorporated Awdaghust into their empire, which became its commercial centre. At the National Museum of Mauritania in Nouakchott, the director, Dr Mamadou Kane, showed me some of the artefacts on display such as ceramics and earthenware dating from the ninth to eleventh centuries, which were excavated from the Soninke quarters of Koumbi Saleh only in the early 1900s. As is so often the case in Africa, archaeologists have been slow in uncovering the continent's rich history, due to a lack of funding and security.

Dr Kane explained to me how Ghana traded gold – weight for weight – for salt with the rulers of North Africa, which had abundant sources of rock-salt bars from salt mines. The people of Ghana greatly valued Saharan salt and used it for food and to treat ailments. At times, it was even used as a currency. They also exported iron and copper to other parts of western Africa. Copper, which was scarcer than gold in Ghana, was priced by its people at 1 gram of copper for 3 grams of gold. Dr Kane pointed out to me the slivers of copper on display that were used as money.

Trade between West Africans and Berber and Arab merchants was constant and extensive. One factor revolutionised trans-Saharan trade: the camel. This animal was brought to the Soninke by the Berbers, who in turn had been introduced to it by the Arabs. The camel had been present in North Africa for some centuries, and its widespread use in trans-Saharan trade coincided with the period of Arabisation and Islamisation of North Africa between the seventh and tenth centuries. Camels are ideal for desert conditions; they can tolerate long periods without water, and stores of fat in their humps can be used for nourishment. By the tenth century, caravans could be made up of thousands of camels. They were as important for desert commerce as ships were for maritime trade. They are still highly valued today, as witnessed when I went to a large camel market outside the Mauritanian capital. It made me think of one of my great-grandfathers, a rich merchant in northern Sudan, who made a fortune out of selling camels; Sudanese camels are among the best in the world and a highly prized export.

I spent a few hours with a family of nomads near the historic key trading town of Chinguetti. Every morning these herders take their camels to graze, fortifying themselves with a good drink of frothy camel milk drunk from large wooden bowls.

As well as major trading centres such as Chinguetti, staging posts were established in places such as Oualata and Ouadane, also in northern Mauritania. I headed to Ouadane, which is about 600 kilometres from Nouakchott, through inhospitable and at times mountainous terrain. Ouadane's old town, dusty and overlooking an oasis, is a seldom visited collection of stone ruins, which serve as the only reminder of the busy metropolis it once was. It was an important camel caravan centre and provided a much-used route for traders.

After centuries of interaction and trade with Muslim Arabs and Berbers, the rulers of Ghana and some of their subjects became Muslim and this helped to spread literacy across West Africa through the teaching of the Koran. I got an idea of just how extensively Islam grew in West Africa when I was in Senegal, which made up part of the Ghana Empire. In the Senegalese capital Dakar, when it was time for Friday lunchtime prayers just about everybody stopped what they were doing and headed to the mosque. Around 95 per cent of Senegalese today are Muslim.

I visited the Grand Mosque in the central district, which is a prominent feature of the city, with its 67-metre-tall minaret dominating the skyline. Richly decorated on the outside and inside, the mosque has a green and white tiled floor, surrounded by a series of arches giving it a distinct Moroccan style. It was built by the late King Hassan II of Morocco in the 1960s as a gift to the people of Senegal. The mosque has an institute dedicated to Islamic research and teachings. Its director, Thierno Ka, described how Islam took hold in West Africa, relating how Sufi religious brotherhoods, under the guidance of a leader known as a 'marabout', were responsible for the proliferation of Islamic teachings from the eighth century. Some marabouts were holy men who might have led a peripatetic existence; others such as the 'Mourides' – one of the main brotherhoods in Senegal – had leaders who enjoyed an extremely high status almost akin to a caliph. The Mouride movement was founded by the Senegalese mystic and poet Cheikh Amadu Bamba Mbacke. In 1895 he set up a global trading company based on three principles: follow Allah; work and provoke no one; and pray and study the Koran. Its followers became known as Mourides and today they number in the millions. You can find many of them in cities across the world selling sunglasses, hats and handbags and they are renowned for helping out one another when in need.

However, the Islamisation of Ghana's rulers diminished their authority over their non-Muslim subjects. Koumbi Saleh, the capital of Ghana, came under attack from the powerful Almoravids of North Africa. The long-established Takrur state, made up of a trading people in the Senegal Valley, had adopted Islam early in the eleventh century, and they sided with the Almoravids against the Soninke in the hope they would be rewarded with a bigger slice of the lucrative trans-Saharan trade. Koumbi Saleh fell to the

Almoravids in 1076. Meanwhile, the chiefs of southern Soninke and Malinke (also known as Mande or Mandinka), who had paid allegiance to Ghana, were becoming more independent, which exposed the southern flank of the empire to rebellion.

There were environmental factors at play too. By the end of the eleventh century, the farmland in Koumbi Saleh was worn out and could no longer support cereal crops. Berber nomads and pastoralists had overgrazed it, so people headed for woodland and savannah to the south and west. The end of the Ghana Empire, through environmental degradation, is also expressed in mythical terms by the story of Bida, the black snake god, who required an annual sacrifice of a female virgin to guarantee the continuing prosperity of the kingdom. One year a beautiful woman, who had been promised in marriage to a young man, was offered as sacrifice. Her fiancé rescued her and as a result Bida took his revenge. A terrible drought descended on the kingdom and its gold mining suffered. Hungry snake god or not, by the end of the twelfth century Ghana had indeed lost its domination of trade and was an empire only in name.

The Soso Kingdom, 1180–1230

After the decline of Ghana, there was an interlude of domination for about half a century by the pagan Soso – a Soninke–Malinke splinter group who were hostile to Islam and opposed the selling of enslaved people to the Muslims. The Soso capital was in a mountainous region near Koulikoro, not far from Bamako (capital of modern Mali), which was occupied by a Malinke clan of blacksmiths.

Sumaoro Kante, r. *c.* 1200–35

One king of Soso, Kemoko, ruled until 1200 and after his death his son Sumaoro Kante (or Sumanguru) took up the reins of power. Sumaoro Kante conquered Soninke provinces and attacked the Malinke, who put up a fierce resistance. The Malinke king, Dankaran Tuman, sought an alliance with Sumaoro Kante. He gave him a kinswoman in marriage, gaining peace and sealing Sumaoro Kante's supremacy.

Sumaoro Kante's virtues were praised by 'griots', and under his rule the 'balafon' (a kind of xylophone) and the 'dan' (a four-stringed guitar) were invented. These were later used in praise songs. Griots are storytellers whose role is to extol the greatness of rulers, heroes and heroines. The griot tradition still exists today and these custodians of Africa's oral culture are an important source of African history. As the Nigerian historian Professor Muyiwa Falaiye explained to me, in most African cultures, individuals do not lay claim to knowledge. It is communal, which is why it is so difficult to work out the provenance of information relayed by the storytellers. Sumaoro Kante, who was said to have been born a magician or sorcerer, inspired such terror that 'men did not dare to meet in conversation for fear the wind might carry their words to the king'.[2]

Eventually the Malinke people revolted against his exactions and appealed to King Dankaran Tuman to help. Mindful of his alliance with Sumaoro Kante, he refused. It fell to his brother Sundiata Keita (sometimes spelled Sunjata) to respond and organise Malinke resistance against the Soso.

The Mali Empire, 1235–c. 1430

Sundiata Keita, r. c. 1235–55

According to the oral tradition of the Mandinka Epic, which dates back to the thirteenth century and has been narrated by generations of griots, Sundiata Keita, so named because he hailed from the Keita clan of the Malinke, had a difficult childhood. He overcame physical disabilities as a youngster and through sheer will had forced himself to walk. But he was persecuted by his older brother, King Dankaran Tuman, who sent him into exile.

Sundiata Keita fled to Ghana, much diminished from its heyday, but still led by a king who recognised and appreciated his qualities. Sundiata Keita brought together the Malinke chiefs and in 1235 led a Malinke army against the Soso, defeating Sumaoro Kante at the landmark Battle of Kirina, near modern-day Bamako. Legend has it that Sumaoro Kante disappeared into the nearby hills never to be seen again.

Sundiata Keita seized the advantage afforded by his victory at Kirina, taking control of the Soninke peoples and much of the former empire of Ghana. Sundiata Keita did not have to resort to much combat. He persuaded other Malinke mansas (village heads) to give up their title and he became the one and only mansa – the religious and secular leader of the Malinke.

Sundiata Keita began building a new and even bigger empire than that of Ghana: the Mali Empire, which encompassed a big chunk of West Africa. It comprised the territory of modern-day Mali, Chad, Burkina Faso, Guinea, Gambia, Senegal, Côte d'Ivoire and parts of Mauritania and northern Nigeria. Sundiata Keita brought together disparate peoples under his rule: his own Malinke community, Muslim Berbers and Tuareg nomads, natives of the Sahel in Timbuktu, Koumbi Saleh and Takrur, and the peoples of the savannah such as the Wolof and the Serer. He ruled through a federation of chiefdoms as Sundiata I and established his main capital at Niani on the edge of a forest near the goldfields of Bure in modern-day Guinea. It was a resource-rich region, a source of kola nuts, palm oil, ivory and gold. There he built himself a compound that included an opulent palace with a dome. He was a just ruler and laid down social and political norms in a proclamation of rights, the 'Mande Charter' of 1236. This was an oral charter that guaranteed 'liberty, dignity and equality' to all citizens of Mali and formed the basis of how Sundiata would govern his subjects. I was discussing the Mande Charter with one of Mali's and indeed Africa's most eminent academics, Professor Doulaye Konaté, sitting under the shade of a tree in the grounds of the National Museum of Mali in Bamako. He agreed that it was a visionary charter that has parallels with the much later motto of the 1789 French Revolution: *Liberté, Égalité, Fraternité* (liberty, equality and brotherhood). Professor Konaté added that when academics make an assessment of a society, advanced and enlightened thinking such as that expressed in the 1236 Mande Charter must count as much as the building of great monuments. Indeed, UNESCO designates Sundiata Keita's Mande Charter as part of humanity's 'intangible cultural heritage'.

Sundiata himself was not a Muslim; he and his community followed traditional religions. Yet there were many Muslims in his kingdom and he restored relations with the Muslim traders who had been viewed as adversaries by Sumaoro Kante. He proclaimed five marabout or holy men clans as guardians of the faith of Islam and made their succession hereditary. This opened the way for the southward expansion of Islam and greatly facilitated its spread, so that subsequent rulers of Mali were predominantly Muslim. Court officials and traders who were more exposed to Muslim merchants accepted Islam more readily than those who worked on the land, but even those who did not convert co-existed peacefully with their Muslim neighbours.

Sundiata liked to flaunt his wealth and enjoyed the trappings of power. He demanded loyalty from his subjects and his reign, roughly 20 years long, was marked by prosperity and stability. Sundiata I died prematurely; he either drowned or was accidentally killed by an arrow during a ceremony. Sundiata's successor was his son Mansa Oulin, who consolidated and expanded the empire to include the middle Niger bend. Sundiata Keita had captured the city of Timbuktu from the Tuareg, the group of nomads from the southern Sahara, but it was under Mansa Oulin that the city became an important centre for traders and scholars.

Those literate in Arabic worked as court scribes just as they had done in the Ghana Empire. The mansa taxed all goods going through his territory. Agriculture was not neglected: there were abundant harvests of sorghum, millet and rice. The mansa and his army had their own state farms, some of which used forced labour, while others were run by peasant farmers. Villages were well supplied, but the mansa had first pick of the crops. To refuse him this privilege was tantamount to rebellion.

The mansa kept a large standing army, with a small elite corps of horsemen and a large body of spear-wielding foot soldiers. It was in essence a defensive army, to protect trading routes and to ensure that tributes from local traditional rulers were paid. Gold miners also had to hand over a large proportion of the precious metal they extracted to the king.

Mansa Musa I, *c.* 1280–1332

Mansa Musa I, who ruled approximately from 1307 to 1332, was the great-nephew of Sundiata Keita. He is the most famous of the Mali kings, and has come to represent the fantastic wealth enjoyed by the mansas of the empire. The incredible riches of Mansa Musa were signalled to the world by his pilgrimage or 'hajj' to Mecca in 1324–5. His entourage comprised his enormous household of 12,000 members, 60,000 porters, 500 personal servants clad in silk, decked in gold and bearing golden staffs, as well as many thousands of enslaved people. His caravan consisted of around 100 camels each bearing a heavy load of gold, estimated at between 10 to 20 tons in total. Mansa Musa set off from his capital Niani (on the modern-day Guinea–Mali border) to the main oasis town of Oualata (Mauritania) and then on to Tuat (Algeria) and Ghadames (Libya) before arriving in Cairo, which was a stopping point for pilgrims heading to Mecca. Legend holds that his caravan was so large that when he arrived at its head in Timbuktu its tail was still in Niani, 1,400 kilometres away!

Mansa Musa's journey to Mecca was a major event that created a sensation in Africa and beyond, and was recorded by several chroniclers. The Arab writer Ahmad al-Maqrizi, who was born in the mid-fourteenth century, described Mansa Musa's arrival in Cairo on horseback: 'He was a young man with brown skin, a pleasant face and a good figure . . . his gifts amazed the eye with their beauty and splendour.'

Mansa Musa was received by the Mamluk sultan of Egypt Al-Nasir bin Qal'un, who accorded him all hospitality and put at his disposal generous accommodation in residential quarters in the gardens of a Cairo suburb. The governor of Cairo was assigned to remain in constant attendance. During his sojourn in Cairo, Mansa Musa was summoned before the sultan. Mamluk protocol required a visitor to the sultan to kneel and kiss the floor before him. Views differ as to whether Mansa Musa succumbed to such an obeisance, which would have been a humiliating experience for the ruler of a powerful and rich empire superior in size to that of the Mamluks. The Arab historian Ibn Fadlallah al-Umari wrote about the visit years later between 1342 and 1349 and used as his source the official who presided over the meeting. He quoted the official thus:

> I tried to persuade him [Mansa Musa] to come to the 'qala' [castle] to meet the Sultan but he refused saying 'I have come to perform the pilgrimage with no other purpose, and I do not want to mix my pilgrimage with anything else.' He kept up his objection on that count. Although I am sure he was apprehensive of having to kiss the floor in front of the Sultan or having to kiss the Sultan's hand. I finally contrived to persuade him to come. When we arrived in front of the Sultan, we asked him to kiss the floor but he again refused saying 'how can this be?' A wise man in his company then muttered something in his ear which we did not understand and then he [Mansa Musa] said on kneeling down, 'I prostrate myself to God who created me and gave me life.' Then he rose and went up to the Sultan who stood up to greet him, sat beside him and they conversed for a long time.

Mansa Musa had found an elegant solution to his predicament, kneeling before the sultan but doing so in the name of God. He bore generous gifts for the sultan, who was an important ally for Mali in helping to counter the power of the North African Berber dynasties. The sultan also sent Mansa Musa 'gifts of clothing for himself, his courtiers and all those who were with him and saddled and bridled horses for himself and his chief officers'.

The sultan ordered that full assistance be given to Mansa Musa to ensure his journey to Mecca progressed without impediment. As al-Umari recorded:

> When the time of the pilgrimage arrived, the Sultan of Egypt sent him a large quantity of drachmas (ancient Greek silver coins), luggage camels, and choice riding camels with saddles and harness. The Sultan caused abundant quantities of foodstuffs to be bought for his suite and his followers, established posting stations for the feeding of the animals and gave to the emirs of the pilgrimage a written order to look after and respect the [Emperor of Mali].

Little is known of Mansa Musa's time in Mecca, except that his men clashed with the Ottomans – swords drawn – inside the Great Mosque. Mansa Musa, observing the fracas from the window of a nearby building, ordered his men to stop fighting, which they did. He also visited the Prophet's tomb in the holy city of Medina and may have spent the fasting month of Ramadan in Mecca. According to tradition, Mansa Musa bought land and houses in both Mecca and Cairo to accommodate pilgrims from West Africa at their final destination as well as en route.

Mansa Musa is believed to have remained in Cairo for a longer period when he made his way back to Mali. During these two stopovers in the city, he was responsible for what must surely qualify as one of the greatest spending sprees in history. He spent lavishly in Egypt and gave away so much gold that he flooded the market, causing its value to plummet globally by up to 25 per cent. It took more than a decade for gold to recover to its previous value.

The merchants of Cairo were delighted with the profits, though it seems the feeling was not mutual. The Arab chronicler al-Umari wrote:

> I was told by a few of the Cairo merchants of the profits they were able to make. They told me that the [Malians] would pay five dinars for a shirt or a piece of cloth which only cost one dinar. They were good hearted and honest and took all that was said to them as the truth. They then lost faith in the people of Egypt after discovering their deceitful disposition . . . Now if they see the most learned of men and they were told he was Egyptian, they would abuse and mistrust him for what they have seen.

Mansa Musa and his entourage must have regretted their excessive expenditure. They ran out of funds and had to borrow money from the Cairo merchants at exorbitant interest for their return to Mali. One debtor pursued Mansa Musa back to Timbuktu for repayment of his loan.

But there was one compensatory development for Mansa Musa during his absence from his kingdom while on his pilgrimage. One of his generals conquered Gao, the capital of the Songhay kingdom to the east, and incorporated it into the Mali Empire. This was a strategic gain for Mali. Mansa Musa wanted to make a majestic impression on the people of the town his troops had conquered, so he commissioned a noted Andalusian architect from Egypt, whom he had taken back to Mali with him, to build and design the Grand Mosque of Gao.

Mansa Musa was also an intellectual and a patron of the arts and music. So it is fitting that the invention of the kora, a string instrument that produces a rich, evocative sound and is still wildly popular all over the world today, is attributed to his era. Toumani Diabaté, an internationally renowned Malian kora player and griot whom I met while in Bamako, the

Malian capital, told me that, as a member of a family of longstanding griots, he uses the music he performs on the kora as a way of keeping his history alive.

Mansa Musa sent scholars to the important university at Fes so that on their return home they would be equipped to set up their own centres of learning, especially at Timbuktu. He ordered the same Andalusian architect responsible for the mosque at Gao to construct the Djinguereber, or Grand Mosque of Timbuktu. A short distance away stands the Sidi Yahya Mosque, which takes its name from one of the city's saints. This was built in 1400, a few decades before the Sankore Mosque. These three mosques of Timbuktu served as Islamic universities, catering for thousands of students from all over Africa, who took part in scholarly exchanges with universities across the Sahara. Mansa Musa also established many Koranic schools.

I was very excited about my trip to Timbuktu. I was familiar with the English phrase 'going to Timbuktu' as a metaphor for going somewhere far away, and indeed my journey to

A photograph of the Djinguereber Mosque in Timbuktu, taken by Edmond Fortier in the early 1900s

Timbuktu was not an easy one because of security concerns after the city was overrun by militants in 2012. Although control was restored by the Malian authorities, the threat remained at the time of my visit and the airport was closed to commercial flights. Undeterred, I hitched a ride with the Malian Air Force. I was also assigned an armed guard of a dozen soldiers as well as my own personal female bodyguard, equipped with a revolver. On our arrival in Timbuktu, the drive to the old town was rather disappointing: an unprepossessing collection of buildings, some with bullet holes in their walls from clashes between the army and militants. I could not reconcile this with the legendary city of my imagination. However, once we reached the old part of the town my faith was restored. The atmosphere was thick with history. The mudbrick mosques built by the Malian kings are reinforced with large wooden logs that poke out of the buildings' facades, up and down their structures, giving them the look distinctive to this part of West Africa. The buildings have the same hue as the sand on which they stand.

Although Oualata was the commercial centre of the Mali Empire, Timbuktu benefited from being accessible by river from West Africa as well as across the Sahara to North Africa, and its library meant it became a multicultural centre for scholars from Africa and the Islamic world, making it the most famous of the empire's towns. Timbuktu acquired its name in the eleventh century when Tuareg nomads settled in the area. One account holds that while the men tended their herds, an old woman was put in charge of the settlement – and her name was Timbuktu, which in the local language means 'mother with a large navel'. Another story relates how the herders went to the river to obtain water and found it infested with mosquitoes and so they dug a well nearby, where they appointed a local woman called Buk to keep an eye on it. The herders would say they were 'going to the well of Buktu', which sounded like 'Timbuktu'.

Whatever its etymology, Timbuktu was a great repository of knowledge. Its libraries, particularly at the Grand Mosque, housed a body of African literature written in Arabic: books on a range of topics, such as law, astronomy, mathematics, culture and science. Writers included prominent African scholars such as Ahmad Baba (1556–1627), who was born in Timbuktu. In one manuscript he argued against the practice of enslaving people: 'Are we not all descendants of Adam? . . . For just the fact of becoming the owner of another person bruises the heart, because servitude is inseparable from the idea of violence and domination, especially when it relates to a slave taken away from his country.'

Mansa Musa's empire consisted of about 400 towns or large population centres. Major urban settlements such as Timbuktu and Djenne, 500 kilometres south, had fine houses with upper floors reserved for male household members. The women and children occupied the ground-floor quarters where the kitchens were situated; separate living areas were and still are common in Muslim households. In towns such as Djenne, Arabic became the language of scholars and the court. Mansa Musa spoke and wrote Arabic well, yet he always used interpreters with his Arab interlocutors.

On his death in approximately 1332, Mansa Musa was succeeded by his son Maghan, but his reign was brief. Mansa Musa's brother Sulayman (r. 1336–58) became king and ruled for more than 20 years. At this time, the Arab traveller Ibn Battuta visited Mali and wrote his book *Al Rihla* – meaning 'The Journey'. He described how the last few years of Mansa Sulayman's reign were marked by intrigue. His first wife Kassi, outraged that her husband had divorced her for a new lover, encouraged her noble kinsmen and allies in court to revolt against the mansa. Her efforts failed and she was banished from the kingdom. Ibn Battuta also recorded how remarkably parsimonious Mansa Sulayman was in contrast to his generous brother, Mansa Musa.

Ibn Battuta wrote about Mali's political institutions, marriage customs, medicines and diet, describing how the people of Mali ate 'pounded millet, honey and milk' and depicting a hospitable people 'who have a greater hatred of injustice than any other people . . . There is complete security in their country. Neither traveller nor inhabitant in it has anything to fear from robbers or men of violence.' He observed that the Muslims of the Mali Empire practised Islam and had a 'zeal for learning the Koran by heart' but he was taken aback by the fact that 'their women show no bashfulness before men and do not veil themselves'.[3]

Mansa Sulayman's son, Fomba, was on the throne for just a year when he was ousted by a kinsman, Sundiata II. The adoption of Islam by the rulers of Mali meant they had gradually moved from a matriarchal to a patriarchal system of heredity and this transition led to successions that were rarely smooth. Sundiata II was a despot, who ruined the empire and exhausted the treasury. He was struck down by sleeping sickness and succeeded by his son Mansa Musa II (1374–87).[4]

The Mossi and the Tuaregs, c.1400–35

By the death of Mansa Musa II in the late fourteenth century, the power of the mansa had so diminished due to a series of feeble rulers, short reigns and dynastic rivalries, that parts of the Mali Empire such as the Songhay of the eastern Niger bend broke away. Raids by the Mossi in the south and Tuareg nomads in the north contributed to Mali's weakness. The Mossi states, which were based in modern-day Burkina Faso, had never come under Mali domination. The people of Mossi had well-armed horsemen who, thanks to their equestrian skills, carried out raids, pillaged and extorted peasants. They profited from their actions and gained an advantage over the declining Mali Empire. Timbuktu, the jewel in the crown of the empire, was raided by the Tuareg around 1402 and captured in 1433. In acknowledgement of its worth and prestige, the Tuareg did not destroy Timbuktu; they maintained its status as a viable commercial centre, levying taxes on traders. The loss of Timbuktu meant the Mali Empire had essentially been reduced to its Malinke heartland. It was an empire no more.

The Songhay Empire, 1435–1592

In its place rose the Songhay Empire. This had existed as a kingdom since the time of the Ghana Empire but had managed to remain outside its sphere of influence. Its name derived from the designation of its ruling caste. The Songhay Empire originated with the civilisation at Gao. These fishermen used canoes to catch fish and hunted hippos too – a perilous pursuit given hippos are famously aggressive. They soon realised that they could use these canoes for military purposes, so they set up trading villages along the Niger and dominated peasant communities there, establishing the Songhay kingdom. By the beginning of the eleventh century, the kings of Songhay moved their capital further north from Kukya to Gao. In 1010, the king Za Kusay converted to Islam and henceforth Songhay's kings were Muslim, and initially Islam was confined to the elite. Songhay society was extremely hierarchical and was divided into three segments. At the top was the ruling class, including the king and his relatives, along with religious and administrative leaders. In the middle were ordinary people who worked mainly in agriculture and in the military. At the bottom of the pile were the enslaved; they could be employed as porters of commercial goods, domestic servants or traded as enslaved people. Sometimes they could be freed to join the ranks of commoners. Gao had been captured during the reign of Mansa Musa I, but most of Songhay remained beyond Mali's tax-collection armies. Only after the mansas' grip on power grew tenuous could the Songhay kingdom develop independently of Mali.

The dynasties of Songhay began with the reign of Sonni Sulayman Dandi in 1435, but it was under his successor Sonni Ali Ber (Ber meaning 'the Great'), who ruled in 1464–92, that Songhay became an empire and totally eclipsed Mali. Sonni Ali Ber was physically strong and a great soldier, as the Tuareg discovered. He seized the prized town of Timbuktu from them in 1468. As a result, he made an enemy out of the Tuareg. They were a constant thorn in his side and mounted regular raids against him. Sonni Ali's formidable army succeeded in warding off all attacks; oral tradition related that Songhay under Sonni Ali was never beaten. As for Songhay's other opponents, the Mossi, they were pushed back deep into their territory.

Sonni Ali enjoyed the same source of funding as rulers of the Mali and Ghana empires: tributes from the provinces, income from royal farms and taxes on trade. Salt was still very important but cowrie shells from the Indian Ocean were also used as currency for internal trade.

Sonni Ali was a secularist and believed in the separation of politics from religion. This created problems, as the holy men of Timbuktu regarded him as a bad Muslim who did not pray regularly and practised sorcery. Sonni Ali is portrayed by Arab historians as ruthless and he did not feature much in their writings, perhaps on account of his lapsed Muslim ways. The Malian academic, Professor Doulaye Konaté, believes that this is why

posterity has not given Sonni Ali the reputation he deserves as
a strong and effective ruler. Nevertheless, in Songhay oral tradition to this day, he is regarded as a great hero and extolled as the
founder of an empire which had a professional army and a civil
service that efficiently ran government departments and minis-
tries; he is remembered as the builder of advanced infrastructure
such as canals and irrigation systems. This is a clear example of
how oral tradition in Africa gives rise to interpretations that can
run counter to the biases of written accounts.

Muhammad Ture, the Askiya dynasty and Timbuktu, 1492–*c*.1740

After Sonni Ali Ber's death in 1492, his successor, Sonni
Baro, was ousted by one of his generals, Muhammad Ture,
a devout Muslim of Soninke origin. He founded the Askiya
dynasty and the Songhay Empire reached the pinnacle of
its power under his rule in 1492–1528. Muhammad Ture
promoted Islam among the people, strengthened the administration of the empire and consolidated territory; the valuable
salt mines of Taghaza became part of Songhay, vastly increasing its wealth and standing. He centralised power and replaced
traditional rulers with loyal appointees who were either members of the royal family or trusted servants. They all had one
thing in common: they relied on the patronage of the king.
Each governor had his own local force, but the king had a
massive standing army of 100,000.

Muhammad Ture restored Timbuktu as a glorious city and
centre of learning, making him the most significant patron
of Islam in West Africa.

Hassan ibn Muhammad al-Fasi, a young Moroccan educated at Fes, visited Songhay in 1510 and 1513. He wrote
under the name 'Leo Africanus' after he was captured by

Christians and forced to convert to Christianity. His description of Timbuktu, during the reign of Muhammad Ture, was detailed and evocative:

> The women of the city maintain the custom of veiling their faces, except for the slaves who sell all the foodstuffs. The inhabitants are very rich, especially the strangers who have settled in the country; so much so that the current king has given two of his daughters in marriage to two brothers, both businessmen, on account of their wealth. There are many wells containing sweet water in Timbuktu and in addition when the Niger River is in flood, canals deliver the water to the city. Grain and animals are abundant so that the consumption of milk and butter is considerable . . . the king has a rich treasure of coins and gold ingots. The royal court is magnificent and very well organised. When the king goes from one city to another with the people of his court, he rides a camel, and the horses are led by hand by servants . . . When someone wishes to speak to the king, he must kneel before him and bow down, but this is only required of those who have never spoken to the king . . . There are in Timbuktu numerous judges, teachers, priests all properly appointed by the king. He greatly honours learning . . . The people of Timbuktu are of a peaceful nature. They have a custom of almost continuously walking about the city in the evening . . . playing musical instruments and dancing.[5]

Needing religious legitimacy to justify his seizure of power, Muhammad Ture went on a pilgrimage to Mecca in 1496 with a military escort of 1,500 (500 of them on horseback) to seek validation as a Muslim leader. When he arrived in Mecca the sharif, the traditional custodian of the holy cities of Mecca and Medina, called him to the mosque in Mecca and 'put a cap and green turban on his head. He gave him a sword and made all those present witness that he [Askiya Muhammad] was a khalifa [holy ruler] in the [land of Songhay] and that he who disobeyed him disobeyed God and his Messenger'.[6] On his way back from Mecca he hired Islamic scholars from North Africa to teach in Timbuktu. Despite his faith he did not force non-Muslims in his empire to convert to Islam, but the religion spread rapidly in any case as trans-Saharan trade was reinvigorated. As Muhammad Ture grew old he fell victim to a betrayal from within his inner sanctum: he was deposed by his eldest son Musa in 1528. Muhammad Ture's large mudbrick tomb, which houses a small mosque, is one of the few monuments remaining from Gao's historic past that visitors like me can see.

There followed a series of dynastic squabbles which led to a gradual decline in Songhay, culminating in a civil war in the 1580s. Drought and disease affected agricultural production and Songhay's control of trade weakened. At the same time, the growth of the Hausa states in what is today northern Nigeria and the Tuareg sultanate of Air drew trade away from Songhay.

The supply of gold was reduced as chiefdoms diverted some of it to European traders on the coast. In 1591, the Saadian Moroccan sultan Ahmad al-Mansour, seeing its weakness, invaded Songhay with 4,000 soldiers and 10,000 camels. The element of surprise gave the Moroccans the advantage when they engaged in battle with Songhay at Tondi near Gao.

The Songhay army, equipped with obsolete weaponry, was outgunned by superior Moroccan firearms and despite severe losses the Moroccans captured the strategic towns of Timbuktu and Djenne. They did not, however, take the whole region, so the Songhay regrouped in their heartland of Dendi under their king Askiya Nuhu and mounted a guerrilla war.

These guerrilla attacks, in combination with intermittent raids by Fulani and Tuareg nomads, exhausted the Moroccans. The sultan Ahmed al-Mansour could barely send enough firearms for his men to fend off the assaults and when he died in 1603 some Moroccans simply gave up and headed home. Others remained and became known as 'Arma'. They mixed with the local community and settled down as the military governors of Songhay. By 1660 they had dropped reference to the Moroccan sultan in Friday prayers in Timbuktu and replaced it with the Arma governor's name. Arma rule collapsed in 1737 when the Tuareg seized Timbuktu.

The territories of the former empire of Songhay were split up into a number of independent kingdoms. One, the Bamana of Segu, was described by a late eighteenth-century Scottish traveller, Mungo Park, as a 'cultivated state ... a prospect of civilisation and magnificence'. In the early 1700s European maritime nations began to assert their presence and supplanted African control of trade routes. The splendid city of Timbuktu fell into oblivion and became a metaphor in English for being a place at the end of the earth.

It is baffling that such a fascinating part of Africa's story is so little known. This was a significant chapter in the continent's history, in which there was a wide range of political formations, from clans to kingdoms to empires. African rulers managed to integrate diverse peoples over large areas. From the twelfth to sixteenth centuries these three West African kingdoms played a role in the global economy. And this at a time when Europe was in the throes of a series of famines and plagues known as the 'Black Death' in England, that were dealing a harsh blow to European populations and wealth.

Mansa Musa quite literally put himself and his empire on

the global stage. He featured on a Catalan cartographer's map of the world in 1375, depicted on a throne, wearing a gold crown, golden staff in one hand and a golden orb in the other.

It was an image that captured the imagination of Europeans at the dawn of the 'Age of Discovery' when explorers such as Christopher Columbus set off on their maritime expeditions across the world. The map is reproduced extensively today as a wall hanging – and I have a copy of it in my own home in homage to Mansa Musa. But there is a sting in the tail of this iconic image of Mansa Musa; maps like this one may well have encouraged later Europeans to invade Africa in pursuit of the riches they depicted.

A portrait of Mansa Musa on a map of the world, made in 1375

Having enjoyed travelling to so many parts of the Ghana, Mali and Songhay empires, in a part of the continent that is now referred to as the Sahel, I find it especially depressing that the region has fallen prey to a vicious brand of jihadism, which has brought instability and bloodshed. I am lucky to have been able to go to Timbuktu and Gao, where unfortunately military activities now prevent visits. According to the 2023 Global Terrorism Index, deaths in the Sahel constituted 43 per cent of the global total in 2022 – more than South Asia, the Middle East and North Africa combined.

There are around seven insurgent groups – including pro-independence Tuareg rebels and ISIS – in the volatile Sahel region, a semi-arid belt south of the Sahara incorporating parts of Nigeria, Niger, Senegal, Cameroon, Chad, Mali, Burkina Faso, the Gambia, Guinea and Mauritania. There are regular reports of clashes between government forces and extremists, especially following the departure of French counterinsurgency troops between 2022 and 2023. The terror group Boko Haram, based in northern Nigeria, made international headlines when in April 2014 militants stole into a boarding school in Chibok and kidnapped nearly 300 teenage girls from the Christian community. Dozens remain unaccounted for.

For insights into jihadist terror groups such as Boko Haram and the Islamic State in the Greater Sahara, I went to Kano in northern Nigeria to speak to a prominent traditional ruler, the then Emir of Kano, Muhammad Sanusi II, who is an economist as well as an Islamic scholar. He traded the boardroom of the Central Bank of Nigeria, where he was governor, for the luxurious palace of an emir.

Kano is the oldest of the historic Muslim Hausa city states which developed between the eleventh and thirteenth centuries in modern-day Nigeria and Niger. It was established at the foot of the Dala Hills and its wealth was based on agriculture, trade and manufacturing, including the export of leather goods to North Africa. Today it is a buzzing city, and as I walked alongside the ancient mudbrick city wall dating back to the late eleventh century, its impressive size was a purposeful reminder of the city's medieval prosperity, when it was one of the most important trade hubs in West Africa and indeed the whole continent. Kano was, and still is, a centre for the dyeing and weaving of cloth, particularly in the distinctive indigo blue produced at the Kofar Mata dye pits since 1498: they are said to be the oldest in Africa. In addition, Kano is also one of the most fertile areas in Nigeria. And so, the conundrum is not the illustrious past of Kano and other parts of the Sahel, but their relatively impoverished present.

The Sahel is no stranger to religious upheavals. In the early nineteenth century, an Islamic revolution coursed across West Africa. Amongst its leaders was Sheikh Uthman dan Fodio (1754–1817). He was a religious scholar and military leader who spurned the trappings of power. Islamic revolutionaries like him were supported by the local populations who were marginalised and resented the oppressive taxation and greed of their rulers. Could history be repeating itself?

In the cool of the evening, I arrived at the emir's palace, a complex of well-maintained buildings in the old part of the city. I walked along manicured and fragrant gardens to the emir's private quarters, and ascended an impressive staircase lit by chandeliers heavy with crystal. His Sanusi dynasty took control of Kano in 1819 and he was the fourteenth in its line. Dressed in extravagant robes and wearing a white turban with a veil that partially covered his face we discussed jihadism in the Sahel and why Boko Haram means 'Western education is forbidden' – taken from the English word 'book' and the Arabic word 'haram', meaning forbidden.

He told me that we must consider how much of the extremism in West Africa is actually religious-based, and how much of it is a reflection of extreme poverty, inequality, corruption and years of bad governance. 'It is difficult to find any serious jihadi tract that recommends killing innocent people, suicide bombings or kidnapping schoolgirls. These are just criminal activities. I hold strongly to the view that many of the conflicts in the world – religious, ethnic and racial – tend to be caused or at least inflamed by grievances rooted in economics. Poverty, unemployment, marginalisation and a general sense of being outsiders combine to bring together individuals who challenge the status quo, often violently'.

The north of Nigeria is the poorest part in the country and the emir believes this makes it easier for people to be co-opted into extremist views. He states: 'Any serious attempt at understanding Islamic radicalisation in northern Nigeria [and the Sahel] cannot avoid discussion of material conditions – poverty, lack of opportunity, hopelessness and economic inequality in general.'

The emir also explained how adherents of extremist groups readily accept a narrative that pits Islam as being in confrontation with the West and Western values. Sometimes their violence is directed at real oppressors, while often it is directed at those who 'are not like us', those defined as the 'other'. Of course, not every poor Muslim is an extremist and there are many militants who hail from affluent backgrounds in Africa and beyond. It is right that jihadist groups in the Sahel and elsewhere are defeated. But a long-term solution must look beyond forceful methods to issues of governance, economic inequality, social exclusion, marginalisation and perceived injustices. As the emir put it to me: 'Certain social and economic conditions are fertile ground for breeding violent movements – be they religious extremists, ethnic militias or just criminal gangs. Religion simply becomes a rallying point and an ideology, but the real discontent lies in politics'. How the fortunes of the Sahel have changed from the glorious days of Mansa Musa.

9

Tippu Tib and the
First Enslavers

As we have seen, the Arabs and Islam wielded huge influences on Africa, but there was also a horrific side to this. Aided by some African Muslim traders, they initiated the first international trade in enslaved Africans.

I was born into an Arabic-speaking family in northern Sudan. A simple DNA test that one of my siblings took showed that nearly 50 per cent of my family's DNA is Arab, from both the Arabian Peninsula and North Africa, and the other half is East African. The Muslim Swahili communities, who come into focus in this chapter, were from further south than I, and although they mixed to a far lesser extent with Arabs than the northern Sudanese, and spoke Swahili rather than Arabic, many also strongly identified with Arab Muslim culture. Some Swahili families trace their lineage back to the Arabian Peninsula, such as the late Zanzibari historian Professor Ali Mazrui.

As the Tanzanian archaeologist and historian Professor Felix Chami put it to me with some force, the fusion of

African and Arab culture and the adoption of Islam created 'a major problem in the history of coastal East Africa'. He argued, and many African academics would agree, that Swahili empathy with Arabs made it easier for some Swahili to acquire non-Swahili African captives for human trafficking.

The participation of some Africans in the trade of enslaved people is a topic most people across Africa find difficult to comprehend. It engenders feelings of shame and guilt among the descendants of enslavers and there are concerns that a franker conversation could foster divisions among communities and perhaps even hinder efforts at nation building.

There has also been little, if any, meaningful discussion in Arab countries on the subject. Arab society and civilisation benefited tremendously over the centuries from the blood, sweat and tears of African labour and there has not been a public debate about slavery reparations to mirror the one in Europe and North America. One leading African academic told me: 'The Arabs are in denial about their prolific and long-lasting slave trade.' However, perhaps the reticence is also due in part to the reluctance of descendants of enslaved ancestors to shine the spotlight on their origins.

The only museum in an Arab state that examines the Arab slave trade is Bin Jelmood House in Qatar, where incidentally slavery was only abolished officially in 1952, and where the continual reliance on migrant labour in a system open to abuse has attracted much international criticism. The museum, built on the site of a former slave merchant's house, opened in 2015 and raised suspicions that it was an attempt to polish Qatar's reputation ahead of hosting football's 2022 World Cup. Bin Jelmood House does at least tackle the subject of the enslavement of Africans by Arabs, albeit within a wider context of labour and human exploitation. Its mission statement lacks explicit mention of the Indian Ocean trade and reads: 'The House pays tribute and acknowledges the social, cultural and economic contribution of formerly enslaved people to the development of human civilisations.'

It is believed that a total of 14 million Africans were shipped out by the Arabs and their partners between the seventh and nineteenth centuries to Arab lands, as well as to the Persian Gulf and India. As alluded to in previous chapters, the kingdoms of West Africa and the North African dynasties also profited from this trade. This terrifyingly huge estimate

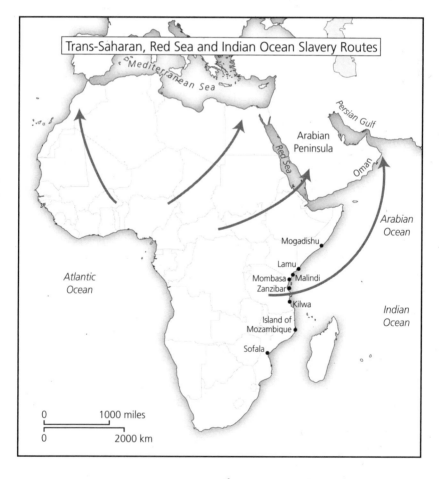

includes all routes: across the Sahara to North Africa, and across the Red Sea and the Mediterranean, as well as the Indian Ocean. The vast majority – nearly 10 million enslaved people – were transported via the Indian Ocean. Although the Arabs also sourced enslaved people from India and Southeast Asia, Africans made up the largest number of the enslaved. Human trafficking across the Indian Ocean is a hugely tragic and over-looked aspect of the chapter of slavery in Africa, with far more attention being given to the transatlantic trade. To give it the focus it is due, we will explore the life of Zanzibari business-man Tippu Tib, who operated in the nineteenth century and was one of the most prolific of the Swahili Muslim traders. He came from the Swahili coast, a rich and exciting meeting point of cultures, with whose history I shall begin.

Swahili Civilisation

Africa attracted outsiders because of its rich natural resources and trade opportunities, and Africans on the east coast had trading networks with the Arabs, Persia, India and China perhaps as far back as the fourth and fifth centuries CE.

The Arabs, mostly from the Arabian Peninsula, were the most dominant external influence on Africa's Indian Ocean coast, which stretches for more than 3,000 kilometres, and the spread of Islam in the seventh and eighth centuries fur-ther boosted connections and interactions. A few of the Arabs who arrived on Africa's east coast from the 700s settled and intermarried with the local Bantu population. Over the centuries, Bantu-speaking people had migrated to the region from the Niger Delta in West Africa through the Congo Basin. Arab writers referred to the main portion of the East African coast as the 'Land of Zenj' (meaning 'Land of the

Blacks') and they traded at eight major ports: Zanzibar, Kilwa, Mogadishu, Mombasa, Lamu, Malindi, Sofala and the Ilha de Moçambique, known in English as the Island of Mozambique. Some local sources suggest that Mozambique is derived from the name of a tenth-century Arab trader called Musa Bek. The Arabs bought goods such as gold and ivory from the interior, but also took part in the trade in humans and found commercial allies among Swahili communities.

By the ninth century, most of the East African coastal towns were predominantly inhabited by the Swahili, and their culture included African, Arab and to a lesser extent Indian elements. With the subsequent arrival of European Christians, there developed what the Tanzanian historian Ali Mazrui described as the 'triple heritage' of Swahili civilisation: African, Arab and European. The Swahili language, with its origins in Bantu, borrowed its script from Arabic as well as words such as *tafadhali* (meaning 'please') and *haqiqa* (meaning 'truth'). It also incorporated some words from the Portuguese, such as *meza* for table and *gereza* for prison (the Portuguese were the first Europeans to arrive in the region). Despite these external influences, Swahili culture and language remain African at heart, and embody a magnificent African heritage.

I wanted to see a range of Swahili settlements for myself, so I chose to go to four of its ancient ports: Zanzibar, Mombasa, Lamu and the Island of Mozambique – Mogadishu was sadly off limits to me during my period of research due to security concerns about the activities of militant groups.

First to Lamu, a beautiful island popular with tourists. Lamu is located in southeastern Kenya about 20 kilometres from the border with Somalia. This charming place has its roots in the thirteenth century, making it Kenya's oldest continually inhabited town. I passed markets bursting with goods, boys pushing wheelbarrows laden with merchandise and walked along alleys so narrow in places that I could stretch out my arms and touch the walls on either side. Roads in Lamu are typically narrow to provide refuge from the rays of the hot sun. In the old town, I met architect Mohammed Mwenje, curator of Lamu Museums, Sites and Monuments and the World Heritage site, who took me on a tour and told me that the historic part is about 16 hectares, and that Lamu started as two independent settlements in the thirteenth century: one in the north and one in the south, which at some point, a century later, combined into one town. Most of the old buildings date to the seventeenth century, some rather dilapidated, but still displaying picturesque arched window frames and beautiful ornate carved wooden doors.

I wanted to meet a local Swahili family to test how far people identified with Arab culture and religion. During my visit, it was the season of Ramadan. One long-term resident of the old town, Muhammad Abdulkader, invited me to break the fast with his wife and two teenage sons. Muhammad chatted to me in Arabic, evidently drawing pride from the fact that he was speaking in the language of the Koran. He said it was not unusual for Swahili men to be reasonably proficient in conversational Arabic. The family were dressed in long kaftans, plus a headscarf for his wife, and I came away feeling that if they were anything to go by, then the impact of the Arabs and Islam was very apparent in Lamu, whose population is almost entirely Muslim.

Mombasa, Kenya's second city, is the largest of the continent's Swahili settlements and its port one of East Africa's biggest. The first capital of British East Africa, Mombasa is a cosmopolitan place. Many of Kenya's 100,000-strong Indian population live in the city, their forefathers having arrived in the nineteenth century from British India as indentured labourers. A large number of them worked on the

Kenya–Uganda railway. Now they form a large part of the mercantile class, and are a close-knit community, retaining their customs and maintaining a high rate of endogamous marriages. Mombasa boasts several historic buildings. The 1570 Mandhry Mosque is a good example of Swahili architecture – a combination of African and Arab styles that features an unusual, rounded minaret.

But for all their picturesque and vibrant qualities today, coastal cities and towns such as Mombasa and Lamu have regrettable pasts: they were holding ports for enslaved people as well as transportation points across the Indian Ocean to Arabia, India, Persia, Yemen and what later became Türkiye.

I had arranged to meet a Mombasa cultural expert over a cup of Kenyan tea and snacks at one of the city's many smart hotels. Amira Said Msellem is a guest lecturer at universities across Kenya. She related how, according to local tradition, the Swahili acquired their name. Apparently, when the Arabs first arrived on the Indian Ocean coast of East Africa, they asked the locals what their community was called, to which they replied that they were the people of an area known as 'Ziwa Hili'. The Arabs took this to mean that they were the 'Ziwahili' people, which became Swahili, though the Arabic word for coastal is 'sawahili'. Amira, like most Swahilis, professed her gratitude to the Arabs for introducing them to Islam. However, when I tried to bring up the topic of how members of her community in the past had participated in the capture and trafficking of their fellow Africans, she seemed reluctant to engage and was instead at pains to explain how the Swahili would accept Africans from inland areas into their community so long as they adopted Islam along with Swahili ways and customs. She implied that Africans who converted to Islam were protected from enslavement, but this was not always the case.

Other conversations about the Indian Ocean trade proved more fruitful. I ventured just outside Mombasa to meet a Kenyan Anglican vicar, Father William Katama, the priest at St Paul's Church in Rabai. An easy-going man with a relaxed countenance, he recounted how as a Christian non-Swahili Kenyan, he had learned about this period of history through stories handed down by his elders and through his own readings. According to him, Arabs along the Indian Ocean coastline enslaved people by capturing or abducting them with the help of local agents, who were most often chiefs from the Swahili coastal community. Arabs would aggrandise potential Swahili collaborators by giving them the means to style themselves as 'chief', so that they would have the 'authority' and resources to employ people to penetrate the interior and enslave people on their behalf. He described how sometimes the Swahili would trick people to come to the coast. There are many accounts of coastal raiders convincing community elders to find them porters to carry goods such as ivory, gold, copper and ebony for many kilometres from the interior of the continent to the East African coast. Sometimes the porters were ambushed en route and then shackled in chains. Many thousands of captives died on the long walk, and those who survived the journey were not released; instead, they were forcibly taken across the Indian Ocean.

Sadly, some Africans cooperated with Arab and Swahili traders, believing they were being employed for other purposes, only discovering the truth when it was too late. The Kasigau communities were exploited in this way. The North African Arab geographer al-Idrisi, who lived in the 1100s, wrote of how merchants would lure children to their ships with goods such as dates and then kidnap them.

Father William also explained how Arab traders encouraged ethnic rivalries by providing guns to various groups in the hope of securing war captives and enslaving them. These tactics were used, for example, in what is now Mozambique and the Lake Malawi region, where some Arab allies such as the Bemba gained military superiority over their rivals.

The unfortunate distinction of being the centre of this trade on Africa's Indian Ocean coast is borne by the island of Zanzibar, a part of modern-day Tanzania that attracts hordes of tourists, thanks to its beaches and the stunning Swahili architecture of its historic Stone Town. After coming ashore, I made my way through beautiful, immaculate gardens, a labyrinth of buildings and the market, with wafting scents of exotic fruits and spices competing for strength and allure. It was such a pleasant walk that I was rather taken aback when I arrived at the site of the former slave market in Zanzibar, where there was a square pit containing life-sized statues in dark stone: men and women with anguished faces and chains around their necks. A gesture towards the misery of millions.

A short distance from Zanzibar is Shimoni, a little fishing village, which means 'the place of the hole', where there are several bat-infested limestone caves that were used as holding pens for enslaved people. They may have originally been used as hiding places by those trying to avoid capture. Once enslaved, men and women were shackled and then fastened by metal hooks to the cave walls to stop them from escaping until dhows (traditional sailing vessels) arrived to take them to the main slave market at Zanzibar. Sometimes entire families were captured and enslaved. Today, you can still see iron shackles and rusty remnants of chains on the walls, and the large wooden crates used to transport the enslaved people. Captives could also be kept in holding houses. The sick and unhealthy would be separated from the others, and those who were unwanted were sometimes thrown overboard once they were taken onto ships.

With coffers swollen from the proceeds of slavery and traded goods, the port-cities of Africa's east coast, including Zanzibar, became prosperous, but their riches also meant they attracted the attention of Europeans. The Portuguese were the first Europeans to arrive in this part of Africa in the late fifteenth century. In 1498 the Portuguese explorer Vasco da Gama landed on the Island of Mozambique and thereafter the Portuguese established themselves there. On the island there is an imposing statue of Vasco da Gama and a replica of the boat that brought him ashore. Looking at them I was at a loss as to what there was to celebrate about his arrival, given the horrors of the transatlantic trade in enslaved Africans that it presaged.

The Portuguese at first wanted to control the gold supply, but when they discovered the wealth of Swahili trade they began demanding that these towns' dwellers become Portuguese subjects. In the face of vigorous opposition by Arab Muslim traders in the region, the Portuguese launched attacks on Swahili coastal towns from the early sixteenth century. Zanzibar put up fierce resistance but Lamu and Malindi capitulated and agreed to pay taxes and tributes to the Portuguese. On the Island of Mozambique and at Sofala, the Portuguese managed to maintain a good foothold from an early stage.

In 1528, the Portuguese gained a big advantage when they seized the port-city of Mombasa. Yet local African communities, Omani Arabs and Ottomans soon contested their control, so that by the late seventeenth century the Omani Arabs had become the dominant force on Africa's east coast, governing most of the region through Swahili proxy rulers. The rivalry between the Portuguese and the Omanis resulted in major military conflict. Mombasa was captured by the Omani Arabs in the first half of the 1700s and it became part of the sultanate of Oman.

The Omani Arabs were prolific traders of enslaved Africans, via the Indian Ocean. This trade differed from the chattel slavery of the Atlantic world in several aspects. First, enslaved Africans could be deployed in a multitude of ways: they could be employed as menial servants, as owning domestic staff was seen as a sign of prestige in Arab culture; they could make a significant contribution in the cultural sphere as poets, craftsmen, authors, musicians and as business assistants; they could serve as sailors or soldiers in the Omani army; or they could be employed as pearl divers in the Gulf (many divers suffered from ruptured eardrums as well as severe skin and respiratory problems). However, although such occupations were open to some enslaved people, the vast majority were put to work in enormous

Enslaved Africans with their Arab slavers

agricultural projects such as date-palm cultivation and salt marsh draining, the latter being a particularly gruelling and punishing activity.

The transatlantic trade only dealt in African victims, but the Arabs obtained enslaved people from many parts of the world, including Europe, although Africans made up the greatest number. Markets operating under strict state regulation opened in every important town throughout Arab lands. The price an enslaved person commanded was determined by their place of origin, gender, age, physical condition and abilities.

In the transatlantic trade, males outnumbered females two to one. They were in greater demand because their strength meant they were more productive as agricultural labourers, and they were mostly put to work on plantations in the Caribbean, and North and South America. By contrast, in the Indian Ocean and eastern trade, female captives were more valued and are believed to have outnumbered males. Enslaved African women could be forced to work as sex slaves or enter the system of concubinage for nobles, which meant it was not uncommon for Arab princes and caliphs to inherit African blood from their mothers. Notably, if an Arab man bore any offspring with an enslaved woman, that child would be born free, and in practice the mother would be released to look after her infant. Yet, in the Americas and the Caribbean a child sired by a white 'master' with an enslaved African woman would generally be born an enslaved person too.

It was prohibited for an African man to have sexual relations with an Arab woman. Additionally, a portion of enslaved men would be castrated by their Arab masters, and as eunuchs they were tasked with keeping watch over the concubines. Castration was a cruel and inhumane process: most young males did not survive the ordeal.

From the very beginning, many Africans forcefully resisted. In fact, a number achieved significant military victories against their oppressors. In one well-documented and very early case, members of forced labour gangs who toiled on farms in Mesopotamia, in present-day southern Iraq, rose against their Arab overseers in 869 CE. Their work and living conditions were so dreadful that the enslaved people who were draining salt in marshes revolted in what became known as the 'Zandj Revolt'. The rebellion lasted nearly 15 years and claimed thousands of lives before it was finally put down.

Centuries after the Zandj Revolt, a group of African women refused to accept enslavement, according to an account that has been handed down through oral tradition and was referred to several times during my discussions about slavery in Africa. It relates to the trans-Saharan trade to North Africa.

The Women of Nder, 1819

Nder, a small Walo kingdom in Senegal, was attacked by Arab slavers in November 1819. At this time Nder was a wealthy and peaceful place. Its inhabitants were farmers, who also traded with North Africans. As was their custom, one day in November, the men had left before dawn to go fishing, or to the fields to farm, leaving the women and children behind in the village.

An anguished voice shattered the tranquillity. One woman carrying water cried: 'I was by the lake and I saw through the bushes that the Arabs were coming.' The women screamed in horror, knowing what fate would befall them. They would be sold as enslaved women to the rich Arab families of North

Africa. They decided to resist, so they dispatched their children to the fields, then went into their huts and took everything they could find to defend themselves: spears, guns and knives. About 100 armed men had arrived at the village. The women had nothing to lose and resolved to fight. They managed to kill or wound many of the Arabs who retreated, but only to regroup.

When they returned, the Arabs first killed any man they came across, then set their sights on the women. One wise woman in the village, Mbaka Dia, who had been wounded in the previous skirmishes, leaned against a tree, and defiantly proclaimed:

> Women of Nder, you are the daughters of Walo. Stand up, dress, put on your scarf and be ready to die. Women of Nder do we have to submit before the enemy? Our men are faraway and cannot hear our cries, our children are in the field and hiding. God will save them but as for we women, what can we do? Where can we hide so that they do not find us? We will be captured like our mothers and grandmothers, taken while we are young . . . We will be taken to the other side of the river and sold as slaves. Is that good for us?

The women's cries stopped.

> Just answer me, instead of standing and crying. What will we say later to our grandchildren and their children? Do you want people to say that their grandmother left the village as a slave or that she was brave until death? Yes, my sisters, we need to die as free women and not live as slaves. Whoever agrees with me follow me into the great hut where the counsel of the wise people takes place. We will all go in there and set fire to it. So, it will be ash that meets the enemy. Let us live as the proud women of Walo.

The sun was high in the sky and a deep silence descended on the village. The women walked slowly to the great hut, which was built with hay and branches. For the last time they turned and looked at their village and its familiar sights: wells, huts, favourite trees. As they entered the hut some of the young women held their small babies tightly to their chest. One of the last to go in was a pregnant woman who was close to giving birth. Mbaka Dia closed the door of the hut, lit the torch, and calmly threw it against the wall. A jet of fire raged almost instantly. The women held onto one another and sang lullabies. The singing was replaced by violent coughing. The heavily pregnant woman decided she wanted to save her unborn child and ran towards the door and kicked it hard. Gasping for air she made a dash into the open, crying and collapsing onto the ground. The women who witnessed her escape did not attempt to move. They thought at least there would be one witness to their hour of history, who would relay their story to subsequent generations and record it for posterity.

The voices of those who were inside the blazing coffin grew weaker and weaker and eventually stopped. The roof collapsed on the women. Massive black clouds appeared in the sky, and everything went dark, as if nature were trying to hide the pain of the fathers, sons and husbands who would be destroyed by despair, hoarse with futile lamentation, and whose cries could not heal. From then onwards in the village of Nder, a festival called 'Talata Nder' is held on a Tuesday in November to remember all the women who perished that day. The villagers avoid any activity that could disturb the silence of the village. The men do not fish, hunt nor farm. The women do not cook and remain in their homes for many hours, praying and paying homage to the heroic sacrifice of the women of Nder.[1]

Sultan Seyyid Said, r. 1804–56

By the 1840s there were about 5,000 Arabs living in Zanzibar out of a total population of around 22,000. In 1840, the Omani sultan Seyyid Said moved his capital from Muscat in Oman to Zanzibar where his possessions were proving more valuable than in his homeland, and he expanded his reach across Africa's east coast. Arab traders had been importing cloves from Indonesia and found that Zanzibar and its sister island Pemba were well suited to their cultivation. Seyyid Said established clove plantations in Zanzibar, for which the island is still famous. Walking around Zanzibar's main market I was immediately overcome – though pleasantly – by the intense and distinctive smell of the cloves on sale. Wandering around the 'House of Wonders', the palace Sultan Seyyid Said built for himself, I instantly appreciated the opulence in which he and his family lived: magnificent staircases, wide corridors with ornate pillars, huge rooms with high ceilings. The Arabs of Zanzibar enjoyed a much higher standard of living than the locals. The old town had separate quarters for the two populations, with poor sanitary conditions for the Africans, who frequently endured outbreaks of diseases such as cholera.

Under Sultan Seyyid Said, the trade in enslaved Africans burgeoned to meet his need for a steady flow of male labour for his plantations. The Arab and Swahili traders who controlled the trade, transported captives in dhows to markets in Arabia and Persia. Sultan Seyyid Said made regular trips back to Oman and in 1856, at the age of about 70, he died at sea as he was making the return journey to Muscat from Zanzibar.

'Tippu Tib' – Hamad bin Muhammad al-Murjabi, c. 1837–1905

Tippu Tib, photographed in Zanzibar *c.* 1890

One of the best known and richest of the Swahili traders in ivory and enslaved African people was Tippu Tib, or Tippu Tip, and his activities were notorious. His real name was Hamad bin Muhammad al-Murjabi, and he was born in Zanzibar around 1837 to parents of Omani and African origin. His father, Muhammad bin Juma al-Murjabi, was an Arab who lived in Kazeh, now Tabora, about 700 kilometres inland from today's Dar es Salaam. His mother, whose first name is not known, was most likely the daughter of Habib al-Wardi, and was relatively fair in complexion, though she had African ancestry. Upon his birth she is said to have remarked: 'How could a son of mine be so dark?' Arabs in East Africa often took African wives so both of Tippu Tib's grandmothers were likely to have been African. Tippu Tib was given a rudimentary education in religious studies at the family farm near Stone Town. He used his mother tongue Swahili on an everyday basis, but was conversant and literate in Arabic. His father stayed in Tabora for long periods of time and used enslaved labour to grow crops, which he would sell to passing caravans.

At around 12 years old, Tippu Tib accompanied his brothers and uncles on trips to trade in a tropical resin used in varnish and ink. At first, he traded in a system based on barter, with items such as beads and bangles exchanged for ivory. Vast profits could be made from ivory, which had growing markets in Asia, western Europe and North America. Many objects, such as the white keys on a piano board, billiard balls, combs, cutlery handles and jewellery, were made of ivory. African elephants were larger than their Indian counterparts and provided ivory of a softer quality, which was more suitable for carving and making jewellery. Elephants had become extinct in China around 200 CE, so the Chinese were also keen to get their hands on ivory. The Arabs rarely killed the elephants themselves for their ivory and generally purchased it from locals.

By the time he was 18 years old, Tippu Tib had progressed to the ivory trade, introduced to it by his father who took him on his first early travels inland. He persuaded his father that he could be entrusted with overseeing the goods. After crossing Lake Tanganyika in dug-out canoes and arriving at the market at Urua Tippu Tib discovered that large tusks were fetching higher prices than smaller tusks. In his autobiography, written years later, he recalled: 'Everyone was buying the large tusks, so I decided to go for the small ones and collected a great number.'[2] He then headed to the market in Zanzibar: 'I was lucky it was the small tusks which were fetching a good price.' Tippu Tib was clearly a man who from an early age swam against the tide. He was a risk taker and he did not take kindly to being given advice. If his kinsmen tried to dissuade him from embarking on what might be a dangerous project, he would tell them 'Maybe I am mad and you are sensible, keep to your own affairs'.

At around 1860, Tippu Tib struck out on his own. His first 'major decision' was to borrow goods worth about US$120,000 today to trade along the coast. By this time Tippu Tib would have been married and by the mid-1850s is believed to have been a father, though it is not thought that any of his children had Arab mothers. He was moderately religious, fasting during Ramadan, and noted 'we were at prayers at dawn before the sun rose'. He was also interested in making the pilgrimage to Mecca. Tippu Tib was organised and vigilant, and ensured that the enslaved, porters and other members of his entourage were adequately provided for. In his autobiography he mentioned that his half-brother Muhammad bin Masoud, whom he had not seen for 12 years, had not done well by slave trading – unlike himself with his 'tremendous profits'.

About 1864, Tippu Tib borrowed an enormous number of goods from Indian merchants in Zanzibar – the equivalent of more than half a million US dollars today – and set off on the trading route connecting Kilwa with Dar es Salaam. During this expedition his porters, finding themselves on home territory, fled his service. A furious Tippu Tib rounded up about 200 hostages from among their relatives and bound them in chains until the porters returned. He ended up with around 800 porters back in his charge, whom he yoked together in iron chains or neck grips to prevent them from escaping again. It was at this time that he acquired his first nickname of 'Kinkugwa', meaning 'the leopard'. Towards the latter part of his life he was called 'Mkangwanzara', meaning 'he who fears nothing'.

From the East African coast, Tippu Tib ventured into the interior and established himself in what became the Democratic Republic of the Congo (DRC). It is not known how many Africans he captured, but he faced regular attacks from communities that he almost invariably overcame. By the late 1860s he was leading large expeditions of around 4,000 men and had amassed vast quantities of ivory. This gave him considerable power and authority over many villages across territories in East and Central Africa. Tippu Tib formed a semi-organised state and set up home in Lasongo, east of the River Congo towards Lake Tanganyika. He confirmed the rule of local chiefs or replaced them with loyal regents. He also established a monopoly on elephant hunting and developed infrastructure such as roads so he could move his goods more easily.

The ivory and slave trade proliferated in areas where there was weak political rule and where power was decentralised, and Tippu Tib's access to firearms allowed him to exploit such environments to the full, as one incident in 1867 illustrates. He had gone to visit the Bemba people in an area that is now part of Zambia, bringing with him 120 men armed with guns. He negotiated with an elderly local leader or 'nsama', whose name was Chipli Chipoka. Tippu Tib presented him with many goods and was given two or three tusks in return. When he requested more ivory, the nsama refused and started cursing Tippu Tib and his entourage, so Tippu Tib and his group retreated. The next day he was invited back by the chief to examine his stocks of ivory. Tippu Tib went into the heavily guarded stockroom with 20 men and 10 enslaved people. The nsama then summoned crowds of people to see the 'Arabs', but once the crowds turned up, there was a kerfuffle and panic ensued with the Arabs firing their weapons. Another account holds that Tippu Tib and his party were suddenly attacked by the villagers, and that he was hit by two arrows, one striking him in the leg. In the subsequent mayhem, Tippu Tib and his men started firing. He claimed he was struck by three arrows, as he wrote later when describing the incident:

> However, our guns were loaded with bullets and buckshot and the enemy were attacked like sardines. One round and they died like birds! When the guns went off, 200 were killed instantly and hundreds of others were trampled to death in a stampede as they fled. In one hour more than 1,000 died. Our casualties were only two slaves killed and two wounded . . . I am not leaving here until I have completely crushed the [Bemba] people of Samu and they bring peace.

The nsama was carried away by his followers, though the battle between Tippu Tib's men and the villagers continued. Within two days Tippu Tib's forces had prevailed and hundreds more villagers had died. Tippu Tib carried off his enormous stocks of ivory and copper. It took him another two months properly to subdue the nsama's forces. In the second half of 1867, the nsama made a pact and gave Tippu Tib 50 elephant tusks as a peace offering. It was after the nsama episode that Tippu Tib acquired the nickname for which he would be known throughout history, because of the sound his guns made – 'tip tip'.

During this conflict he came across an Englishman, as he noted in his autobiography: 'a big fellow, by the name of Livingstone, his first name David. He and the ten members of his party had almost been killed and a number of the locals came with him. Some of my men brought him to camp'. David Livingstone was the British missionary turned explorer who was trying to find the source of the River Nile. The idea that Europeans 'discovered' parts of Africa is a misconception. Africans such as Tippu Tib had long traversed large portions of the African interior and were familiar with its topography and terrain. In fact, Tippu Tib wrote that when he found Livingstone, he was in such dire straits that he had 'neither good options'. An opponent of the slave trade, Livingstone travelled under Tippu Tib's protection for a few months in 1867.

Tippu Tib's autobiography is short on facts and dates, and the second half is almost entirely devoted to his dealings with the Welsh explorer, Henry Morton Stanley, who was in the Congo on behalf of the Belgian king Leopold II. He travelled with Stanley in a major expedition in 1876 for two months along the Congo River, providing him with both protection and knowledge of the territory. Stanley, who like Livingstone, was searching for the source of the Nile, described Tippu Tib in his writings as:

a tall black bearded man of negroid complexion, in the prime of life, straight and quick in movements. A picture of energy and strength. He had a fine intelligent face with a nervous twitching of the eyes and gleaming white and perfectly formed teeth . . . He reclined vis à vis while a buzz of admiration of his style was perceptible from the onlookers. After regarding him for a few minutes I came to the conclusion that this Arab was a remarkable man – the most remarkable man I had met among the Arabs, WaSwahili [those who speak Swahili as their sole mother tongue], and half castes in Africa. He was neat in person; his clothes were a spotless white. His fez cap was brand new; his waist was encircled by a rich dowel; his dagger was splendid with silver filigree and his tout ensemble was that of an Arab gentleman in very comfortable circumstances.[3]

One British writer, A.J. Swann, wrote of him in 1882: 'He possessed a frank, manly character enlivened by humour and loved immensely to play practical jokes upon his intimate friends . . . He enjoyed conversation and had a curiosity for politics in Europe and America.'[4]

In the 1880s, towards the latter part of his life, Tippu Tib saw that the balance of power was shifting in favour of the Europeans and managed to maintain good relations with them. It helped that they believed him too significant to challenge. By then, the Belgians were the major force in the Congo and they approached Tippu Tib to work with them but he replied: 'I can do nothing except on the authority of my ruler', meaning Sultan Barghash of Zanzibar, son of Sultan Seyyid Said. Yet some Arabs suspected that he had sold out to the Europeans. Stanley had agreed to make him governor of a large area of the Congo and sure enough signed a deal in 1887 making him governor of its eastern part. Tippu Tib became even richer and more powerful, but Leopold II, King of the Belgians, was intent on gaining control of all of the Congo. The Belgians engaged in battle with the Arabs and pushed them out. Tippu Tib's son Sayf was killed in the fighting, with Tippu Tib recalling, 'I realised that all was up'.

By the 1890s, the power of the Arabs had evaporated. Sultan Barghash still claimed some kind of sovereignty over his lands up to and beyond Lake Tanganyika but the Europeans in Central Africa were now the dominant force. Central and East Africa were partitioned between the Belgians, British and Germans, which led to the departure of the Arabs. Only in Zanzibar did the sultan maintain his authority, but then in 1890 Zanzibar became a British protectorate. Tippu Tib returned to Zanzibar that same year and managed his clove plantations there. These were said to be the second largest in Zanzibar – he was one of the richest men in East

Africa, probably 'owning' thousands of enslaved people. The slave trade had been abolished in 1876 in Zanzibar, but slavery remained there openly until ownership of enslaved people was abolished in 1897, though the practice continued for some years into the twentieth century. Tippu Tib also began to dictate his autobiography in Swahili, which was written in the Arabic script and was 70 pages long. By now in his late fifties, it seems it was recorded mostly from memory.

Although Tippu Tib had gained enormous wealth through ivory and slave trading, even he was reluctant to engage on the topic. British soldier and adventurer Colonel Richard Meinertzhagen, who saw him in January 1903 wrote: 'I tried to get him to talk of his slave-raiding days, but he clearly did not like it.'[5] Tippu Tib died in 1905 of a cerebral haemorrhage, probably as a result of malaria, at his home in Stone Town. *The Times* newspaper in London recorded his death on 14 June: 'Hamid Bin Mohammed alias Tippoo Tib was the famous Arab merchant and slave trader of the Upper Congo.'

The impact of the Indian Ocean trade was widespread and destructive. Inter-regional trade declined. Traditional systems of networks and alliances were disrupted. Trust between African communities was eroded, conflict and migration increased, farmsteads were abandoned, and internally displaced people carried out raids for food. People sold their children into slavery to survive. Many others simply starved to death.

By the late nineteenth century, the region was mostly under British control, though the Portuguese managed to retain their hold on what became Mozambique, which was the last of the four Swahili settlements I visited. I walked along the gleaming beaches – some of the best in Africa – and came across a gate that marked the exact spot where enslaved Africans were taken across the Indian Ocean. On the other side of the gate is a garden of remembrance, with terracotta busts of men and women mounted on plinths surrounding a rectangular bed of earth. Adjacent to it is an empty pit where the captives would have been held – a silent memorial to the nameless millions taken from Africa during 1,000 years of enslavement by Arabs and their partners.

I wanted to find out how the ordinary inhabitants of the Island of Mozambique remembered their past and so I sought out Fatimata Moumdi, a cheerful widowed mother, who worked as a housekeeper at a hotel, and whose passion was dance. I accompanied her to her weekly session on the beach with the Asante dance group, comprising around eight women who perform their routines to the accompaniment of three male drummers. I was struck by how the women used dance as an expression of their history and their perceptions of it. They were Muslim but were from the indigenous Bantu, who made up large cohorts of enslaved people in the past.

Sitting in front of a fishing boat, on the white sandy beach at dusk, the women at first swayed in unison, and then got up on their feet. Two wielded a skipping rope as the others danced in turn, each falling onto the ground. The pair holding the rope then proceeded to gently whip those on the ground, in a re-enactment of a trader punishing his captives. Then one woman deftly removed her skirt revealing loose pantaloons underneath, and donning an Arab-style head-covering to depict herself as an Arab master, moved aggressively among her fellow dancers in a show of dominance. One woman pretended to faint, a metaphor for the capture of a captive as well as for the displacement that enslaved people experienced. The dances I observed were a demonstration of a collective memory of suffering, handed down through the centuries.

The arrival of the Arabs on Africa's east coast in the seventh century marked the first time that Africans were captured and sold in an international, extensive and organised trade. The Arab presence also redrew the identity of the east coast of Africa, with Arab and Muslim cultures becoming inextricably linked with that of indigenous Africans. As Dr Djaffar Moussa-Elkadhum, a UNESCO official, explained to me, this has led to ambivalence: on the one hand, African Muslims are faithful adherents of Islam and are grateful the religion spread to Africa; on the other hand, many millions of Africans were enslaved by Arabs, who looked down on them. Another factor Africans have to come to terms with is that fellow Africans were involved in the slave trade.

The dance troupe on the Island of Mozambique was proof that the agony of slavery is still very much alive in the memory of the victims' descendants. I wonder if there is a similar awareness among the descendants of the perpetrators? In 2001, one of Tippu Tib's great-great-grandchildren, Ummi Mahsoudha Ali Hammid, gave an interview in which she said she was neither 'proud nor ashamed' of him, just as she would not have felt pride nor shame at being 'the descendant of a slave; they were victims of the slave trade just like I would be a victim if I am made accountable for what my forefathers did . . . It was the trend of the time, that was business, purely. You either be a slave or a slaver. You choose the lesser of two evils. And if you are in a position to be a slaver, why should you be a slave?'

As well as encouraging a wider discussion between African communities, the legacy of all Arab involvement in the trade of enslaved Africans should stimulate further debate about mutual perceptions of Africans and Arabs, as well as the treatment of African migrants in the Arab world and the intersection between enslavement and racism. Comments made in March 2023 by the Tunisian president Kais Saied that sub-Saharan Africans in his country were part of a 'conspiracy' to 'change the demographic composition' of Tunisia left some African migrants subject to violence and verbal abuse in the country, and it is one recent example of how prejudice and racism still exist towards black Africans in the Middle East and North Africa. The Arab slave trade in Africa is a part of global history that requires more research and informed discussion both in Africa and beyond.

I saw a poignant image at the National Museum of Kenya in Nairobi: five African men and one woman with a baby on her back, all in chains walking in line through thick vegetation, some carrying elephant tusks, under the supervision of two bearded Arabs. The Arab in the foreground of the picture is lashing a young screaming man with a whip that appears to be made of an elephant's tail. A simple drawing that speaks a thousand words, but the silence must be broken.

10

Cast in Bronze

A grainy black-and-white photograph shows a group of smiling British officers, surrounded by precious artefacts, a collection of elephant tusks at their feet. The picture is captioned 'LOOT'. In 1897 British troops invaded the Benin Kingdom, massacring its people, ransacking the king's palace and eventually burning down the city. The 'loot' in the picture was among 5,000 artefacts, metal plaques and sculptures pillaged at this time, including what are known as the Benin Bronzes (Benin here refers to a part of southern Nigeria, and should not be confused with the country, the Republic of Benin).

The Benin Bronzes are perhaps the most iconic body of art found south of the Sahara, and they have become even more famous thanks to their huge significance in the restitution debate. The bronzes date from the thirteenth century, though the ones held in Western museums are more likely to be from the sixteenth century. One of my favourite pieces is the alluring bust of Queen Idia, which I have admired many times over the years at the British Museum in London.

When I visited Benin National Museum, a strikingly circular building in the state capital, Benin City, its director at the time, Theophilus Umogbai, pointed out a copy of Queen Idia's bust. Should the original be sent back to Benin? Demands for African art to be repatriated have been made for decades, but the debate has shifted tremendously in the last few years, in large measure due to an important study commissioned by the French government in 2018. Its authors, the Senegalese academic and writer Felwine Sarr and French art historian Bénédicte Savoy, estimated that a colossal 90 per cent of Africa's cultural heritage is in the West, and they added their voices to calls for France to return objects it had acquired during the colonial era. The report's publication had been preceded by a speech made in November 2017 in Burkina Faso by the French president Emmanuel Macron, in which he signalled that he would like to see the 'permanent or temporary return of African heritage back to Africa . . . there are historical explanations for it, but there is no valid, lasting and unconditional justification'. France was one of the two major European colonial powers in Africa, along with Britain, and so Macron's speech seemed a turning point in the debate, moving the needle somewhat in favour of the politicians and activists in Africa and elsewhere who had long fought for restitution.

Nearly all Africans from every walk of life with whom I have discussed the topic, including in the diaspora, support the repatriation of treasures, either through the transfer of ownership or long-term loans.

The knotty issue of restitution naturally extends beyond Africa and there are implications for treasures from other parts of the world held by Western museums, most notably the Parthenon Marbles in the British Museum. There are many issues to consider and assessments need to be made on a case-by-case basis, but when it comes to African artefacts in particular, I have at times noticed an unpalatable undertone to some of the counter-arguments being deployed. In August 2021, an article about the Benin Bronzes published by *The Spectator* stated: 'The fact that the objects were taken from a West African kingdom that could hardly be confused with a pacifist, vegan commune – Benin grew rich on the Atlantic slave trade and the slaying of elephants; it practised human sacrifice and possibly ritual cannibalism – does not quench the appetite of those demanding their return.'[1] The implication is that the people of Benin are not worthy recipients of their historic works of art because of the 'sins' of their predecessors. The same people who hold these views usually reject the notion that present-day Europeans should be held responsible for the 'colonial sins' of their forefathers. Such paradoxes speak for themselves.

Although interventions such as the above are mercifully rare, and do not reflect the majority opinion in the UK, the myth of 'primitive Africa' has proved remarkably persistent. One would think that the following opinion espoused by a former Regius Professor of History at Oxford University, Sir Hugh Trevor-Roper, had been consigned to the past. This is a quote, from his book *The Rise of Christian Europe*, published in 1965, during the period of rapid decolonisation in Africa:

It is fashionable to speak today as if European history were devalued: as if historians in the past have paid too much attention to it; and as if nowadays we should pay less. Undergraduates, seduced, as always, by the changing breath of journalistic fashion, demand that they should be taught the history of black Africa. Perhaps, in the future, there will be some African history to teach. But at present there is none, or very little: there is only the history of the Europeans in Africa. The rest is largely darkness . . . And darkness is not a subject for history . . . If all history is equal, as some now believe, there is no reason why we should study one section of it rather than another, for certainly we cannot study it all. Then indeed we may neglect our own history and amuse ourselves with the unrewarding gyrations of barbarous tribes in picturesque but irrelevant corners of the globe.

The late Hugh Trevor-Roper was held in high regard by many. But to think he was an active member of Oxford's academic body when I was an undergraduate there makes me feel quite indignant. Incidentally, Hugh Trevor-Roper doubled down on his views in 1969, extending his observations and calling the whole of Africa, including the Maghreb, Egypt and Ethiopia, 'unhistoric'. The teaching of history in UK universities has come a long way, but there is still more to be done to ensure that studies on African history draw on the scholarship of African intellectuals from the continent and diaspora. I am not at all suggesting that the credible and authoritative work of Western historians of Africa today – the Africanists – should be supplanted. I am merely advocating that we should supplement it with more local perspectives in order to achieve a greater understanding of the past. As one eminent Nigerian historian, Professor Muyiwa Falaiye at the University of Lagos, told me:

A black person needs to write their own history, speak for themselves, to give a different perspective from what is orchestrated by the West, and I say this against the backdrop of the fact that no one can explain your history better than yourself. If you look at the history of Africa and its belief system with the mindset of the West, you are bound to misunderstand what the African stands for. You need to understand what Africans do, why they think the way they do. For me this is of utmost significance: telling the history is not enough, understanding the mindset of the African is more important.

I want to dispel preconceptions about Africans by providing a more holistic understanding of their history; one that moves beyond gratuitous mentions of cannibalism and human sacrifice, intended to denigrate the culture and devalue the history of an entire continent's people.

Some may object that by downplaying such gory practices I swing the pendulum too far in the other direction and put forward an Elysian view of Africans. But I would point the reader to a multitude of writings on these subjects that have attracted a disproportionate amount of attention, and that must now be counter-balanced. Indeed, these very practices were used to justify the murderous excesses of European colonialism. Sir Richard Burton, the British soldier, diplomat and traveller who visited Benin in 1863, decided that the occasional human sacrifices were the most compelling aspect of its culture. Painting a picture of evil, he presented the invasion of Benin as a 'civilising mission'. This mission also became a convenient excuse for imperialists to stop what Burton described, apparently without a trace of irony, as the oba's 'interference' with trade 'far beyond the borders of his kingdom'.[2] Oba is the title used for the kings of Benin.

Given the prominence of the Benin bronzes in current discussions about art and colonialism, I wanted to delve deeper into the history of the kingdom that gave rise to these treasures, and I sought out the expertise of Professor Osarhieme Osadolor at the University of Benin, whose knowledge informs much of this chapter.

The Benin kingdom lay in a forest region to the south and east of Ife towards the Niger Delta, where the Edo-speaking people live. It was established in 600 CE by a ruler known as Igodo, who took the title Osigo, meaning the 'king with wisdom from the sky above'. By the early seventh century, Benin was essentially a city-state made up of around 30 smaller entities. Throughout history most Africans have lived in rural areas, and this is still true today (though patterns of urbanisation are increasing). The kingdom of Benin, however, was an early example of a major urban civilisation on the continent.

The first dynastic ruler in Benin was Oronmiyan in 1200. In the mid-1200s Oba Ewedo made Benin City his capital, which it has remained ever since. He was likely succeeded by Oguola, who ruled in the late 1200s. It was a divine form of kingship. Past kings were regarded as gods and when they died their descendants would appeal to their spirits to watch over them and the kingdom. The Benin people also worshipped their own deities: Ogiso was ruler of the sky, Olokun was the sea god and Ogun the god of war and iron, who presided over the making of tools and equipment from metals. Osun was the spiritual force behind medicinal plants and other natural products. Sacrifices were made to appease the gods; one bronze relief shows a cow being killed for ritual purposes: animal sacrifices were more common than human ones, which occurred once a year.

Oguola is credited with two achievements: he was the first oba to fortify his kingdom by digging moats around it to protect it from invaders; and it was he who breathed life into the ancient skill of bronze making by founding Benin's royal Guild of Bronze Casters, which was not allowed to produce bronzes for any other person without permission from the oba's palace. Craftsmen were lavished with gifts under this royal patronage, long before the start of the European Renaissance.

The Benin Kingdom really came into its own in the mid-1400s under Oba Ewuare I, or Ewuare the Great (r. c. 1440–73), who built an army and turned Benin into a powerful kingdom. Until then, the oba had limited authority. Ewuare I surrounded the city with protective layers of walls and moats and the nine gates into it were guarded and locked at night so that nobody could enter until morning. The walls of Benin City and its surrounding kingdom are recognised as 'the world's largest earthworks carried out prior to the mechanical era' and at one point extended 16,000 kilometres – four times longer than the Great Wall of China.[3] Ewuare I appointed his own district chiefs and had his son recognised as his official heir. He had chief administrators in different parts of his kingdom from which he received tributes, increasing his wealth and resources. These vassal states would also mobilise soldiers to fight on the oba's behalf.

It was at this time that the Guild of Bronze Casters started making bronze heads. During my tour of the Benin National Museum, its director at the time, Theophilus Umogbai, showed me the few historic bronze plaques and reliefs that Benin retained – elaborately decorated cast plaques depicting animal and human figures, used to decorate the walls of the oba's palace. There were also bronze vessels, wood and ivory carvings, artefacts, furniture and instruments as well as exquisite jewellery. Although the phrase 'Benin bronzes' implies that they are made of bronze, which is an alloy of copper and tin, some of them in fact are made of brass – an amalgam of copper and zinc that is far easier to work with. There were also terracotta heads of nobles; only kings and the queen mother could have a head made of bronze.

Theophilus encouraged me to go and see how a Benin

bronze is made by the bronze casters who maintain this prized skill, handed down through the centuries. So I set off to Igun Street. At its entrance, overhead there was a terracotta-coloured arch bearing the words 'Guild of Benin Bronze Casters World Heritage Site'. As I walked along, I could see dozens of bronzes for sale on either side of the road, and behind the shopfronts were open areas where the bronze casters were working their magic. If not for their modern clothes and the music being emitted from a radio, I could have imagined that I had been transported back to the sixteenth century. The bronze casters sat on low stools, surrounded by scrap metal, furnaces and metal sticks. Jeff Eholor, a member of the guild, greeted me and explained the painstaking efforts required for the process, which is called the 'lost wax method'. First, an object is modelled in beeswax. Encased in a ceramic shell, the mould is heated on a fire. While baking hardens the clay, the beeswax melts away (it is 'lost'), leaving a hollow mould into which the liquid metal is poured. After a few hours, once the metal has managed to set and cool down, the mould is broken to extract the casting. Only then does the bronze caster find out how good his product is. The piece is then finished and decorated finely by hand, and no two artefacts are the same. It was with great delight that I bought a newly made bronze head from this ancient guild, which now has pride of place on a mantelpiece in my sitting room.

Queen Idia's bust, arguably the best known of Benin's bronzes, depicts a woman with elegant features and a long, slim neck. Her hair is styled in a conical fashion, resembling a parrot or chicken's beak – a style believed to have been invented by her – and her head is covered by a netting of coral beads, a symbol of royalty and wealth. There are rectangular incisions between her eyebrows. Idia was beautiful, and Oba Ozolua (r. c. 1481–1504) wanted to marry her. But

Queen Idia's bust

her parents were opposed to the marriage because they did not want to lose her to a king, so they scarred her face with markings between her eyes to disfigure her beauty and make her unworthy of a royal betrothal.

Another theory handed down through oral tradition holds that the scars depict the point where thought and power are concentrated and that they indicate a person in possession of great spiritual power. Either way, Ozolua was so taken with Idia that he married her. As queen, Idia would have been expected to perform her duties within the confines of the palace. Obas had several wives and the relationship between the co-wives could be competitive. Idia and her fellow wives would have titles reserved for them that referred to a particular body part of the oba – his eyes, spirit or feet – and these titles would be conferred on them by the oba himself. This was an honour he bestowed on his favourite wives, though one that was fraught with peril: if he died before them, they could be buried with him. A royal wife's status was gained through giving birth, but a childless queen would not be cast out; she could remain in the palace and train new wives, providing them with a crash course on how to be a queen. Once a queen bore an oba a first-born son, she was not expected to have any more children, and would dedicate her life to bringing him up. This was the case until as late as the reign of Oba Akenzua II (r. 1933–78). So an oba's wife reached her peak status as a widow of the king and the mother of the new oba.

Idia's husband, Ozolua the Conqueror, was a soldier renowned for his military skills, and he was often portrayed in carvings in full-length chain mail. The people of his kingdom farmed or were artisans and craftsmen. They engaged in trade, and cowrie beads were used as a form of currency. The first Europeans to arrive in Benin were Portuguese traders in 1486, who found an established kingdom with an economy already equipped to deal with international trade. The oba controlled all imports and exports and Ozolua traded extensively with the Portuguese, which gave him immense economic power. The Portuguese were mostly missionaries and traders interested in goods such as pepper, ivory, cotton, textiles, palm oil and enslaved people. European consumers would place orders for Benin goods such as fine salt cellars carved out of ivory. According to Professor Osadolor, the obas of Benin did not sell their own people into slavery but embarked on wars of conquest to enslave people for Europeans. In return they received metalwork, firearms, weapons and luxury goods, with which they could expand the boundaries of their empire.

When Oba Ozolua died, two of his sons wanted to

succeed him. One, called Esigie, was his second-born son and was based at the capital Benin City. The other, Arhuaran, the king's first-born, lived in Udo, a significant urban settlement about 30 kilometres away.

By custom, Arhuaran should have succeeded his father Ozolua. However, at a young age he had been sent to Portugal to be educated while Esigie had remained in Benin. This gave Esigie – and his ambitious mother, Idia – the advantage. He was better versed in the ways of the court than Arhuaran and familiar with the oba's army. A civil war ensued between the two, and while Benin was preoccupied with its fraternal feud, the neighbouring people of Igala seized the advantage and entered northern Benin. The future of the kingdom was in the balance. Idia raised more troops and went into battle on behalf of her son. She is the only woman in Benin's history to have done so and is lauded with the aphorisms 'No woman but Idia, mother of Esigie ever went to war' and 'Idia, mother of Esigie, fought with a double-edged sword'. The double-edged sword might be an allusion to the fact that along with her combat skills, Idia was a traditional doctor. Possessing a strong spirituality, she is credited with using her knowledge of the occult to win the throne for her son. In any case, Esigie defeated his brother Arhuaran, pursued the Igala invaders out of his territory and became the oba of Benin in 1504.

Once a queen's son became the oba, tradition required that his mother would not set eyes on him ever again. It would still be her duty to provide him with guidance and all maternal support, but she would only be allowed to communicate with him through intermediaries.

However, Oba Esigie was so devoted to his mother and grateful for her help seizing the throne that he established a new custom. He honoured Idia as the first ever queen mother of Benin, the *iyoba*, meaning literally the 'mother of the oba'.

Esigie built a palace for Idia (the 'Eguae-Iyoba') just outside Benin City in Uselu, from where she could exercise independent authority through officials under her control. From then on, the role of mothers of kings in Benin was significant, with subsequent obas following Esigie's lead and observing this practice. The position of iyoba gave the queen mothers the ability to acquire wealth and prestige in a male-dominated system of kingship that would otherwise have denied them an official role.

Idia advised her son, kept a watchful eye on his health, and maintained her own regiment in the army to assist his men when they carried out raids. She also supported him in the day-to-day process of running the government and adjudicated in legal cases.

Oba Esigie enjoyed a long and prosperous reign. He expanded Benin so that by 1500 its territory stretched from the Niger Delta in the east to the coastal lagoon of Lagos in the west. As it prospered, the kingdom became widely known, featuring on maps of Africa drawn up by Europeans from the 1500s. Esigie could speak Portuguese fluently and cultivated ties with the Portuguese, who became important allies. He bought guns from them and employed Portuguese mercenaries in his battles against rivals. There are bronze reliefs depicting Portuguese soldiers and visitors – their features and clothing clearly that of Europeans.

As diplomatic relations between Benin and Portugal took hold, there was an exchange of ambassadors and a Portuguese embassy was established at the court in Benin City. In 1516 the Portuguese ambassador Duarte Pires wrote a letter to the king of Portugal, Manuel I:

> The favour which the king of Benin accords us is due to his love of your highness; thus he pays us high honour and

sets us at table to dine with his son, and no part of his court is hidden from us but all the doors are open. Sir, when these priests arrived in Benin, the delight of the King of Benin was so great that I do not know how to describe it and likewise that of all his people; and he sent for them at once.[4]

At some stage towards the end of his reign, Esigie's beloved mother Queen Idia died. A heartbroken Esigie ordered a memorial head to be made by the Guild of Bronze Casters and he kept it at an altar in his palace. Queen Idia was the first woman to be given the honour of being depicted as a bronze memorial head – 90 per cent of Benin bronzes are of men. Idia's fame in the modern era has, ironically, eclipsed that of Oba Esigie, the son to whom she dedicated her life.

After Idia there was a proliferation of artwork pertaining to the iyobas. Nearly all art commissioned by the Benin court of royal women was of queen mothers and their retinue, and included works in bronze, wood, terracotta, iron, coral beads and cloth. The creations could be used as regalia by male and female courtiers and chiefs, and some artefacts associated with the queen mother were used outside the palace, in shrines for instance.[5]

Ordinary women who had performed honourable or remarkable deeds could also be remembered through sculptures. Emotan is one early example. She was a trader who helped look after the children of others and was kind and protective of Oba Ewuare I before he became king in 1440. She had helped the young prince win back the throne from his brother who had usurped it. Emotan died soon after Ewuare became oba and he marked her grave with a tree so that people could pay homage to her burial site. In Benin, women who were transformed into these kinds of heroine-deities were represented through nature, sometimes as trees or rivers, inspiring local cults.

When Esigie himself died in 1550, he was succeeded by his son, Oba Orhogbua (c. 1550–78), who is believed to have commissioned many of the reliefs to mark his father's long reign. Bronzes were not merely decorative, but were objects of record: history immortalised in art, not just art for art's sake. Some of the reliefs that I saw in the Benin National Museum portray court musicians such as hornblowers, and many are of court dignitaries. Some depict important battles, with military commanders dressed in tunics with leopard skins, wearing necklaces made of leopard claws, swords in raised hands or smiting enemies. The leopard was a symbol of the oba, and leopard hunters were highly valued in Benin. The obas themselves are depicted wearing beads and bearing swords. Three incisions marked above each eyebrow were a sign of royal identity as well as being representative of thought. The Benin people believed that a person's head was the focal point for receiving wise advice from otherworldly or supernatural forces. The oba's head was therefore of paramount importance – the kingdom's security and prosperity depended on his wisdom.

Benin became an increasingly militaristic kingdom and as time went by it expanded beyond its core heartlands to the east, west and towards the Atlantic Ocean in the south. Esigie's son (Orhogbua) and grandson (Oba Ehengbuda, who reigned c. 1578–1606) consolidated Benin's territory. Orhogbua established Lagos, and ensured that the first oba of Lagos was installed by him. Indeed, the Yoruba royal family of Lagos still pays homage to the oba of Benin. The Yoruba kingdom was established in the eighth century by the first king, Oduduwa, who had originated from Benin. The Yoruba are among the best known of West Africa's groups, and are spread across Nigeria, Benin, Ghana and Togo, numbering around 40 million.

I had the honour of meeting the queen mother (or 'erelu kuti') of the Yoruba people of Lagos at her ancestral palace on Lagos Island. Her Royal Highness Erelu Abiola Docemo was decked out from neck to toe in a dazzling long white gown, with gold necklaces and earrings, and pearls glinting on her wrists and feet. Given the number of people waiting to see her, she clearly commanded a great deal of respect and affection, as did the queen mothers of the Benin kingdom best typified by Idia. She spoke to me about her role and status:

> As the erelu kuti or the queen mother of Lagos, I have a specifically defined role within the royal family. I preside over ceremonies, the installation of a new king, I act as a bridge after the passing of one king to another, I am a kind of anchor; because I am the most senior royal on the king's council, I lead the process to determine who the eligible successors are, who is fit to be king. In the Yoruba language the literal meaning of becoming a king is that "you have eaten the king!" So the installation ceremony is shrouded in secrecy. It is done in privacy, as though you were having dinner. You do not go on the rooftop to eat your dinner, after all, so the process is all done with decorum and privacy . . . I have been the erelu kuti for nearly five decades, and when a new king accedes to the throne, he wants to put his own stamp on it, so naturally there is a little bit of tension between us. But in the end we get to understand each other and we extend mutual courtesies.

To this day the Yoruba people venerate the oba of Benin, and their art, beliefs and traditions – including the role of the queen mother – reflect their deep shared history with the Benin kingdom.

Benin enjoyed a sophisticated and complex system of government, as alluded to by Dr Andreas Joshua Ulsheimer, a German doctor writing about his voyage to West Africa in 1603–4: 'Of this kingdom and its inhabitants, especially their system of justice, their regulations and laws, warfare, marriage and so on, there would still be much to write'. He described how the palace doors were covered in brass foil, lintels and beams, and 'on the walls of the palace there hung hundreds of brass plaques' depicting historical events. There were terracotta plaques too, and ivory decorated altars.[6]

As the city of Benin grew in stature, so did its architecture. Even by the early 1400s, Benin was a walled city with wide streets up to 40 metres wide. By 1602 it boasted fine houses, its streets illuminated by tall metal lamps fuelled by palm oil.

In 1688 the Dutch writer and physician Olfert Dapper described the royal palace of the Benin court as having 'beautiful and long square galleries about as big as the exchange at Amsterdam, some bigger than others, resting on wooden pillars, covered from top to bottom with cast copper, on which deeds of war and battle scenes are carved.'[7]

In 1691, the Portuguese naval captain Lourenco Pinto wrote:

Great Benin, where the king resides, is larger than Lisbon; all the streets run straight as far as the eye can see. The houses are large, especially that of the king, which is richly decorated and has fine columns. The city is wealthy and industrious. It is so well governed that theft is unknown and the people live in such security that they have no doors to their houses.[8]

Benin's palaces were divided into male and female quarters – a reflection of the kingdom's cultural practices. Children of either sex could wander freely around both areas.

At the extreme back of the women's quarters was the 'house of menstruation', where women were banished during their periods, because menstrual blood was seen as unclean.

Those in power in Benin could hold hereditary or non-hereditary titles, and members of the royal family had a significant role to play in the administration. The top officials were the seven *uzama* or kingmakers. The non-hereditary titles were held by four town chiefs who presided over a large group of administrators. Three high-ranking officials ran the palace associations that oversaw the complex system of the devolution of power. One palace association, the 'Iwebo', was in charge of the king's personal belongings and all his regalia for ceremonies. This included supervision of the craft guilds: the bronze casters, ivory carvers, weavers, costume makers and leatherworkers. The royal drummers and hornblowers as well as the executioners and priests were also part of this association. The second palace association, the 'Iweguae', oversaw the duties of the king, his personal staff, attendants, sword bearers, healers and guards. The third palace association, the 'Ibiwe', was in charge of ensuring that the needs of the wives and children were met.

In the eighteenth century, the kingdom became decentralised and chiefs and warlords gained ascendancy, weakening the power of the oba. Oba Ewuakpe (r. *c.* 1701–12) managed to restore some authority and resources for the kingship by trading ivory with the Dutch. Akenzua I (r. *c.* 1713–40) tried to suppress squabbles over the succession by establishing the title of crown prince, or *edaiken*. His son, Oba Eresoyen (r. *c.* 1740–50), deployed the Benin tradition of making bronze sculptures, associating himself with the glorious reigns of the sixteenth-century warrior-obas. He commissioned a large proportion of Benin's bronze art.

Internal rivalries challenged the power of the oba but a bigger external threat loomed: the increasing military presence of the British in this part of Africa. Ovonramwen, who became oba in 1888, had to contend with Britain's Niger Coast Protectorate, established in 1884, which enshrined trade deals between the British and local chiefs and undermined the oba further. A fraudulent treaty was imposed on Ovonramwen by the British, which he refused to sign. When its terms were hence not fulfilled by him, a British mission forced its way into Benin City in 1897, even though the oba had requested a meeting at a later date. The party was attacked by men loyal to the oba, and seven out of nine Europeans and two hundred African 'carriers' were killed. This triggered the British into action. The Foreign Office in London authorised a punitive military expedition to prove that white men could not be killed with impunity and within weeks British troops sacked the city of Benin. The oba's forces tried to repel the attack but their spears and arrows were no match for the sophisticated British weaponry. British historian Dan Hicks described the tragedy as 'massacres of towns and villages . . . primary among the war crimes was the scale of the killings and bombings of civilian targets'.[9] Benin was wrecked, including the city walls and palace, and nearly all of its treasures and art was looted. Jewellery, bronzes and other magnificent objects shipped overseas ended up in museum and private collections, mostly in Europe and North America.

Oba Ovonramwen was exiled to Calabar near the border with modern-day Cameroon, but while he was there his son, who eventually became Oba Eweka II (r. 1914–33), employed carvers. The oba may have been banished from his kingdom but his kingship would live on through Benin's traditional art. At the Benin National Museum, Theophilus Umogbai showed me a wooden stool carved with figures depicting the oba

Some of the looted bronzes, catalogued for the Pitt Rivers
Museum in Oxford

with attendants holding his hands, two servants by his side. It was an expression, he said, of how the oba had been betrayed by insiders within his own kingdom and served as an example of how art was used to record events.

Ovonramwen was the last independent oba of Benin. Between 1897 and 1914 there was no oba officially on the throne in Benin itself; the British had taken over the administration of the kingdom. As British colonialist Sir Ralph Moor declared, 'There is only one king in the country and that is the Whiteman'.[10] Ovonramwen died in January 1914, and his sword was returned to the kingdom to be given to his

Oba Ovonramwen with his household

rightful heir, symbolising that as far as the people of Benin were concerned the succession was unbroken. During his exile there had been efforts to ensure that the kingship of Benin would continue and indeed Oba Eweka II regained the throne in July 1914 in a newly formed country: Nigeria, under the authority of British colonial rule. Eweka rebuilt the royal palace and restored the craft guilds to replace artefacts that had been snatched away by the British. He had deliberately chosen the throne name Eweka after the thirteenth-century founder of the dynasty, Eweka I, the son of Oronmiyan.

Today, Ewuare II, who became oba in 2016, is one of the most widely respected monarchs in West Africa because he represents a lineage that goes back centuries. His palace, a white building with a terracotta tiled roof, is relatively modest and stands in a large courtyard. Two simple columns adorn the entrance. I met courtiers dressed in white robes, with cowrie shell necklaces around their necks and hair shorn, save for a ring above their foreheads, who instructed me on how to greet the oba. I was told I would have to kneel and rub my hands in a show of deference, at the same time proclaiming in the Edo language 'Oba gha t'okpere,' meaning 'Long may the oba reign.' So, desperately practising the words in an unfamiliar language, I entered the elegant reception room with high ceilings and pictures of Oba Ewuare II on display. I sat on one of the golden chairs that lined either side of the room, along with others granted an audience, such as a beauty pageant that happened to be in town; it made for a rather glamorous affair!

As we waited for Ewuare II, the atmosphere was charged with anticipation. The oba came in, a tall imposing man dressed in white and yellow robes, an elaborately decorated red hat, and coral beads around his neck and wrists. A pair of reflective sunglasses perched on his nose added a modern touch. He looked every inch a king, sitting regally on the padded red velvet seat of his golden throne, and there was a flurry of excitement as we all chanted the well-rehearsed words. Some courtiers also raised their fists in greetings. Large metal sculptures of animals flanked his throne on either side.

When Nigeria became independent in 1960 all the former kingdoms that had existed on its territories were brought together in a new modern state with a constitution that left traditional rulers such as the oba with weakened powers. However, to this day, many citizens of Benin hold the oba in greater reverence than they do the 'here today, gone tomorrow' federal governments in the national capital Abuja. The oba is seen as the custodian of the history, culture and heritage of Benin; he is still called on to resolve disputes among his subjects and is expected to protect their interests. During my audience and conversation with Oba Ewuare II, he projected himself as an advocate for his people, stressing how much he wanted to see development and investment pour into Benin. On the restitution debate, he stated that he has consistently requested that his kingdom's art be returned, insisting it would be put on public display in a palace museum as a way of attracting visitors. The oba added, however, that he would also like to see a portion of artefacts remain abroad so that they could act as 'ambassadors', as he put it, for his kingdom. As a former Nigerian ambassador in Europe, including in Rome, Oba Ewuare II was keenly aware of the significance of cultural heritage.

Theophilus Umogbai told me that by putting the spotlight on Benin's bronzes, the debate has increased interest in his culture. He believes that the body of art produced by Benin, epitomised by Idia's memorial head, counters any interpretation of Benin's history as being nothing more than 'uncivilised'.

When I left Benin City, having met Oba Ewuare II, toured the museum and seen the bronze casters at work, I found myself wondering how anybody could reconcile Benin's so-called 'uncivilised past' with the artistry and sophistication of a society that had so impressed those who had visited it. The thousands of bronze, brass, ivory, terracotta and wooden artworks for which the kingdom is renowned, represent a fairer picture of Benin's achievements. Of the many museums I visited in Africa, there were more people – of all ages – at the Benin National Museum than anywhere else. One local leader, Patrick Agbaza, spoke effusively: 'I am a champion of Benin cultural heritage. It is fantastic. I appreciate what we have and treasure it. We feel sad when it is said that our civilisation started with the arrival of white men, this is murdering historical facts.'

The Benin bronzes are not just objects of art to be admired, they are important sources of history. In the Edo language of Benin, the verb to remember, *sa-e-y-ama*, means literally 'to cast a motif in bronze'. Oba Esigie wanted his mother Queen Idia to be remembered and she is immortalised in her bronze memorial head. As Professor Osadolor told me: 'The past that we cherish so much is not with us here, what represents our past and its accomplishments, in terms of great artworks that reflect the history of our people and what we have contributed to African and world civilisation, is somewhere else, and we feel bad about this, we believe that this lost past must be regained.' The yearning I heard in the professor's voice still echoes in my ears. For me, he epitomises how historians can also be activists, advocating for a cause.

History is not only about the past, and the debate about the Benin bronzes raises a significant issue, as articulated by Aindrea Emelife, the curator of the Edo Museum of West African Art:

> Restitution is meaningless if it does not connect the present and the future. The return of objects does not reach its maximum impact if we, as a globalised art world, do not link this moment with the vibrancy of Africa's contemporary art scene and come together to support its overdue rise and those working within it. Restitution addresses the injustices of history and is symbolic as it reintroduces missing pieces into our artistic canon. But it is not static. The enthusiasm to return and the self-congratulation that accompanies it should metamorphose into a new connection with the countries from where the works originate. The return of objects such as the Benin bronzes is not the ending of the relationship; it should be the beginning.[11]

I wholeheartedly agree: the restitution debate should redouble the growth of Africa's vibrant creative sector, and bring new engagement with it from inside and outside the continent.

For my part, I am full of hope that as dialogues blossom between museums and the communities from which their collections originated, a new era of cooperation and collaboration will dawn.

11

Southern Kingdoms

It was a bright sunny day when I saw the stone complex for the first time. My heart rose up in awe at the magnificent sight. Yet unlike the first European visitors, who in their ignorance could not believe it was built by Africans, my wonder was mixed with pride.

The imposing and extensive stone structures of Great Zimbabwe are the largest set of ruins in sub-Saharan Africa. Established in about 1100 CE, Great Zimbabwe is located 240 kilometres east of Bulawayo in modern-day Zimbabwe, and it was the capital of a great southern African kingdom. But rather like Ancient Egypt, achievements of the magnitude of Great Zimbabwe could not be accepted by later Europeans as having emerged from an 'African' civilisation.

In 1871 the German geologist Karl Gottlieb Mauch held that the stonework was too sophisticated and the culture too advanced to be the work of Africans. He opined that Great Zimbabwe had been built by Phoenician or Israelite settlers under the instruction of the Queen of Sheba, to whom he assigned a non-African lineage. And in 1891 the British mining magnate Cecil Rhodes commissioned the English explorer and archaeologist James Theodore Bent to carry out an investigation to prove that Great Zimbabwe had been built by a Semitic people. Bent spent two months at the site studying the edifice and concluded:

> The ruins and the things in them are not in any way connected with any known African race ... The cumulative evidence in favour of this race being one of the many tribes of Arabia is very strong ... a northern race ... closely akin to the Phoenician and Egyptian.[1]

In 1895 Cecil Rhodes gave W.G. Neal of the Ancient Ruins Company a commission to exploit all Rhodesian ruins (in the late nineteenth century, Rhodesia was named after Cecil Rhodes as the territory was chartered to his British South Africa Company). As world-renowned Zimbabwean archaeologist Dr Webber Ndoro puts it, 'Neal and his rogues pillaged Great Zimbabwe and other Iron Age sites, taking gold and everything of value, tearing down structures and throwing away whatever was not valuable to them (pottery shards, pots and clay figurines).'[2] James Theodore Bent had also discarded 'clay and metal artifacts, including Persian and Arab trade beads, as insignificant' and his excavations at the site destroyed crucial evidence, making it more difficult to make sense of its age.

The Rhodesian Front Party, an all-white party led by Prime Minister Ian Smith, censored all books and material on Great Zimbabwe from 1965 until 1980, reflecting an attitude which Dr Webber Ndoro describes as being 'pervasive in colonialist Africa: the continent had no history, no sophistication; its people and tribes were unchanging, unable to develop, culturally barren'. A crucial aspect of white-settler propaganda was that they had appropriated empty tracts of land inhabited by people with no culture or history – *terra nullius*. Ian Smith's government instructed its employees 'that no official publication may state unequivocally that Great Zimbabwe was an African creation'.[3]

Dr Webber Ndoro, who has trained archaeologists and heritage managers throughout Africa, explains how, at the turn of the twentieth century, respected archaeologists such as David Randall-MacIver excavated Great Zimbabwe and concluded that it had been built by native Africans. Subsequent research by J. F. Schofield and Gertrude Caton-Thompson in the 1920s supported the theory of indigenous construction. However, most white settlers and visitors rejected such archaeological evidence.

Pressure was brought to bear on any archaeologist who demurred, leading to several departing from their posts in protest at the assault on their academic freedoms. Some white archaeologists who remained in the country, such as Helmut Silberberg, conceded that Great Zimbabwe had been built by Africans, but denigrated their achievement: 'it cannot possibly have been built by one of the famous old civilizations or any "civilization" worth of this appellation', Silberberg wrote in an article in 1978.[4]

Among the most prominent and vocal opponents of the white government's censorship was archaeologist Peter Garlake, who argued that the site had been built by the ancestors of the current inhabitants of the area. Garlake was forced into exile in 1970, after which he relocated to Nigeria and then London, before returning to Zimbabwe upon black majority rule in 1980.

The reality, as Garlake and others proved, is that Great Zimbabwe was a fundamentally African development. Its monuments were built of local raw materials by Africans according to age-old African styles of architecture. Great Zimbabwe has become the physical embodiment and expression of Zimbabwe's national identity, an image of a pre-colonial golden age. Indeed, in 1980 the country assumed the name Zimbabwe – meaning 'stone buildings' (*dzimba dzamabwe*) in the Shona language spoken by two-thirds of the country's population. At the independence celebrations the new president, Robert Mugabe, pledged to give the nation 'a new perspective, and indeed a new history and a new past'.

I was fortunate to enjoy the expert guidance of Professor Emeritus Ngwabi Bhebe, from Midlands State University, when I visited Great Zimbabwe. We mused on the scepticism about Great Zimbabwe's origins and how it connects to the outmoded beliefs that Africans somehow remained on the sidelines, spectators and observers to others making history.

According to Professor Bhebe, it is difficult to identify Great Zimbabwe's construction with one particular ethnic group from southern Africa, because constant patterns of migration meant populations were fluid. The original inhabitants of the region were the San and Khoikhoi. At the time of Great Zimbabwe's initial construction, the main community in southern Africa was the Bantu, who emigrated at different times from Central and West Africa and mixed with the local San. The people who built Great Zimbabwe were most likely the predecessors of the Bachwana, Shona or Nguni people. Some of the Nguni people were known as Zulus, others as Swazis, but they all had similar ancestry.

Leopard's Kopje, c. 900s

By the late tenth or early eleventh century, a culture known as Leopard's Kopje emerged. It would form the bedrock for kingdoms such as Great Zimbabwe. Leopard's Kopje was named after the site where it was first identified, in Zimbabwe about 25 kilometres from Bulawayo, and the culture covered parts of modern-day Zimbabwe, Zambia, South Africa, Mozambique, Malawi and Botswana.

From the tenth century, the remaining hunter-gatherers who used stone tools were either absorbed by agricultural communities or pushed out of the region. Most of the ethnic groups in southern Africa kept cattle, generating a 'cattle economy' that fostered conflict. Communities would seek to conquer others in order to acquire their cattle. They were a source and symbol of wealth: the bigger your herd, the richer and more powerful you were, so cattle were rarely slaughtered for food.

As well as tending to their livestock, people farmed and terraced hillsides to prevent the erosion of fertile soils. Food was plentiful, and southern Africa was known for its deposits of valuable metals such as gold – just as it is today. The same elites who owned lots of cattle would likely have forced people to go down the mines to obtain precious metals. Miners would dig shafts 30 metres deep or more, and young children were often deployed to venture further into the shafts. We know this because children's skeletons have been found in the mines.

However, much of the mining that was done in the early years was normally along riverbanks. When it rained, alluvial gold, iron and copper were exposed. People were adept at distinguishing an ordinary rock from a mineral that was worth taking.

Mapungubwe, 1075–1220

The Leopard Kopje culture reached its height in about 1075 at Mapungubwe in the northern part of modern-day South Africa. A network of stone settlements was established, each a power base for regional councillors. Ordinary people hunted and farmed, growing crops such as sorghum, millet and vegetables. But they were not allowed to venture up the remote and rugged hill at Mapungubwe, which was a sacred site occupied by the king and his household, who lived in comfortable houses made of clay. In order to reach the summit, holes were cut on both sides of a rock to anchor tree branches, which were used as a ladder to climb up and down the precipice. There was a system of sacred leadership, and the king or paramount chief had both religious and political authority over their citizens.

The elite grew rich from the sale of gold, copper and ivory, and we know that Mapungubwe traded with Arabia, India and even China, importing goods such as Indian cloth and Chinese ceramics (some, found at the site, date to the thirteenth and fourteenth centuries, notably Chinese porcelain teapots). The people at Mapungubwe also made their own exquisite objects, probably for royal use, such as a wooden rhino covered in gold leaf, a golden sceptre and a gold headdress that resembles an inverted bowl. The tombs of the rulers, high up on the sacred hills, containing their golden treasures, clay pots and beads, have been looted throughout the centuries, depriving archaeologists of vital evidence that could have expanded our knowledge of the civilisation.

Nevertheless it seems that Mapungubwe was the first stage in the development of the kingdom of Zimbabwe, laying down its important trading, economic and political

Some of the treasures at Mapungubwe

foundations. Mapungubwe lasted for the best part of a hundred years, and then at some point in the thirteenth century became absorbed by Great Zimbabwe, which lay 250 kilometres to the northeast.

Great Zimbabwe, 1100s–1450

The rulers of Great Zimbabwe built on the stonemasonry traditions of Mapungubwe and established elaborate settlements to display their wealth, power and prestige. The city itself is about 7 square kilometres, and is made up of three parts: the Hill Complex, the Great Enclosure and the Valley Ruins, the latter consisting of a number of dwellings, mostly made of mudbrick and wattle. Positioned between the goldfields of the western plateau and the Swahili trading post of Sofala

Great Zimbabwe

on the Indian Ocean coast in modern-day Mozambique, it was a fertile setting, and today it is still gorgeously verdant.

The city was most likely developed on a settlement that dated back to the sixth century, and archaeologists have found a number of iron tools and artefacts suggesting it was established by a metalworking population. At up to 1,100 metres above sea level, the area offered respite to both cattle and herders from being bitten by the tsetse fly, which transmits the dangerous disease sleeping sickness, making it an attractive location for settlers.

At its height in the fourteenth century, Great Zimbabwe may have had a population of 18,000. Professor Bhebe and I both felt dwarfed by the 7-metre-high Great Enclosure, which, uniquely for an African structure of its size, was built without mortar. I found it mind boggling as I walked around the vast stone complex that a staggering 1 million stone bricks weighing 15,000 tons were needed just for the main granite walls of the Great Enclosure. Circular in form, it was built in the fourteenth century, with carefully cut rocks used to maintain the shape of the construction. Inside the enclosure is a second set of walls, and as I made my way along the narrow passageways of their inner confines I felt cocooned by the weight of history. What a feat of construction this must have been! At the end of the Great Enclosure is a stone tower about 10 metres high, which may have been used as a royal granary. I climbed up the steep stone steps of the Hill Complex, the oldest part, dating originally from perhaps the tenth century. As in the Leopard Kopje culture, as if to emphasise their superiority the kings resided high up in a stone palace, away from their subjects down below.

The earliest written description of Great Zimbabwe probably comes from the Portuguese sea captain Vicente Pegado in 1531:

Among the gold mines of the inland plains between the Limpopo and Zambezi rivers, [there is a] fortress built of stones of marvellous size and there appears to be no mortar joining them . . . This edifice is almost surrounded by hills, upon which are others resembling it in the fashioning of stone and the absence of mortar, and one of them is a tower more than 12 fathoms high. The natives of the country call these edifices 'Symbaoe', which according to their language signifies court . . . When and by whom these edifices were raised, as the people of the land are ignorant of the art of writing, there is no record . . . In the opinion of the Moors who saw it, it is very ancient, and was built there to keep possession of the mines.[5]

Great Zimbabwe's location made it a thoroughfare for trade in gold and ivory from the interior of Africa to the southeastern coast, generating wealth and making it an important political and economic centre. A succession of rulers accumulated wealth through the taxation of trade as well as tributes in ivory, gold and food from local chiefs. Blacksmiths, metal smelters and workers fashioned tools and weapons from iron, and used gold and copper for more decorative artefacts and adornments. The kings of Great Zimbabwe asserted their dominance over their neighbours, increasing their wealth by forcing people to pay tributes, cementing their hold on power. Indeed, the kingdom had about 150 ancillary fiefdoms.

Little is known about the exact belief systems at Great Zimbabwe, but people most likely pursued traditional African beliefs and worshipped gods through the intercession of the king. According to Shona legend, only kings can communicate with royal ancestors, who take the form of crocodiles during their passage through deep pools to the spirit world.

The kings of Great Zimbabwe were therefore not seen as mere mortals by their subjects, but as possessing spiritual and priestly powers. The kings would have presided over religious ceremonies assisted by priests and traditional dancers, and would have been expected to intercede with the rain god in particular, as their citizens' livelihoods depended on rain-fed agriculture.

It is believed that about eight consecutive kings occupied the compound at Great Zimbabwe with their armies and close relatives. Below in the Great Enclosure were the quarters of the senior wife, who lived with her own entourage and children. The kings were polygamous, and whichever wife was on conjugal duty would ascend the hill to spend a lofty night or two with the king.

King Mutota, r. *c.* 1420s–50s

One of the kings of Great Zimbabwe, Nyatsimba Mutota, who probably reigned there in the 1420s, is believed to have had 200 wives and no doubt a great number of children, though Professor Bhebe could not verify this! Mutota decided to leave Great Zimbabwe in the late 1420s or early 1430s, and accompanied by his people and a very large army travelled north to the Dande region. Professor Bhebe related how Mutota had left in search of salt, which was an extremely valuable commodity and was consumed in huge quantities, leading to a shortage. Mutota's army was so big that it was likened in oral tradition to 'a plague of locusts'. It travelled through various territories, defeating communities such as the Tonga and Tavara along the way. Mutota settled at Chita-kochangonya Hill in northern Zimbabwe and established a new independent kingdom called Mutapa. Over the following years Great Zimbabwe was eclipsed politically and economically by Mutapa and the striking stone edifices that had been the beating heart of the civilisation were abandoned and deserted by 1450.

Mutota gave up on Great Zimbabwe for a number of reasons, including the depletion of natural resources, which meant that trade routes gradually shifted northwards. Traders were mostly dealing with people in the Zambezi Valley, and if Mutota wanted to maintain his control of trade he would also have to shift to the north. Furthermore, the kingdom became a victim of its own wealth; the massive herds of Great Zimbabwe had overgrazed the land. As a result, many cattle keepers moved southwards out of their overpopulated settlements to an area south of the Limpopo River, drawing the curtain of history on Great Zimbabwe and paving the way for the Mutapa Kingdom to become the dominant force in the region.

The Mutapa Kingdom (sometimes called Monomotapa), c. 1450–1629

King Mutota settled among the Shona people around the Mazoe valley in the province of Tete in modern-day Mozambique, giving him a supply of gold. He became 'Lord of the Metals' and, with his son Matope, quickly established control over the northern Shona. Mutota took the title of Mwene Mutapa, meaning 'Conqueror' or 'Master Pillager', which gives us an idea of how he vanquished communities and gained territory. This became the title for subsequent rulers of Mutapa. Mutota's new kingdom, which in time stretched across portions of modern-day South Africa, Zimbabwe, Lesotho, Eswatini (formerly Swaziland), Mozambique, Namibia, Botswana and Zambia, was rich in agricultural resources and was well positioned to take advantage of trade both on the coast and further inland. Mutota governed through a system of vassalage, divided among vassal lords known as 'fumos', as well as chiefs. He appointed the fumos from among his relatives, favourite advisers and generals, and they stayed in post for as long as it pleased him.

As Father Monclaro, a missionary from the Fathers of the Company of Jesus, who visited the kingdom around the 1560s wrote: 'The greater part of this [empire] is governed by fumos and petty rulers and though it has powerful kings whom it obeys, it nevertheless has these fumos and headmen by whom the people are governed.'[6]

Several of these positions became hereditary and even survived the later collapse of the kingdom. The fumos would be present at the Mwene Mutapa's court during special occasions such as festivals and ceremonies and their sons might work at court as messengers or similar posts. Mutota had to ensure the loyalty of his fumos so he gave his appointees land that was exempt from tributes and afforded them the right to use labourers.

In time the Mwene Mutapas forged alliances with some of the fumos and even entrusted them with monitoring long-distance trade in their areas. Ultimately they won themselves relative autonomy. They were tasked with running the territories on behalf of the king, supplying him with soldiers, maintaining law and order, and administering justice. Mutota promoted economic ties with neighbouring settlements and boosted their wealth. One such beneficiary was Ingombe Ilede in modern-day Zambia near the border with Zimbabwe – about 150 kilometres north of the capital Lusaka. The site of Ingombe Ilede is picturesque. Lying close to Lake Kariba on a hill by the confluence of the Zambezi and Lusitu rivers, it means the 'sleeping cow' in the local Tonga language, because a fallen baobab tree at the location looks like a cow lying down – from a certain angle! Archaeologists have discovered textiles, ceramics, copper ore and gold at Ingombe Ilede, dating from the seventh to the sixteenth centuries, suggesting that the area was the site of a small commercial state or chiefdom whose principal item of trade is presumed to have been salt. However, Ingombe Ilede really flourished through commercial links with the Mutapa kingdom in the fifteenth century.

The unity and continuation of the kingdom depended on the Mwene Mutapas' popularity, diplomacy and wisdom. They were more interested in dominating trade, and their power derived from that rather than from the political control of their territories. Surrounding states were encouraged to join Mutapa voluntarily, in exchange for a position on the Great Council of the kingdom. To his subjects, the kingship of the Mwene Mutapa was divine in nature: he was 'Lord of the Sun and the Moon, King of the Land and the Rivers and Conqueror of Enemies'. He owned the land, which could only be exploited with his permission.

The Mutapa kingdom did not necessarily operate on the basis of primogeniture: a favoured junior son could be designated heir by his father and a successor could be barred if he had a physical disability such as blindness or a disease such as leprosy. Whenever a new Mutapa was installed, the 'fire ritual' was held: old fires were extinguished and fresh ones lit to receive the new Mutapa, symbolising the passage of power.

The riches of the Mutapa kingdom caught the attention of Europeans. First to notice were the Portuguese, who had arrived in southern Africa in the late fifteenth century. Stories about the abundance of mineral wealth in Mutapa were widely known in Portugal, and in 1505 the Portuguese set up trading posts on the Indian Ocean coast of Africa at Sofala and began expanding trade in the region. They were also interested in finding sailing routes to India. Initially the Portuguese paid the rulers of Mutapa for the use of their trade routes, but then they took control of trade from Swahili merchants from East Africa and forced the Mwene Mutapa to trade with them instead.

The Africans were exposed to new products, as the Portuguese brought cloth, beads and other items from India and also introduced maize, which is widely consumed in Africa to this day. Mutapa developed a comparatively strong relationship with the Portuguese, and an enthusiastic exchange of goods and ideas developed by the 1560s. Ominously, however, as time went by the Portuguese became frustrated by restrictions on their trade activities and, spurred on by the killing of a Jesuit in Mutapa in the 1560s, invaded in 1571. They were quickly defeated by disease, drought and determined resistance from the locals, and so the Mutapa kingdom ended the sixteenth century as the dominant power in the region.

Nevertheless, a conflict of interests had been exposed, which pointed forward to European domination. The Mwene Mutapa decided it would be wise to reach an agreement with the Portuguese and so they were allowed access to the region's resources. Increasingly, the Portuguese exploited these and then took over the management of long-distance trade under the auspices of Mutapa.

At first, the markets where transactions took place were supervised by Mutapa agents. The Portuguese captains and merchants had to obtain permission from the capital and the Mwene Mutapa himself to leave for the villages with their goods. They were required to approach the king barefooted, without weapons, and prostrate themselves before him. A 'captain of the gates' to the market would be chosen by Portuguese traders and formally presented to the king, who would bestow upon him a spear mounted on black wood about a metre long and a gold bracelet, symbols of jurisdiction. The captain of the gates would have to keep order in the market, facilitate fair trading by ensuring that measurements and weights were accurate, and collect all royal taxes.

There was no cash and chiefs would share surpluses of goods and produce within the community. Such largesse was a way to project their high standing and help them cultivate social relations. Throughout the fifteenth century, the Mwene Mutapas' authority was sovereign, but from the sixteenth century their power started to decline, so that by the late seventeenth century it had all but rotted away. Civil wars ensued, which led to some of Mutapa's rivals appealing to the Portuguese for military support, allowing them to exploit the unrest to their own advantage. In time, the Portuguese became power brokers and the Mutapa kings became their puppets. They had lost the respect of their citizens, rendering them incapable of maintaining law and order, and their kingdom soon disintegrated.

Changamire Dombo, r. 1684–95

Around the mid-1680s, a military leader called Changamire Dombo gained power over the Zimbabwean plateau. For more about him, I turned to Dr George Karekwaivanane, a young Zimbabwean historian who had recently moved to the University of Edinburgh in Scotland. He told me that Dombo, a man of great political cunning, was a skilled military strategist and one of those significant characters that are so often missing from our understanding of African history. Changamire was the title of the rulers of the Rozvi Empire.

Dombo was originally a humble herdsman who caught the attention of the Mutapa king and gained his favour. As a result he was granted a great deal of land, which he used to build a power base. But then he turned against his patron. Unhappy with the domination of the Portuguese and the Mutapa kings' subservience, he rebelled against the Mutapa kingdom, headed south, and conquered communities in a large area of southern Africa. Dombo established a new kingdom of his own, the Rozvi (1684–1830s), having defeated Mutapa in a battle in 1684. Dombo absorbed Mutapa into Rozvi and his influence extended over much of present-day Zimbabwe, northeastern South Africa, and parts of Mozambique and Botswana.

Changamire Dombo had an immense suspicion of foreign traders, and did not want to be overly reliant on commerce for his survival and wealth. He wanted his people to be independent and self-sufficient, and so he encouraged them to be active in farming, fishing, cattle rearing and hunting. Nevertheless, the Portuguese were a persistent, menacing presence; they had wasted no time in establishing several trading posts in his resource-rich territories. The scene was set for a clash.

Changamire Dombo's combined military and economic might earned him a fearsome reputation. He equipped his army with a variety of weapons: bows and arrows, daggers, shields, battle-axes and cudgels. One Portuguese source said the Rozvi fighters used the cudgel 'with such deadly accuracy they can throw it from a long distance away and the blow is almost always fatal'.[7] The Rozvi army was huge and its fighting effective, with its soldiers favouring close face-to-face combat. In 1684, Dombo's unconventional tactics helped him overcome the Portuguese at the battle for Mahungwe. Despite the heavy fatalities inflicted by superior Portuguese technology and firearms, Dombo rallied his men and at sunset the battle was undecided. At one o'clock in the morning, the Portuguese army found itself suddenly surrounded by the enemy; their African auxiliaries fled and Dombo merely had to pick up the booty.

In 1693, Changamire Dombo again routed the Portuguese and their African allies at Dambarare, where they had a trading fort, and he almost succeeded in seeing them off entirely from his kingdom. His soldiers were said to have supernatural powers that could kill their enemies, and a magic oil that could kill through touch.[8] Father Conceição called Dombo a 'most skilled wizard' and wrote: 'He was so wily and cunning that after being defeated by our arms he vanquished us with stratagems.'[9] Changamire Dombo forced the Portuguese to acknowledge him as the ruler of Rozvi and pay him tributes, and his control of his mineral-rich lands became absolute.

Dr Karekwaivanane concedes that the Portuguese had not been able to unleash the full force of their might on Changamire Dombo because they were preoccupied with their military engagement for dominance with the Omani Arabs along the Indian Ocean coast. Nevertheless, he insists this should not detract from Dombo's immense abilities as both a soldier and ruler. In 1695, suddenly, and at the peak of his powers, he died. His unexpected death meant the Rozvi kingdom was rocked by repeated succession disputes, which weakened it and made it vulnerable to invasion from other communities moving into the Zimbabwean plateau.

With their formidable opponent out of the picture, the Portuguese could now entrench themselves in the region. They built a fort in the late eighteenth century at Lourenço Marques, now Maputo, to defend their positions and interests.

In the Rozvi kingdom's wake rose the Gaza kingdom (1830–97), founded by Soshangane, also known as Manukuza, who ruled from 1821 to 1858. Soshangane had some success in weakening the Portuguese and was able to repel them on a number of occasions. He extended his new kingdom's borders across much of modern-day Mozambique, South Africa and parts of Zimbabwe, with his capital in what is now southern Mozambique.

By the time Soshangane's reign was ending, large numbers of young men had begun migrating to Kimberley in South Africa to work in the diamond mines there. This deprived Soshangane's successors of labour, revenue and a fighting force. By the 1880s, the Gaza kingdom had become so weak that in 1895 the Portuguese were able to defeat in battle the last king of Gaza, Soshangane's grandson, Ngungunhane (1850–1906). He was imprisoned and then deported to Portugal where he died in exile in 1906. Ngungunhane's body was repatriated after Mozambique gained its independence in 1975, and his remains have been housed in Maputo Fortress since 1985. I went there to see his burial chamber under the supervision of the fort curator Moises Timba. Moises told me the elaborately carved wooden coffin had been designed by a Mozambican sculptor, who had fashioned a likeness of Ngungunhane's face on the exterior. Moises was at pains to explain that although he had failed to see off the Portuguese, Ngungunhane was nevertheless a hero in the eyes of his people. He had not surrendered but had resisted occupation by a foreign force, refusing to sign a treaty with them to avoid the exploitation of his land and resources.

In the courtyard of the fort, besides the relics of canons on display, is a larger-than-life statue of a Portuguese general on horseback and a bronze wall relief, both commissioned by the Portuguese colonial government in the twentieth century. Ngungunhane is depicted with head bowed, a group of Portuguese soldiers in front and behind him, one brandishing a sword at his feet in a decisive gesture, indicating that Ngungunhane had been brought to heel. To me, he looked dignified but resigned to his fate, truly befitting his title 'the Lion of Gaza'. To the Portuguese he was a king humiliated and conquered; to his subjects he was a legend. After all, as a proverb from southern Africa says, 'When the lions have historians, then the hunters will cease to be heroes.'

As Dr George Karekwaivanane passionately described, the kingdoms of southern Africa were important civilisations. They were led by rulers who built diversified economies, sophisticated political systems and complex urban areas with impressive architecture such as that of Great Zimbabwe. These civilisations were made up of various ethnicities in southern Africa and so today provide cultural and historic connections between citizens of different African countries, as national boundaries in the modern era can separate communities who share common pasts and glories.

The teaching of this history has been neglected, but this is changing as younger generations in Africa demand a greater knowledge of their past. My travels through Zambia, Zimbabwe, Mozambique and South Africa, and my extensive conversations with people for this chapter, have convinced me of this thirst for information about their roots. People are so proud of their heritage. The recognition of Great Zimbabwe as a UNESCO World Heritage site in 1986 mattered enormously to Zimbabweans. Eight bird soapstone sculptures, recovered from Great Zimbabwe, have given Zimbabwe its national symbol, the Zimbabwe Bird, which features on the country's flag.

Despite the site's significance in the national psyche, Dr Webber Ndoro laments the lack of attention and resources that archaeology receives in Zimbabwe and across sub-Saharan Africa as a whole:

> It is clear that cultural legacies are being lost as monuments decay and artefacts are taken out of various countries. If contemporary cultures, fragmented and ruptured by centuries of colonialism, are going to be able to piece together and to reconnect with their severed past, archaeology will need to assume a more important place in African society.[10]

According to Dr Ndoro, there are only about ten archaeologists responsible for the preservation of Great Zimbabwe and all of the 35,000 other archaeological sites in the country – notably the hilltop Khami ruins of the Butua kingdom, established by the Torwa dynasty (*c.* 1450–1683) outside the city of Bulawayo, in southwestern Zimbabwe, which display some of the fine stonemasonry traditions of Great Zimbabwe.

In Zimbabwe, a nation wracked by misrule, corruption and widespread poverty, I should imagine that heritage champions such as Dr Ndoro have a tough time making the case for more investment in the preservation of cultural sites – understandable perhaps, but regrettable.

I recall an exchange with Professor Bhebe. I asked: 'When you were at school, in what was then Rhodesia, what were you taught about the people who built Great Zimbabwe?' He answered: 'Nothing at all. I was only taught about the activities of the white colonisers, missionaries and explorers.' 'So when did you find out about it?' I continued. 'When I became a professor of history, I must confess that it was relatively late in life . . . It was very exciting for me to teach students about the rise of Great Zimbabwe and other kingdoms.'

Professor Bhebe's comments are hardly surprising; he was born in 1942 and was schooled during the years of white rule. One of the most popular history textbooks at the time was T.R. Batten's *Tropical Africa in World History*. Most of it is dedicated to the Roman and British empires, with some history of ancient Egypt. When Batten eventually gets round to mentioning Africa, he expresses sentiments such as: 'no great civilisation began in tropical Africa. Nor did the people there learn very much from civilised peoples until quite recently.'[11]

Professor Bhebe is one of Africa's most distinguished historians, and has taught in several countries across the continent, publishing books and articles extensively and serving as chairperson of the University of Zimbabwe's history department. He also represented Zimbabwe on the UNESCO board preparing the *General History of Africa*, describing the task as 'one of the most successful and difficult international cooperation projects ever undertaken in the world': to teach African history from the perspective of Africans. Beaming in satisfaction, he declared himself 'proud to have been part of such a mission', and for my part I will be delighted if I can contribute to that same endeavour.

I 2

Asante Ascent: Osei Tutu and Abena Pokou

The Asante know how to throw a party. One of their most spectacular celebrations is the 'Akwasidae' festival. Held every six weeks on a Sunday in the grounds of the royal Manhyia Palace in Kumasi, the capital of Asanteland, it is dedicated to the memory and noble deeds of past kings, chiefs and queen mothers. An atmosphere of jubilation pervaded the area when I attended in 2019. Kings, princes, senior chiefs and royal Asante women decked out in sumptuous clothes, festooned with gold jewellery, made a grand entrance into the compound, to a chorus of hornblowers, drums and singers. Ordinary members of the Asante community milled around, eager to see the Asantehene, the 'king of kings', Osei Tutu II, who assumed the title in 1999, while also seizing the opportunity to catch up on the latest news. I watched rapt as a man bearing a large urn containing herbs on his head walked solemnly into the compound to clear the congregation of evil spirits; two others carried a collection of enormous ancient metal keys, symbolising the Asante-hene's arrival. Soldiers holding antique ceremonial muskets representing past Asante rulers served as a reminder that they were not only kings but also military leaders, and a man bearing silver caskets full of gold was on hand, should the Asantehene need to distribute it.

When I attended the Akwasidae there was extra security on account of two VIP guests, the then Prince Charles and his wife Camilla, the Duchess of Cornwall, who sat in a marquee with electric fans and air-conditioning units engaged in fierce battle with the scorching Ghanaian sun. The Akwasidae is one of the highest profile, most frequent and extravagant manifestations of African regal tradition, a precious example of an ancient, august African institution that has withstood the pressures of centuries of social change and the depredations of colonialism.

In Africa as elsewhere, culture and heritage are vitally important aspects of identity for forging a sense of nationhood. However, as the last chapter also showed, the arbitrary creation of modern African states, with illogical borders, obscures shared histories that transcend national boundaries. Indeed, the Asante have come to define a large part of the culture of two neighbouring West African countries, Ghana and Côte d'Ivoire.

Who are the Asante? They form part of the Guan ethnic group, itself part of a much larger community known as the Akan, who make up nearly half of the population of Ghana and a third of Côte d'Ivoire; they speak related languages with similar structure and vocabulary.

The origins of the Asante (sometimes called Ashanti) date back to between 8,000 and 10,000 years ago when people migrated in stages from the Chad region in Central Africa to West Africa. They crossed the lower Niger River and then went through present-day Benin and Togo and settled along riverbeds, rock shelters and caves, both in the open plains and in the forest belt, over an area stretching from central Liberia to beyond the lower Niger River. They survived by hunting, foraging and fishing.

Archaeological remains indicate that between 600 and 1100 CE they began to live in villages, and farmed crops such as yam, which is particularly rich in carbohydrates and so a valuable source of nutrition. They also utilised the palm fruit, which they cooked. The trunk of the palm tree was used for palm wine and its branches were handy for thatching huts. However, before they could farm, these settlers had to embark on the monumental mission of creating agricultural land by clearing large tracts of forest using only hand-axes and extreme perseverance. The open water holes and discarded farm products in agricultural villages became ideal breeding grounds for malaria-infected mosquitoes. Likewise, the roofs and eaves of thatched huts provided perfect conditions for the mosquitoes to lurk in during the day before emerging at night to glut their fatal appetites. Plenty fell victim to disease.

By about the seventh century CE, the population had gained a degree of protection from malaria through the emergence of the sickle cell gene. We do not know precisely when or how the sickle cell gene mutation took place, but if a child received the gene from both parents then it was very likely to die in childhood from sickle cell disease, a condition where unusually shaped red blood cells do not carry enough oxygen and can block blood vessels. However, if a child did not inherit the sickle cell gene at all, then there was a big risk they would die from malaria. The best situation was to inherit the gene from just one parent; a child would then have a large measure of immunity against malaria, without the health complications from sickle cell disease. Even today people of West African descent can carry the sickle cell gene.

Notwithstanding the scourge of malaria – the biggest killer disease in history – by the twelfth century the Guan people were well settled in a forest and savannah environment straddling the middle and southern parts of Côte d'Ivoire and the coastal parts of Ghana.

From around 1200, kingdoms were already taking shape. Power among the Akan was typically matrilineal, inherited through the female line. One common explanation for this is that the identity of mothers is certain, unlike that of fathers. Until the fifteenth century, when clans were still isolated and autonomous, the founders and rulers of kingdoms would have been queens. This gradually changed as greater interaction between groups and rival kingdoms brought about more armed conflicts. The word 'Asante' means 'because of war' and originated at a time when several communities came together in a union. The elders said they were uniting because if there was a war their combined strength would be advantageous. Men were judged better suited to govern during conflicts on account of their physical strength, and so kings replaced queens as rulers. Moreover, women were required to focus on repopulating communities that had lost men in combat by bearing and raising sons who could become future soldiers. Although queens no longer reigned directly, the matrilineal system of succession was preserved, and the most important king would be chosen from the eligible candidates by the queen mother and senior chiefs.

At the Akwasidae, I spoke to a prominent female member of the Asante royal family, Nana Rawlings, a former first lady of Ghana, and author of a 2018 book called *It Takes a Woman* about the role of women in her country. 'For us it takes a queen to make a king,' she said with a chuckle. 'The king is important, but the queen mother has the power to mobilise support, to decide who is king, and she also provides wise counsel and guidance on how to govern.' I asked if she herself dispensed advice to the Asantehene, Osei Tutu II, who is her first cousin, and she nodded vigorously. 'As chancellor of the Kwame Nkrumah University of Science and Technology, he wants to improve the quality of life in Asanteland and to encourage investment in the region, and I back him in all his efforts.'

The Asante believe a person inherits his mother's blood and his father's spirit. So, while a father is important, his significance is trumped by the mother. Sexual relations between any blood relatives are forbidden. In modern Asante culture the queen mother and the wives and daughters of the king are still vested with considerable power, and the birth of a daughter is welcomed with delight in royal circles. Nana Rawlings told me how, whenever she goes back home to Asanteland and enquires about a recent birth in the extended family, people respond with a cry of 'Oh, how fantastic it is a girl.' What a contrast to the male primogeniture system in many other royal and noble circles where the first-born son was traditionally the heir. In Europe, the lack of a son meant thrones and estates could be inherited by distant male relatives to the detriment of the deceased's daughters; indeed, this centuries-old practice still endures in many countries today. For example, male primogeniture exists for the succession of the emperor of Japan, the king of Thailand and most British hereditary peerages, although the practice was abolished for the British monarchy in 2011.

The Asante, like other Akan groups, worked and traded in gold. The precious metal came from forests and savannahs, in reefs, sand and river gravel. Peasant farmers obtained alluvial gold from the river, especially after flooding, when floodwaters washed earth down hills and made it easier to pan for nuggets and grains of gold. They sold the gold to passing Akan traders, who were often agents of local rulers. These traders used the gold to buy a range of goods, including cloth and metal. Even remote villages were part of this network. Between the eleventh and early seventeenth centuries, West Africa provided the international community with its biggest supply of gold, and at its peak during the seventeenth century it accounted for almost two-thirds of world production, around 1.2 tons a year. The Asante not only traded gold, but also accumulated vast reserves of it in their treasury, giving them the means to buy substantial quantities of European weapons and ammunition from coastal traders. This, along with their military acumen gave them a decisive edge over their rivals, the Aowin and Denkyira, so that by the seventeenth century the Asante kingdom was firmly dominant.

Osei Tutu, c. 1660–1717

Osei Tutu is enshrined in Asante oral tradition as the founder of their nation. He was a charismatic, ambitious and warlike ruler of an Asante clan, the Okoyo. Having gained control over a trading centre near Kumasi in Asanteland, he grouped other clan chiefs around him and used this as his base to conquer surrounding Akan chiefdoms. His authority grew as he gained the backing of key religious figures: priests were important social leaders in Akan culture and provided a crucial source of support and legitimacy for a ruler. The Asante practised an indigenous African religion, primarily worshipping a god who resided in Lake Bosomtwe, Ghana's only natural lake, about 40 kilometres from Kumasi. Osei Tutu benefited enormously from his alliance with one influential priest: Okomfo Anokye – the Great Prophet.

According to folklore, Okomfo Anokye assembled all the Akan kings and decreed that whoever received a gift from the heavens would be the paramount king. He prayed multiple times that it would fall to his friend, Osei Tutu. A golden stool then appeared from the sky and landed at Osei Tutu's feet. The stool became known as the 'Sika Dwa Kofi', meaning 'the Golden Stool born on a Friday', and Okomfo Anokye granted its custody to Osei Tutu and his successors. According to oral tradition, Okomfo Anokye told Osei Tutu: 'If this is ever captured or destroyed, then just as a man sickens and dies without his soul, so will the Asante lose their power and disintegrate into chaos.' To this day the Golden Stool is the ultimate symbol of Asante kingship in which the soul of the Asante nation resides. The stool is so precious to the Asante that when a king is crowned he is said to be 'enstooled'. It is carried to him on a pillow, since only the Asantehene can hold it, and the king, with his courtiers' support, touches the Golden Stool three times with his rear, but does not sit on it. The stool is still central in Asante culture. Every Asante family should possess a stool, usually made of wood. A father presents his son with a stool as his first gift and a wife gives her husband one upon marriage. A chief inherits his stool from his predecessor, and it is always preferred that a chief dies on his stool. Presumably once it was known that a chief's demise was imminent, he would somehow be placed on it!

Although Osei Tutu was the most powerful ruler of the Akan in the late 1600s, his federation was still a loose grouping of chiefdoms. The Asante, like many other African peoples, have a tradition of praise songs and poems. Oral tradition relates how some of Osei Tutu's opponents challenged his efforts to conquer them by asking: 'What did you come to do?'

Osei Tutu would boldly answer: 'I serve nobody. I have heard your [message]. So what?'

The highest glory in Asanteland came from victory in war. Osei Tutu notched up success after success on the battlefield and in one major war to the southwest, in about 1700, he defeated Denkyira, a rich and mighty Akan state. Okomfo Anokye was considered to have been instrumental in this conquest. According to the account written by a nineteenth-century Asantehene, Prempeh I (of whom more in the next chapter), the priest worked his 'magic' to the advantage of the much smaller Asante army:

> All the soldiers of the Ashanti kingdom cannot be compared to the smallest wing of the Denkyira kings, so I will change the mind of half of their armies in such a way that, during the fight, half of them will come to you [Ashantis] and the other half – I will discourage them so that you will be able to fight and defeat them . . . I will surely make you defeat the enemy.[1]

It was an iconic victory and one which left the Asante as the dominant Akan power. The power of the Golden Stool is expressed in a special invocation which the king makes during the Odwira festival:

> Stool of Kings, I sprinkle water upon you, may your power return sharp and fierce. Grant that when I and another meet [in battle] – grant [that] it be as when I met Denkyira; you let me cut off his head . . . May the nation prosper. May the women bear children. May the hunters kill meat. We who dig for gold, let us get gold to dig, and grant that I get some for the upkeep of my kingship.[2]

By the following year, Osei Tutu had overcome local opposition in 70 realms. He united these domains into one kingdom and established his capital at Kumasi, assuming the title Asantehene, 'king of kings'. Today in Kumasi, which is about 250 kilometres north of the capital Accra, a statue of the priest Okomfo Anokye in a short white tunic presides over a roundabout on a busy matrix of roads in the heart of the city. Holding aloft the Golden Stool, he is a perpetual reminder to all visitors of how the Asante kingdom was founded. Kumasi was a suitable location for Asanteland's capital because it was located on the edge of the rainforest, allowing access to both forest and savannah, and it was well situated between the commercial routes linking the coast to the interior. This allowed Osei Tutu to control the trading ports as well as most of the goldfields of the forest.

As I observed at the Akwasidae, the Asante kings and the elite have become associated with the lavish use of gold jewellery: necklaces, rings, bracelets, ankle and toe rings, often styled in the shape of animals. Osei Tutu, like his successors, used his gold royal regalia to inspire awe and majesty. Gold craftsmen were lionised in Asante culture and the king's considerable collection was guarded by a chief gold-keeper. The king had his own artisans and whatever style they crafted for him could not be reproduced for anyone else. He would wear gold breastplates and the sheaths of his ceremonial weapons were decorated with gold. The gold mask of the Asantehene Kofi Karikari (*c.* 1837–84) is rare in having survived, for gold objects were melted down and reused, meaning much of the jewellery of the Asante kings has been lost. Asante jewellery is freighted with meaning. For instance, jewels for a funeral might include symbols to ward off evil spirits and allow the safe passage of the deceased. Human and animal figures sometimes represent popular Asante proverbs; for example, one gold weight is fashioned in the form of a cartridge belt to represent the saying: 'The cartridge belt of Akowua [a famous Asante soldier] has never been known to lack bullets' – meaning a person can use their wits to get out of difficult circumstances.

Osei Tutu's kingdom had such a powerful cultural reso-nance that it has become one of the best known in Africa. His leadership was based on a concept of 'divine kingship'; a king's sovereignty was sanctioned by the priesthood, and not prescribed to him by godly divine right. Osei Tutu came to embody the identity of the whole nation, which revelled in his heroic deeds. Praise poems dedicated to him and handed down through oral tradition usually began with 'Behold the Great One!' A contemporary praise poem lauded him thus:

> The king is above all a hero. A hero is above all things, a fighter. As a fighter he is fearsome and fearless. He is of great strength and nimble in his movements. He is a supreme strategist; ruthless, capable of great mental and physical endurance; unpredictable; dependable and pitiless. He is a jealous guardian of his own, but generous to his servants and he can inspire even the weak to great deeds. As a tri-umphant warrior trailing tribulation in the wake of his ceaseless wars, the king must expect and be able to endure calumny and hatred . . . Man among men. Hero. Royal of Royals. The king is the embodiment of the highest virtues, and these are essentially those of the soldier.[3]

Backed by military strength, Osei Tutu developed a con-stitutional, political and financial administrative structure through which to govern. He brought together all the kings and chiefs into one council under his leadership. It was not a meritocratic system; a person could only be vested with influ-ence if they bore the correct rank and met the king's approval. All those who held authority were elders, and a common challenge within court circles was: 'What right do you have to participate in public affairs?'

Osei Tutu divided his Asante kingdom into metropolitan and provincial parts. The metropolitan consisted of all the former states within a 70-kilometre radius of the capital Kumasi. These were represented by their own leaders on the council, which was the governing body of the Asante confederation. The conquered kingdoms, reduced to vassal states, made up provincial or Greater Asante. They had no representation on the council nor access to the Asantehene. If they paid their annual tribute and participated in wars fought by the Asante they were accorded autonomous status in return. The chiefs of the provinces collected taxes from villages and were obliged to share the earnings with Osei Tutu. Each married villager also had to pay a tax. Osei Tutu further benefited from the judicial system in which, if a person was found guilty of a crime, they would have to pay a fine in gold. They could also buy their acquittal. Perhaps less reasonably, even if a person was found innocent, they would be expected to make an offering in gratitude for the verdict! The chiefs of provincial Asante also gave Osei Tutu some of the gains from their goldfields and provided him with soldiers.

Notwithstanding the folklore attached to the origins and customs of the Asante kingdom, and the praise poems sung in Osei Tutu's honour, in 1717 the Akyem dared to challenge him. The Akyem were an Akan forest people, located in what is today southeastern Ghana, who had broken away from Asante during the period of its formation as a centralised kingdom – the name Akyem means 'breakaway'. A war ensued between the two and, by now an elderly combatant in his late fifties, Osei Tutu was killed. A contemporary Dutch account noted: 'there were reports of a great lack of food in the Ashantee [sic] army and a considerable mortality among them from smallpox, attended by the death of their Head

Chief, which caused them to decide to avoid battle with the Akims and to retire quietly'.[4]

Osei Tutu was succeeded by his nephew, Opoku Ware I, who had to contend with the fact that the Asante's military prestige had suffered a major blow after the war with the Akyem. Rival Akan states such as the Aowin in the south-west and the coastal Fante became emboldened by the defeat and launched battles against the Asante. Around 1718–19 the Aowin sacked Kumasi and returned home with booty and captives, including members of the royal family. Opoku Ware fought on with such resolution and assiduity that by the end of his long reign, in 1750, he had succeeded in expanding the boundaries of Asanteland until it included most of modern-day Ghana.

During these eighteenth-century wars of conquest, the Asante rulers did sell their captives as enslaved people to Europeans and North Africans, but they were not economically dependent on the trade, as they still derived their wealth primarily from the sale of gold, and benefited enormously from their solid agricultural base. In the early 1800s a British envoy, Thomas Bowdich, described the richly decorated court of the Asantehene Osei Bonsu:

> the royal stool, entirely cased in gold, was displayed under a splendid umbrella, with drums, sankos [similar to a harp], horns, and various musical instruments, cased in gold, about the thickness of cartridge paper; large circles of gold hung by scarlet cloth from the swords of state, the sheaths as well as the handles of which were also encased ... various attendants were adorned with large stars, stools, crescents, and gossamer wings of solid gold.[5]

Kente Cloth

Apart from their extravagant use of gold, the Asante are also renowned for arguably the most famous cloth in Africa: kente, which was originally worn only by Asante royalty, including Osei Tutu. Kente literally means 'whatever happens to it, it will not tear'. Traditionally it has been woven by men and the cloth can be single, double or triple woven. Its colour and design indicate status and clan allegiance, and it is not cheap, with one garment costing the equivalent of hundreds of US dollars. Every colour has its own purpose: during funerals, mourners wear red or black kente, which denotes that the wearer is in mourning; on a happy occasion, such as a marriage or a child's naming ceremony, the Asante wear kente that has a white background with a decorative weave predominantly in white. On an ordinary day, kente in any colour can be worn. Designs have varying names. 'My heart's desire', for instance, can be bought by a bridegroom for his bride. The tradition of naming patterns continues, and one is called 'Queen Elizabeth' after the late British queen, while another is called 'Clinton', following a visit to Ghana by the former US president. Senior chiefs can wear a kente cloth with symbols of eyes, meaning they are the eyes of the Asantehene and keep watch over his interests. Asante kings commission the best designers to make special kente cloth for them, whose pattern cannot be replicated for anyone else to wear. The first multicoloured kente was made for Opoku Ware. It dates to 1720 and is wrapped around the body like a toga. Kente cloth is popular with many African Americans – including former first lady Michelle Obama – who wear it to demonstrate their links with the continent of their ancestors.

The Akwasidae

At the Akwasidae, I met up with local historian Osei Bonsu. We waited for the Asantehene and scrambled for the best vantage point as he entered the compound. His enormous headdress made of eagle feathers represented his power. The Asantehene and his chiefs dress to impress. They don their most elaborate regalia and march in to a drumbeat. The Asante used a talking drum or *atumpan* as a means of communication: everyone would understand the meaning of the drumming and, if necessary, act on its message. Osei Tutu II, flanked by numerous attendants, made his way slowly through the adoring throngs, acknowledging well-wishers as he went. I managed to get a good view of him. I saw a tall, handsome middle-aged man, his multicoloured robe fastened over one shoulder, his black headdress decorated in gold stars and crescents perched atop his head, with a chunky gold ring on his right hand. A vast parasol, held high by an assistant, cast shade over him. The king began to exchange gifts ceremoniously with his chiefs. If the Asantehene has matters of state to discuss, then he will gather his chiefs around him, and sitting on a wooden stool embossed in gold, listen to their deliberations and offer his pronouncements. His word, naturally, is final.

The chiefs were, like the Asantehene, also under the cover of enormous parasols to shield them from the intense heat of the sun. The use of parasols or umbrellas has been popular for centuries in Asante royal circles. After Osei Tutu I's victory over other Akan kingdoms, he was given an umbrella by a Dutch official and a few years later the Dutch presented him with an Indian umbrella lined with calico. In 1707 Sir Dalby Thomas, a British merchant and writer, urged the

Osei Tutu II

English to send the Asante umbrellas of 'scarlet cloth, embroidered, lined and well fringed. A bird or beast on top of the stick. The umbrella to be made to play up and down the stick, for their way of managing them is by turning them round and round and laying them up and down, which is, as I suppose to give air to the person that goes under them'.[6] Later in the 1820s, Thomas Bowdich attended a reception in Kumasi and noticed that 'at least a hundred large umbrellas, or canopies, which could shelter thirty persons, were sprung up and down by the bearers with brilliant effect, being made of scarlet, yellow, and the most shewy [sic] cloths and silks'.[7] In time, the Asante developed the craft of making their own umbrellas or canopies and Bowdich recorded that there was an umbrella-making village just northwest of the Asantehene's palace.

As, finally, the dignitaries departed amid the same commotion that their arrival had generated, I reflected on Osei Tutu I's achievement: an accomplished military strategist, he had established a wealthy kingdom and governed it through an efficient and elaborate bureaucratic system of his own design. But along the way, he also laid the foundations for cultural practices that are gloriously undiminished by the passage of centuries.

Abena Pokou, c. *1720s–60*

The wars associated with the rise of Osei Tutu's kingdom caused a great number of Akan people to flee into the forests of what is today Côte d'Ivoire, as they sought to escape his mighty army – propelled at times by a need to avoid capture and perhaps enslavement in the transatlantic trade, the subject of Chapter 14.

After the death of Opoku Ware I in 1750, another notable migration took place, led by an Asante princess called Abena (meaning Tuesday-born female) Pokou, who was Opoku Ware's sister and hence the niece of Osei Tutu I. When Opoku Ware I died, a struggle for succession broke out in Kumasi. The Asantehene should have been succeeded by his younger brother but an uncle from a different part of the royal family staked his claim to the Golden Stool with the vital support of the council of elders. Together they launched a brutal military expedition against Abena Pokou's branch of the family, killing her brother, mother and cousins. Her husband had died in an ambush, leaving her widowed with a young son. Abena Pokou was the only senior survivor of her clan and so she was appointed its leader. Seeing that it would be futile to try to take on the powerful new Asantehene, she gathered her supporters in secret and hatched a plan to leave Asanteland in the dead of the night when her foes would be sleeping. Dozens of men, women and children, and a few soldiers, ventured northwest into the unknown with Abena Pokou at their head. As they marched on their long journey, villagers deserted their homes and joined them on the walk to liberty. Assailed by sickness, attacked by wild beasts and deadly insects, and pursued by the Asantehene's men, the group arrived at the Komoé River. On their side of the bank was Asanteland, across the river was freedom: territory that lay outside the Asante kingdom's domains.

But calamity struck: rain had swelled the river's waters and it was flowing in torrents. Unable to swim across the cascades, Abena Pokou and her party stopped at the river's edge, at a loss. The Asante king's men were not far behind and were bound to kill them. So, in keeping with Asante practice in times of peril, Abena Pokou sought the advice of a priest in her entourage. According to oral tradition, he told her that the spirit of the river was demanding an offering in exchange for safe passage. Abena Pokou asked the priest if they could give him some of the provisions they were carrying: kola nuts, palm oil, palm wine, chickens and oxen. The soothsayer mulled this over and then pronounced that the river god wanted something more valuable than food. Upon hearing this all the women in the group removed their gold and ivory jewellery and the men opened their boxes displaying the treasures inside, in the hope this would appease the god. The priest considered this propitiation, but rejected it, for not even these were their most precious possessions.

Then came the shocking news: the priest conveyed the sombre message that the river god was demanding the sacrifice of a boy. Silence fell upon the group. No woman offered to surrender her child. Abena Pokou hoped that perhaps a sickly boy, close to death, might be presented, but she was met with a wall of silence. She knew that time was pressing and that the king's men could not be far. It was a grim choice: either they all succumbed to the enemy or one child, who would be killed in any case, could be sacrificed. Perhaps knowing that her own royal son – not yet three – would be the first to be slain alongside herself, Abena Pokou handed him over to the priest. The soothsayer took the infant, uttered a prayer and then threw him into the water. The river almost immediately became calm, allowing Abena Pokou and her followers to swim across it. Other oral accounts state that after the child's sacrifice, a huge tree bent its branches across the river, so that people could step over the water. Once the last person had reached the other side, it is said the tree straightened and the river became turbulent once more. A short time after Abena Pokou and her group had reached safety, the king's soldiers arrived at the river. Frustrated with their inability to swim across, they abandoned their murderous mission.

Meanwhile, a relieved but grieving Abena Pokou and her party paid homage to their ancestors and commemorated the death of the boy that had brought them salvation. They settled in Sikasso, just north of Yamoussoukro, the capital of modern-day Côte d'Ivoire. When Abena Pokou was asked by her people what the name of their new state would be, she replied 'Baoule', meaning 'the child is dead'. The sacrifice she had made would forever be linked with the kingdom she had founded.

Abena Pokou became the first queen of the Baoule kingdom and ruled with courage and wisdom. She wanted her subjects to be self-sustaining and so she ensured that the land was properly cultivated. She laid down a highly centralised political, administrative and social structure, remarkable for its blending of Akan traditions with those of their new home. Abena Pokou established a leadership role for women, who could reach the highest positions as chiefs and rule as queens. The system of succession was a matrilineal one; when Abena Pokou died in about 1760, she was succeeded by her niece, who expanded the kingdom of Baoule, making it one of the most significant communities in the region. In the years to come, Baoule became less centralised and split into smaller chiefdoms. Abena Pokou is still a highly revered figure who commands respect and affection across West Africa. On my journeys in Côte d'Ivoire, I frequently came across depictions of her in statues and pictures, and in conversations it was evident that her name evokes memories of heroism and self-sacrifice.

Today, there are more than 60 ethnic groups in Côte d'Ivoire, most of which have ethnic and cultural links with groups living in surrounding nations, just as we saw in the previous chapter. The migration story of Abena Pokou illustrates a common feature of most African populations: that national borders drawn up during the nineteenth century by colonial Europeans divided peoples with a shared history and heritage. Few, including myself, would argue for a redrawing of these borders. What is done is done, and Africans must look to the present and future.

Dr Kodzo Gavua of University of Ghana goes further in this argument: while in favour of maintaining traditions such as the Akwasidae, he told me:

Communities in Ghana and elsewhere in Africa have mixed and remixed over a long period of time and subdividing ourselves on the basis of ethnicity and tribes will not help us move forward, because we face common challenges as Ghanaians and Africans. Differences are celebrated by those who wield power because it serves their cause to do so. It rallies people around, but for what purpose? Just to have a big celebration – what does that translate to? Identity without improving standards of living becomes meaningless. I am part Ewe and part Asante, but I am Ghanaian; I have to think about my nation and ultimately I am just an African.

Dr Gavua presented an interesting conundrum: what does the preservation of identity, culture and traditions mean if it does not result in making people's lives better? I believe that Africans can be proud of their heritage and revel in their traditions, without allowing ethnicity to hinder nation building. Each African country constitutes a 'multicultural community of communities' where differences can be celebrated, not used to polarise and divide. Dr Gavua is right that ethnic differences must have no place in political, social and economic decision making, and he calls for fellow feeling beyond ethnic divisions and pride in a shared history. As we will see in the next chapter, every Ghanaian, Asante or not, was encouraged by the first leader of an independent Ghana, Kwame Nkrumah, to draw pride from the achievements of one outstanding Asante woman who took on the forces of imperialist Britain.

13

Asante Courage: Prempeh and Yaa Asantewaa

As we have explored, in the 1700s the Asante kingdom was the dominant power in a region that extended beyond the borders of modern Ghana. In the late eighteenth century it underwent a further period of consolidation and centralisation. The Asantehene Osei Kwadwo, who ruled from 1764 to 1777, introduced a more cohesive system of administration. He abolished the federation of chiefdoms, and instead officials were appointed or promoted on merit rather than by birth. Hereditary chiefs also saw a reduction in their financial power; much of the provincial collection of taxation was removed from their control and transferred to officials judged on their capability. The army too was restructured and centralised. Asante kings continued with the campaigns of conquest, piling up ever more wealth through the first decades of the nineteenth century.

Kumasi in the nineteenth century was a masterpiece of urban planning, its wide streets swept regularly and always kept clean and tidy. I visited one typical Asante home from the nineteenth century, just outside the city centre. Now a museum, it has features common to the period: a steeply pitched thatched roof, walls made of mud plastered onto a timber frame, which was painted white; the lower parts of the walls an attractive terracotta hue, decorated with geometrical designs.

The palace complex was in the centre of the city and was made up of intricate passageways and courtyards. The palace roofs were topped with brass, the windows and doors were plated in gold and the doorposts and pillars were made of ivory. One account by the British historian and explorer William Winwood Reade in 1874 described the upper rooms as containing rows of 'Books in many languages, Bohemian glass, clocks, silver plates, old furniture, Persian rugs, Kidderminster carpets, paintings and sculptures, numberless chests and coffers. A sword bearing the inscription "From Queen Victoria to the King of Ashantee".[1] There were plenty of rooms in the palace for the Asantehene, his family and concubines, as well as offices for his officials.

Asanteland's agricultural sector was thriving; captives were put to work as farm labourers, helping to produce food in abundance, and they traded with the Portuguese and then the British, who had been present since the early 1800s in this part of West Africa. The British wanted to diminish the Asante hold on coastal trade, and rejected Asante claims on coastal areas ruled by the Fante. Despite the best efforts of the Asante, the Fante had maintained their sovereign existence during the eighteenth century by utilising diplomacy. The Fante had formed into independent states as far back as the tenth century, moving to the central region of modern-day Ghana, from where they then dispersed along the Cape Coast, organising their matrilineal societies around chieftaincies and councillors under a constitution. The Fante tried to extract taxes and revenue from the Asante, who refused to cooperate and disputed the legitimacy of any such action. To resist the Asante, the Fante turned to the British for help in the 1800s.

The Fante and British alliance, along with the drop in revenues from the slave trade (which was gradually declining), eroded the Asantehene's standing and wealth. At the same time, British power increased, facilitating the establishment of the British Gold Coast in 1821 under Governor Charles MacCarthy, who in 1823 declared war on the Asantehene Osei Tutu Kwame. Setting off to Asanteland with about 80 men of the Royal African Colonial Corps, 170 from the Cape Coast militia and 250 Fante fighters, Brigadier-General MacCarthy was due to be joined by thousands of reinforcements, but his camp came under Asante attack. Outnumbered by 10,000 Asante soldiers armed with muskets, MacCarthy's troops were almost entirely wiped out in what is known as the Battle of Nsamankow in January 1824. MacCarthy was wounded and died by suicide rather than be taken captive. His head was cut off and kept as a war trophy by the Asante. Later, his skull would be used as a drinking cup by Asante royalty.

The so-called 'Bond of 1844' was the first formal grant of power to the British by Fante chiefs to exercise jurisdiction within certain coastal areas. But the Anglo–Asante Wars continued for decades and although the Asante emerged victorious in some of these conflicts, the wars eventually reached a horrific conclusion in February 1874 when British troops marched into Kumasi and sacked the city. The treasury in the king's stone-built palace was emptied, after which the royal compound was blown up. The remainder of the city was burned to the ground. A British official, R. Austin Freeman, passing through in 1888 noted that Kumasi was:

nothing more than a large clearing in the forest, over which were scattered, somewhat irregularly, groups of houses. The paths were dirty and ill-kept, and between the groups of houses large patches of waste-ground intervened, and on these, amidst the tall coarse grass that covered them, were to be seen the remains of houses that had once occupied them.[2]

The city was pulverised. Its prosperity vanished. Asanteland and the ruins of its capital were now under British control.

Prempeh I, c. 1871–1931

In the same year that the British official made his observation, a new Asantehene, Prempeh I, emerged. He wanted to recover his kingdom, reunite the Asante people, and raise

Prempeh I

them from despondence and humiliation. Born around 1871, he became Asantehene in 1888. A young and charismatic man, Prempeh drew legitimacy from claiming to be a direct descendant of the Oyoko clan – the founders of the Asante nation – and succeeded in mobilising the Asante behind him. Prempeh's own writings indicate he believed that the British would accept his authority in Asanteland and provinces of the kingdom that had broken away provided he accepted 'missionary' education. He wrote that a British envoy told him,

> His Excellency [the British governor] wishes to construct a mission house at Kumasi and His Excellency is sure that when the missionary has started his work, peace and tranquillity would reign; secondly His Excellency would appoint King Prempeh to be the king of all the Africans; thirdly that he would not interfere with any law of the country; fourthly he would hold himself responsible to fight any other nation who would attempt to invade Ashanti.[3]

Prempeh, who referred to himself in the third person, said the offer was reiterated by another British envoy: 'the Governor further states that if you accept these terms, he would then unite and hand over all the departed Ashanti provinces to King Prempeh'. In reality, the British viewed the young royal as an obstacle to their growing ambitions for full control over the Gold Coast. In 1891, when Britain offered the Asante protectorate status, he responded:

> The suggestion that Asante in its present state should come and enjoy the protection of Her Majesty the Queen and Empress of India I may say is a matter of very serious consideration and I am happy to say we have arrived at this conclusion, that my kingdom of Asante will never commit

itself to any such policy. Asante must remain as of old – at the same time to remain friendly with all white men.

In 1895 Prempeh sent a mission to England to 'plead to have all the Ashanti provinces which are under the control of the English be restored to King Prempeh as before'. The Asante ambassadors were not accorded an official audience and they returned home ignored and thwarted. However, Prempeh I did not abandon diplomacy in his efforts to achieve sovereignty. On the return of the failed Asante mission, he offered to negotiate with the British. Instead, the British authorities assembled thousands of soldiers and prepared to march on Kumasi. When asking what the purpose of the expedition was, Prempeh was informed that it was 'coming to arrange everything', and that Prempeh should bear the costs of the military expedition. He understood the implications of the demands – recognise the British flag, or face seeing the Asante nation destroyed.

Later, Prempeh wrote about this period:

On Monday morning, King Prempeh and the Chiefs went to the meeting, and they found the British flag being hoisted in the square and King Prempeh and the Chiefs caught hold of the mast and said, 'we now receive the flag'. When they had all assembled the Governor [William E. Maxwell] asked the King and Queen to come and kneel before him . . . they complied accordingly by taking off the crown and royal sandal. When the King and Queen got up from their knees, they were asked to pay the balance of the war indemnity . . . King Prempeh replied that he had not been asked for this amount before, and that it was only two days previously on Saturday that he had come to know of it. And moreover, the amount was allowed to be paid by instalments and so for the present, he is ready to give £2,720 [about £450,000 today] as remittance and ask for 7 days to return the remainder of the amount. And during the 7 days, the 2 sisters of the King would be given to be surety. The Governor refused both the remittance of £2,720 and the surety of 2 sisters of the King up to 7 days to return the balance. The King then asked to be allowed to return to his house to take the same remittance. The Governor refused to allow the King to go home and said that unless the amount is paid to him in full at the very moment – he will be taken prisoner.

And so, on this pretext, in February 1896 a stunned Prempeh I, King of Asanteland, was suddenly arrested and taken to Elmina Castle at Cape Coast, escorted by a battalion of the West Yorkshire Regiment. He was held there for several months. His prison conditions, though not comfortable, were considerably better than those of other prisoners at the castle, who were kept in small cells, fed once a day for just two minutes and kept in total darkness. Many did not survive their ordeal.

Prempeh was imprisoned along with his mother, a brother, two of his wives and several attendants. His quarters were cleaned twice a day and he was allowed the use of an old bathtub; he and his entourage could obtain and cook their own food. Prempeh, who would have been in his mid to late twenties, was described by the Elmina district commissioner as being 'about 5 feet five and a half inches tall, brown, with slight beard, whiskers and moustache, black hair, large eyes, high forehead, broad face and strongly built'. The doctor who examined him remarked that he had 'much superfluous fat'.[4] During his captivity at Elmina a pair of Kumasi chiefs engaged two African lawyers from Cape Coast to file a suit for Prempeh's release. The petition accused the British of acting in bad faith. It was a useless endeavour. The British decided that so long as Prempeh remained in the Gold Coast he would be a source of instability, so at the end of the year they sent him into exile to Sierra Leone, along with the two lawyers.

The acting chief justice wrote about the reaction of Prempeh and his entourage on being told of their fate:

> They calmly received the news, but in spite of their self-control, I could see that they were disconcerted by it, being so different from what they expected, and Prempeh burst into perspiration ... Prempeh as spokesman asked me to beg the Governor not to send them to Sierra Leone, that they preferred to remain in Elmina Castle with their liberty restrained than go to Sierra Leone to enjoy the liberty they would have there. He further stated that I was to assure His Excellency that if he would send them back to Kumasi, not only would the indemnity be paid, but they would also place themselves entirely under the Resident, obeying all his commands.[5]

Prempeh's plea fell on deaf ears. He arrived in Sierra Leone in January 1897, accompanied by his family and around 30 attendants. His mother Yaa Akyaa was described by the Reuters news correspondent as 'much more reserved' than her son and was 'always smoking, a pipe or a cigarette being scarcely ever out of her mouth'.[6]

While Prempeh lived in relative freedom in Sierra Leone, he pined for his homeland and continued to file petitions requesting his repatriation. Asanteland was restless and did not abandon hope for the return of its traditional and rightful ruler, who was regarded as the embodiment of its customs and history. The British governor of the Gold Coast, Sir Frederick Hodgson, intent on weakening the spirit of the Asante, opined that if he could seize the Golden Stool – the Sika Dwa Kofi (or Asikadwa) – it would spell the end of the Asante kingdom, as the seventeenth-century soothsayer Okomfo Anokye had decreed.

During a visit to Kumasi from Accra, the seat of British rule in the Gold Coast, Hodgson met a group of Asante leaders and demanded to sit on the Golden Stool to demonstrate Queen Victoria's sovereignty over the Asante 'Where is the Golden Stool? Why am I not sitting on the Golden Stool at this moment? I am the representative of the paramount power: why have you relegated me to this chair? Why did you not take the opportunity of my coming to Kumasi to bring the Golden Stool and give it to me to sit upon?'[7]

Sir Frederick's speech was received in silence by the assembled chiefs. The South African-born anthropologist Edwin W. Smith wrote in 1927 that it was 'A singularly foolish speech! An excellent example of the blunders that are made through ignorance of the African mind!'[8]

Yaa Asantewaa, c. 1840–1921

One Asante leader who would not capitulate to the governor was Yaa Asantewaa, the queen mother of the Asona Royal Court of Ejisu, a few kilometres northeast of Kumasi. A life-size statue of her is displayed at the museum attached to the Manhyia Palace in Kumasi, which I visited with its curator Justice Brobbey. The terracotta-coloured statue shows Yaa Asantewaa wearing a dark robe, sitting down, hands at her side, with a steely stare and elegant features, cropped hair and a determined air. Justice Brobbey spoke of her with beaming pride.

Yaa Asantewaa was descended from a heroic Asante lineage. When her grandson was sent into exile with King Prempeh, she, despite being in her late sixties (elderly by the standards of the time), gathered Asante men around her and admonished them for watching the immiseration of their homeland without putting up a fight. According to oral tradition, she urged them to organise their troops and said that, like her, they must be ready to die for the Asante nation:

> How can a proud and brave people like the Asante sit back and look while the white men took away their king and chiefs and humiliated them with a demand for the Golden Stool. The Golden Stool means money to the white men; they have searched and dug everywhere for it. I shall not pay one 'predawn' [£8] to the governor. If you, the chiefs of Asante, are going to behave like cowards and not fight, you should exchange your loincloths for my undergarments . . . Now I have seen that some of you fear to go forward to fight for our king. If it were in the brave days, the days of Osei Tutu, Okomfo Anokye, and Opoku Ware, chiefs would not have sat down to see their king taken away without firing a shot . . . Is it true that the bravery of the Asante is no more? I cannot believe it. It cannot be! I must say this, if you the men of Asante, will not go forward, then we will. We, the women, will. I shall call upon my fellow women. We will fight. We will fight until the last of us falls in the battlefields.

Shamed into action, some Asante men answered Yaa Asantewaa's heroic call. In 1900 she raised an army of 20,000 soldiers to challenge the British and their African auxiliaries on the coast, assuming the role of commander-in-chief, wearing the traditional war dress – the *batakari kese* – of the kind first worn by Osei Tutu in the late 1600s. This garment is similar to a smock, with pouches in varying shapes and of different materials, such as leather and cloth, stitched on to it, laced with silver and gold. The pouches are each embedded with sacred

Yaa Asantewaa in war dress – the *batakari kese*

writings, charms and amulets endowed with powers to assist the wearer in battle. The *batakari kese* is now only worn twice in the life of an Asante king: at the burial of the former king and by the new Asantehene during his coronation or enstoolment.

The Asante attacked the British fort in Kumasi, which had been rebuilt by the British in 1897 and was being used as a base for launching military campaigns against the Asante. The governor was under siege. This engagement – the last of the Anglo–Asante Wars – culminated in a big battle known in British quarters as the 'War of the Golden Stool' or the Yaa Asantewaa War. Yaa Asantewaa's forces blocked all routes into Kumasi; it is believed she herself took to the battlefield bearing arms, saying: 'I have loaded my gun, and not for nothing'.

For all her bravery, Yaa Asantewaa was confronting British forces equipped with far better weapons. They deployed the newly invented Maxim gun, for example, the first automatic firearm in the world and the forerunner of the machine gun. Nevertheless, the British did not secure an easy victory. The Asante soldiers erected barricades as protection from the Maxim gun. For seven months from April to November 1900, the British and their forces held out at the fort. Many of them, starved of resources, died in the siege. The tide only turned against the Asante when Governor Sir Frederick Hodgson managed to escape from the fort and returned with reinforcements: more guns and men from the Gold Coast Colony, Lagos and Sierra Leone. Yaa Asantewaa lost one of her best generals, the trenches built by the Asante were demolished, and she and her senior officers were captured at the end of the year and imprisoned at the fort.

The Asante had lost the Yaa Asantewaa War. Or had they? When a British official demanded the Golden Stool be surrendered, Yaa Asantewaa was one step ahead. In a story handed down over generations, she is credited with having the presence of mind to hide the Golden Stool deep in the forest. Some accounts suggest that a fake one was presented to the British; others state that the British continued to search for the Golden Stool for another 20 years.

Even in military defeat, Yaa Asantewaa had succeeded in ensuring that the Golden Stool did not fall into British hands. She was sent into exile to join Prempeh I. As she was being led off, she made a bitter parting shot: 'Asante women, I pity you,' she cried. When an Asante man asked her: 'What about us, the men?' She replied: 'Which men? The men died at the battlefront.' In 1902, the Gold Coast formally became a British colony until independence in 1957.

Eventually, the Golden Stool was discovered in the forest by a group of labourers, who stripped it of its gold and ornaments, except for the gold plate on its face. In 1921, the violated stool was found at a local market by Kumasi chiefs who recognised it for what it was. News of the desecration of the Golden Stool spread across Asanteland and plunged the nation into mourning.

British anthropologist Captain R.S. Rattray wrote at the time, perhaps a little superstitiously, that it was a relief that the British had not seized the Golden Stool: 'I believe that so far from benefitting, had we ever taken this Stool – which would have been little more than a "trophy" to us – that its power would then have worked against us.'[9]

Fourteen men, accused of the crime of damaging the Golden Stool, along with those who received the stolen ornaments, were tried under a traditional Asante justice system. Six men, according to the judgement, were condemned to death on the grounds that they,

> being natives of Ashanti and subjects of the Golden Stool of the Ashanti Nation did expose, steal, destroy, sell and otherwise unlawfully deal with and use the said Golden Stool, thereby betraying the Ashanti Nation and laying it open to disgrace and ridicule, and debasing the name and fame of Ashanti, much to the annoyance and provocation of all people, young and old.

The sentence of death was revised to one of banishment from Asanteland and the others found guilty were given prison sentences. Although the Golden Stool had lost most of its gold, it was still intact and so the soul of the Asante people had not been destroyed, and the priest Okomfo Anokye's prophecy had not come to pass. The British waived all claims on the Golden Stool of Asante, so Yaa Asantewaa's mission to save it had not been in vain.

Meanwhile, during his 28 years of exile, Prempeh had continually and persistently petitioned the British authorities to be allowed to return home. He regarded himself as the Asantehene and believed he was the victim of British injustice and perfidy. When the Yaa Asantewaa War had broken out in 1900, the British had blamed Prempeh. Governor Hodgson had decided that Prempeh 'was too much in touch' with his people and decreed that he should be banished entirely from West Africa and sent further away to the Seychelles. Prempeh appealed against being moved to so distant a land; at least in Sierra Leone he could discuss events in his homeland with people who understood and knew the region. It was to no avail. He was moved to the Seychelles, but he never gave up hope of returning to his people and kingdom. In 1923, Prempeh again asked to be released and wrote that of his original entourage 'there remain six chiefs and out of the six, one is blind, and the remaining are old and ill'.[10] The *Gold Coast Leader* newspaper in February 1924 stated that the 'general sentiment of the whole country and of Ashanti is for his early release'.[11]

Finally, at the end of 1924, after many years of exile, Prempeh I was allowed to return to Asanteland on the condition that he do so as a private citizen and not try to claim his throne. He sailed home from the Seychelles with his remaining attendants. The *Gold Coast Leader* newspaper reported in November: 'Thousands of people, white and black, flocked down to the beach to welcome him . . . A charming aristocratic-looking person in a black long suit with a fashionable black hat held up his hand to the cheers of the crowd.'[12] People wept with emotion on Prempeh's return home.

Two years later, in 1926, the British allowed Prempeh to be enstooled – but only with the diminished title Kumasihene, 'King of Kumasi', and with his authority drastically curbed by colonial rule. However, for him and his subjects, he was Asantehene, pre-eminent king of the whole of Asanteland, not just its capital Kumasi.

Prempeh demanded the repatriation of the remains of all

those Asante who had died in exile in the Seychelles, including Yaa Asantewaa, who had passed away in 1921. Her body was sent back to Asanteland and given a royal burial in 1930. Prempeh I himself died the following year. In 1935 the British allowed his son Prempeh II to reassume the title of Asantehene. Although vested with some autonomy, the king was much reduced in power. Nevertheless, the position retained the veneration accorded to it in the kingdom's heyday.

Prempeh I and Yaa Asantewaa serve as powerful examples of how Africans fought to preserve their heritage, institutions and traditions through times of great adversity. Prempeh I remained steadfast in claiming his birth right as Asantehene. Yaa Asantewaa's courage has made her an icon – not just for the Asante but for the whole Ghanaian nation and the continent of Africa. The British portrayed her as a dangerous subversive and for a long time banned any commemorations to her. When in 1952 the Ghanaians were given control of the National Museum of Ghana in Accra, its first exhibition included exhibits from the Yaa Asantewaa War; after independence in 1957, statues of her were erected. The cell in which she had been imprisoned in Kumasi Fort was converted into a public exhibit, and a new Ghanaian narrative of her was fashioned, portraying her as a fearless and principled woman – a model of African resistance to colonial aggression.

Ghana's first independent leader, Kwame Nkrumah, who was from the Nzema community, not the Asante, was especially keen to ensure Yaa Asantewaa was seen as the 'mother of the nation'. He was instrumental in naming a secondary school for girls in Kumasi after her and giving it the mission of inspiring young women to become leaders. In later years, Yaa Asantewaa's image was minted on Ghanaian money and imprinted on postage stamps. Her status as a great Asante queen and symbol of nationhood has been employed by the Ghanaian state to make of her an icon to unite all Ghanaians, regardless of ethnic affiliation.

Data published in 2021 by the Accra-based pan-African polling organisation Afrobarometer – the only African entity that carries out such surveys – showed that the number of Ghanaians who identify equally with their ethnic group and the nation-state has risen dramatically to two-thirds in the last ten years, compared with only 11 per cent who cite greater attachment to their ethnicity.[13] Just as Yaa Asantewa's achievements transcend divisions within Ghana, they can resonate continentwide: her tale is one for all Africans, and indeed men and women worldwide who prize heroism, determination and vision in the face of injustice. Ultimately, African history and African traditions are not to be measured by their economic value, but by the sense of joy, pride and identity they bring to Africans, and by the vast opportunities for instruction they bring to the rest of humankind.

14

Slavery and Salvation

We must now turn in more detail to the trade in enslaved Africans across the Atlantic Ocean. We have seen how the Asante were among African communities who were involved in the trade, selling war captives to Europeans and keeping some for their own use. However, although the transatlantic trade was abetted by some Africans, it was driven by its principal beneficiaries, the Europeans.

The trade was as catastrophic as it was extensive. Between the sixteenth and nineteenth centuries at least 12.5 million enslaved Africans were brutally ripped from their homes and sent across the Atlantic Ocean. It is likely that as many as 2 million did not survive the arduous journey. Those who did faced a life of extreme hardship, degradation and humiliation. Much has been written about slavery in Europe and the Americas, but less about its impact on Africa and how Africans, including in the diaspora, resisted it and contributed to its abolition.

I have had long discussions about slavery with my good friend, the Cameroonian-born academic Professor Augustin Holl, head of the UNESCO committee supervising the *GHA* project, whose extraordinary erudition across a range of topics ranks him as one of Africa's foremost polymaths. Professor Holl believes more research is needed into how the transatlantic trade has had long-lasting effects on people in Africa, the Caribbean and the Americas:

> The memories of the pressures of daily survival in an environment of centuries of enslavement shifted African minds into self-preservation mode . . . This has had some impact on how modern African states function. Poor governance afflicts many African nations, and part of the reason may be attributed to the fact that once an ethnic group achieves power they look after themselves and their community first – often to the detriment of others, and this can hinder efforts at nation building.

Histories of slavery from an African perspective are a precondition of the kind of research that Professor Holl advocates; the voices of enslaved Africans must be heard from beyond the grave, and the actions of many brave enslaved people who resisted their plight must be recognised.

Indigenous Slavery

Slavery is as old as humanity and is not confined to any one culture or people. It has therefore sometimes been cynically claimed that the presence of slavery in Africa before the arrival of the Europeans mitigates the evils of the transatlantic trade, as if Europeans were simply participating in an activity that had already existed for centuries in Africa. While slavery of all kinds is reprehensible, not all kinds are morally equivalent. Africans were treated very differently in indigenous slavery compared to how they were put to use across the Atlantic, as two leading Ghanaian professors, Akosua Perbi and Esi Sutherland-Addy explained to me at the University of Ghana in Accra.

In indigenous slavery, war captives could be used as unpaid labourers, soldiers or domestic servants, just as has been the case for centuries across Europe. An African male could also be forced into enslavement to repay a debt, which was not dissimilar to practices of bonded labour in Asia and indentured labour and serfdom in Europe. Naturally, being an enslaved person in Africa meant hardship: men had to toil on the land or in the mines for little or no recompense, though their enslavement did not necessarily last a lifetime. In indigenous slavery, women could be acquired at slave markets, sought as wives to bear children – especially following times of war and high casualty rates – and to help with household chores. In fact, women were more valued in indigenous slavery than men; in the transatlantic trade men fetched a higher price because they were used as agricultural labourers.

Once an African 'master' had children with his captive, those children would become part of the family and fully integrated into the community. Among the Akan people of West Africa, including the Asante, chiefs were expected to swear an oath stating they would make no distinction between children born of enslaved women and their other offspring. This aspect of assimilation into the community is an important difference with the 'chattel' slavery of the transatlantic trade, which conferred 'slave' status to the children sired by white males with enslaved African women. Significantly, there was an absence of an ideology of racism in indigenous slavery – the enslaver did not believe he or she was racially superior to their captives and enslaved people were not regarded as being sub-human; it was a matter of who happened to have power over whom.

Nigerian Professor Muyiwa Falaiye from the University of Lagos expressed rather emphatically to me a commonly held view in Africa: 'It is more tolerable and acceptable for people of the same colour to enslave one another. It is less visible, less tangible and it is not based on racism.'

The belief in the intrinsic inferiority of Africans, once widespread in Europe and the Americas, could lead to the inhumane treatment that most enslaved Africans were subjected to. Nevertheless the longstanding practice of indigenous slavery helped to enable the transatlantic trade, because chattel slavery could build on and benefit from it.

Transatlantic Trade, c. 1510–1868

The origins of the transatlantic trade date to the mid-fifteenth century, and I went to Cabo Verde, or Cape Verde, to see for myself the site of these early markets, finding it hard on arrival to reconcile the beauty of this island nation off the west coast of Africa with the earliest beginnings of the atrocity. Cabo Verde lies about 500 kilometres off the coast of Senegal and today consists of ten islands, all but one inhabited. They look like a colourful necklace draped across an endless expanse of water. These volcanic islands, which surge up from the seabed, are home to remarkable landscapes and remarkable people. Vast fields of volcanic rubble are otherworldly, barren but for the occasional tree, which reaches forth like inverted lightning. Elsewhere, in greener fields, lizards lie in the shade, licking the air and watching the passing traffic. Cabo Verde's markets throb with laughter and conversation in rich Creole dialects, born through the Africanisation of old Portuguese. It is Africa's most western point, lying on the Atlantic crossroads linking Africa, Europe and the Americas. The Atlantic covers 17 per cent of the earth's surface and a quarter of the world's maritime space. This gives it a strategic position – an advantage apparent to early settlers.

The first Europeans to arrive on the Atlantic coast of West Africa were a group of Portuguese sailors in the early 1440s. They disembarked on a small island, which they named Île de Palme. Later it became known as Île de Gorée and today it is part of Senegal. They were trying to find routes from Africa to India for the spice trade and so they only stayed temporarily. However, enslaved Africans were taken to Europe as early as this, a good 60 years before the actual transatlantic trade began. It is believed that nearly a thousand enslaved people were shipped from West Africa to the Portuguese port of Lagos in the first half of the 1440s. On witnessing the unloading of about 230 enslaved Africans, the Portuguese chronicler Gomes Eannes de Azurara wrote in 1444:

> But what heart could not be so hard as not to be pierced with piteous feeling to see that company? For some kept their heads low and their faces bathed in tears ... others stood groaning very dolorously looking up to the height of heaven, fixing their eyes upon it crying out loudly ... And though we could not understand the words of their language the sound of it right well accorded with the measure of their sadness.[1]

In 1462, around 100 settlers – mostly Portuguese and some Spanish – arrived on one of the islands of Cabo

Verde, which were then entirely uninhabited. They called it Santiago and established trading posts on it. The Europeans had been denied the opportunity to settle on the mainland by local African chiefs and so they set their sights on this strategically positioned archipelago. They designed their town in a similar style to those in their home countries.

I walked along a narrow street called 'Banana Road' that retains its historic features, with a series of single-storey thatched cottages dating back to the sixteenth century. It is the oldest road in the oldest town established by Europeans in West Africa – and despite the ominous period of history it foreshadowed, the old quarter of Santiago is one of the most picturesque spots in Cabo Verde. The settlers of Santiago grew crops for themselves and reared domestic animals, so they were relatively self-supporting. But they had not gone to Africa just to farm – they also wanted to make money. So they planted lucrative cash crops, such as sugar cane, coffee and cotton, for export to Europe where they were then in high demand.

However, if they were to cultivate these crops on a large scale, the settlers realised they would need a labour force; and since they wanted to make significant profits they would need a multitude of unpaid workers. Hence the settlers imported thousands of enslaved people from some of the main communities in West Africa, whom they had bought from indigenous traders.

The Portuguese settlers soon grasped that the Africans were not only important as a pool of labour but also as a source of knowledge – a fact that is often passed over. Their expertise in weaving and spinning cotton was a crucial factor in Cabo Verde's growing prominence. At the Ethnographic Museum in the capital Praia, which is housed in a nineteenth-century building formerly owned by an enslaver, the director Adilson Dias put on his protective gloves to handle some of the cotton material on display, telling me how the cotton grown by enslaved people was woven into fine cloth, called *panu di terra*, by enslaved skilled weavers, which was highly valued and even became a chief currency of trading. The dye was extracted from plants according to indigenous practice. Ironically, cotton cloth produced by enslaved people was then used to purchase more enslaved people. However, the settlers were still not content with the profits of their export of cotton and foodstuffs from Cabo Verde, and so they turned to two other activities. First, they used Cabo Verde's strategic position to repair and resupply ships. And second, and most devastatingly they also began to trade in enslaved people to sell to Europeans.

The Portuguese were supplying a market with a high demand for workers. Sugar cane plantation owners in Spain and Portugal and in the Canary, Azores and Madeira islands were all desperate for forced labour. Moreover, by the early sixteenth century the Spanish, French and English were clamouring for enslaved labour for their plantations in South America and the Caribbean. The native populations of the Americas had already been decimated by enslavement and sickness, and so Africa was seen as a new source of labour; plantation workers from West Africa were much less susceptible to malaria, yellow fever and other diseases. The Portuguese on Cabo Verde needed a base to handle all the trade and so they used African labourers to build a huge and magnificent fortress, Forte Real de São Filipe, which still stands in the old town of Santiago – a vast and sprawling stone structure that engulfed me with an eerie silence on my visit there.

I stood by a simple white marble column in the main

square that marks the spot where enslaved Africans were brought from the mainland of West Africa to be sold by the Portuguese, who dominated the trade at this stage. Enslaved people who were considered disobedient were whipped at the *pelourinho* ('whipping post') to set an example to others who might be contemplating rebellion. Surrounding the whipping post were colourful market stalls, with local merchandise to tempt passing browsers – innocent transactions today compared to those of yesteryear.

The Portuguese held their captives at the *alfândega*, a storeroom, where they would be branded on their necks with a hot iron. Santiago evolved entirely around its function as a hub for the sale of enslaved Africans.

Soon after, on the Atlantic coast of mainland Africa, the Portuguese established another important slave trade centre on the Île de Gorée. The island became one giant warehouse composed of more than a dozen slave houses. The boat ride from the Senegalese mainland to Gorée is pleasant and the walk to the main slave house is picturesque. As I approached the famous House of Slaves, the atmosphere seemed to change and darken. Once inside I made my way to the house's most striking feature: the 'door of no return', a large, heavy wooden door studded with metal hinges that opens onto a very short gangway, which would have led directly to the waiting slave ships, the point of departure across the Atlantic Ocean to a life of misery.

Once the Portuguese and Spanish had officially begun trading in enslaved people in 1510, the trade attracted several European nations. The English began their transatlantic trade in 1562, the Dutch in 1626, the French in the 1640s, and the Danes and Swedes in the 1650s. In the mid-seventeenth century, the French established St Louis in what is today Senegal as the main base for their operations in West Africa; these extended across the region including modern-day Côte d'Ivoire. Britain eventually became the world's foremost slave-trading nation. In his 2013 book *Freedom's Debt*, historian Dr William Pettigrew stated that the Royal African Company, set up by the royal Stuart family and London merchants in 1660, 'shipped more enslaved African women, men and children to the Americas than any other single institution during the entire period of the transatlantic slave trade'.

European nations established their forts, warehouses, castles and other holding centres up and down West Africa's coastline. On Ghana's Atlantic coast there are 80 old slave-trading forts, castles and lodges along a 250-kilometre stretch of beach built by the European powers. These buildings were at various times used by different European states all vying for captives. One example is Cape Coast Castle, an impressive complex with an imposing stone staircase that can be mounted from either side. The outer perimeter of the castle displays a line of cannons and cannonballs, deployed to see off rival powers seeking to gain control over the castle and the slave trade. Cape Coast Castle was originally built by the Danes in 1653 but it changed hands five times over the next decade. It was acquired in the 1660s by the British, under whom it was reconstructed in the mid-1770s. Slave dungeons were built in the castle basement; directly above was a church where the slavers and officials held sermons and prayed – a striking juxtaposition. On the day that I visited Cape Coast Castle with my superb local historian guide, Nkunu Akyea, I saw a group of young men on a school trip descend into the dungeon – a couple of hundred years ago their forebears would have been taken against their will and forced down those very same steps in very different circumstances.

A plaque on one of the castle's walls bears the inscription, 'In everlasting memory: Of the anguish of our ancestors, may those who died rest in peace, may those who return find their roots, may humanity never again perpetrate such injustice against humanity. We the living vow to uphold this.'

Nkunu told me how the enslaved Africans would be sorted and separated by gender. Hundreds at any given time were confined in gloomy, dank and overcrowded dungeons as they awaited shipment, sometimes for months on end. They would be fed a basic diet of starchy food such as yam, and also given salt to replace the amount of fluid they lost through heavy perspiration as a result of their stuffy and cramped incarceration. I could see the shallow channels that served as toilets – basically open sewers. Even centuries later the marks on the walls left by human waste were clearly visible. Many Africans died either while being confined or during their 'passage', but with a plentiful supply of enslaved Africans there was little incentive for the slavers to keep their captives in better conditions.

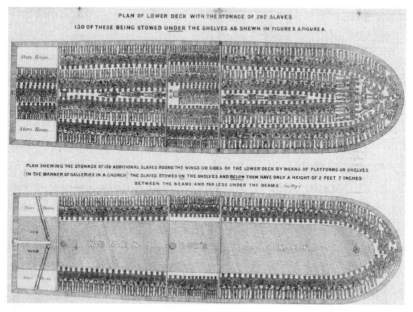

A 1788 diagram showing how enslaved people were stowed on the British slave ship *Brookes*

An English trader's sales manifest, published in the *Columbia Herald* in Charleston, South Carolina, on 30 May 1785, serves as an example of how Africans were perceived as 'human goods' to be bought and sold:

> A cargo of 152 prime healthy young negroes, just arrived in said ship from the River Gambia, after a passage of 35 days. The negroes from this part of the coast of Africa are well acquainted with the cultivation of rice and are naturally industrious. Conditions of sale: To approved purchasers, bonds payable the first of January, 1786, and to those who make immediate payment in cash, rice or any other produce a proper discount will be made thereon. Robert Hazlehurst & Co.

The men had been taken on the ship *Mentor* to Charleston, which was the main port of entry for enslaved Africans in the United States.

Men were valued for their strength and endured back-breaking work on plantations; most had a lifespan of seven or eight years. As hinted at in the manifesto, their expertise in crop cultivation was also recognised. Enslaved females, however, had to endure the grim additional threat of sexual assault. The Portuguese fort of Elmina on Ghana's Cape Coast is particularly associated with this kind of abuse. Elmina dates back to the late fifteenth century, which makes it the oldest surviving European structure in sub-Saharan Africa. It was not originally built to hold captives but to defend Portugal's sphere of influence against other Europeans; but once the transatlantic trade became entrenched it was used for this nefarious purpose.

The Portuguese governor was notorious for surveying the latest delivery of enslaved women. I climbed the stairs to his elegant and luxurious living quarters and peered down from his balcony to the courtyard below, as he would have done to view and select whichever woman, or indeed girl, caught his fancy. She would then be bathed, dressed in clean clothes and sent up to the governor's bedroom to be raped by him. If an African woman became pregnant by him, or indeed by any other European, the governor might release her from captivity and she could live as a free woman, unlike enslaved women in the United States who found themselves in a similar predicament.

The transatlantic trade was part of a wider network known as the 'triangular trade'. A naval ship would set sail from Europe with weapons, whisky, beads and other goods to buy enslaved people. The enslaved Africans would then be transported to the Caribbean, South America and North America; this was known as the 'middle passage'. Then the ship would be loaded up with sugar, cotton, and other products from the Americas and the Caribbean and would return to Europe.

Africans were not only acquired from coastal areas but also from the interior of the continent. The kingdom of Kongo, which included territory today that makes up the Democratic Republic of the Congo, Angola and the Republic of the Congo provided great numbers of enslaved people. The colony of Luanda was established by the Portuguese in 1575. They had conquered the coastal areas of this part of Africa, and Luanda was the biggest of their slave trading hubs. More enslaved Africans were sent by the Portuguese to Brazil than anywhere else. By the 1780s, 40,000 enslaved people were exported annually from Angola alone to Brazil, and these numbers increased between the 1810s and 1830s. Today, more than half of the 210-million-strong Brazilian population claims some African ancestry, making it home to the world's biggest African diaspora.

While Europeans carried out their own slaving raids,

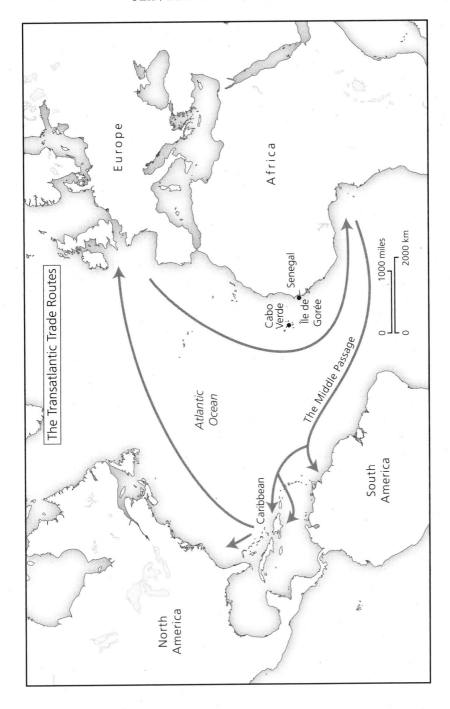

The Transatlantic Trade Routes

Europe

Africa

Senegal

Île de
Gorée

Cabo
Verde

Atlantic
Ocean

The Middle Passage

Caribbean

North
America

South
America

1000 miles

2000 km

especially at the beginning, they realised that it would be easier to acquire enslaved people through negotiation and purchase, and they sought the cooperation of chiefs and allies.

While many Africans refused to sell their fellow human beings, there is little doubt that African elites played a dominant role in the capture and sale of Africans to European merchants. One of the main kingdoms in West Africa that was deeply involved in the trade was Dahomey, now part of the Republic of Benin. It grew rich from the slave trade and was famed for its female soldiers, the Agojie or Ahosi, often referred to as 'Amazons'. A female army was established in Dahomey in the seventeenth century that lasted until the end of the nineteenth century. The Agojie were fierce, fearless and renowned for their military prowess. Before enslaved people were dispatched across the ocean from Dahomey, they were made to march six times around a large tree counterclockwise, so that they would forget who had enslaved them, thereby preventing their souls from returning to Dahomey and haunting those who had captured them and sent them into a life of slavery across the ocean.

The Malinke, Mandinka or Mandingo people, whose community spanned West Africa, were traded as enslaved people by other groups such as the Wolof. They accounted for a large portion who were taken to the United States. These were the very same people whose ancestors had drawn up the Mande Charter of human rights in the 1200s. However although some Africans willingly participated in the trade, others were often also threatened and coerced so that they had little choice but to obtain enslaved people. African oral accounts handed down over the centuries in the Ewe area of what is today eastern Ghana relate stories of how Europeans would deceitfully entice people on board their ships and then set sail with them as captives.

A common misperception is that Africans bartered their fellow Africans for trifling amounts or frivolous items. This may seem the case when viewed through a Western lens, but within the African cultural system, objects deemed by Europeans to be of no consequence were ascribed value. For instance, Africans accepted beads as payment for humans because these were regarded as valuable goods by West Africans, who used beads and shells as a currency and as a means of projecting wealth and prestige.

Some coastal Africans who had maritime skills, such as the Kru people of West Africa, were more likely to have actively participated in the transatlantic trade than those living in the hinterland, and some communities and kingdoms prospered greatly from the trade. Another relevant factor for African participation in the trade was the discovery of huge gold reserves in Brazil in the 1690s. This depressed demand for African gold and encouraged Africans to resort instead to selling enslaved people.

Along with coastal people, communities who had become acculturated into European ways – such as the *signares* of Senegal – provided collaborators in the trade. The *signares* were powerful women who owned houses and businesses. They were the offspring of wealthy European merchants and African women, and they played a substantial role in both the civic life and the economy of their communities. Some of the *signares* kept enslaved people themselves.

One of the best-known women of mixed-race heritage who made a huge personal fortune from slave trading was Ana Joaquina dos Santos e Silva, popularly known as Dona Ana Mulata. Born around 1788 in present-day Angola, she 'owned' large numbers of enslaved people who worked on her agricultural holdings, as well as domestic servants. As a member of the Afro-Portuguese elite, she enjoyed a leading position in Luanda. She died in 1859 in Portugal while undergoing medical treatment.

Slavery also created a kind of intermediate class between masters and the enslaved. It was not unusual for some enslaved people in Africa to have significant roles, including as foremen and interpreters. Some of them wielded power and requested recognition and reward from the Europeans with whom they dealt. For instance, in 1546 in Cabo Verde the Afro-Portuguese mixed-race community asked Portuguese officials if they could share civic power with them in the local government – a request that the Portuguese refused.

The trade had an immeasurably detrimental impact on Africa. It fuelled conflicts between communities and gave victors the opportunity to sell those whom they defeated; this meant that communities became suspicious of one another, conflict became endemic and people increasingly looked to their own ethnic group for protection, leading to the atomisation and polarisation of African societies.

In July 2018 the novelist Adaobi Tricia Nwaubani wrote in the *New Yorker* magazine about her sense of shame over her great-grandfather Nwaubani Ogogo Oriaku, who was prolific in his capture of and trade in fellow Igbos in what is now Nigeria in the nineteenth century. She described how her family in 2017 participated in a cleansing ceremony with their Anglican priest and that at the end of it, her mother Patricia said: 'People did all these evil things but they don't talk about it. The more people confess and renounce their evil past, the more cleansing will come to the land.'[2] It is a sad fact that the descendants of people freed from enslavement in southern Nigeria, called *ohu*, still face significant stigma today within Igbo culture.

Although many Africans were complicit or proactive in the acquisition of captives, the barbaric treatment and racism that enslaved people endured while awaiting transport across the Atlantic and at their final destinations were perpetrated by white slavers. The cruelty meted out by white people has been the subject of books, films, plays and much public discourse. But the first-hand written accounts by captives taken from Africa provide the most moving and illuminating narratives; these are the exceptional stories written by those who were either literate before their captivity or were lucky enough to learn how to read and write.

These include the memoirs of Ayuba Suleiman Diallo (1701–73), a man of noble birth who was captured in 1731 near the River Gambia. Diallo was sent to the English colony of Maryland in North America but was later released by his owner and returned to Africa via London and died in Senegambia in 1773.

Charles Ignatius Sancho (c. 1729–80) was born on a slave ship in the Atlantic and sold into slavery in the Caribbean. He subsequently arrived in England as a child, working for 18 years with a family in Greenwich. He ran away and managed to start a business as a shopkeeper. He wrote essays, plays and books, and his portrait was painted by the celebrated English artist Thomas Gainsborough.

Ottobah Cugoano (c. 1757–91) was sold into slavery when he was captured in his early teens while in a field on the Gold Coast, and sent to the Caribbean in 1772. There he experienced terrible suffering on a plantation. Soon after, he was purchased by a merchant who took him to England where he learned how to read and write and was freed. In London he joined the abolitionist movement and wrote *Thoughts and Sentiments on the Evil and Wicked Traffic of the Slavery and Commerce of the Human Species*.

Omar ibn Said (c. 1770–1863) was born and raised as a Muslim in West Africa and was educated and literate in Arabic. He was 37 years old when he was kidnapped and taken to the US in the 1800s. He wrote his autobiography in Arabic in 1831 in which he described his capture: 'Then there came to our place a large army who killed many men and took me and brought me to the great sea ... and we sailed upon the great sea a month and a half when we came to a place called Charleston' – the main entry point in the US for those who had been enslaved.[3] He was sold to a 'small and wicked man' called Johnson in North Carolina. Omar ibn Said's erudition marked him out and he eventually gained his liberty with the help of abolitionists and missionaries.

One of the most compelling narratives of slavery is that of Olaudah Equiano, a friend and fellow anti-slavery campaigner of Ottobah Cugoano. His eighteenth-century testimony is particularly significant because it sheds light on the experience of being both a victim of internal African slavery and the transatlantic trade.

Olaudah Equiano, c. 1745–97

Olaudah was born around 1745 in Igboland in what is today southeastern Nigeria. He described a happy childhood, as the youngest son of a village elder. 'I was trained up from my earliest years in the art of war, my daily exercise was shooting and throwing javelins; and my mother adorned me with emblems after the manner of our greatest warriors.'[4] Olaudah was snatched at about 11 years old, along with his only sister: 'One day when all our people were gone out to their works as usual, and only I and my dear sister were left to mind the house, two men and a woman got over our walls, and in a moment seized us both, and without giving us time to cry out or make resistance,

A 1789 engraving of Olaudah Equinao

they stopped our mouths and ran off with us into the nearest wood.'

Olaudah described how the only comfort he and his sister drew was 'being in one another's arms . . . and bathing each other with our tears. But alas! We were soon deprived of even this small comfort of weeping together. The next day proved a day of greater sorrow than I had experienced for my sister and I were then separated, while we lay clasped in each other's arms.'

Olaudah ended up living with a chief in what he called a 'very pleasant' place. The chief had two wives and several children. He said the first wife treated him very well and was something of a mother figure. They spoke the same language and his principal employment there was working the bellows for his 'master', a smith. After about six months he was taken to the coast and in 1754 was put on board a European slave ship. It took him first to Barbados in the Caribbean and then to Virginia in North America.

Through his voice speak many. On boarding the ship he saw

a multitude of black people of every description chained together, every one of their countenances expressing dejection and sorrow, I no longer doubted my fate; and quite overpowered with horror and anguish, I fell motionless on the decking and fainted . . . I was soon put down under the decks, where I received such a salutation to my nostrils as I had never experienced in my life: so that with the loathsomeness of the stench, and crying together I became so sick and low that I was not able to eat.

On refusing the food offered by a white crew member he was 'severely flogged'. The traders had invested in their human cargo and wanted them to arrive at their destination in a relatively passable state.

Olaudah made this important comparison of being a victim of the internal African system of slavery with that of the transatlantic trade: 'If ten thousand worlds had been my own I would have freely parted with them all to have exchanged my condition with that of the meanest slave in my own country . . . and I even wished for my former slavery in preference to my present situation which was filled with horrors of every kind.'

As the ship continued its journey across the Atlantic, he recalled:

I would have jumped over the side but I could not, and besides the crew used to watch us very closely who were not chained down to the decks, lest we should leap into the water; and I have seen some of these poor African prisoners most severely cut for attempting to do so . . . The white people looked and acted, as I thought, in so savage a manner, for I had never seen among any people such instances of brutal cruelty . . . The shrieks of the women and the groans of the dying rendered the whole scene of horrors almost inconceivable . . . I began to hope to soon put an end to my miseries. Often did I think many of the inhabitants of the deep, much more happy than myself. I envied them the freedom they enjoyed and as often wished I could change my condition for theirs. Every circumstance I met with served only to render my state more painful and heighten my apprehensions and my opinion of the cruelty of the whites . . . Many a time we were near suffocation, from want of fresh air, which we were often without for whole days together.

In this extract, Olaudah wonders aloud how people could subject their fellow humans to such cruel treatment:

O, ye nominal Christians! Might not an African ask you, learned you this from your God? Who says unto you, Do unto all men as you would, should do unto you? Is it not enough that we are torn from our country and friends to toil for your luxury and lust of gain? Must every tender feeling be likewise sacrificed to your avarice? Are the dearest friends and relations, now rendered more dear by their separation from their kindred, still to be parted from each other, and thus prevented from cheering the gloom of slavery with the small comfort of being together and mingling their sufferings and sorrows? Why are parents to lose their children, brothers their sisters, or husbands their wives? Surely this is a new refinement in cruelty, which while it has no advantage to atone for it, thus aggravates distress and adds fresh horrors to the wretchedness of slavery. Slaves are sometimes by half-feeding, half-clothing, over-working and stripes [lashes] reduced so low that they are turned out as unfit for service and left to perish in the woods or expire on a dunghill.

Enslaved field workers were notoriously overworked from sunrise to sunset and most died while still in their early twenties. Olaudah only remained in Barbados for a few days before setting sail for Virginia in the USA, where he was put to work on a plantation.

Olaudah was then sold to a British sea captain, Michael Henry Pascal, who was visiting the house in Virginia and took a liking to him. He bought him for about £20 or £40 and gave him the name Gustavus Vassa. Olaudah stayed with the captain for seven years, during which time he learned to read and write, and saw action in key naval battles as Britain competed for imperial power with its European rivals.

Olaudah recounted how shocked he was when in 1762 Captain Pascal announced that he was parting ways with him: 'Indeed I almost loved him with the affection of a son . . . He used to say that he and I could never part.' A baffled Olaudah described how Captain Pascal had suddenly and inexplicably turned horribly against him and sold him to Captain James Doran, on a ship called *Charming Sally*, bound for the Caribbean island of Montserrat. There he was sold to a plantation owner, Robert King. Olaudah was educated and this helped him avoid the brutal treatment that other enslaved people had to endure. 'Mr King soon asked me what I could do . . . I told him I knew something of seamanship, and could shave and dress hair pretty well; and I could refine wines . . . and that I could write and understand arithmetic tolerably well.'

While he worked for Mr King, he witnessed

cruelties of every kind . . . it was almost a constant practice with clerks and other whites to commit violent depredations on the chastity of the female slaves . . . I have even known them to gratify their brutal passions with females not ten years old and these abominations with some of them practised to such excesses … One Mr Drummond told me he has sold 41,000 negroes and that he had once cut off a negro-man's leg for running away … he then said his scheme had the desired effect – it cured that man and some others of running away … A load of heavy iron hooks hung about their necks …the iron muzzle, thumb screws &c. are so well known as to not need a description and were sometimes applied for the slightest faults. I have seen a negro beaten till some of his bones were broken, for only letting a pot boil over. Why do you use those instruments of torture? Are they fit to be applied by one rational being to another? And are ye not struck with shame and mortification to see the partakers of your nature reduced so low?

If a white enslaver had children with a captive African woman, the children could be put to work, as Olaudah observed: 'An account of a French planter, who shewed many Mulattoes [mixed race] working in the fields like beasts of burden … these were all the produce of his own loins.'

Olaudah worked on Robert King's trading vessels and travelled widely in the Caribbean and North America. Over three years he managed to save enough money to buy his freedom and in 1766 he departed for London. There, he first trained as a hairdresser and improved his education a little more, and then he worked as a personal servant and ship's steward, travelling to the Mediterranean and America. On his return to London in 1777 he again took up a domestic post before returning to sea once more in 1784.

About two years later, Olaudah went back to London and joined the campaign for abolition. In 1787 he founded 'Sons of Africa', made up of formerly enslaved individuals living in London such as Ottobah Cuagano. The group worked closely with the British parliamentarian and abolitionist William Wilberforce. They lobbied Parliament, delivered lectures and wrote to newspapers to persuade politicians and the public to support the emancipation of enslaved people in British colonies. Olaudah also became a public advocate for poor black people living in the capital. He was appointed the 'Commissary of Stores' for the Sierra Leone relocation scheme for African returnees. This was effectively a civil service post and would make him the first black civil servant in Britain. However, he did not last long in the role, since he drew attention to what he believed were corrupt financial practices and was sacked for whistleblowing. He asked for compensation and was awarded £50. By 1788 he had become a prominent abolition campaigner and a year later he published his memoirs, *The Interesting Narrative of the Life of Olaudah Equiano, or Gustavus Vassa, the African*. Its timing was critical, coming just a fortnight before the British parliament began debating the slave trade.

Olaudah Equiano went on book tours around Great Britain and Ireland and his memoirs were translated into several languages. In 1792 he married a white Englishwoman from Cambridgeshire called Susanna Cullen. He had two daughters with her, one of whom died as a small child. Susanna herself died in 1796 and the following year so did Olaudah. His burial place is unknown.

Some have questioned whether Olaudah Equiano was indeed born in Igboland. But whatever his provenance, his autobiography is an unforgettable work, and his status as an articulate and energetic abolitionist who drew on his first-hand experience of enslavement is beyond doubt. 'Tortures, murder and every other imaginable barbarity and iniquity are practised upon the poor slaves with impunity. I hope the slave trade will be abolished,' he wrote at the end of his memoirs.

By the time of his death in London in 1797, calls for abolition were gaining momentum in both Europe and the Americas. Equiano's account of enslavement played an important role in highlighting the horrors of slavery and furthered the abolitionist cause. Contributions by black abolitionists such as his are too frequently overshadowed by the efforts of establishment campaigners like William Wilberforce.

Abolition

Many did not wish to see the end of the trade. The advocates for abolition had argued that if there were no buyers then the trade would immediately cease to exist. The slavers on the other hand insisted that it was the regular supply of enslaved people from Africa that sustained the external demand for them, so according to this counterintuitive argument the Africans themselves were primarily to blame for the persistence of the trade and there was somehow a constant supply of Africans waiting to be shipped overseas. The time, effort and money that went into the construction of huge European slave forts, and the size and profitability of plantations in the Americas and the Caribbean strongly suggest that it was demand from Europeans and Americans that fuelled the supply of enslaved people.

Legislation abolishing the trade was enacted first by Denmark in 1803, Britain in 1807, the United States a year later, the Netherlands in 1814, France in 1818, Brazil in 1850 and Portugal as late as 1878. However, slavery itself did not end with abolition of the trade. It continued until 1838 in British colonies, until 1888 in Brazil, and slavery persisted in the southern US states until the end of the American Civil War in 1865; and as we saw in Chapter 9, the

Indian Ocean trade under the Arabs and their allies continued for decades after the transatlantic trade ended.

The main impetus driving the abolition of slavery will continue to be discussed and contested. I am grateful to two brilliant Liberian academics for their guidance on this topic: professors Carl Patrick Burrowes of Cuttington University and William Ezra Allen of the University of Liberia.

There were undoubtedly powerful moral arguments by white abolitionists, such as William Wilberforce, based on the belief that God created all men equally, which triggered widespread discussion, much heart searching and guilt in Europe and the Americas. However, new economic realities also lay behind abolition. There was a transition away from mercantile capitalism as European nations and North America began to industrialise in the early nineteenth century. And for the Industrial Revolution to succeed, large quantities of raw materials, such as palm oil, which was vital as a lubricant for factories and machines, needed to be imported. Since tropical materials such as cotton and rubber could be acquired in Africa, the argument for keeping the enslaved labour there instead of transporting such people elsewhere was a compelling one.

There is a strong consensus among African intellectuals that the economic motive was instrumental, even paramount, for the abolition of slavery. As Professor Allen pointed out, 'the very nations that had been involved as beneficiaries of the slave trade, Britain and the United States, were the ones leading the transition to industrial capitalism'. Certainly the continued exploitation by Europeans of African workers (even forced labour) in the decades after abolition undermines the argument that abolition was a triumph of morality.

Furthermore, the role played by regular slave revolts in

achieving abolition has been overlooked. These occurred from the very beginning of the trade. As the mood against slavery hardened, such rebellions demonstrated the cost and difficulties of maintaining it. Africans could turn against their crew masters when they were loaded onto ships and were waiting for it to fill up – sometimes for weeks – before it set sail. Although escape was difficult once the ship set off, there are examples of Africans overpowering the crew on various occasions and directing the vessels back to Africa. In 1729, the enslaved people on board the *Clare* mutinied, successfully drove the crew from the vessel, and returned it to the West African coast. In some cases, the ships would sink with the enslaved Africans on board.

One prominent mutiny took place in 1839, when about 50 Africans – mostly adult males – were taken from West Africa to Cuba. They were put on board a slave ship, the *Amistad* (ironically meaning 'friendship' in Spanish), bound from Havana in Cuba to a sugar plantation in Puerto Principe. During a storm, the Africans found sugar cane knives in the hold and staged a mutiny under the leadership of one of their number, Sengbe Pieh, also known as Joseph Cinqué, killing the captain and a crew member. Two other crew members either were thrown overboard or swam away. The two Cubans who had purchased the enslaved people were on board and were ordered to sail back to West Africa, but instead they diverted the ship to the North American coast. For two months the *Amistad* remained at sea, and around a dozen of the enslaved Africans on board died. Eventually the USS *Washington*, a vessel of the American navy, spotted the *Amistad* and escorted it to Connecticut. The Cubans demanded the return of their 'human property', and the Spanish government asked for the extradition of the Africans to stand trial for murder. North America had abolished the trade by this time, so a group of American abolitionists assisted the Africans and argued they had been illegally captured. They took the case through the American court system and in 1841 the Africans won their freedom and passage back to Sierra Leone. Tellingly, Cuba acquired the bulk of its enslaved Africans to work in its burgeoning sugar industry after the abolition of the trade – more than in all the preceding years combined.

The impact of Haiti's national rebellion against slavery was also of paramount significance: its success reverberated across the Caribbean, Europe and the Americas, and emboldened Africans everywhere to resist their enslavement. In 1791, enslaved people led by Toussaint Louverture, a free man with military experience, revolted against their French owners in what was then known as Saint Domingue. Louverture said: 'I was born a slave, but nature gave me the soul of a free man.'[5] He did not live to see the day of freedom. He died in prison in 1803. The birth of Haiti in 1804 made it the first independent black republic in the history of the world. However, Haiti was isolated and undermined for seeking its freedom and sovereignty, with the US trying to cut it off from the start, refusing to recognise its independence until 1862. In 1825, Haiti was made to take out a loan by France in order to compensate the French colonists. Formerly enslaved people were forced to compensate those who had enslaved them; the irony is devastating. The exorbitant interest from the debt meant it was not paid off until 1947, resulting in Haiti having to pay out more than twice the value of the colonists' claims; unsurprisingly, given its beginnings, today it is the most impoverished nation in the western hemisphere.

After abolition one question loomed large: what to do with the huge numbers of freed Africans? Most former enslaved people, especially those who had gone to South

America and the Caribbean, stayed put. But some of those emancipated were sent from North America and Europe to Sierra Leone in West Africa. A philanthropic settlement for freed Africans had been founded by the British anti-slavery movement in 1787–8, and provided a chance for people of African descent to return to the continent of their forebears. In 1802, Sierra Leone was taken over by Britain as a colony. One of its most famous residents was Samuel Ajayi Crowther. His life provides a good example of the vicissitudes that could befall Africans at the time. Captured in 1821 in what is today Nigeria, he was sold to Portuguese traders. Put on board a ship bound for the Americas, he was freed by an anti-slaving British naval squadron ship and taken to Freetown, the capital of Sierra Leone. Later, Samuel Ajayi Crowther received a remarkable education in England and eventually returned to Lagos, where he became an Anglican bishop.

While Sierra Leone was a British colony, neighbouring Liberia was the part of West Africa that a society of predominantly white Americans chose as a new home for emancipated African American enslaved people. Liberia was established in the early 1820s by the American Colonization Society, the ACS. It was originally called the 'Society for the Colonization of Free People of Color of America'. However, this was not a project based on moral or humanitarian grounds; it was essentially motivated by a desire to reduce the influence of emancipated black people in the United States.

Many Americans regarded free Africans as potential instigators of insurrections: a threat to the institution of slavery. So the formation of the American Colonization Society was established to remove free African Americans – not enslaved ones – from the United States, in the belief that if enslaved African Americans saw their 'free brothers and sisters' then they would also aspire to be liberated. The aim was to eject emancipated people from the US in order to maintain and optimise the enslavement of others.

In the 1790s Thomas Jefferson, who would become president of the US, had concluded that it would be impossible for enslaved and free people to live together in harmony and that a revolution could be triggered, in which the enslaved would become the master. Such a view laid the foundations for the establishment of the ACS in 1816 by enslavers such as Bushrod Washington, the associate justice of the US Supreme Court. James Monroe, who became president in 1817, was supportive of the initiative; as a former governor of Virginia he had been appalled when there was an insurrection by enslaved people there and he made funds available to the ACS to send an exploratory mission to Africa to find a suitable location for black Americans. In 1822, the first settlers from the United States, as well as a few from the Caribbean, arrived in Liberia. They disembarked on Providence Island, a green stretch of land by an inlet of water to the Atlantic.

At first there were a few hundred settlers and then their number grew to about 2,000. They occupied an area that later became the capital Monrovia – named after James Monroe. The population swelled: between 1822 and the early 1900s around 20,000 settlers arrived in Liberia. About a third of that number were not emancipated African Americans, but enslaved people who had been told they could be freed on condition that they left the US for good.

These settlers craved the political rights they had not enjoyed in America, and so very quickly became politically active. One of the most prominent of these early settlers was Joseph Roberts, a highly intelligent man with striking features. He was born in the US in 1809, emigrated to Liberia at the age of 20 and became a merchant, then an adviser to the governor of the colony. From 1824 to 1847, Liberia was administered by the American Colonization Society. Roberts himself became governor in 1842, and in 1848 he was appointed the first president of the newly independent republic of Liberia, which then consisted of 11 towns.

The African Americans did not arrive in an unoccupied land. There were long-standing indigenous communities, such as the Mandingo, the Kpelle and the coastal Kru. The structure of these societies differed from others in West Africa that were kingdoms and empires based on trade; these were autonomous, independent and locally governed entities. The new settlers were urban dwellers and so they did not seek to acquire much land from indigenous groups, and this helped defuse potential tensions. However, interactions with the coastal Kru people remained cool and distant, due mostly to the fact that the Kru were known to have been involved in the transatlantic trade. They did not capture or sell people, but did transport them from the coast to waiting ships on the Atlantic.

Relations between settled communities and the immigrants eased somewhat because the Americans immediately recognised aspects of their culture as practised by their grandparents, which helped emphasise similarities rather than differences. Popular African American spiritual songs were imbued with a sense of melancholy at being displaced from Africa, including, as relayed to me by Liberian professor Carl Patrick Burrowes, 'Sometimes I Feel Like a Motherless Child'. Nevertheless, the Americo-Liberians, as they came to be known, began to dominate the ruling class, although they only represented 5 per cent of the population. This led to resentment, as seen in the resistance by the Kpelle in the early 1900s and the Kru in the 1920s. The conflicts of the 1980s and 1990s also had their roots in these early tensions. From Liberia's independence in 1847 until

1980, when Samuel Doe became president, the country had been continuously ruled by Americo-Liberian presidents.

Yet Liberia is not the only African country still defined by its history: the legacy of the trade continues to have wide effects on Africans and the diaspora today. As Professor Augustin Holl has said, there must be a more concerted and extensive debate and more research on its consequences in the continent itself. I recall the words of my Ghanaian guide Nkunu Akyea, a man in his late sixties: 'When I was at school the subject of slavery was not discussed. We spoke of it only in hushed tones because of the pain involved.' Indeed, apart from the academics I interviewed about slavery, I found people were generally reluctant even to broach the topic. It was hinted to me that some people with fairer skin might be unwilling to be reminded that their female forebears may have been raped by white enslavers.

Slavery stunted development and laid the foundations for some of the problems with which the continent still wrestles. In 1850, the population of sub-Saharan Africa was about 100 million; it would have been double that if there had been no slave trade. The trade brought about massive disruption by dislocating families and communities, who were forced to scatter and form small, isolated groups in order to avoid wholesale capture, which fragmented their economic activity. Many of the youngest and the strongest people were sent into a life of captivity, depriving Africa of its powers of productivity and procreation, leading to economic, social and cultural devastation. The vast majority of enslaved people were men, which skewed the gender ratio in Africa, further arresting its development. Northern Ghana, for example, has been more impoverished than the rest of the country because it was a hunting ground for the capture of people for enslavement. The architecture in that part of Ghana reflects the fear that inhabitants felt at the prospect of being hauled off to the next waiting slave ship. The houses there are still raised from the ground with flat roofs; the entrance is accessible only by climbing up a ladder, and the opening into the hut is small, so it is not easy to peer inside from the exterior. Nkunu told me that areas known to be locations where slave raids took place are often deserted even to this day, with many reluctant to settle there because of the painful memories handed down through the generations. The shadow cast by the giant events of centuries ago is long and malignant. As Professor Burrowes put it to me, 'How do we disentangle the cultural and intellectual web that was foisted on us, that questioned our humanity and assumed our inferiority?'

The legacy of the transatlantic slave trade therefore cannot be blithely consigned to distant history, for its end did not mean real emancipation for Africans. Rather, they were subjected to a different form of coercion, control and domination: colonisation, which endured well into the twentieth century and extended beyond areas of Africa affected by the transatlantic trade. In the case of southern Africa, the subject of the next chapter, white rule continued until the very end of the last century.

For this chapter, I visited many locations connected to the transatlantic slave trade and spoke to dozens of people across Africa – Ghana, Nigeria, Liberia, Gambia, Senegal, Cabo Verde, Angola and the two Congos – and found that today those who call for reparations both for Africans living in Africa and in the diaspora are no longer seen as an extreme minority. This is a controversial issue, which excites powerful sentiments on both sides of the argument.

However, there is greater international engagement on the topic than 20 years ago, including in the US Congress. African leaders and citizens are increasingly urging European nations to make some form of reparations to Africa for the slave trade, which as Ghana's president Nana Akufo-Addo said in August 2022 had stifled the continent's 'economic, cultural, and psychological progress'. The African Union, consisting of 55 members, has been trying to create a dialogue with European countries and is working on a plan that sees African countries affected by the trade, mostly in western, southwestern and central Africa, coalesce around a common position on reparations. Ghana is joined in the vanguard of such efforts by Mia Mottley, the feisty and plain-speaking prime minister of Barbados.

According to opinion polls, the majority of diaspora Africans consistently support some form of reparations, even if there is no agreed method about how this might be delivered. Indeed, some more extravagant suggestions have perhaps led to a deviation from more serious discussions.

One of the most coherent calls for reparations emanates from Caribbean nations. When I visited Barbados, the eminent economic historian, Professor Sir Hilary Beckles, vice-chancellor of the University of the West Indies, talked at length with me about the subject, pointing out that when in 1833 Britain 'emancipated' its enslaved people, the government raised the equivalent of US$25 billion today to compensate 46,000 enslavers for the 'loss of their human property'. The interest on that money was only paid off by the British government in 2015. Nothing was given to freed men and women. They were told liberty was their reward.

As the inaugural chair in 2013 of the CARICOM Reparations Commission, the Caribbean Community grouping with a combined population of around 16 million, Sir Hilary believes an apology and reparations are long overdue. In a ten-point plan, which he helped to draw up, CARICOM calls for reparations to be paid in the form of development assistance and the cancellation of international debt. 'We have argued in the Caribbean that reparatory justice is about development and that Britain and Europe do indeed owe a debt to this region, a debt that is recognised, that can be computed, that is historically sound in terms of its legitimacy.' He says that the issue can no longer be swept under the carpet and that there should be 'immediate negotiations about how to repair the harm and suffering that continues to be the legacy of slavery in the Caribbean today'. The reader can make their own judgement but Sir Hilary, who has long been involved in the fight for reparations, is adamant that it is only a matter of time before they are made.

15

Land, Gold and Greed

After Europeans ceased to trade in enslaved Africans, a new period of exploitation of Africa's rich resources and mineral wealth began. Southern Africa best epitomises how Africans fell victim to the conquest of their land and subsequent displacement by European settlers: the most beautiful and bountiful African territories were those most coveted by outsiders. Endowed with an abundance of natural resources, southern Africa became a magnet for white settlers spurred on by a desire for land, gold and diamonds, and hence its people endured some of the worst oppression. We will therefore focus on what are today South Africa and Zimbabwe. The tight political grip of white settlers was maintained until relatively recently: Zimbabweans and South Africans had to wait until 1980 and 1994 respectively to enjoy full citizen rights and black majority rule. It is legitimate to question whether black enfranchisement has reduced the economic dominance of white industrialists and farmers, and whether it has brought peace, prosperity and equality to the citizens of these two countries, but few if any of their black populations would wish to turn back the clock to a time when they were accorded inferior status simply by dint of their race.

We will also focus on African figures in a period of southern Africa's history in which coverage has been dominated by rivalries between the colonisers, such as the Anglo–Boer Wars in the late nineteenth century, and by accounts of the activities of Europeans such as the British mining magnate Cecil John Rhodes.

The first Europeans to reach the Cape in southern Africa in 1488 were the Portuguese, as was usually the case, as we have seen in earlier chapters. However, the beginnings of European settlement in the area date to the early 1650s. Standing at the top of the 1,000-metre-high Table Mountain – a prominent landmark overlooking Cape Town in South Africa, which afforded a marvellous view of the mountainous landscape that lay beyond – I could see the strong ocean waves rhythmically beating the sand. I imagined the Dutchman Jan van Riebeeck coming ashore three and a half centuries before at the head of the small expedition dispatched by the Dutch East India Company and thought of the upheaval that he portended. Only the craggy coastline remains the same.

The VOC – the Dutch abbreviation for Vereenigde Oostindische Compagnie – was a conglomerate of several rival Dutch trading companies and was established as a chartered company in 1602 under government sanction to trade with India. Van Riebeeck arrived at Table Bay, which lies strategically close to the point where the Atlantic and the Indian oceans meet. Its turbulent waters gave it the name the Cape of Storms – a fitting metaphor for South Africa's history once Van Riebeeck sailed in. It was a useful route to the east for the spice trade and so Van Riebeeck initially established a Dutch station to supply provisions for ships bound eastward, which then became a permanent settlement. The typical Dutch settler was of a peasant or low-class background and would have joined the VOC out of poverty and desperation. In fact, many were not Dutch but of mixed Dutch–German descent, and there were also some French settlers among them. They all had staunch Protestant Christian beliefs in common.

For perspectives on this chapter I sought out two prominent South African academics: Dr Thula Simpson from the University of Pretoria and Professor Nigel Penn from the University of Cape Town, as well as local Zulu cultural experts such as Bongi Thabede and Prince Mangosuthu Buthelezi.

The Khoisan

The original inhabitants of the Cape in southern Africa were the pastoralist Khoikhoi (sometimes just the Khoi), later pejoratively referred to by Dutch settlers as the Hottentot; and the San, who were hunter-gatherers and received the derogatory name of 'bushmen'. Collectively they are known as the Khoisan. Their lives had continued peacefully for many hundreds of years, and their history was uneventful, because history that is devoid of conflict often is. But the arrival of the Europeans meant their centuries-old way of life was irrevocably disrupted.

Initially, Jan van Riebeeck was instructed by the VOC to maintain cordial ties with the Khoikhoi and not be tempted into enslaving them. Indeed the Khoikhoi and San people welcomed and traded with Europeans during their first encounters from 1488 onwards, supplying them with provisions such as water and fresh meat. When the number of Europeans was modest, there was not much friction and it was a mutually beneficial relationship. The Europeans began to farm and became known as 'free burghers'. However, after about five years, the Dutch settlers began to dominate the Cape Peninsula, and were establishing agricultural land holdings in order to farm produce that they could sell to ships sailing around the Cape.

The Khoikhoi were deeply unhappy by this encroachment of their ancestral land. They told the Europeans, 'Why are you ploughing up the land? Why don't you go back to your own country? What would you think if we came to your country and began to take over your land?'[1]

The Dutch ignored their entreaties and the Khoikhoi saw their territory slip into the foreigners' hands. The Western Cape had what could be described as a Mediterranean climate, with winter rainfall that allowed the cultivation of crops favoured by Europeans, including grapes to make wine, so it was particularly attractive to them. Unable to prevent the loss of their lands, the traditional Khoikhoi leaders saw their prestige and authority diminish and their political and social structures decline. In addition, smallpox and other new diseases introduced by the white settlers from the East Indies led to crushing pandemics and mass deaths among the Khoikhoi in the late seventeenth and early eighteenth centuries.

Witnessing the disintegration of their society, the Khoikhoi fought back. A guerrilla war began. The Khoikhoi saw that the Dutch had superior military hardware and technology so they relied on their better knowledge of the terrain to engage their enemies at close quarters. But they were outgunned and it was a lost cause.

Some of the Khoikhoi migrated north but most were forced to work for Dutch settlers as herdsmen, hunters and labourers for extremely low wages. Sometimes they were not paid at all and were just given food and clothing. They were effectively reduced to being servants of the Dutch settlers, although they were not officially enslaved nor bought and sold in a slave market.

Professor Penn told me the Europeans' first impressions of the Khoikhoi were based 'largely on prejudice rather than objective observation'. In fact, he said, the Khoikhoi were wealthy:

> they owned cattle and sheep, they had structured societies, lived communally in huts and had their own religions. They had all of the things which you would think the Europeans would recognise as constituting a civilised society; instead, they highlighted the fact that the Khoikhoi did not build towns, lacked visible forms of worship and that they were mostly naked. Bias led the Europeans to see in the Khoikhoi only what they wanted to. They accused the men of being cannibals and the women of being promiscuous. It was an archetypal depiction of savagery.

Later, the fate of Sara Baartman (*c.* 1789–1815), whose African name is uncertain, would serve as a tragic example of how the Khoikhoi were exploited. Sara was taken by two white men to England as a freak attraction in shows in the early 1800s in Europe and given the name the 'Hottentot Venus'. Exoticised, she was exhibited naked, and her body shape and intimate parts became the subject of lurid and racially charged discussions in salons. Sara died penniless in Paris, in her mid-twenties, possibly of syphilis or smallpox.

Yet, miserable as their situation was, as pastoralists, the Khoikhoi were treated better than the San. The San were hunter-gatherers, so were not valued as labourers and were regarded as a threat to livestock. According to Professor Penn, the Europeans saw the San as a 'form of vermin that ought to be exterminated, and so frequently commanders were sent out against San or other hunter-gatherers who had killed the livestock of the colonists. The men were hunted down and slaughtered. There was almost a genocidal warfare waged against resisters.' Thousands were killed. Those women and children who were spared were absorbed into the Dutch workforce as labourers and domestic servants.

Both the San and Khoikhoi resisted. One leading opponent was the Khoikhoi chief Autshumao (c. 1611–63). At first, he was an interpreter for the Dutch, learning not only to speak that language but possibly several other European ones, including English. The Dutch called him 'Harry the Strandloper', which means 'beach walker'. His linguistic skills made him useful and he was paid for his services, which greatly boosted his wealth and standing within his own Khoikhoi community. When a dispute over cattle ownership between the Khoikhoi and the Dutch broke out, conflict ensued and Autshumao sided with his people, turning against the Dutch in 1658. The Khoikhoi lost and Autshumao was imprisoned by Van Riebeeck on Robben Island off the Cape. (Centuries later Nelson Mandela would be held captive there in a tiny cell by the descendants of the Dutch settlers.)

In 1660 Autshumao managed to steal a rowing boat and sailed away from the island along with a fellow prisoner. It is likely that this was the first and last time that any inmate managed to escape from Robben Island. Autshumao died in 1663, a broken man. He was a failure in his own eyes, because his people had been betrayed by the Dutch and he had not succeeded in securing freedom for them. In reality, the Khoikhoi never stood a chance of winning this asymmetric war.

In order to consolidate its position, the VOC began the construction of the Castle of Good Hope in Cape Town. Today, this is an impressive and sprawling complex of stone fortresses: a church with spires, workshops and living quarters for the European inhabitants, beautifully manicured quad gardens with cannons poking out menacingly between walls. Inside the compound were several prison cells, small and cramped, still displaying the chains and equipment used to torture prisoners. The VOC had one particular cell called the 'Donker Gat', Dutch for 'dark hole', where a prisoner awaiting trial would be kept in solitary confinement in complete darkness, ready to confess to any alleged crime once he emerged. The castle was completed in 1679 and is the oldest existing European building in South Africa.

In 1806, the British finally seized control and established their authority. The VOC had ceased to exist in 1799 and most of the Dutch settlers accepted that they had a new government. They were prepared to tolerate the British as long as they helped them to fight the Africans and 'keep order' among the Khoikhoi and the San.

Unlike other parts of Africa, which saw the export of enslaved people to Europe and the Americas, southern Africa used labourers imported from elsewhere on the continent, as well as from Malaya, Indonesia, Madagascar and the Indian subcontinent. The Cape Colony under the Dutch was a slave society, with vast numbers of enslaved people. These groups of labourers all mixed with one another, giving rise to a new community later known as the 'Cape Coloureds'.

Tensions between the British and the Dutch came to a head after the British introduced around 5,000 settlers into the Eastern Cape in 1820. These educated British middle-class immigrants were encouraged to settle on farmlands, to act as a buffer between the Dutch settlers and the local population. Some had agricultural backgrounds and became significant landowners, rearing sheep for the production of wool, which was the mainstay of the Cape economy and became its biggest export between 1835 and 1882, before diamonds overtook it.

Another issue of contention was the fact that by the early 1830s slavery had been abolished and the British wanted to discourage the practice, while the burghers wanted to continue using enslaved labour. And so, from the mid-1830s, although the majority initially remained, thousands of Dutch settlers and their African servants began to leave the British-controlled Cape for new areas in the interior. This mass movement of settlers was known as the 'Great Trek'. The burghers moved north and east to regions such as KwaZulu-Natal, the land of the Zulus. They travelled in ox-drawn wagons and on horses, armed with their guns and carrying their bibles. These were the first of the Voortrekkers or Trek Boers, shortened to just the Boers. Voortrekkers means 'wandering farmers' in Afrikaans – the version of Dutch spoken by the Boer settlers. They were self-sufficient and isolationist, with a narrow view of the world. They held austere Protestant Calvinist beliefs and thought they had a duty to 'civilise' their black neighbours, just like Christians in the Confederate states of the US used a 'religious' imperative to justify their dominance over and enslavement of black people.

Once the Boers had established republics in the interior, they were seen as a threat to the British project of imperialism and control of mineral-rich land. The rivalry between the British and the Boers led to a series of battles known as the Boer Wars, which began in the late nineteenth century. The discovery of gold by the British tipped the balance in their favour. Not wanting the Boers to exploit this massive source of wealth, the British were spurred on to defeat the independent Boer sovereignties. Much ink has been spilled about the conflict between the British and the Dutch in what is today South Africa and how it came to shape the country's future, but the competition for dominance between white settlers came against the background of a critical phase within black African history: the rise of the Zulu kingdom in the early nineteenth century.

Zulus

The Zulus, with their military renown, are among the most famous of Africa's ethnic groups and South Africa's biggest. They are a subgroup of the Nguni people, who include the Thembu, whose most illustrious son is Nelson Mandela. The Nguni moved from western into southern Africa as part of the Bantu migration, eventually extending all the way up to the boundaries of the present-day Western Cape. The Zulus occupied a large area of land known today as KwaZulu-Natal, which is a southeastern coastal province. Flying to Durban, its biggest city, I could see the long shoreline on the Indian Ocean, famous for its beaches and savannah populated by big game. It is a generally mountainous region, with rocky outcrops.

Just outside Durban, Bongi Thabede, a Zulu guide, took me to a cultural centre to explain how Zulus today enthusiastically embrace their heritage and rich folklore, especially through their use of the Zulu language. She showed me an example of an *iQukwane*, a thatched Zulu hut, made from grass. The Zulu people were originally cattle herders, their crops farmed mostly by women. Zulus are proud of their distinctive ritualistic dance, the *uMhlanga*, which was suppressed during apartheid and has now been re-established. It is a dazzling spectacle to behold: a vigorous stamping of feet launches the earth beneath the dancers up into the breeze. The Zulu fighters are colourfully adorned, dressed in animal skins and holding their shields and spears aloft. Sporting a profusion of beaded jewellery, Bongi told me how the skill of beadwork is important for the Zulus. Their kings wear intricately worked chest decorations just like Shaka did centuries earlier.

Shaka Zulu, *c.* 1787–1828

Shaka, king of the Zulus, was one of the most iconic and influential rulers in southern Africa. A hero to many Africans, he was also a fearsome foe both to his African rivals and to European settlers. Much of what we know about uShaka kaSenzangakhona, to give him his full name, comes

An 1824 sketch of King Shaka, appearing in Nathaniel Isaacs's travelogues. Isaacs did much to establish European perceptions of Shaka as 'a savage'

from European sources. Although some of these recognise the military and state-building achievements of the Zulus, others paint a strikingly different picture of him from that related by the Zulus. Shaka's people hold him in the highest esteem and have handed down rich accounts of him through the generations. Shaka has been the subject of several films, with the 1964 British epic *Zulu* being one of the best known. More modern interpretations of his story by Africans, such as the 2021 award-winning animated film *Shaka Inkosi Yama-Khosi*, directed by South African businessman Manzini Zungu, present a more holistic portrait of him. Zungu said he wanted to bring to life fundamental aspects of Shaka's character which have been omitted: 'Shaka over and above being a military tactician and having prophetic gifts was a musician, songwriter and composer. He would often comfort his people with music and inspire his troops in song (amahubo)'.[2] In the early nineteenth century Shaka prophesied that the 'white man' would seize control of the Zulu kingdom he had founded – a prediction which devastatingly came to pass.

Shaka was the son of Senzangakhona. When he was an infant, a traditional doctor had foretold that he was destined to be a powerful king, and in a nod to the adult valour for which he would be renowned, it is said that Shaka never cried as a baby. As a child, however, he was mocked by the older herd boys on account of his illegitimacy. His mother Nandi had conceived him out of wedlock, and though she subsequently married his father, Senzangakhona nevertheless rejected them, banishing both her and Shaka from the village. After years of travel with his mother, wandering from place to place, they settled among their herdsmen kin in Mtetwa. There Shaka joined the army of the prince Dingiswayo and trained as a fighter. He excelled so much that he was appointed commander of his regiment. Later, between 1816 and 1818, after his father's death, Shaka returned to his home village. Even though he had no claim to the chiefdom, the recognised heir Sigujana was deposed and Shaka was installed as chief. While still remaining as Dingiswayo's vassal, Shaka consolidated his power base by expanding his army, which then numbered about 500. Shaka was reportedly intelligent, shrewd and brave, and building on the foundations that his father had established he made his clan a strong military force. In 1818 Dingiswayo was killed in battle by a rival chief and the Mtetwa confederacy fell apart, giving Shaka the opportunity to incorporate it into his territory.

In 1819 Shaka saw off a key rival, which allowed him to establish himself as the ruler of a single all-powerful kingdom, even empire. Community after community succumbed to his rule through force and intimidation. His philosophy was that 'might is right'. Shaka proclaimed: 'Though many bandit nations have been tamed, there still remain those who cause disorder and violate custom and bully the smaller nations.'[3] Men were either co-opted into his army or expected to work with the women in cultivation and cattle rearing. The Nguni lavished great care on their cattle, their diet consisting mainly of meat and milk; their wealth was measured by how many cattle they owned. Shaka wanted to forge a new identity among his conquered peoples, so he gave them his clan's name, the Zulu, and addressed them thus: 'My brothers, our journey is now pointless. Everywhere we go we find only those who acknowledge our authority. Zulu power no longer issues from conquest, but from a bond of all embracing nationhood. We must turn back to our homes'.

In the early 1820s, in the space of just a few years, Shaka extended his domain across modern-day KwaZulu-Natal – a region the size of Portugal. Written sources about the Zulus and Shaka from European traders and missionaries depicted him as a 'savage warrior'. In 1836, one British adventurer, Nathaniel Isaacs, described Shaka as 'an insatiable and exterminating savage' and wondered if 'history, ancient or modern can produce so horrible and detestable a savage'. He wrote to a fellow author, Henry Francis Fynn, urging him to smear Shaka and his successors:

> Make them out to be as bloodthirsty as you can and endeavour to give an estimation of the number of people that they have murdered during their reign and describe the frivolous crimes people lose their lives for. Introduce as many anecdotes relative to Shaka as you can; it all tends to swell up the work and make it interesting.[4]

This depiction of Shaka has subsequently been perpetuated by some European writers, who saw him as a villain, driven by an illegitimate birth, an unhappy childhood and rejection by his father.

For a Zulu perspective, I arranged to meet Shaka's great-great-great-nephew Prince Mangosuthu Buthelezi at his office in Durban, who is related to Shaka through his mother Princess Mgogo. As leader of the Inkatha Freedom Party, Chief Buthelezi, who died in September 2023, played a polarising role in South African history in the 1980s and 1990s during the transition from apartheid. But it is his dominant role within the Zulu nation that is relevant to this chapter. Dressed in a smart blue suit and tie, his ninetieth birthday imminent, he beamed with delight as he told me that he had learned about Shaka from his mother and her family. In Zulu folklore, Shaka is regarded as a great king. His profound military acumen, his transformation of Nguni pastoralist societies into a state and other achievements are transmitted in an oral tradition of songs and stories that exults him to this day.

Shaka's conquests were ferocious and came at colossal

cost to human life and resources. He built a large army, quashed internal opposition and launched a series of wars in the 1820s against rival southern African communities, in what was known as the Mfecane, or the 'crushing', among the Nguni, and the Difaqane, meaning the 'scattering', among the Sotho-Tswana people. Whole villages were obliterated and many fled their lands in different directions.

This military campaign by the Zulus is contested among historians. Numerous African academics, including Dr Thula Simpson, believe the description of the Mfecane as laying waste to African communities creates a very convenient myth from a colonial point of view, especially the idea that black-on-black conflict created a depopulated interior, enabling white settlers to move into 'empty' land and develop it. They believe the Mfecane was more a continuation of a pattern that had existed for a number of centuries: different communities competing for land and cattle, with populations moving around. It is also likely that Africans shifted increasingly *into* the interior to avoid capture by slavers who were combing parts of the southern African coast. One prominent South African industrialist told me his grandmother, born in the 1920s, would talk of how her own grandfather spoke in terrifying terms about people being captured and taken away in ships. In any case, the Mfecane was undoubtedly a phenomenon that remoulded southern Africa, creating new identities and cultural and historical consciousness that influenced African responses to the European conquest of southern Africa.

During the Mfecane various rival chiefs fled elsewhere in the region. At its height one chief, Moshoeshoe, established a new kingdom, Sotho, in what became Lesotho. This was a loose confederation of chiefdoms and Moshoeshoe introduced a complex web of strategic marriages to maintain unity. He sent gifts to Shaka to deter him from pursuing him. Another

Nguni chief who founded a new kingdom was Soshangane, founder of Gaza, as seen in Chapter 11; and a prominent chief of Zulu origin called Mzilikazi had set up his kingdom in Matabeleland, in part of what was later Zimbabwe. Mzilikazi is widely regarded as the second greatest Nguni fighter and leader after King Shaka. He had defied Shaka and refused to be cowed, telling him: 'I will create my own nation.' Exceptionally, Shaka allowed him to retain his title and keep his own armed forces.

Shaka maintained absolute control. He was king, commander-in-chief, supreme justice and chief priest. All state property belonged to him, as did natural resources, cattle and people. He could distribute state wealth through gifts, patronage and pensions. He appointed royal officials to oversee newly conquered lands and replaced any local chief who opposed his rule. Rivals or even those deemed merely useless could be eliminated. His word was final. He governed through his advisory council and could discuss issues for weeks on end. Upon meeting the king, subjects would have to shout, 'Bayete! Wena we Ndlovu,' meaning 'Hail the father of the nation, hail his majesty.' In the king's presence one would have to kneel and not address him directly but through court clerks. He appointed army commanders on merit, which incentivised soldiers to do well on the battlefield so that they could be promoted to positions of leadership, and posts were open to all regardless of ethnicity, which also helped develop a sense of nationhood. Skill in combat enhanced the Zulu reputation as fighters, and perhaps encouraged a cult of youth. It is believed that Shaka bought black hair dye from European settlers so he could colour his grey hair!

Shaka had to be disciplined and single-minded to maintain such consummate control. He did not marry so that he could dedicate his life to being a soldier and ruler. Zulu oral tradition maintains that Shaka remained celibate all his life and pushed unwanted female attention onto his younger brother Mpande, who clearly benefited from this for he had scores of wives. Shaka also expected his active soldiers, who were kept in barracks, not to marry until they were discharged and sent back to their original villages at the age of 40. He may have asked them to refrain from sexual relations or he may have forbidden them from impregnating women, which gave rise to accounts of how to have intercourse without conception. Shaka insisted he had to abide by the rules of celibacy too: 'What example would I be setting for the army? What wise general would ask of his men what he himself would not do?'[5] Other accounts hold that Shaka discreetly indulged in sexual activity and secretly gave his children to relatives or had them removed. Prince Mangosuthu told me that from everything he had heard about Shaka, he believed that he had indeed remained celibate.

At the peak of his powers, Shaka had about 15 regiments comprising thousands of soldiers including a large female regiment in which he placed senior women, who specialised in gathering intelligence. Men and women were strictly kept apart until they were discharged. The regiments were supported by the state: soldiers received their land, weapons and cattle from Shaka's royal coffers, although they were also expected to contribute to the treasury through donating some of their spoils of war. Young boys were recruited from diverse villages. They would have to start at the bottom, first as herdsmen and then baggage carriers until they had completed their training as soldiers.

Shaka achieved countless successes on the battlefield because he was an effective military strategist, and he earned the Zulus their reputation as a war-like people, renowned for speed and surprise when mounting attacks, usually at dawn.

The soldiers were trained barefoot to toughen them. Shaka is credited with inventing the short spear, the assegai, which was much more effective as a fighting tool in close combat than a long one. The Zulus were adept at iron-working which helped them make better weapons. Their fighters would position themselves some distance from their opponent and use their sturdy cowhide shields to deflect the spears being hurled at them. They would then draw closer to their enemy and kill them with their short stabbing spears. Losing a spear could incur a severe penalty. Shaka also devised the 'bull or cow horn' fighting formation, which meant the enemy would be completely encircled by his men, cutting off any escape. The centre regiment would then charge into the enemy, while the reserves would wait behind for relief. Meanwhile, two other regiments formed horns to surround the opponents on the left and right. If a Zulu soldier deserted service, mutinied or displayed cowardice it amounted to a crime punishable by death. As well as the physical abilities of his soldiers, Shaka also made extensive use of spies and psychological warfare. He appointed certain men as 'rousers' or agitators, to motivate his soldiers before battle. Shaka established his capital KwaDukuza about 80 kilometres north of Durban. In the Zulu language this means 'place of the lost person'. From there he ruled for several years.

When Shaka's mother Nandi died in 1827, he was grief-stricken. She had been a dominant force throughout his life. 'I have conquered the world but lost my mother.' To mourn her passing he decreed that no crops should be planted for a year, and no couple should allow a pregnancy to occur. And anyone who he deemed had not cried enough was liable to lose their life. His ruthlessness eventually alienated even those close to him. For a soldier-king, death on the battlefield would have been fitting, but that was not how Shaka died.

Treachery from within his inner circle brought about his demise, much in the vein of Julius Caesar's death; Shaka also had his 'Et tu, Brute' moment.

On 24 September 1828, Shaka was sitting on a rock in his compound in KwaDukuza awaiting visitors. Two of his half-brothers, Dingane and Mhlangana, along with Shaka's servant, Mbopha, approached him carrying spears. According to oral history, one of the brothers, aiming for Shaka's heart, instead stabbed him in the arm. Shaka tried to deflect his brothers from their murderous mission by warning them that if they killed him it would lead to the defeat of the Zulu kingdom by the white man. 'Ye children of my father, what is the wrong? What have I done to you? So, my brothers you are killing me? And you too Mbopha, son of Sithayi? You think you shall rule Zululand after my death? No, you shall never rule. Only the swallows shall rule over it.' He got to his feet and confronted his brothers but they stabbed him repeatedly until he fell to the ground. Zulu tradition holds that to be stabbed in the back denotes a cowardly death; it would imply a person was running away from his attackers rather than facing death like a soldier.

Shaka's body was wrapped in the skin of a black ox and buried. Afterwards his brother Dingane burned Shaka's compound to the ground. To stand by Shaka's grave, in a small garden plot at the spot of his old homestead, is a rather noisy affair. Situated on a busy road, cars hurtling by, it is not a place for quiet reflection. His grave is enclosed by a small fence inside a walled garden. A black rock is next to it, reputedly the very same one Shaka was sitting on before his death. A bust of Shaka atop a marble pillar bears testament to his legacy as the acme of African militarism. Many Zulus mourn his murder, but perhaps these words from his brothers show

how others had grown weary of Shaka's appetite for war: 'The insatiable war-thirst of Shaka gives us no peace, those who applaud the endless campaigns only do so to please. We have the right to the destiny of our nation. We too are the children of the king. No nation was ever built only on wars. The greatness of a people lies in the richness of their lives. The sacrifice of war is to ensure a better life for their children.'

Shaka was undoubtedly ruthless and at times cruel, but he also radically changed society in southern Africa through a complex revolution that overturned traditional orders and created a new and dynamic nation based on meritocracy and militarism. New elites based on the soldier-citizen were formed. The concept of honour and valour became ingrained in the national psyche.

Shaka's successors

Shaka was succeeded in 1828 by Dingane (*c.* 1795–1840), the brother who had murdered him. For good measure, he had also killed his co-conspirator Mhlangana to become sole king. Although he was accorded respect, he couldn't escape the perception that his act of betrayal was cowardly and wrong, and Dingane lacked Shaka's leadership qualities. Although the Mfecane continued under him, the depletion of available land led to the breakdown of discipline in the Zulu army and widespread pillaging by his soldiers. Dingane wiped out scores of Boer trekkers who were led by Piet Retief in 1838. Retief was seeking to negotiate with Dingane over access to land in his domain. He met Dingane for discussions, only to be killed immediately afterwards, along with his entire delegation, by Dingane's men.

Dingane's brother, Mpande (1798–1872), who became

king in 1840, managed to rebuild the Zulu kingdom as a militarised state. He tried to avoid conflict with the white settlers
but the Boers were encroaching on his land and the threat of
war was ever present. Upon Mpande's death in 1872, his son
Cetshwayo (1826–84) ascended the throne. Cetshwayo was
regal, tall and broad chested, but it was not an easy time to
become king. The Zulus not only had to deal with the Boers
but had to contend with an ever-growing threat to their sovereignty from the British. The following year, Cetshwayo
invited to his coronation the British representative in charge
of natives' affairs, Theophilus Shepstone, who described
him as: 'A man of considerable ability, much force of character and has a dignified manner. In all conversations with him
he was remarkably frank and straightforward. He is naturally
proud of the military traditions of his family especially the
policy and deeds of his uncle and predecessor Shaka.'6

But Shepstone proved to be a fickle friend and turned on
Cetshwayo; the British decided to seize his lands. Cetshwayo
expressed his concern: 'I hear of troops arriving in Natal
that they are coming to attack the Zulus and to seize me.
What have I done wrong that I should be seized like an
"umtakata" [wrongdoer]. The English are my fathers. I do
not wish to quarrel with them but to live as I have always
done at peace with them.'7

The British gave Cetshwayo conditions that they calculated
he would never accept. He was told to disband his army and
abolish the military system on which his kingdom was based.
They were right; as a Zulu king, he could not agree to such
terms, and this gave them the pretext for war. In January 1879,
the British assembled an army and crossed the Buffalo River
into the Zulu kingdom at Rorke's Drift, where they selected a
giant rocky outcrop called Isandlwana and set up camp. A
20,000-strong Zulu force attacked them and killed 870 British

troops and 490 African auxiliaries drawn from Cetshwayo's enemies. Only 55 British soldiers survived.

It was one of the most famous victories by Africans in British colonial history and is one from which Zulus today draw considerable pride. The British attack, which came after King Cetshwayo tried unsuccessfully to sue for peace, was seen by the Zulus as unjustified and warmongering. But the British resolved to dismantle the Zulu kingdom and bring it under their sway. 'What have I done? I want peace. I ask for peace,' Cetshwayo said in exasperation.[8] Just a few months after the iconic Zulu achievement at Isandlwana, the British retaliated in July. The Zulus were subjected to a massive attack with gun and artillery fire for five months at the Battle of Ulundi, which was Cetshwayo's capital: more than 1,000 Zulus were killed, while only a handful of officials and dozens of men died on the British side. The kingdom built by Shaka Zulu was now in the white man's hands, just as he had predicted before his murder.

After his defeat at Ulundi, King Cetshwayo's palace was burned down and he was imprisoned along with two of his wives in the castle built by Van Riebeeck in Cape Town. He was then exiled to London, where he made a plea to Queen Victoria to be allowed to return to his kingdom, but to no avail. Cetshwayo's kingdom was broken up and divided into 13 fiefdoms, and the British installed loyal rulers as 'kinglets' in each one of them. Cetshwayo never recovered his throne, but soon before his death in 1884 he was allowed to return to Zululand. The remains of the wagon that bore his body to his burial site are today kept in a museum near Ulundi.

The defeat of the Zulus and other communities at this time provided white settlers with greater security, and enabled them to exploit the natural resources of the whole southern African region. South African history became defined by the discovery of diamonds in Kimberley in the northern Cape and gold around Johannesburg, in what became known as the 'mineral revolution' in the 1870s and 1880s. This shifted the economic centre of gravity from the Cape, which had been significant for its role in international trade routes, to the interior. It also accelerated the establishment of the segregation system under white supremacy that became known as apartheid.

In 1886, gold was discovered in Witwatersrand, a lightly populated rural part of the Boer republic of the Transvaal. Within months the city of Johannesburg was laid out, and its population boomed. By 1907 the mines of Witwatersrand were producing a third of the world's gold. At first, for many Africans the mines were a place where they could go to earn money in order to purchase cattle, ploughs and land, and become important figures in their home territories. The majority stayed for brief periods of up to six months, working for white miners or holding other jobs in the camps. They returned home after they had enough money.

Kimberley, capital of Northern Cape province, was the first place in what is now South Africa to offer up its treasures. Until the eighteenth century, when the first mines were opened in Brazil, all diamonds came from India or Borneo. Relatively scarce until then, by the nineteenth century they were the most precious of all gemstones. So the discovery of diamonds in Kimberley led to frenzied excitement. The open mine, which covered 42 acres, was opened in 1871 and became known as the big hole. The site is now a museum which welcomes visitors. I felt as if I was staring into the abyss as I looked 240 metres down into its deep cavernous interior, trying to fathom the unimaginable toil of the labourers who excavated it – astonishingly – by hand. Obviously, many lives were lost. Many arrived at the diamond fields starved and utterly exhausted, having travelled on foot for weeks to get there. In the early 1870s, the mines drew 50,000 Africans each year.

The British and Boers, though engaged in a bitter rivalry, separately launched attacks against the local populations in the areas surrounding the diamond fields in order to control them. It was a brutal rush motivated by greed. As the conquests and encroachment expanded, land for the Africans became ever more scarce, leaving them no alternative but to offer their services to white settlers for ever lower wages.

The extraction of diamonds was based on the exploitation of labour: the contract holder held the mining rights, and the labour was carried out by miners who worked under often merciless supervisors. At the end of each day, the African workers were thoroughly searched, their every orifice checked for smuggled diamonds. Their movements were restricted while they were under contract and their living conditions in cramped dormitories were basic. The rural-to-urban migration of these workers separated them from their wives and children, which had devastating consequences for family life and structure, creating fractures in society that persist to this day. The onsite reproductions of these dormitories were chilling, and as I looked at photographs of miners from that era, I was haunted by the sight of young men made old before their time – some not even yet men, their faces scarred with a resignation that spoke of suffering and despair. By the time the Kimberley mine closed in 1914, it had remarkably yielded nearly 3 tons of diamonds, about 14.5 million carats' worth – a mined 1-carat diamond is valued at anything between US$1,500 and $10,000 today.

The diamond deposits in Kimberley were deep underground, unlike diamonds washed away by water into rivers and seas in what are known as alluvial mines. Therefore, to extract the diamonds in Kimberley, investments in technology were needed of a scale that few were able to bring. Britain, as a major industrial power, had the wherewithal to do so, and so it annexed the area for itself and claimed the rights over the diamonds.

The best known of the mining magnates was the Englishman Cecil John Rhodes. He is a prominent figure in British colonial history, and did much to consolidate British colonial power in southern Africa. Rhodes had come to southern Africa in the early 1870s as a young man. Quick to spot the opportunities to make big money, he ended up at the helm of the famous De Beers mining company, owning it with his associates. The company took its name from the farm of a Boer called Johannes de Beer, on whose land diamonds were found.

Rhodes understood that as more and more diamonds were produced, their value would diminish, which would depress his profits; to prevent this, he gained control of other diamond-mining sites, so that from 1889 De Beers had a total monopoly on diamond production in South Africa, accounting for 90 per cent of global supply.

At the site in Kimberley stands a Pullman coach. Built in 1898 it was used by the directors of De Beers when they travelled on the main lines of the South African railways. Walking alongside and peering in on my tiptoes, I could see the sumptuous interiors: tables laden with period silver champagne buckets, crystal spirit decanters and glasses, and ornate ashtrays for cigars – an evocative illustration of the lifestyle enjoyed by men such as Cecil Rhodes, while African labourers were strictly controlled and enclosed in fenced compounds.

Lobengula, c. 1845–94

Cecil Rhodes's business interests stretched into Matabeleland in what is today Zimbabwe. Gold was discovered there and this drew his attention. To fully exploit opportunities there, Rhodes needed to conquer the Ndebele people of Matabeleland, ruled by Lobengula. He was the son of King Mzilikazi, who had earlier defied Shaka and set up his own kingdom, centred within a radius of 80 kilometres around Bulawayo. Lobengula became king between 1868 and 1870, after a violent succession struggle in which his brothers were killed. His kingdom was a heavily militarised state, which raided and to some extent absorbed defeated communities, from whom they collected tributes.

An 1880 engraving of King Lobengula

Among the most impressive experts I met on my journeys around Africa was an elderly Zimbabwean by the name of Pathisa Nyathi. He told me how oral tradition relates that Lobengula was a clever man, who would carefully weigh up situations before making a decision. However, in 1888, despite the misgivings of his chiefs, due to his illiteracy, he voluntarily signed a concession for mining rights of minerals on his lands. Soon after, he tried to retract his agreement and, desperate, sent a delegation to London to plead his case. But the British ignored it and allowed Rhodes to press on. Rhodes interpreted the concession as allowing him to annex land for white settlement in order to exploit the minerals. At first, he avoided Lobengula's heartland by settling the Shona lands to the east.

In 1893, Ndebele fighters moved against the Shona population. They did not threaten white settler communities but this confirmed the view among Cecil Rhodes and his fellow white settlers that Lobengula was an obstacle to their consolidation of power in the region. Rhodes paid the huge sum of £50,000 (equivalent to approximately US$10 million today) to mount a war effort, recruiting settlers from across southern Africa to fight with the promise of land as a reward. Rhodes and his allies wanted war, land and control. Lobengula wanted peace and asked to negotiate. He was realistic and, according to Pathisa, described himself as a fly and Cecil Rhodes as a chameleon.

In October, the white army, accompanied by auxiliaries from the Shona community, moved towards Bulawayo, Lobengula's heartland. His Ndebele forces of up to 6,000 men attacked the invaders, but despite having a good number of rifles were unable to outgun the Maxims of their opponents. It was a short battle; hundreds of Ndebele fighters were wiped out. Lobengula and his followers burned their settlement at Bulawayo, took their livestock with them and moved northwards. But they were pursued by Rhodes's army, who were aiming to capture and kill the king. About 150 kilometres north of Bulawayo near Lupani, Lobengula lost hundreds more men and most probably died sometime in 1894. However, Ndebele tradition merely relates that he disappeared; that feeling humiliated by his ignominious defeat, he took poison and asked his faithful followers to bury him in a place that would not be found by the white imperialists. Lobengula's death is still mourned, as an Ndebele song that Pathisa sang to me relates: 'In the past our life was different and not like this. Our nation was ruled by King Mzilikazi. We went to the river Shangani and knelt down to pray there. Then King Lobengula disappeared. The rains came. But still our king was not with us . . . He had disappeared.'

With Lobengula out of the way, Cecil Rhodes and his associates handed out farms to white settlers. Lobengula and the other rulers of southern Africa had lost their battles, but not their spirit. Uprisings by the Ndebele and the Shona in the east continued in the late nineteenth century. Nevertheless, the Ndebele were pushed into near arid land to eke out a living as best they could. They suffered from more conflicts with the white settlers, as well as from famine, disease and the mass loss of livestock. The immense wealth of the few, such as Cecil Rhodes, was gained at the expense of the many black Africans who were dispossessed from their lands and consigned to a life of misery toiling in the diamond and gold mines of southern Africa. Rhodes became a symbol of British imperial ambitions in the late nineteenth century. Interestingly, some southern Africans fought alongside white settlers against other Africans. There were rivalries between African kingdoms and it was at times convenient for Africans to ally themselves with their 'enemy's enemy'. Increasingly, as the system of 'apartheid' or white supremacy was established, people began to define themselves as 'black', and unity began to assert itself among erstwhile warring communities.

While other parts of Africa also suffered conquest, land appropriation and exploitation, the nineteenth-century mineral revolution in what became South Africa and Zimbabwe drew in unprecedented thousands of outsiders to develop mines and industry, including from within Africa itself. It brought rapid industrialisation and urbanisation, and shifted the centre of gravity from the ports of the Cape to the mineral-rich interior. The fundamental pillars of apartheid, such as segregation, migrant labour and limitations on freedom of movement in urban areas, were laid down during the mineral revolution. It was a watershed moment in the region's history that ushered in a racist system, entrenching white minority rule until the very end of the twentieth century.

This century could see a new 'mineral revolution' for Africa, which, particularly in the south, has the largest such reserves in the world. I can only hope that this time it will bring economic windfalls that can be used to achieve key social goals and fund nationwide development in an equitable and sustainable manner. Seventeen key metals – known as rare earth elements – are crucial for our way of life today. They are used in all kinds of technology, from televisions and smartphones to jet engines and military defence systems, as well as renewable energy technology such as solar panels.

According to the Brookings Institution in the US, in 2021 global demand for rare earth elements reached 125,000 metric tons; by 2030 it is forecast to reach 315,000. Production of rare earth minerals has been dominated by China, which accounts for 60 per cent of global production and 85 per cent of processing capacity. The US and many other countries have been looking for alternative sources, and so once again Africa, which has huge and untapped potential in rare earth minerals, could prove to be a magnet for outside interest in its natural resources. The Steenkampskraal Mine in South Africa, for instance, has some of the best-quality rare earth elements in the world. The Democratic Republic of the Congo has more than 70 per cent of the global cobalt supply. Dismayingly, due to corruption and economic mismanagement, Africa's wealth has so far been used to fill the pockets of its ruling class and their foreign collaborators. I fear that this is a pattern that will continue, though I do not cease to hope that perhaps this new 'mineral revolution' will also give Africa added ballast as it tries to build strong global trade partnerships. Natural resources can be a blessing, not the curse they have so often proved to be.

16

The Kingdom of Kongo and the Scramble for Africa

As the previous chapters have explored, the so-called 'Scramble for Africa' was a disaster for the continent. It corresponds roughly to the period between 1884 and 1914, when European colonisers partitioned Africa into protectorates, colonies and 'free trade areas'.[1] Dozens of conferences were held in the latter part of the nineteenth century in which European countries, corporations and individuals vied for control of African territories in order to exploit their natural resources. The Berlin Conference of 1884–5 is the most infamous. During the conference, the European powers established the principles along which they would divide the continent without clashing with one another. This was a key event in global history, for it coincided with soaring commodity prices due to the demands of Western industrial revolutions. European nations were using new technology, such as the steamboat and train, which sped on a burgeoning of trade.

Perhaps the most egregious example of the ruthlessness of European hegemony is the treatment of the Congo, which has given rise to a huge body of academic work. The Congo has come to represent this period of Africa's history in part because of the public attention it captured following Joseph Conrad's 1899 novel, *Heart of Darkness*. The six months Conrad spent in the Congo led to his reflection that its treatment constituted 'the vilest scramble for loot that ever disfigured the history of human conscience and geographical exploration'.[2] Many accounts of the Congo naturally gravitate towards this period of its history, but it has a long and vibrant past, which long predated colonial rule.

The Kingdom of Kongo, 1390–1800s

The Kingdom of Kongo, which included what are today parts of the Democratic Republic of the Congo (DRC), Angola, Gabon and the Republic of Congo, was established in about 1390. Its influence extended to neighbouring kingdoms such as Ndongo and Matamba, whose most prominent ruler was Queen Njinga (sometimes Nzinga). Njinga's towering historic importance is embodied in a monumental bronze statue erected at a former Portuguese fort in the Angolan capital Luanda after decolonisation in 1975. Njinga formed powerful alliances and was in constant warfare with the Portuguese for the best part of 25 years. She was a deft diplomat, a skilled negotiator and a brilliant military tactician.

Kimpa Vita, a noblewoman of the Kongo Empire, is also noteworthy if less celebrated. She stands in bronze in front of the provincial assembly in Lubumbashi, the capital of Katanga province in the DRC. She opposed the Portuguese and

Standing next to the bronze statue of Njinga in Luanda

founded a religious movement, fusing Christian and African traditions, that survives to this day and has spread far and wide. These likenesses and others are fittingly picturesque mementoes of the Kongo Empire and its vassal kingdoms.

The kingdom gave its name to the Congo River, the world's deepest river and second largest by volume of water. Inhabitants of modern-day DRC and Angola pushed northwards from the late 1400s to settle in modern Gabon and the Republic of Congo (also called 'Congo Brazzaville') and take over a huge area of wet grassland and thick forest. The region had been inhabited for millennia by the Bantu, though ethnicities often became mixed due to population movements.

Professor Emeritus Isidore Ndaywel è Nziem of the University of Kinshasa was generous with his time, and as we stood overlooking the city he told me that what we know about Kongo comes from two main sources: oral tradition

and Portuguese accounts. The founder of the Kongo kingdom was Lukeni Iua Nimi. He was a member of a skilled
ironsmith clan and was known as the 'blacksmith king' or
Mwene Kongo, which means 'Lord of Kongo' in the Congo
language, with *congo* meaning iron; the Portuguese version
was *manikongo*. Lukeni Iua Nimi was originally a member of
the royal family of a small kingdom called Boungou, situated
in what is now the Republic of Congo. Upon realising that
he would not become king there, he crossed the Congo River
and through his status as a blacksmith established a new
kingdom, a loose federation of small polities that expanded
as conquered territories were integrated. Towards the end of
the fourteenth century, the king founded his capital on the
border between modern-day northern Angola and the DRC,
at Mbanza Kongo, now a UNESCO World Heritage site.
The Mwene Kongo exploited this densely populated area for
manpower.

While the village had a localised matrilineal group, a head
male was chosen from the dominant lineage. But hierarchies
were otherwise egalitarian; there was no noble class. Since villages, inhabited by both enslaved and free people, could be
large, they were divided into districts ruled by an official who
relied entirely on the favour of the king or provincial governor
for his legitimacy. Each regional clan or group specialised in a
craft, such as weaving, basket making or pottery. Trade was
based on a system of barter that included agricultural products,
textiles and cowrie shells. By the second half of the 1400s, less
than a century after the Kongo kingdom was established, it is
estimated to have had a staggering 3 million subjects – England
in the same period had a population of around 2.5 million.

In the meantime, Portuguese sailors had been relentlessly
pushing down and along the west coast of Africa until, in 1483,
a fleet headed by Diogo Cão arrived at the court of the Mwene

Kongo Nzinga-a-Nkuwu. The African traders were keen to obtain exotic textiles and novelties such as alcohol. Relations developed apace between the two. Ideas flowed with goods, and so profound was this exchange, and so assiduous the efforts of the Portuguese missionaries, that the king and his son Mvemba were baptised as Roman Catholics only eight years later, in 1491. The Mwene Kongo took the name João I and his son became known as Afonso. However, not all members of the royal family adopted Christianity. Another of the king's sons maintained his African religion and even when the Kongolese did adopt Catholicism this was mixed with their African beliefs.

Soon after the start of Afonso's reign in the first decade of the 1500s, the Portuguese began enslaving Africans both to work in their newly established colony of São Tomé, an island nestled in Africa's bend, and also to sell in Cabo Verde to settlers in South America. The Portuguese had come with words of friendship and a spirit of cooperation, but very quickly the Africans grasped that their true agenda was economic gain at their expense, and that the Portuguese were altogether more interested in trafficking enslaved people than spreading religion. At first the enslaved people were prisoners of war and criminals, but then Portuguese demands increased exponentially, leading to extensive slave raids throughout the kingdom.

By 1514 special military campaigns and kidnappings were mounted with the specific objective of acquiring captives to sell. A new class of Portuguese-backed procurers called *pombeiros* arose. Some were mixed race, some pure African, but all endeavoured to feed an ever-more insatiable market for enslaved people. By 1520 the kingdom of Kongo was exporting up to 3,000 people per year.

King Afonso I, in his desperation, sought to prevent people from being illegally enslaved, and wrote to the Portuguese king João III in 1526 appealing for an end to the trade:

Many of our people, keenly desirous as they are of the wares and things of your Kingdoms, which are brought here by your people, and in order to satisfy their voracious appetite, seize many of our people, freed and exempt men; and very often it happens that they kidnap even noblemen and the sons of noblemen, and our relatives, and take them to be sold to the white men who are in our Kingdoms.[3]

Afonso I tried to insist on the removal of all Portuguese merchants, to no effect. To compound the kingdom's problems, a succession crisis followed his death in 1542, leaving a power vacuum that the Portuguese could exploit for their benefit. Contested successions were not uncommon at the death of a Mwene Kongo, and sometimes factions would compete for power for many years. Eventually, in 1568, Nimi a Lukeni Iua Mvemba or King Álvaro I (r. 1568–87) secured the throne, but at a great cost: he only managed to do so with the military backing of the Portuguese. Beholden to them, Álvaro had little choice but to allow them to extract their pound of flesh from him and his people. He granted the Portuguese the right to settle in part of his territory – a promontory that spears into the Atlantic and encloses a placid bay, helpfully close to the Cuanza River, which twists its way inland. This site would eventually become modern-day Luanda. Today it is a picturesque spot – quite a contrast to the horror and degradation of centuries past. For, by 1575, the Portuguese had established a new slave-trading colony at Luanda Bay. The kingdom of Kongo provided a seemingly endless supply of human cargo. It covered a vast expanse of land divided into six provinces and included some client kingdoms such as the Ndongo kingdom of the Mbundu people to the south. Local opposition to the slave trade soon grew and spread across the kingdom.

Queen Njinga, 1583–1663

In 1583, in the royal household of Ndongo, excitement greeted the birth of a baby whom traditional belief marked out as special: she came out feet first, with the umbilical cord wound around her neck. This was Njinga, who became one of the most prominent opponents of the Portuguese in the Ndongo and Matamba kingdom.

Perhaps the story of her birth influenced her Kongolese name, Njinga Mbandi, from the word *kujinga* meaning 'to twist'. Even as a child she displayed strong leadership qualities. Her father, King Ngola Kia Samba, recognised early on that she was clever and possessed great strength of character. Portuguese gunfire often echoed in the background as the king coached his favourite child in matters of state, so she grew up to the sound of Portuguese guns and her childhood was characterised by constant wars. She excelled at military training, showing exceptional aptitude at wielding the fighting axe. Njinga was allowed to attend judicial and military councils that her father presided over – a privilege normally reserved for male heirs. The king ruled through a system of nobles, or sobas, with specific advisers.

Njinga had a voracious sexual appetite and took on many lovers, bearing a child with her favourite one, Kia Ituxi. Njinga did not take criticisms lightly and was ruthless with anyone who dared offend her, attracting jealousy from her less able siblings. After Njinga's beloved father died, he was succeeded by his son, Ngola Mbande. Fearful of his rivals, he had his brother and nephews murdered, including Njinga's infant son. Njinga, enraged with grief, harboured resentment but pledged allegiance to Mbande. The new king sent her to negotiate with João Correia de Sousa, the Portuguese governor of Luanda, on the royal family's behalf. She asked her brother to provide her with a large entourage for the long journey west to Luanda –250 kilometres from their capital Kabasa. She went bearing many gifts for the Portuguese officials she was due to meet.

Dressed in her best clothes and sporting lavish jewellery on every limb, Njinga would have cut quite a figure. The Portuguese governor was seated on a velvet-covered chair embroidered with gold; he expected Njinga to sit on the floor on a rug to reflect what the Portuguese saw as her subordinate status. Affronted, Njinga commanded one of her female attendants to go down on all fours and she sat on her instead. The poor woman had to remain in that position for hours as Njinga conducted her negotiations with the Portuguese. She wanted them to stop their aggression against Ndongo and to cease enslaving its people, for many thousands were being snatched from Ndongo every year.

The governor assured Njinga that they would maintain good relations with her kingdom. Njinga believed she had achieved her objectives and said she experienced 'a profound happiness and an extraordinary peace' during her sojourn of several months in Luanda at the largesse of a Portuguese judge who was hosting her and her delegation. She described a banquet held in her honour as an event of 'festivity and gaiety and splendour'. During her diplomatic mission Njinga was baptised a Catholic, under the name Anna Njinga, the governor became her godfather and the judge's wife her godmother. But despite her public acceptance of Christianity she never really abandoned her traditional Mbundu religious beliefs.

In 1624 Njinga's brother, the king Mbande, who suffered from depression and was becoming increasingly ineffectual as a ruler, either died or committed suicide. There is also some speculation that Njinga may have had him murdered.

Queen Njinga, sitting on her female attendant while
negotiating with the Portuguese

His son was the legitimate male heir, but he was still only eight years old and so Njinga became regent for him. However, not content with ruling indirectly, rather like Queen Hatshepsut in Egypt, centuries before her, she decided to seize the opportunity afforded by the king's death. Upon her instructions, the boy heir was killed, and she assumed power as queen, ruling in her own name. It may have been an act of retribution for the murder of her own son years earlier.

Njinga had used her diplomatic talents to bring some

much-needed warmth to the royal family's dealings with the Portuguese, and even a sense of equality, but she knew that this was a convenient illusion: her kingdom was in reality a vassal state of the Portuguese. Now that she was queen in her own right, this was too much for Njinga to stomach. She rallied to her side all those in Ndongo who opposed Portuguese rule. Conditions were ripe for action: Njinga adroitly exploited the deep well of resentment against the Portuguese, who had forced thousands to fight and had enslaved many tens of thousands of others.

The Portuguese monitored these developments with growing anxiety. They installed a rival of Njinga as a puppet ruler of the kingdom. After all, she had many enemies within royal circles who had become alienated from her after the murder of her nephew, the young heir – an act of regicide. The Portuguese tried to delegitimise her on the grounds of her gender, pointing to the fact that Ndongo had never had a female ruler before. However, through diplomacy, defiance and at times outright military confrontation, Njinga maintained her claim and hold on her throne.

In 1626 the Portuguese resolved to take stronger measures against her. They assembled a substantial army and attacked her forces. After a long and bloody campaign, Njinga thought it wiser to seek a settlement. Although the Portuguese had prevailed, this had come at great cost: they were exhausted by the fighting, had suffered many losses and their provisions were running low. Promisingly for Queen Njinga, they initially agreed to negotiate. But after receiving reinforcements, they hardened their position and lost interest in a diplomatic settlement. Njinga, now pushed into a corner, faced the prospect of capitulation. But she had one major bargaining chip: she held six Portuguese prisoners of war whom she could leverage to avoid annihilation. Njinga agreed to hand over the hostages and to appear in person in the Portuguese camp to proclaim publicly that she had accepted vassal status. However, while the Portuguese general awaited her arrival, Njinga and her followers fled into the countryside and hid in caves. Her supposed overlords, wrong-footed, set out in fruitless pursuit. The loyalty of the locals and her unmatched knowledge of the vast, impassable terrain made her capture impossible.

People had good reason to be reticent: they resented that the king, Ngola Hari, had been installed by the Portuguese. They perceived him as a subservient puppet king and Njinga as a brave resistance fighter. So the Portuguese searched in vain. Njinga did not wish to remain a fugitive, and so, again, she offered to negotiate with them through her emissaries. This time their impatience and desire to replenish their supply of enslaved people made Njinga an obstacle that needed to be eliminated. Ignoring her overtures, in late 1628 the Portuguese renewed their campaign to track her down. Initially she was nowhere to be found but eventually, in May 1629 after she had been in hiding for three years, a contingent of 150 Portuguese soldiers, aided by an even bigger number of local fighters, managed to find Njinga's camp. It seemed the game was finally up for Njinga.

She and her bowmen fled headlong until they reached a rocky precipice – what to do? Oral tradition relates a story more at home in a comic book or on a cinema screen than in a book of history. Although by now at least in her late forties, Njinga took hold of a liana, or strong vine, abseiled down from the top of the precipice, and escaped to the safety of the valley. Many Portuguese soldiers fell to their deaths as they tried to get to the other side. The Portuguese troops and acolytes who managed to navigate the precipice continued to chase Njinga a while longer – but without success. Her freedom was still intact, for now.

The Portuguese, keen to claim some shred of victory, attacked the camp where some of Njinga's relatives, including her two sisters Kambu and Funji, had relocated. The Portuguese killed many, perhaps out of sheer exasperation, vengeance and rage. Njinga's sisters were captured and taken to Luanda where they were presented naked to the governor in an act designed to humiliate them, but they remained defiant. The two women were held prisoner, forcibly baptised, and given the names Barbara and Graça. Njinga was deeply saddened by the fate of her sisters.

In the coming years, though her power was greatly depleted, Njinga engaged in battle after battle with the Portuguese – always succeeding in staying one step ahead of them. Around 1631, in an effort to bolster her strength, she recruited the fearsome Imbangala fighters to her cause. Disdaining allegiance to any ruler, they were a kind of mercenary force, courageous, ruthless and devoted to warfare. Njinga adopted their way of living to a large extent, though she never fully abandoned her own heritage. She became their leader and dressed as a man, perhaps forever haunted by the fact that her gender had excluded her from the throne in favour of her male relatives. She enjoyed the trappings of masculine power and was either polyandrous or indulged in the services of male concubines whom she required to wear female clothing and address her as king. Her status as an Imbangala leader made her the most powerful African in the region. Njinga personally led her troops on the battlefield, and according to the Portuguese soldier and chronicler António de Oliveira, who witnessed her behaviour behind the battle lines, Njinga was adept at managing arms. As a result, she attracted many followers and fighters, and launched attacks against her rivals in Ndongo and surrounding areas.

Through the 1630s, Njinga scored one military success

after another, seizing land from the Portuguese. In acknowledgement that they could not defeat her, the Portuguese
changed tactics and extended an olive branch by releasing
her sister Kambu as an incentive for Njinga to lay down her
arms. Njinga herself was also keen to negotiate and in 1637
she sent the Portuguese gifts of enslaved people and ivory.
Like many African elites, Njinga actively procured members
of rival ethnic communities for the transatlantic trade.

The Portuguese sent two emissaries to hold talks with her:
a Luanda resident called Gaspar Borges Madureira and a
priest, Father Dionísio Coelho. They arrived sometime in
late 1639 or early 1640 to Njinga's court in Matamba and
were entertained with sumptuous feasts. They made her an
offer of an alliance, which she reflected upon and then
rejected. Njinga insisted on her independence but told them
she was willing to extend her friendship. The two negotiators
gave up – no deal was struck – and for his pains Madureira
was poisoned while at her court, and only survived because
he was given an antidote when he got back to his base.

A new twist was in the offing. The power dynamics
between Njinga and the Portuguese were radically influenced
by the presence of another European nation. By the early
1640s the Dutch, buoyed by their successful landgrabs in
Brazil, had arrived in Africa, keen to secure a slice of the
slave trade. By the end of that decade, they had secured control of parts of what is today Angola. The Portuguese saw
the Dutch as a menace and rival, and tensions soon erupted
into violence. On the basis that her enemy's enemy was her
friend, Njinga allied with the Dutch and enlisted their support to help her in her longstanding conflict with the
Portuguese. Their combined power almost succeeded in
expelling the Portuguese from Central Africa. Crucially, the
Dutch conquered the port at Luanda and were only pushed

out with the help of Portuguese reinforcements arriving from Brazil.

Portugal just managed to save its Central African colonies and the Dutch withdrew, much to Njinga's surprise and dismay. Out of vengeance, the Portuguese killed Njinga's sister Funji, who had been sending letters informing her about her enemy's movements. Her other sister Kambu was recaptured in 1646. Saddened and running out of options, Njinga retreated to her stronghold of Matamba, where she seized two Italian monks and decided to use them as emissaries to negotiate once more with the Portuguese, whom she had now given up on defeating militarily. She established firm control of land between Matamba and Ndongo, and accepted its status as a Christian kingdom. In about 1656 she secured her surviving sister's release by sending 130 enslaved people; the Portuguese had demanded 200, but Njinga told them that over the years she had given many enslaved people to various governors and their representatives. Njinga, anxious that the Portuguese might double-cross her, held one official hostage until 'I can see with my own eyes my sister arriving in my court.'[4]

In 1656 she signed a peace agreement with Portugal, which crucially made no mention of an annual tribute to the Portuguese; Njinga had maintained her honour. That year, her sister Kambu was finally freed after years of captivity. It was an emotional reunion. The two women embraced each other repeatedly amid public celebrations. In 1657, in a Christian ceremony, Njinga married a man decades younger, and around the same time wrote to the Pope asking to be recognised as a Christian monarch. After many letters and a long wait, in 1661, Pope Alexander VII granted her request: Anna Queen Njinga was acknowledged as a Christian sovereign.

She now took to wearing silks, velvet and brocade in the European style.

By October 1663 Njinga's health had deteriorated. A severe chest and throat infection rendered her incapable of speaking except in a rasp. An abscess developed on her throat, which spread the infection to her lungs. Njinga had a high fever and said she felt that death was near. She wanted to die a Catholic and regretted the fact that she had not left a son to succeed her, but stipulated that she wanted somebody of her blood and lineage to inherit her kingdom. On her deathbed she asked the priest for forgiveness, lost consciousness and died in her sleep in December. She was in her early eighties. After she passed away, her 20,000 soldiers gathered to view her body as it lay in state. A page held up her head bearing a crown. Njinga was given a Christian burial, but her funeral ceremony was traditional. Months of mourning followed and her longtime enemies, the Portuguese, held a ceremony in Luanda to honour her – she had been a worthy and determined opponent. Within 24 hours of Njinga's death, her sister Kambu was pronounced queen and she ceremonially adopted the royal symbols of the vine and the bow and arrow. However, Njinga's young husband opposed the succession and the Ndongo kingdom was handed to another branch of the royal family.

Soon after Njinga's death, the entire kingdom of Kongo – of which the Ndongo was a part – fell into the grip of civil war. This time, wary of allowing another Njinga to arise, the Portuguese played off one faction against the other. Two years after Njinga died, the Portuguese killed the *manikongo* Nvita a Nkanga, or António I, at the key battle of Mbwila along the Ulanga River. The kingdom was now a vassal state of the Portuguese.

Kimpa Vita, 1684–1706

About 20 years after Njinga's death, Kimpa Vita Nsimba was born in 1684 in the village of Songololo close to the town of Bakongo, in the kingdom of Kongo. She hailed from a noble family of early converts to Christianity. Her father was a commanding officer of the king's army. She herself was baptised Donna Beatriz. Kimpa Vita was deeply religious; she would dream of angels and was credited with having spiritual gifts. She became a Nganga Marinda, a person who can communicate with spirits. Her comments on falling ill with fever in 1704 give a sense of her outlook: 'I was sick, about to die when I saw a brother dressed like a monk and he told me I had to go and preach to my people and go forward. I felt rejuvenated.'[5] Kimpa Vita gave away her wealth and renounced worldly goods. She believed she had a direct line to St Anthony of Padua, a major Portuguese saint of the early thirteenth century, who urged her in a dream to found her own Christian movement. So she established Antonianism or the Antonine sect, which rejected baptism, confession and prayer, and incorporated certain African practices such as ancestor veneration.

Kimpa Vita urged people to convert to her style of Christianity, telling them that Judgement Day was coming. She was regarded as a prophetess by her followers, who included Hippolyta, wife of Nusamu a Mvemba (Pedro IV), the Portuguese-backed king of Kongo, and many of the farming population. Kimpa Vita was worried that the Christian faith preached by missionaries was predicated on their sense of superiority over Africans and assigned no value to African practices. She pointed to a lack of African saints in the Catholic Church, and instead preached that Jesus Christ was African. Moreover, unlike Njinga, she was a bitter opponent of the slave trade and was hostile to Roman Catholic missionaries, whom she considered to be too aligned with Portuguese interests.

Basing herself at the capital Mbanza Kongo, she urged the rulers of the divided Kongo to unite a kingdom beset by civil wars, which the Portuguese fuelled through their support of Nusamu a Mvemba. She chided the latter for not resolving the conflicts within Kongo; these, she said, facilitated the slave trade by creating pools of captured people who could then be sold into enslavement. Kimpa Vita's message resonated, raising the morale of many people. Her charisma and the appeal of her special form of Christianity threatened the influence of the Catholic Church and that of Nusamu a Mvemba himself. In 1706 Kimpa Vita instigated a heroic but doomed revolt against the Portuguese. She was arrested and tried, under the authority of Nusamu a Mvemba, for witchcraft and heresy on the grounds that she had given birth to a child, and that as a 'vessel of God' she should have remained chaste. She was burned to death under the watchful eye of Capuchin priests. Although Nusamu a Mvemba ended up defeating other contenders for the kingdom, civil war became the rule not the exception in Kongo.

After Kimpa Vita's death, her Antonian movement was led by her mother, Ngumi andi Kimpa Vita. One account by a European priest, Father Lorenzo da Lucca in 1709, who knew Kimpa Vita, described how enslaved people in the ship *Nossa Senhora do Cabo* wore symbols of Kimpa Vita: in this way, Antonianism spread as far as the Caribbean and Brazil. Drawing parallels between people's lives is an exercise fraught with difficulties, yet I find there are striking similarities in Kimpa Vita's life with that of Joan of Arc (*c.* 1412–31), who was born in France and is honoured as a defender of the French nation. Like Kimpa Vita, Joan claimed to be acting on divine guidance. She made an appeal to her king to save the people from foreign domination and became a military leader herself, rallying troops to her cause. Joan was also put on trial for heresy, burned to death at a young age, and is remembered as a heroine and icon of freedom.

Kimpa Vita's story is important because, as one of Congo's leading academics, Professor Scholastique Dianzinga, told me as we chatted in a leafy courtyard in the capital Brazzaville, the role of women in African history books is overlooked: 'We tend to talk for example of the fathers of independence but rarely of the mothers. There were many women who resisted foreign rule; and we need more public memorials of these women, like those to Kimpa Vita and Njinga. We need to give them more visibility.'

By the late 1800s, wracked by conflict, most of the Kongo kingdom had been reduced to decentralised trading villages bereft of meaningful leadership. In Kongo as elsewhere in Africa, violent encounters with Europeans enervated political systems, priming them for the total domination that the late nineteenth century would bring.

The Scramble for Africa

After my meeting with Professor Dianzinga in Brazzaville I made my way to the centre of the city to see a tiled arch memorial depicting scenes of European hegemony and African resistance. One portion showed European leaders sitting around a large table with claws for hands – the Berlin Conference.

The Berlin Conference of 1884–5 marked a dramatic and new period of destruction for Africa. It was attended by European nations, as well as the United States and representatives of the Ottoman Empire. It was organised by the German leader Otto von Bismarck, at the request of the Belgian king, Leopold II, a first cousin of Queen Victoria. The conference largely focused on the boundaries of Central Africa, and crucially laid down the foundations and principles of how the whole continent would be divided between key powers. By the start of the twentieth century, five European nations – Britain, France, Belgium, Portugal and Germany – had seized almost the whole continent, awarding themselves 30 new colonies and protectorates with 110 million African subjects. The Berlin Conference did not set in motion the Scramble for Africa; rather, it formalised a process that had long been underway on the ground.

The British prime minister, Lord Salisbury, summed up the mood well when he said: 'We have been engaged in drawing lines upon maps where no white man's feet have ever trod; we have been giving away mountains and rivers and lakes to each other, only hindered by the small impediment that we never knew exactly where the mountains and rivers and lakes were.'[6]

The eminent Nigerian historian, Professor Emeritus Anthony Asiwaju, a key contributor to UNESCO's *GHA*, whom I was fortunate enough to meet in Lagos, believes the evidence supports an 'accidental rather than a conspiratorial theory of the marking of African boundaries'. He also states that 'it was essentially a European affair: there was no African representation and African concerns, if they mattered at all, were completely marginal to the basic economic, strategic and political interests of the negotiating European powers.'

The Scramble for Africa resulted in catastrophe for Africans, and for the Kongo kingdom in particular. Kongo's former territories fell to the Belgians in the Congo and the Portuguese in what became Angola. Portugal's rule of Angola resulted in an economy based on various forms of forced labour, which lasted until the mid-1900s; slavery itself was not banned by the Portuguese until 1868.

The vast fertile areas around the Congo Basin had long

caught the eye of King Leopold II. In 1876, nearly ten years before the Berlin Conference, Leopold had convened an international conference of explorers and geographers at his palace in Brussels, and he invited one man, the British explorer Henry Morton Stanley, to be 'his man' in Africa. By the late nineteenth century, thanks to the activities of their explorers, Europeans began to know far more about Africa and its interior, terrain, resources and economy, as well as the strengths and weaknesses of its states and societies — knowledge that was critical in the conquest of African territories by Europeans. For the next five years Stanley travelled up and down the waterways of the Congo Basin, setting up trading posts and striking deals with local chiefs such as Tippu Tib. Some of these agreements appear to have been subsequently doctored and put to very good use by Leopold.

He managed to secure control of the Congo by convincing delegates at the Berlin Conference of his philanthropic goals in the area, such as ending the enslavement of Africans by Arab and Swahili slave traders — the subject of Chapter 9. The vast territory, rich in resources such as rubber, was named the Congo Free State (CFS) and designated as a trade zone for actors from other European nations.

As the price of rubber reached an all-time high, it became a particularly attractive resource. The rubber trade was not as dependent on large armies and centralised power as the slave trade had been; what was essential for its production was a small and mobile workforce that required no training. Rubber grew wild in inland areas and so large parts of the population moved into the interior to harvest and sell it to European traders. It was needed for a multitude of commercial purposes, such as inflatable bicycle or car tyres, for industrial belts and gaskets, and for coating telephone and telegraph wires. It was a booming and lucrative trade that needed little capital investment.

Contrary to the agreement struck at the Berlin Conference, Leopold regarded the CFS as his personal colony, and he set about using it to amass a great fortune for himself. In order to maximise his profits, King Leopold declared in 1891 and 1892 that all the land and raw materials in the region were the property of the CFS. He divided the CFS into several parts: his private domain, a portion of which was marked out as a distinct crown property, and a third area which was to be settled as circumstances dictated, with the rest of the country remaining a free trade zone. Leopold designated concessions to dozens of European companies, the biggest ones being Anversoise, based in Belgium, and Abir, the Anglo–Belgian rubber company, which were publicly listed on the Antwerp and London stock exchanges respectively.

Under Leopold's auspices, a vicious system was introduced by the concession companies to ensure labourers were terrified into extracting the rubber. They used militias made up of sentries from other parts of the Congo, who were expected to use force to ensure labourers collected the rubber. It should be stressed that although Congolese sentries carried out the bulk of the atrocities, they were commanded by the European corporations and their actions were sanctioned by King Leopold. Some rubber gatherers worked until they collapsed to death as they tried to meet their quotas. Chiefs would be punished, imprisoned or even killed if their villagers did not reach their targets. On average, a man would have to deliver about 4 kilograms of dried rubber every fortnight, in a process that was exhausting and time consuming. Many escaped and abandoned their villages and farms for the rainforest, where they starved. Desperation led to constant revolts, which were savagely suppressed by a steel shower of gunfire. It was not only the sentries who were responsible for the violence; European agents would also engage in the barbarity. To prove he had not wasted a bullet, a sentry would have to cut off a hand of each person he had shot dead, preserve it with smoke, and place the severed hands in a basket to show its gory contents to his European agent. If he missed a shot, he would simply cut off the hand of a local to account for the

Two Congolese with severed hands

missing bullet. There are scores of photographs of Congolese with severed hands, attesting to this degenerate practice.

The Belgians (and other Europeans) were drawn especially to the mineral-rich province of Katanga, which Leopold managed to acquire in an agreement with the French. Katanga became the focus of exploitation because the price of rubber had dropped after the establishment of rubber plantations in Asia. Accompanied by Dominique Munongo Inamizi, a politician and member of the Bayeke royal family in Katanga, I visited the graveside of her forebear King Msiri (*c.* 1830–91) at the Munema cemetery in the village of Bungaya about 200 kilometres north of Katanga's provincial capital Lubumbashi; visibly moved as she laid flowers at his tomb, Dominique told me about the circumstances leading to his death.

King Msiri made a brave stand against the officials of King Leopold II when they visited him in Katanga in 1891 and insisted he hand over his land and copper mines. Msiri refused and was instantly shot dead by a Belgian captain called Omer Bodson. On seeing the king mown down, one of Msiri's kinsmen in turn shot dead Captain Bodson; whereupon the young man himself was promptly killed by another Belgian officer. Captain Bodson's strange last words were: 'I do not mind dying now that I have killed Msiri. Thank God my death will not be in vain. I have delivered Africa from one of her most detestable tyrants.'[7]

The real tyrant of the Congo was King Leopold. His regime was so brutal that in due course the Belgian government bowed to international pressure and ordered the king to relinquish the territory to them. He did so in 1908, but not before he had demanded and received compensation for the loss of his 'private colony'. Abir and Anversoise had stopped their operations there two years earlier, having severely depleted the Congo's natural rubber supplies. The impact of the frenzy for rubber had devastating consequences for the Congo. With farmers unable to tend their land, famine became widespread, and it is estimated that between 1880 and 1920 about 10 million people – approximately half of the population – died directly or indirectly at the hands of Leopold and the Belgians, through killings, overwork, starvation or disease.

Although they disagreed with the manner of Leopold's handling of the CFS, the Belgian government, like other European nations in Africa, was still enthusiastic about exploiting the Congo. European industry had an insatiable appetite for Africa's raw materials, and what better way of efficiently extracting these products than to control the people and territories of Africa? In 1870 most of Africa was – at least nominally – in the hands of the Africans, but by the late 1880s that was no longer the case: the majority of African lands had fallen under European control.

The Europeans had devastatingly superior firepower and technology, which gave them an unassailable advantage across the continent. As the early twentieth-century English poet Hilaire Belloc wrote: 'Whatever happened we have got / The Maxim Gun, and they have not.'[8]

Once the Africans were overcome militarily, the Europeans set about governing them. They justified their conquests by claiming it was to 'civilise' and 'Christianise' them, and indeed some may have sincerely believed that. But overwhelmingly they wanted direct rule in Africa to be able to exploit its resources. In addition to rubber, they wanted palm oil for industrial goods, cotton for textile mills, copper, tin, cobalt, zinc, precious metals and diamonds, as well as cash crops such as cocoa, tea and coffee beans. In Kenya, which was part of Britain's East Africa Protectorate, formed in 1895, Europeans were given thousands of square kilometres of the best farmland, the so-called 'White Highlands', mostly on the slopes of Mount Kenya and in the Great Rift Valley. Locals were dispossessed of land on which they had toiled for generations, and Kenyans were heavily encouraged to migrate to work for meagre pay on the European-owned farms as labourers. Often, they had little choice but to do so, for they had no other means of income.

European rule also brought Africa the railway, for example in Kenya and Uganda, where the railway was built by imported Indian labour. However, roads and railways were designed to consolidate colonial rule in Africa by providing the means to transport produce to and from the continent, connecting its mineral-rich interiors with ports. Such infrastructure did not bring substantial community links within countries nor between African nations. To this day, it is often cheaper to move goods from Africa to Europe than across the continent. Whatever benefits the railway brought were collateral rather than planned to the Africans' advantage.

North Africa was in quite a different situation: much of it had been under the Ottoman Empire, which typically ruled through local proxies. Algeria was the centre of Ottoman North African territories, which included Egypt, parts of Sudan, Libya and Tunisia. There was a rivalry between the Ottomans and the French, who had been present in the region since the first half of the nineteenth century, as well as with the British in Egypt and Sudan, and the Italians in Libya. The Ottomans sided with the Germans in the First World War. After Germany's defeat in 1918, their long-lived empire was finally disbanded, and the Republic of Turkey – now Türkiye – was established by Mustafa Kemal Atatürk. Former Ottoman territories in North Africa were divided mostly between France and Britain, though the French had controlled Algeria as early as 1830. By 1914 the domination of Africa was all but concluded through military conquest.

Apologies

In 2020, Leopold's great-great-great-nephew King Philippe of Belgium wrote to the Congolese government stating:

> This history consists of shared achievements, but also painful episodes. During the Congo Free State, violent and cruel acts were committed which continue to weigh down on our

collective memory. During the subsequent colonial period, suffering was caused, and humiliations inflicted as well. I would like to express my deepest regret for those wounds of the past.[9]

In 2022, on King Philippe's first trip to the Democratic Republic of the Congo, he reiterated his regret, but stopped short of making a full apology. The distinction between the two may seem trivial, but while regret expresses sadness at what happened, a full, unambiguous apology carries greater weight because it entails assumptions of responsibility. Some people find the element of culpability troubling, given that nobody alive today was involved in the atrocities to which King Philippe referred. There has been a vigorous debate in Belgium, as in other countries with a colonial past, about whether there is a need for such apologies. As we saw in the previous chapter, Caribbean nations have made a formal request for an apology from former slave trading nations.

Many who object to such apologies being made believe the sins of the past should not be foisted on current generations. There is also a concern among governments that a formal apology could trigger compensation claims, and indeed when in 2021 Germany apologised for massacres by its colonial forces in Namibia in the early 1900s, its government agreed to pay around US$1.3 billion to Namibia over 30 years for development projects in what the then German chancellor Angela Merkel said amounted to a gesture of *reconciliation* and not reparations. Incidentally, the Herero and Namaqua people, the two communities that suffered the most at German hands, have expressed their dismay at not being involved directly in the negotiations with Berlin and have contested the settlement.

Apologies, reparations and statues from the colonial era as

well as restitution of African artefacts are different aspects of one huge postcolonial debate that generates much heat. In the early twenty-first century, statues of Leopold II such as the one in Place du Trône/Troonplein in Brussels have been regularly vandalised, and in 2018 a square in Brussels was named after Patrice Lumumba, the first leader of independent Congo, who was assassinated in 1961 with the complicity of Belgian officials. When I was a member of the 2021 Oriel College Commission on the future of the Oxford college's statue of Cecil Rhodes, I was forced to pick through a minefield of competing considerations. We may have been deliberating in a modern context, but our discussions about the retention, relocation or complete removal of a statue were not new: as we saw in an early chapter about the kingdom of Kush, memorial images of its kings were wiped out by subsequent Egyptian pharaohs; and Roman emperors and emblems of the *anciens régimes* were thrown off their pedestals after revolutions in France and Russia. The commission on which I served proposed (among many other recommendations) that the Rhodes statue be relocated from its public position on the High Street to an inner quad of Oriel College; the *place* where a statue or memorial is displayed is also significant.[10] After Congo gained its independence in 1960, a statue of King Leopold II mounted on his horse was moved from its prominent position outside the state palace to the grounds of the national museum in Kinshasa.

Whatever your personal stance might be, it is important to acknowledge that the debate about the legacy of slavery and colonialism will remain in the foreseeable future and it demands measured responses devoid of prejudice, emotion and tin ears on all sides.

In 2019 a United Nations commission, 'Experts on People of African Descent', backed apologies for the wrongs committed during the colonial era. Overcoming this legacy will require much more than apologies and the mere toppling of statues, however. The carving up of the continent into artificial states has contributed to vicious cycles of violence that play out to this day. Furthermore, ethnic partitioning by colonial powers within these new countries – a practice known as 'divide and rule' – had devastating consequences, none more so than in Rwanda. A small land-locked nation in central East Africa, Rwanda was a German protectorate from 1899 until the First World War, when it was placed under Belgian administration.

Rwanda

In 2016, on a visit to Rwanda, I went to the Genocide Memorial in the capital, Kigali, the resting place of about 250,000 victims. I wanted to find out more about what happened in 1994, when around 800,000 people were massacred (then about 10 per cent of the population). Those killed were mostly from the minority Tutsi community, but the dead also included moderates from the majority Hutus. I was affected on a personal level. I could not erase from my mind the image of a lively, mischievous-looking boy of about five, whose grin extended cheerfully from ear to ear. His photograph was among those of the victims of the genocide. He bore a striking resemblance to the youngest of my four children, then about the same age. I flew back to the UK that evening and spent most of the plane journey home with tears pricking my eyes. The photographs were troubling to look at but they brought home the fact that behind the statistics real people were killed. I could put faces to the numbers.

Throughout its history, the Great Lakes region of which

Rwanda is a part, although not entirely free of conflict, exhibited no trend of violence between Hutu and Tutsi communities. In pre-colonial Rwanda, after centuries of inter-marriage and a shared common language, Kinyarwanda, the terms Hutu and Tutsi were descriptions of economic class rather than ethnic origin.

Historically, the Tutsis were cattle owners, and hence enjoyed greater prominence and wealth. The Tutsi king ruled over a highly organised society with a hierarchy of chiefs who were both Hutu and Tutsi. However, under Belgian rule, policies were introduced that distinguished Hutus from Tutsis. The latter were favoured by the Belgians, just as they had been under the Germans. From the mid-1920s, the number of cows one possessed became the dividing line. Those who owned more than ten cows were designated Tutsi, and all others Hutu. Identity cards based on ethnicity were issued by the Belgians, who introduced a system of forced labour, using the Hutu as workers and Tutsi as their overseers. In time, Hutus became alienated. They resented their servitude and began to resist Tutsi authority. As one Tutsi army officer Joseph Nzabamwita put it, speaking after the 1994 genocide: 'The teachings of the colonial administration left the permanent impression that those of the Hutu ethnic group could never cross the line to become Tutsi, and those in the Tutsi ethnic group would remain permanently Tutsi – whereas in actual fact even their own brothers who are poor are Hutus. This created a very big socioeconomic disruption in Rwandan society.'[11]

Then in 1959, in an abrupt volte-face, the Belgians began to promote Hutus, replacing Tutsi administrators with Hutu ones. Violent clashes subsequently broke out between the two groups, and more than 20,000 Tutsis were killed. The Belgians agreed to abolish the Tutsi monarchy in 1961 and the following year Rwanda became independent, with Hutus assuming control of the government. Tutsis were heavily discriminated against, facing job restrictions and limits to educational attainment. Many were forced to flee the country. By the mid-1960s nearly half a million Tutsis had left for neighbouring Uganda, Tanzania or Burundi.

In 1973 a Hutu general, Juvenal Habyarimana, seized power. Although he initially won favour with both communities, in time he reinforced anti-Tutsi sentiments. Rwandan Tutsi refugees viewed with growing dismay the treatment of their community and formed the Rwandan Patriotic Front (RPF), led by one Paul Kagame. The RPF invaded Rwanda in 1990, provoking a massive response from the army, cementing anti-Tutsi hatred. Despite a peace agreement with the Tutsi rebels in 1993, the unrest continued, encouraged by radio propaganda that incited violence against Tutsis.

On the evening of 6 April 1994, a private Falcon 50 plane carrying President Juvenal Habyarimana was shot down. It crashed in the grounds of the presidential palace as it prepared to land at Kigali International Airport. Everybody on board, including the president of Burundi, Cyprien Ntaryamira, a Hutu, died. Tutsis were blamed for Habyarimana's death, something Paul Kagame has always vehemently denied. The recriminations were immediate, and a campaign of violence ensued. The speed and scale of the mass killings both astonishes and disturbs. Government forces and an armed militia known as the Interahamwe led the attacks and distributed machetes to the Hutu community. Neighbour turned against neighbour, friend against friend. It was a concerted and brutal effort to exterminate the Tutsi, who in 1994 made up about 14 per cent of the population, with the rest Hutu.[12] Many moderate Hutus who tried to help their fellow Rwandans were also killed. The wave of slaughter lasted 100 days, and only ended when the RPF, under Paul Kagame, fought, won, and became the dominant political force in the country. Paul Kagame has been the president of Rwanda since 2000. The international community took no action to stop or slow the genocide. In 1998, US president Bill Clinton apologised for the collective failure to halt the massacres.

I sought the views of the former Rwandan government minister Louise Mushikiwabo, a member of the Tutsi community, for her thoughts on the impact of Belgian actions on Rwanda. Her brother Lando Ndasingwa was the only Tutsi minister in the Habyarimana Hutu-led government and was killed at the beginning of the genocide. 'My brother Lando, along with other opposition figures in Rwanda, was under the protection of the UN, or so they were told. For three or four months before the genocide actually started, he had armed guards at his home and in his car. But when the massacres started on 7 April 1994, the UN soldiers guarding him fled. They just left him and his entire family to be killed by the Presidential Guard.'

Louise was living in Washington, DC, when she received the news that her family members had been killed. She has written a book about the tragedy, called *Rwanda Means the Universe*, and when I spoke to her the first fact she wanted to drive home to me was that prior to Belgian rule, there were no tensions between Hutus and Tutsis. Even today she is loath to describe the genocide in ethnic terms, or as what is still sometimes anachronistically referred to as 'tribalism'. 'The genocide was committed by the state. Whatever is meant by Hutu or Tutsi was a term just used by people who were power hungry and who were not ready to share resources. There were a number of people in Rwandan society who had nothing to do with the killings. There were a number who went along with it and later expressed regret. And there were Rwandans who disobeyed orders to kill their neighbours.'

Louise was profoundly offended by descriptions of the massacres as some 'mindless ethnic slaughter and "tribal" violence instead of the politically motivated, long-planned, systematic mass extermination of a people by Presidential Guards and the death squads acting under orders. The genocide was not spontaneous. It was not a savage outburst of innate African tribalism. It was the outcome of a methodical, state-orchestrated campaign over decades to dehumanise Tutsis as a means to amass power.'

The Rwanda genocide stands out as a hideous chapter in recent African and indeed global history. Its aftermath still plagues the eastern part of the Democratic Republic of the Congo, where millions struggle to find enough to eat and thousands are subjected to regular campaigns of violence perpetrated by Hutu militias and other groups. Two million Hutus, many of whom were involved in the genocide, had escaped across the border into the DRC in 1994. Burundi also has a Hutu majority population and gained its independence from Belgium in 1962. It has witnessed similar atrocities such as the mass killings of Tutsis in 1993, and human rights abuses continue today. Rwanda and Burundi are two egregious examples of how conflict in Africa can have an ethnic dimension. Here as elsewhere, colonial powers, by reifying existing differences for their own purposes, entrenched them so that they survived into the post-colonial era. But is there evidence that ethnic loyalties are diminishing in Africa?

One morning in August 2022 I travelled about 230 kilometres from Nairobi to County Meru in eastern Kenya. I was there as a member of the 20-strong Commonwealth Observer Group for the country's general election. We were dispatched in teams of two or three to different parts of Kenya. My companion was the former Principal Judge of the High Court of Uganda, James Ogoola, one of Africa's leading jurists – a man of great knowledge, intellect and wisdom, who incidentally loved writing verse in his spare time. He regaled me with tales about his time as a young lawyer during the era of President Idi Amin in the 1970s. For instance, when General Amin wanted to pass a law banning the miniskirt, the young James had to determine with the help of a ruler what a correct hemline should be!

Having been briefed for an entire week on the Kenyan political landscape by a variety of politicians, officials and activists, by the time we monitors were on the road we were fully apprised of the issues at stake. Past Kenyan elections have been marred by ethnic violence. The 2007 poll, for example, left 1,300 dead and 600,000 displaced in clashes between supporters of the then incumbent Mwai Kibaki and those of his opponent Raila Odinga. In 2022 Raila Odinga was making his fifth attempt to win the presidency, this time against the sitting vice president William Ruto. On our arrival at Meru city, Justice James and I trudged from one polling station to the next observing the run up to the vote as well as the count itself. We even visited Meru County Prison, where unlike in the UK, inmates are allowed to vote. Following the result, which delivered victory to Wiliam Ruto, it seemed that for the first time Kenyans were no longer voting along clear ethnic lines, but on bread-and-butter issues. My fellow Commonwealth observers and I sincerely wish that Kenya will continue to prove that elections can be conducted in a free and fair manner, devoid of violence and without ethnic loyalty being the determining factor in how citizens cast their vote.

Whether ethnic adherence trumps national affiliations in Africa is a subject that has attracted much attention and research. There are leaders across Africa who play on such differences and exploit them for their own political advantage. However, a study carried out between 2021 and 2022 by the Accra-based pan-African polling organisation Afrobarometer, on whose advisory council I serve, showed that only a small minority of respondents in the 36 African countries surveyed stated that they felt more affinity for their ethnic group than their nation. Only Nigeria and South Africa showed a sizeable minority – a quarter of respondents – who said their ethnic identity was more important to them than national sentiment.[13] Further studies by Afrobarometer show that ethnicity is becoming less politically relevant across Africa. I hope this continues, since it can only benefit durable nation building.

African states are relatively young: colonial powers drew the boundary lines for most, prioritising their own needs over those of Africans and paying little heed to ethnic, religious and cultural divides. It should be no surprise, then, that these artificial creations did not immediately function as organic, cohesive wholes. However, as we will see in the next chapter, all Africans were united in a common cause: casting off the colonial yoke.

17

Africa's Resistance and Liberation

As European incursions into the continent increased, African resistance redoubled from the 1880s onwards. By the early twentieth century only Ethiopia and Liberia were sovereign countries, although the influence of private concessionary companies in Liberia acted as a severe constraint on real independence. Africa, now a continent of 54 countries – of varied landscapes, peoples and languages – shared a common experience of foreign subjugation and resistance, which propelled nationalist movements right across the continent, and encouraged the development of pan-African ideals.

The following quote from the *GHA* refers to the transatlantic slave trade but could equally apply to Africans living in every corner of the continent during the colonial era: the African 'has been accustomed to so many alien dictates coming from outside that even if he lived far from the slave coast or nearest white officer, some part of his soul was bound to be marked with the annihilating brand of the serf . . . but it would be wrong to assume that these changes were easily made or African identity easily manipulated'.[1]

As we have seen throughout this book, Africans opposed foreign incursions and invasions over several centuries, but resistance gained momentum after the First World War, and gathered pace after the Second World War. However, the roots of anti-colonial nationalist sentiment go back further, so in this chapter I want to provide an outline of the forces that helped propel Africans into independence and give a brief overview of the struggles of some countries. At times, Africans had to resort to arms in the face of discrimination, oppression and bloody crackdowns by colonial powers, most notably in Algeria. However, contrary to popular belief, independence was won mostly through peaceful and organised mass resistance, demonstrations, strikes and political rallies. Countries that gained independence through the power of protest, Ghana for instance, went on to enjoy better levels of democracy than those forced to do so through armed rebellions like Algeria, where violence was used as a form of political dissent.[2]

Resistance

First, I turn to the northeast of the continent, arguably the part of Africa that most successfully resisted European occupation in the period 1880–1914 when colonial rule initially took hold. I start in Sudan, where I was born, with a victory whose significance resonated across the continent and stiffened the resolve of freedom fighters. This chapter of African history was the subject of the 1966 British epic feature film *Khartoum* starring Laurence Olivier as the Mahdi and Charlton Heston as his adversary, the British general

Charles Gordon. The movie was described by the Arab intellectual and writer Edward Said as a piece of pro-colonial propaganda that cast 'a despotically violent Arab masculinity against a noble, rational Western one'.[3]

Although I have lived in the UK since I was an infant, I grew up with tales of the valour of the Mahdi as a great nationalist leader. I recall watching *Khartoum* at the cinema in London as a young child with my parents and being utterly confused as to who was the 'good or bad guy', with General Gordon clearly being portrayed as being on the side of right! I learned the lesson early in life that one person's villain can be another's hero.

The following is an account of this episode of history from the Sudanese perspective, drawing heavily on the memoirs of a follower of the Mahdi, Sheikh Babikr Bedri (1861–1954), a vital and little-known source.

The Mahdi, 1844–85

Muhammad Ahmad ibn Abdallah was a charismatic and religious leader who proclaimed himself 'The Mahdi', or the 'Chosen One'; that is, a divinely appointed guide. He was born in northern Sudan near Dongola and was the son of a boat builder, though he moved later to Aba Island on the White Nile, south of Khartoum. The Mahdi received a religious education and was a member of the Sammaniya Sufi order. In Sudan, there was a number of such orders as well as holy men known as 'fakis'. Some of them were attributed supernatural powers and commanded huge followings. The Mahdi had spent many years living as an ascetic, spurning material goods and leading a simple life governed by religion. In 1881, the Mahdi – by now in his late thirties – had gained a reputation as a religious thinker, and attracted many

The Mahdi

adherents from across Sudan. Contemporary accounts describe him as being dark-skinned with handsome, fine features and startling white teeth with a large gap at the front.

Sheikh Babikr Bedri's memoirs provide insights into how the Mahdi captivated his supporters. He describes one encounter in the mid-1880s:

I and my mother . . . journeyed to the Mahdi, full of single-hearted devotion and eager desire. I had known him, as I said, and believed in him when he used to visit Rufā'a [eastern Sudan] to see his relatives, accompanied by his disciples and deacons with their shining faces and spotless clothes. Often when we were students we would attend the sunset prayer with him and listen to him reciting the Koran in his reverent, humble voice . . . Once when he was reciting the Chapter of the Calamity during the first part of the service, and when he came to the verse 'A day will come when mankind will be as a cloud of scattered moths', he fell down unconscious in a trance, and one of his disciples came forward in his place to finish the prayer. I was among the worshippers, and when we left he was still unconscious.[4]

Once he had declared himself the Mahdi, Muhammad Ahmad ibn Abdallah began a 'jihad' or 'holy war' against the Ottoman Egyptian administration, in pursuit of an Islam that he described as 'purged of heresies and accretions'. Ottoman rule was in its last throes in Sudan. It had begun with Muhammad Ali Pasha (1769–1849), who was the Ottoman viceroy of Egypt. He had advanced southwards into Sudan in 1820, capturing much land there. Most of the administrative hierarchy was held by Turco-Egyptians, although a few locals filled some bureaucratic posts. This Turco-Egyptian period saw the unification of the territories that comprise the modern state of Sudan. Muhammad Ali was a modernising force, but his ideas were incompatible with Sudanese traditional society, and his administration was corrupt and oppressive, which made him and his successors unpopular.

By the time the Mahdi came onto the scene, the local population was heartily fed up with foreign rule. They were ready for his call to arms. The Mahdi's first armed conflict with the Turco-Egyptian administration was in 1881, but then in 1882 the nature of the opposition changed: the British took possession of Cairo, occupied Egypt, and the royal dynasty established by Muhammad Ali was thereafter reduced to constitutional status and shorn of its power.

The Mahdi, who had by now based himself in the west of Sudan, had formed a devoted army known as the Ansar, and in November 1883 they engaged in battle at Shaykan in the woods outside El Obeid in Kordofan. They were confronted

by an army of around 8,000 to 11,000 mostly Egyptian soldiers
under the command of a retired British officer, Colonel William Hicks. Only a few hundred survived – Hicks himself
died in battle. Winston Churchill described the army as 'perhaps the worst army that has ever marched to war'.[5] The
Mahdi's victory galvanised other parts of Sudan into joining
the revolution and the Battle of Shaykan also marked a turning point in British policy towards Sudan. Britain now believed
their imperial interests would be better served by an Egyptian
withdrawal from Sudan and in 1884 sent General Charles
Gordon to ensure the full evacuation of Egyptian garrisons
and civilians. Gordon had been employed previously in Sudan
by the ruler of Egypt, Khedive Ismail, and from 1877 he had
enjoyed a two-year stint as governor general of Sudan.

This time he was appointed to the same position by Britain, and he based himself in Khartoum. However, Gordon,
an eccentric and deeply religious man, had a different interpretation of his mission and exceeded the mandate he had
been given by the British government. Gravely underesti-
mating both the power and popularity of the Mahdi, he
argued that the Egyptian garrisons needed relief, not evacuation. The Mahdi besieged Khartoum, Gordon inside.
Gordon managed eventually to persuade the government to
send him a relief expedition of around 10,000 men from
Egypt. He waited for them in a part of the city he had fortified with defences, trapped with around 8,000 soldiers and
civilians. It was a long wait; the siege lasted from March 1884
until January 1885. Life became desperate: people were driven
to eating anything they could lay their hands on, including
dogs and donkeys. The Mahdi based himself across the river
in Omdurman, with around 50,000 troops, and sent Gordon
a letter urging him to surrender.

Babikr Bedri was in the Mahdi's camp, and recalled the

standoff: 'I was in the most advanced of the positions surrounding Khartoum, so that at night we could see the glow
of the enemy's cigarettes and hear their conversation; nor
could we leave our trenches in the daylight to get water, but
only at night.'

He explains how as time passed General Gordon became:

> fully aware that things had come to a crisis, and saw no
> reason for those to remain in the city who did not share in
> the defence but only in the consumption of the stores of
> food, and who would die if food was refused. So, he gave
> them permission to leave and go where they would, and
> many of them did, and spread the news of the famine in
> Khartoum . . . Gordon no longer sent his troops to fight us
> outside the fortifications but confined his attention to the
> problem of feeding those in Khartoum, and economizing
> his ammunition against the coming of the relief expedition.
> As the people suffered more and more from the pressure of
> the siege and the flames of hunger, he tried to cheer them
> with all sorts of specious words and tricks. What else could
> a good general do? But human care is no match for fate.

The Mahdi, after consulting his advisers, decided to hurry
on with the capture of Khartoum before the relief force
from the north could arrive, and so in January 1885 the Mahdi
gathered his army and

> harangued us, mounted on his camel. Part of what he said,
> before the final oath of allegiance, was that the enemies of
> God had dug the ditch surrounding Khartoum very wide
> and deep, and had placed in it iron teeth, each with four iron
> spikes on three of which it stood, leaving the fourth spike
> upright to pierce the feet of men or the hooves of horses.
> Then he said, 'Swear allegiance to me unto death!' and was

silent for a moment, when the whole army with one voice sounded three times, 'We swear allegiance to you unto death.'

Then he said, 'If God grants you the victory, Gordon is not to be killed . . .' He said, 'If a man throws down his arms do not kill him, and if a man bars his house against you do not kill him' . . . Then the flags were unfurled and we were on our way to the fortress . . . I was among the foremost and did not realise that I had passed the ditch until I found myself close to a machine gun that was firing on us. When we neared it, those who were manning it ran to a nearby tent and let it down over them, but we killed them under it. Then we continued to advance along the edge of the inner ditch, until we reached the spot opposite Gordon's palace, where we met other Mahdist soldiers who had entered the city from a different direction . . . We turned towards the palace, and there found Gordon struck down and covered with blood, and were very angry at whoever had killed him, for only two hours earlier the Mahdi had proclaimed in the loudest of voices that he was not to be killed. It was then about 4 o'clock in the morning. Then we took the road along the Blue Nile bank until we arrived opposite the mosque to which we turned, and the sun rose as we reached it.

The relief expedition arrived two days after the Mahdists had overtaken the city and, after a brief military engagement with Mahdist forces, retreated. Gordon's death caused instant outrage in Britain, and helped contribute to the fall of the government of the prime minister, William Gladstone.

The Mahdi's victory in January 1885 marked the start of a Mahdist state, comprising northern Sudan and large parts of the west and the southwest. The Mahdi set up his capital in Omdurman but would alternate between living there and in Khartoum. However, within just six months of his victory at

Khartoum, the Mahdi died in June 1885 of a fever, probably typhus. Babikr Bedri had had a premonition in which he wrote that he dreamed that he saw the Mahdi walking, and then 'He just vanished, in open plain, from quite near, in full daylight.'

The Mahdi was succeeded by one of his companions, Abdullahi al-Khalifa, who had commanded a large part of his army. The Mahdi had not lived long enough to expand his jihad beyond Sudan, though that had been his ambition, so it fell to the Khalifa to attempt to push into Egypt and Ethiopia. In 1888 his forces invaded Gondar in Ethiopia and killed the Ethiopian emperor, Yohannes IV, but they failed to make any lasting inroads there and the Ethiopian monarchy was restored under Menelik II. The Khalifa's attempt to invade Egypt in 1889 was catastrophic and his forces suffered defeat at the hands of Anglo–Egyptian troops at the Battle of Tushki. The Khalifa abandoned his efforts to export the Mahdist revolution, but the campaigns had weakened him and religious fervour for the holy war in Sudan was beginning to wane. This provided the British with an opportunity to avenge both the death of Gordon and satisfy their imperialist ambitions. A reinforced British–Egyptian army, led by General Herbert Kitchener, engaged with Sudanese forces from 1896, culminating in the Battle of Omdurman in September 1898. The Sudanese showed magnificent courage. One ditty composed at the time by a famous Sudanese poet Al Khadari was defiant: 'The men are united / And one is worth five / When we come little white man / You'll not stop alive'.[6]

But the Sudanese were annihilated: their traditional weapons and shields were no match for the 26,000-strong British–Egyptian force and their Maxim guns, as well as a fleet of ten gunboats and five transport steamers. A total of about 11,000 of the Khalifa's 40,000 men were killed in the

Battle of Omdurman alone – and thousands more were wounded. Babikr Bedri recalls the day after the battle: 'we saw corpses lying in al Hijra street, and no one knew who they were or who had killed them'.

Kitchener, who had lost about 500 men, set up his base inside a mosque in Omdurman and ordered the destruction of the Mahdi's tomb. His remains were dug up and thrown into the River Nile. Only his skull was kept. Years later his grandson Sadiq al-Mahdi described this as an act of 'vindictiveness'. In January 1899, de facto British rule in Sudan was established under what was known as the Anglo–Egyptian condominium.

The Khalifa evaded capture in the west of Sudan for a year, but he was finally defeated at the Battle of Umm Diwaykarat in November 1899 and was found dead on his sheepskin prayer rug. It was the official end of his resistance movement.

The Mahdi's resistance ultimately failed but the nationalist sentiment it had engendered spurred Sudan towards independence in 1956.[7]

Sayyid Mohammad Abdullah Hassan, 1856–1920

Like the Mahdi in Sudan, one imam in Somalia, Sayyid Mohammad Abdullah Hassan, derived authority from religion. He was greatly inspired by the Mahdi. Al-Sayyid was born in 1856 and studied Islam in East Africa, including in Mogadishu. He then embarked on a period of travel, including to Arabia and Palestine, where he was greatly impressed by Islamic revivalism – a group of movements that sought to reinvigorate society by redoubling its commitment to Islamic principles and restoring lost traditions. Back in Africa, he began to preach adherence to a strict interpretation of Islam and urged a rejection of colonialism by Christian Europeans.

He formed an army of around 12,000 loyal clansmen and in 1899 launched a major offensive in British Somaliland. The British were assisted by the Italians, and over the next 20 years he fought a war against them both, warning the British in a letter in 1899: 'Now, choose for yourselves. If you want war, we accept it, but if you want peace, you must pay us a protective tax.'[8] At one stage the British government even considered paying off al-Sayyid in order for him to stop his attacks. His response: 'why should I now accept your offers of paying our due blood money? Rather I shall lay my vengeance upon them. As long as my deathbed does not take me!'[9]

By 1905, al-Sayyid's forces were weakened, and he signed a treaty with the Italians. He was down, but not out. In 1908, he rallied and five years later scored a significant victory against the British, whom he continued to fight until his death, probably from influenza, in 1920. Although his campaign against colonialism was long and hard, in the end he failed to rid the Somalis of alien rule. Nevertheless, Sayyid Mohammad Abdullah Hassan is known as the father of Somali nationalism. A statue of him on horseback, arm outstretched, sword in hand, stands on a high plinth in Mogadishu. And the many poems he composed are still recited today in Somalia. In one he curses 'those who of their own volition chose to be the doormat of the coloniser; again, not out of coercion but of their own volition, they strive to coddle to the coloniser.'

Somalia fell to the British and Italians, with the bulk of the country coming under Italian rule and the British controlling the northwest. In 1960, the two areas gained their independence and merged to become the United Republic of Somalia. In 1991 Somaliland, an autonomous region in the north of the country, broke away and declared independence; it is self-governing but its sovereignty is not recognised by Somalia, the United Nations or the African Union.

Ethiopia

Somalia's neighbour, Ethiopia, then known as Abyssinia, also drew the attention of the British and the Italians. Ethiopia, a country with a royal dynasty dating back many centuries, had staved off numerous attempts by Europeans to subdue it. Under Emperor Menelik II (r. 1889–1913), a huge army of around 100,000 inflicted a major defeat on the Italians at the Battle of Adwa in March 1896. This heroic battle is still a source of great pride for all Ethiopians. At least 4,000 Italians were killed – about half of their army. Menelik's forces also suffered heavy casualties, but the Battle of Adwa's significance is more than military. It is symbolic of how the Ethiopians resisted European domination and indeed Ethiopia is the only country in Africa that has never been colonised. After the battle, Abyssinia's independence was acknowledged by Italy and the European powers, although the Italians were able to hold on to Eritrea. Ethiopia became an icon for African sovereignty, and later in the twentieth century its emperor Haile Selassie was for many inside the continent and among the African diaspora an important advocate of independence, during his long reign from 1930 to 1974. However, increasingly less admired at home, Haile Selassie met an ignominious end in 1975, probably suffocated to death while in detention following his overthrow by a military junta.

There were many Africans – brave men and women – who right across the continent took a stand against colonial rule. In East Africa, one of the first large-scale movements of resistance was against the Germans in Tanganyika, in what later became part of Tanzania, in the early twentieth century. This was known as the Maji Maji Rebellion and consisted of a mass movement by peasants against their exploitation. The

Germans adopted a scorched earth policy to put down the uprising between 1905 and 1907. The deaths probably numbered in the hundreds of thousands; most died from starvation.

In the west of the continent, in modern-day Senegal, the resistance of Lat Dior against the French in the late nineteenth century serves as another illustrious example. Lat Dior was from a ruling dynasty in the Wolof empire – the dominant ethnic community in Senegal – and died fighting the French at the Battle of Dekhele in 1886, on his legendary horse Maalaw.

There are numerous examples that I cannot cover adequately but, as the *GHA* states, many African historians believe there has been a tendency in the West to describe those Africans who did not resist colonial rule as peace loving and those who fought back as being bloodthirsty. In fact, there was resistance in virtually every region of European advancement. The rebellions were 'just wars' of liberation, and usually commanded the support of the majority of the population.

Sometimes communities were either unprepared or unable to defend their land from the invaders, or cooperated with European colonialists to weaken their own rivals. For instance, the kingdom of Buganda in what is today Uganda allied itself with the British in the last decade of the nineteenth century because its king or kabaka, Mwanga II, saw that his interests aligned with those of the British. As historian Dr Pamela Khanakwa at Makerere University in Uganda put it to me: 'Buganda became the British base in the area, from which rule was extended to other parts. The use of the Buganda people as colonial agents led to other ethnic groups seeing the kingdom of Buganda as "favoured" by the British.' Dr Kenneth Ombongi from the University of Nairobi believes that although there were 'collaborators' such as Buganda, this did not mean that its people actively supported foreign domination.

At other times, some communities found ways of circumventing the dictates of colonial rule. For instance, in the village of Wanzarba near Tera in modern-day Niger, where the succession to the chieftaincy was matrilineal, attempts by the French colonial power to install a man as a puppet chief backfired when locals instead transferred their allegiance to the village priestess. France controlled Niger from the early twentieth century but was present in the region much earlier than that. During our convivial conversation in his office in Abidjan, Alassane Ouattara, president of Côte d'Ivoire, spoke proudly of his forebear Sekou Ouattara of the Kong Empire who fought the French in the early 1700s, and of Samori Touré, who resisted French colonial rule from 1882 until his capture in 1898. Kong consisted of parts of what are today Côte d'Ivoire, Mali, Burkina Faso, Togo and Ghana; its Grand Mosque in northern Côte d'Ivoire was built probably in the mid-1700s with mud and logs, and bears a striking resemblance to the mosques of the Mali Empire. As President Ouattara told me, according to oral tradition whoever prays at the Kong mosque on a Friday has their wishes granted. 'It is true,' he said, 'because I went to pray there when I was in the opposition and two years later I was elected president.' No wonder it is such a draw for the people.

To Europeans, opponents such as Sekou Ouattara were seen as a force that had to be subdued through defeat. At times the violence used was extreme. To reprise a case cited in the previous chapter, the Germans created an oppressive system where they used local agents to force the Herero and Namaqua to work in the many farms that they were establishing. German domination of the Herero and Namaqua in southwest Africa (modern Namibia) involved bloody clamp-downs on revolts. In 1914 the Germans killed tens of thousands of Herero and Namaqua in retribution for an uprising. Some were killed outright. Many were left to starve to death.

Liberation

By the advent of the twentieth century, Africans' resistance to colonisation was deeply embedded in the continent, and this gained momentum through their increasing inclusion in world events. Interactions between Africans and diaspora Africans, such as the prominent thinker Edward Blyden (1832–1912), born in the Caribbean, and African American sociologist Dr W.E.B. Du Bois (1868–1963), led to a sharing of knowledge, insights and inspiration and contributed a great deal to the development of pan-Africanism and theories of black empow-erment and negritude. Bonds of solidarity and parallels between Africans seeking independence and black Americans fighting racism and discrimination helped to boost and unite Africans into actions to gain their independence. African intel-lectuals who became the first presidents of their new nations, such as Senegal's Léopold Senghor, Kwame Nkrumah of Ghana, Dr Hastings Banda of Malawi and Tanzania's Julius Nyerere, had often lived and studied abroad in either Europe or the United States, and been influenced there by ideas and ideologies that helped them to develop their political revolu-tions, like the 'African brand of socialism' of Nyerere and the industrialisation programme of Nkrumah. One very impor-tant aspect of negritude, as expressed by Léopold Senghor, who was instrumental in framing and promoting it, was that it allowed Africans to affirm a cultural identity of their own through which they could project themselves on the global stage. Senghor hosted the First World Festival of Black Arts in the Senegalese capital, Dakar, in 1966.

The world wars were among the most significant catalysts in generating nationalistic sentiments in African colonies. It is estimated that more than 2 million Africans contributed to the First World War and more than 1 million to the Second. Africans fought alongside white soldiers and endured the common experience of the suffering of war. The African Carrier Corps, who played a vital but underrated role in the First World War, found that exposure to British soldiers meant that both sides could learn that they shared the burdens and the frailties of humankind and held similar fears. Black Africans nurtured expectations that once the war was over, they would be granted their rights and accorded equality as human beings. When this did not happen, it only intensified the hunger for independence.

After risking their lives on the battlefront, many found the economic and social disenfranchisement they faced on their return intolerable. For example, when East Africans who had enlisted in the King's African Rifles in the First World War went back home to Kenya, they found that the colonial government rewarded British veterans who had been settled in Kenya with land, but that African veterans were not similarly remunerated.

France, which had formed *tirailleurs* (riflemen or sharpshooters), a corps of colonial infantry recruited from West and North Africa, relied on thousands of these men for various wars in the nineteenth and twentieth centuries, including the two world wars, and thousands died in battle for France. After the Second World War ended, some 1,600 Senegalese *tirailleurs* arrived back in Dakar. When a revolt over missing pay ensued, French soldiers killed at least dozens of the Senegalese veterans.

Increased education was also an important factor. After the First World War there was a drive by the colonial authorities to educate some Africans so that they could perform basic clerical duties in their administrations. Schooling immediately improved rates of literacy, which had been very low. English, French and Portuguese could be of use as lingua francas across ethno-linguistic lines. On the other hand, colonial education was expedient; for the most part it was aimed at producing a subservient African who would serve the colonial regime. Until the 1950s most Africans were given access only to basic rudimentary education. Nevertheless, it helped broaden minds and ideas, and proliferate nationalist sentiment.

The international climate also changed after the Second World War: Europe had been weakened by the ravages of war. In particular, France's occupation by the Nazis dealt a further blow to the air of invincibility that this major colonial power had cultivated before the twentieth century. The independence of India in 1947 also spurred on Africans' pursuit of sovereignty. If the 'jewel in the crown of the British empire' could throw off the shackles of imperialism, then so too could they.

The rise of the anti-imperialist United States as the lead post-war nation strengthened African determination. In the aftermath of the Second World War, the 1953–61 administration of President Dwight D. Eisenhower saw Africa's resources as essentially an extension of the American Marshall Plan to rebuild western Europe, and therefore Africa, was critical to its recovery. However, when President John F. Kennedy took office in 1961 he forged a new diplomacy based on opposition to European colonial rule. He accepted Africans' non-aligned position and offered economic development packages, and the Africans gained a powerful ally who was sympathetic to their goals of self-rule.

By the end of 1966, nearly two-thirds of African countries – that is, 40 – had gained their independence, mostly through peaceful means. The growth of trades unions and greater literacy had helped facilitate the spread of demonstrations, strikes and political rallies.

Ghana

The first example of a comparatively smooth transfer of power in Africa south of the Sahara was the Gold Coast, which on independence in 1957 was renamed Ghana – after the ancient West African kingdom, though in reality it was never part of it. The man who led the Gold Coast to independence was Kwame Nkrumah. He was born in 1909 and was a schoolteacher. Having lived for more than a decade in the US and two years in the UK, he became a great proponent of pan-Africanism. Like many Africans, Nkrumah was affronted by the invasion and brief occupation of Ethiopia by Italian forces during the Second World War, which received wide press coverage. Nkrumah was a student at the time and was visiting England.

> At that moment it was almost as if the whole of London had suddenly declared war on me personally. For the next few minutes, I could do nothing but glare at each impassive face, wondering if these people could realise the wickedness of colonialism, and praying that the day might come when I could play my part in bringing about the downfall of such

a system. My nationalism surged to the fore; I was ready to go through hell itself, if need be, in order to achieve my objective.[10]

The main pro-independence party in the Gold Coast was the United Gold Coast Convention (UGCC) and in the mid-1940s Nkrumah joined its ranks, bridling with nationalist fervour and enthusiasm. With his strong organisational skills he excelled at setting up branches around the country. Nkrumah was a man in a hurry; he wanted independence in the shortest possible time. The UGCC had a gradualist approach and soon he chafed and set up his own party, the Convention People's Party (CPP), and helped orchestrate a campaign of mass disobedience and protests.

One demonstration in the main square in Accra by former Second World War servicemen in February 1948 led to several deaths at the hands of the colonial authorities. The country was irate. Nkrumah became the focal point for the discontent. His arrest became inevitable. He was imprisoned in the old British slave fort at Jamestown overlooking Accra. While incarcerated, Nkrumah worked out his strategy for independence, writing it on pieces of toilet paper. The British, aware the tide was turning, held elections in 1951, in which his party was the overwhelming winner. Nkrumah was too significant a player to be behind bars, so he was released after nearly two years in jail. There then followed a period of power sharing with the British, during which two more elections took place in 1954 and 1956. Won decisively by Nkrumah's CPP, the results confirmed that the majority of voters backed independence.

When it was formally proclaimed in March 1957, Nkrumah, ever the pan-Africanist proclaimed: 'The independence of Ghana is meaningless unless it is linked up with the total liberation of Africa.' He also believed that the Sahara Desert should not divide Africa between the Arab north and the rest, so he forged ties with strong, patriotic leaders who shared his vision, such as Egypt's Gamal Abdel Nasser. At Nkrumah's instigation, Nasser arranged a marriage for Nkrumah, now close to 40 years of age, with an Egyptian Coptic woman, Fathia, who was in her mid-twenties. It was a personal gesture of solidarity forged in a spirit of pan-Africanism.

When we met in Accra, Samia Nkrumah, one of the three children that resulted from the marriage, recounted the first meeting between her parents: 'Mother . . . meets this man Kwame Nkrumah, who was waiting for her . . . and she says he was the most charismatic man she had ever met, very charming. After the pleasantries, the two sit together, and mind you what is remarkable is that they could not speak the same language – they did not have a common language at the time. Mother spoke Arabic and of course French and our father spoke English and of course our African languages. So, they had to sit and communicate with interpreters and dictionaries – she tells us – and after a few hours they decided there and then to get married. Love at first sight, destiny, call it what you will, because obviously it was a politically arranged marriage, but it worked. That marriage contributed so much to bringing North Africa closer to the rest of Africa.'

However, in 1966 during a visit to China, Nkrumah was overthrown in a coup and never again saw his beloved Ghana. His wife and children left for Egypt after he was removed from power. Nkrumah was offered exile by President Ahmed Sékou Touré in Guinea, where he died in 1972. Nkrumah's reputation was later redeemed, as I could judge on seeing the impressive marble mausoleum where his remains lie in downtown Accra. Erected in the early 1990s, the memorial is in a

Kwame and Fathia Nkrumah with their son Gamal and daughter Samia

peaceful location, surrounded by water and fountains in 5 acres of park. It stands on the very spot where Nkrumah made his declaration of independence. His statue bears his oft-repeated mantra: 'Forward ever, backward never'.

Ghana's transition from colonial to self-rule was virtually blood free. This was not always the case, however.

Kenya

In the 1940s, Kenyan nationalists mostly from the Kikuyu ethnic group formed the Mau Mau – an organisation that took arms against the British authorities and white settlers who dominated the colonial government. Mau Mau is an acronym for 'Mzungu aende ulaya, Mwafica apate uhuru', meaning 'The white people

441

should go back to the west so the Africans can have freedom'. The movement won support from rural communities who had been expelled from their land so that it could be given to white farmers. In 1945 there were fewer than 25,000 white settlers in Kenya out of a total population of just over 5 million.

People were confronted with brutal options: work as cheap labour on the white-owned farms, try to eke out a living from the unyielding land they had been allocated, or move to urban areas such as Nairobi and face an uncertain future. This era of dispossession was recalled by a woman farmer in her seventies whom I visited outside Nairobi. On enquiring how her farming activities were going, she replied that she was content with the state of affairs, with her son and grandchildren assisting her in growing a cornucopia of crops: 'So much better than when I was a little girl and the farms we had were practically barren,' she remarked in her native Kikuyu language.

The Mau Mau stepped up their campaign in the early 1950s with attacks on white settlers as well as those Africans who were seen as their collaborators. The colonial authorities responded brutally. Hundreds of Mau Mau fighters were hanged, tens of thousands of Mau Mau sympathisers were herded into concentration camps and at least 10,000 were killed. The Kenya Human Rights Commission states that 90,000 were killed, tortured or maimed during the British counterinsurgency. Among those imprisoned was Hussein Onyango Obama, the grandfather of the former US president Barack Obama. Onyango, who was from the Luo ethnic group, had served with the British Army in Burma, now Myanmar, during the Second World War. On his return to Kenya, he found a job as a military cook, hoping like many veterans for a better life. When this did not materialise, resentment turned to anger and he became involved with the Mau Mau. Onyango was arrested in 1949 on charges of being a member of a banned organisation, and imprisoned for two years during which he was tortured. According to his widow, Sarah Onyango, British soldiers forced sharp pins into his fingernails and buttocks, while his hands and legs were tied together with his head facing down. This, along with other forms of torture to which he was subjected, left him permanently scarred.[11]

When Onyango's grandson Barack was still president in 2016, Boris Johnson, then the Mayor of London, wrote an article in the British tabloid *The Sun*, speculating whether the Obama administration's decision to remove a bust of Britain's wartime leader Sir Winston Churchill from the Oval Office could be perceived as either 'a snub to Britain' or 'a symbol of the part-Kenyan President's ancestral dislike of the British empire'. Onyango's treatment was not atypical. Gitu wa Kahengeri, a very elderly former Mau Mau leader and the secretary general of the Mau Mau War Veterans Association, talked to me in the outskirts of Nairobi. Sitting on a wooden chair in his pristinely kept garden, and dressed in a long red jacket that bore the words 'Mau Mau

Walking with Gitu wa Kahengeri in his garden

hero', he told me how he was imprisoned with his father for seven years in the 1950s. Speaking slowly and with great clarity, Gitu wa Kahengeri, now white haired with misty eyes that matched the haze of the late afternoon, said:

> We wanted to remove the dictatorship and subjugation because the European settlers were treating us like animals in the land of Kenya. They even told us that our children did not have brains in their heads but porridge. I saw them beating my father in front of his wife – my mother. I saw them taking him to go and work for the European farms without being paid anything. For a Mau Mau leader, like me – I was given a job as a strategist during the Mau Mau struggle movement – it meant that when I was detained, there was a routine that every morning I must be beaten from eight to ten o'clock, and then I could go for my *uji* [porridge] . . . after I had been beaten thoroughly. They used to beat us with anything they could find, such as a hoe, anywhere on our bodies, legs, buttocks and head. The women were also sometimes raped. Sometimes they inserted hot water bottles into their private parts. What can you call somebody who does that kind of thing to other human beings – other than a savage?

Although the Mau Mau had been all but defeated by the mid to late 1950s, their rebellion had succeeded in helping to propel Kenya into independence, because they showed how untenable and expensive colonial rule there would be. If the white farms were not sufficiently profitable they could not defray the costs of colonisation. The British government had spent a colossal £55 million – amounting to more than half a billion pounds today – to suppress the Mau Mau. In a speech made in 1960 the then British prime minister Harold Macmillan indicated that he understood that African independence was inevitable. 'The wind of change is blowing through this continent. Whether we like it or not, this growth of national consciousness is a political fact.'

Kenya became independent in 1963 under Jomo Kenyatta, the nationalist political leader, who had not been a member of the Mau Mau but whose aspirations for freedom had been assisted by their actions. In 2013, after a legal battle, the British government agreed to pay nearly £20 million in compensation to more than 5,000 Kenyans whom it had tortured and abused during the insurgency, including Gitu wa Kahengeri; and in 2015 it unveiled a Mau Mau memorial statue in Nairobi as a symbol of reconciliation. By 2019 there were about 70,000 Europeans in Kenya, most of them Kenyan citizens, in a population of around 53 million.

In October 2023, King Charles visited Kenya and expressed his 'greatest sorrow and deepest regret' at the 'abhorrent and unjustifiable acts of violence committed against Kenyans as they waged ... a painful struggle for independence and sovereignty'.[12]

Algeria

If the numbers of dead are used as a measure, then the fight for freedom was at its most extreme in Algeria. First, up to a million died in the French conquest in the nineteenth century, and then 1.5 million more perished in the battle for freedom in the twentieth century. The French were the dominant colonial power in North Africa. They took control of Algeria in 1830 and Tunisia in 1881, and Morocco became a protectorate in 1912, though the Spanish maintained some territory in the latter. Italy had invaded Libya in 1911 and during a protracted series of battles finally managed to gain control in 1934. Algeria underwent the bloodiest of these experiences.

Algeria fell from Ottoman rule to the French, who from 1848 designated it 'an integral part of France', that is, no different in constitutional administrative status from France itself, in contrast to Tunisia and Morocco. In fact, by the turn of the twentieth century the French were producing so much wine in Algeria that this Arab Muslim nation improbably became the world's largest exporter of wine. Emir Abdul Qadir al-Jazairi (1808–83) was the father of Algerian nationalism, and although he failed to defeat the French, he laid the foundations for the war of independence in the mid-twentieth century.

I have already described the significance of the Second World War on African sentiment, but nowhere did the Nazi occupation of France in 1940 have a bigger impact than in Algeria. France, the country that had portrayed itself as the protector of liberty, was now under the pro-Nazi French leader Marshal Philippe Pétain, detonating its imperial standing. Algerian nationalism was galvanised. Moreover Algeria itself, which was after all seen as 'part' of France, was attacked by the US and Britain during the war. Matters came to a head in 1948, west of Constantine in Setif and Guelma, when French officers struck out at Algerian nationalists during a protest. Tens of thousands of Algerians were murdered, compared to a few dozen French deaths. The National Liberation Front (FLN) became the main organisation and catalyst of Algerian nationalism in 1954. While it had promoted secular national ideals, it recognised the significance and value of religious identities. Its manifesto called for 'the restoration of the Algerian state, sovereign, democratic, and social within the framework of the principles of Islam'. The FLN was ruthless in pursuit of its goals and was responsible for killing many tens of thousands of Algerians who did not support their movement, especially those who sided with the French.

I wended my way through the alleys of the Casbah – the traditional quarter of the capital, Algiers. I had come to meet an elderly retired businessman who intimated he had been an FLN member, though he never stated this explicitly. Time had clearly not assuaged his anger: 'We were not treated like second- or third-class citizens, it was more like tenth-class citizens. We had no rights whatsoever. We only had guns with which to fight the French, while they had military jets and a well-organised army. And the French soldiers had another advantage; at the end of a day of fighting they would go back to base whereas our poor men would have to sleep out in the open exposed to the elements. There was a huge disparity between us. We paid a heavy price for our freedom. The French did not grant us our liberty, we had to seize it by force.' People like this man were inspired by major leaders in the Algerian nationalist movement such as Mostafa bin Bullah Eid (1917–56). A rich businessman from Batna, a town in northern Algeria, he used his wealth to arm the resistance against the French in 1954. Mostafa bin Bullah died in his late thirties in 1956 and never saw Algeria win its freedom. Today in his hometown there are many buildings that date back to the French era. Some are dilapidated, but some, such as the old town hall, have been restored. Beside this building a statue of Mostafa bin Bullah stands.

In 1955, the FLN began their own campaign of violence to counter that of France. One hundred and twenty people – mostly French – were killed in Philippeville (now Skikda) in northeastern Algeria. The French escalated their offensive and a number of Algerians (1,200 according to the French, and 12,000 according to the FLN), mostly civilians, were killed in French reprisals. In 1956, bombs planted by three Algerian women in the capital, in public areas frequented by the French, led to an eruption of violence in Algiers. Algeria

effectively fell under French military rule, with torture, sum-
mary executions and mass imprisonments carried out to
quash the revolts. France even bombed neighbouring Tunisia, where FLN leaders were based in exile.

Eventually the public mood in France turned against the
war. The US was opposed to the French campaign, and
France's president General Charles de Gaulle, who had
grown increasingly aware that control of Algeria was untenable, declared in 1959 that 'self-determination' was necessary.
The *pied-noirs* (literally meaning 'black feet', used to describe
white French settlers and their descendants) were aghast.
Nevertheless, negotiations began in 1961 and Algeria gained
its independence in 1962, with Ahmed Ben Bella (1916–
2012), a former soldier in the French Army turned FLN
member, becoming president. The long and complex Algerian war was an important one in the history of Africa's
decolonisation. It drew the attention and sympathy of revolutionaries and activists across the continent, and the world.
Even while the FLN was waging its war it supported other
struggles, such as that of the ANC in South Africa. Indeed,
in 1990, one of the first trips abroad that a newly liberated
Nelson Mandela made was to Algeria.

Guinea

By the mid-twentieth century, the forces of resistance and
nationalism, and the costs of colonialism both in blood and
cash, were too great for the Europeans to overcome. Africa
was gaining its freedom. Transitions were mostly smooth, but
at times independence was granted begrudgingly. Guinea had
rejected membership of the 'French West Africa' federation in
a referendum in 1958. Established in 1895, this was made up

of French colonial territories in the west of the continent. Its capital was in Saint-Louis in Senegal.

After the Guineans voted to leave, France instantly withdrew financial and economic support, stripping Guinea of its public records, equipment and all movable objects. What could not be shifted was destroyed. Telephone lines were severed. The country would have collapsed had it not – in an act of pan-African solidarity – received a £10 million loan, equivalent to about £240 million today (about US$400 million), from Ghana, which had significant revenues from the sale of cocoa, gold and timber. No surprise then, that when Nkrumah was ousted from power in 1966, it was Guinea's leader Ahmed Sékou Touré who offered him sanctuary and named him honorary co-president. Incidentally, Ahmed Sékou Touré was the great-grandson of Samori Touré, the man referred to by President Alassane Ouattara as an opponent of the French.

The year 1960 was a landmark one for Africa; 17 countries won their independence throughout the 12 months, including the former French West African colonies and Nigeria, now Africa's most populous state.

However, although most of Africa was politically free by the end of 1966, external powers, keen to maintain their stake in Africa's economic riches, still exerted influence, and at times this had a malign and destabilising impact.

The Cold War between the US and the Soviet Union in particular created proxy conflicts in Africa, with each arming its supporters in the new nation-states. Some of these had had their boundaries arbitrarily drawn and this exacerbated internal community rivalries, which could be exploited by outsiders. The ideological battle between the communism of the Soviet Union and the free capitalism of the US meant that on independence there were two economic models for African nations to pursue. Initially, 'African socialism' was popular with leaders such as Ghana's Kwame Nkrumah and Tanzania's Julius Nyerere – after all, citizens who had endured years of neglect needed economic development, and fast. However, within the context of the Cold War, which lasted until the Soviet Union broke up in 1989, any mention of socialism was seen by the West as an expression of support for the Soviets.

Congo

The Congo, as we saw in the previous chapter, attracted much foreign economic interest. After the First World War, European and American corporations had invested heavily in the Belgian Congo across a range of sectors: in large plantations that grew cotton, palm oil, coffee and cocoa, in rubber and livestock farms, and in mines of gold, diamonds, copper, tin, cobalt and zinc. Later, during the Second World War, the country had become an important source of uranium for the US, so Western nations had huge vested interests in the Congo.

The Congolese worked in mines and plantations as indentured labourers and infrastructure such as roads and railways was built by forced labour – no surprise then that there were regular revolts. In 1958, the first nationwide Congolese political party, the Congolese National Movement, was launched by Patrice Lumumba (1925–61), a former postal clerk, and others. They were anxious to secure economic as well as political independence, and Lumumba's speeches were littered with references to social problems and inequality. This gave him a distinct socialist hue that did not go down well in Western capitals, who saw it as a pro-Soviet bias.

Lumumba had a large popular following. He was a powerful orator who espoused nationalist and pan-African beliefs.

After a spell in prison following an anti-colonial protest, in 1959 Lumumba and his party outmanoeuvred the Belgian colonial government and independence was declared in 1960. His speech at the ceremony before the Belgian king Baudouin struck a discordant note: 'No Congolese will ever forget that independence was won in a struggle, a persevering and inspired struggle carried on from day to day, a struggle in which we were undaunted by privation or suffering and stinted neither strength nor blood. We have experienced forced labour in exchange for pay that did not allow us to satisfy our hunger, to clothe ourselves, to have decent lodgings or to bring up our children as dearly loved ones ... Together we shall establish social justice and ensure for every man a fair remuneration for his labour.'[13]

Lumumba became the Congo's first independent leader, but he faced a growing secessionist movement in the mineral-rich Katanga province. Unable to secure weapons from the West to quell the rebels, he turned to the Soviet Union for help, which gave him military supplies. This triggered worries,

Patrice Lumumba captured in 1960, shortly before his murder

especially in the US, that the Congo would go the way of pro-Soviet Cuba, and the army chief Mobutu Sese Seko was given the green light to carry out a coup to depose Lumumba. In January 1961, Lumumba was executed by firing squad by his political rivals; he had been in power for a matter of months. Mobutu went on to become one of Africa's richest and most notorious dictators, with his rule becoming a byword for corruption and mismanagement.

My meeting with Patrice Lumumba's son, François, a businessman based in Kinshasa, was moving. He related the aftermath of his father's assassination. He was nine years old when his father was killed. The family had been given refuge by President Nasser of Egypt and were in Cairo when they learned the news of his death: 'It was a tragedy we lived through . . . we never believed that he had been assassinated, we thought he would pull through . . . it was a shock especially for a child. When they assassinated him, he never went down on his knees, he never cried, he constantly looked his enemies in the eye.'

The plot to kill Patrice Lumumba was backed by the United States and Belgium, the former colonial power. In 2000, Gerard Soete, the Belgian police commissioner, 'confessed that he had dismembered Lumumba's body and dissolved it in acid'.[14] He had retained a gold tooth as a memento, which was seized by the Belgian authorities and returned to the family for burial in 2022, allowing Lumumba's soul to rest in peace finally according to African custom.

A Free Africa at Last

By the end of the 1970s, all of Africa was free from colonial rule except a handful of states in southern Africa – where

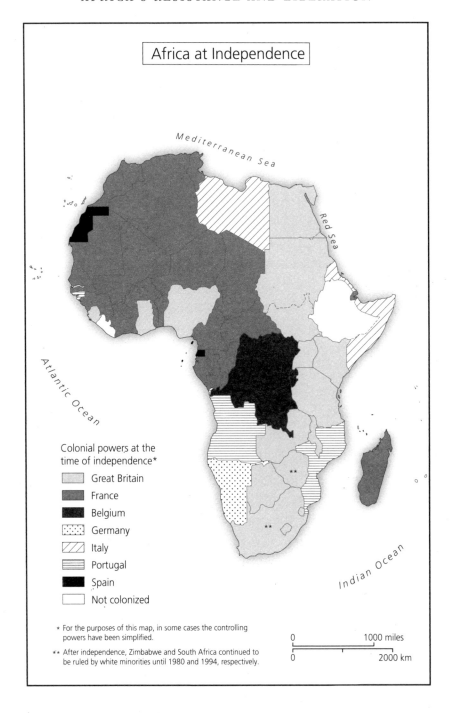

Africa at Independence

Mediterranean Sea

Red Sea

Atlantic Ocean

Indian Ocean

Colonial powers at the
time of independence*

- Great Britain
- France
- Belgium
- Germany
- Italy
- Portugal
- Spain
- Not colonized

* For the purposes of this map, in some cases the controlling
powers have been simplified.

** After independence, Zimbabwe and South Africa continued to
be ruled by white minorities until 1980 and 1994, respectively.

0   1000 miles

0   2000 km

there was a strong colonial presence and dominant white population. Although South Africa and Zimbabwe are considered to have broken away from colonial rule in 1910 and 1965 respectively, they did not attain black enfranchisement until much later. The final country to become free of white rule was South Africa, gaining independence when Nelson Mandela (1918–2013) was released in 1990. He became the first black president in 1994. Mandela had paid a heavy personal price: following a sham trial in the capital Pretoria, he was locked up for 27 years, mostly in a tiny prison cell on Robben Island, forced to wear shorts as his prison uniform, lest he forget that he was regarded as a 'boy' and not an equal by the state.

To borrow the title of Mandela's autobiography, it has been a long walk to freedom for Africa. Slavery and then colonial rule have profoundly marked the continent in myriad ways, as I have attempted to outline in this book. Colonisation and its artificial and arbitrary drawing up of borders have made some countries more prone to ethnic tensions, conflict and underdevelopment.

Perhaps UNESCO's *General History of Africa* is right that those who believe colonialism was an unmitigated disaster and brought *nothing* but servitude, suffering and underdevelopment are overstating the case. Colonial economics, which later became 'development economics', did bring about more efficient agricultural practices, with increased mechanisation and irrigation, and new sources of energy were explored and small-scale industries were established. And yet the dozens of African intellectuals whom I have met unanimously agree with the *GHA*'s conclusion that the evidence shows that exploitation far outweighed economic development, and that on balance the colonial era was a period of economic growth without development, an era of lost opportunities and of humiliation for the peoples of Africa. In 2017, Jakaya Kikwete, former president of Tanzania, said his country on independence in 1960 had three medical doctors and two engineers. Such startling statistics are by no means the exception for Africa south of the Sahara; the Congo had three native university graduates on its independence.

As the charismatic and brilliant Kenyan historian Dr Kenneth Ombongi put it to me in the peaceful grounds of Nairobi University: 'I would largely agree with the assessment that colonialism was more of a liability than an asset to post-colonial Africa. Imperialism alienates, dominates and seeks to control. The bottom line was that the colonial system was totally oppressive.'

I did not intend to embark on detailed arguments about the impact of colonialism on Africa in this book – many tomes have already been written on the subject. And my aim was not to write a book that pits the 'African against the European'. Nor do I ascribe all of Africa's problems to its colonial past. My goal, as expressed in the introduction, was to examine aspects of Africans' history from an African perspective and to highlight and celebrate the achievements of a people – sometimes in the face of great adversity.

Before I turn to the last chapter, an epilogue on Africa today, I would like to say to the non-African reader of this book that I hope I have demonstrated that Africa has a history, that it is a fundamental part of our global story, and one that is worthy of greater attention and respect than it has so far received. And to African readers, I hope I have managed in some small way to increase your knowledge of – and pride in – the great history of your continent. My project was inspired by the memorable words of the late Kenyan environmentalist and Nobel Peace Prize laureate Wangari Maathai: 'You cannot enslave a mind that knows itself, that understands itself, that values itself.'[15]

Epilogue: A New Africa

I have embarked on a panoramic sweep across Africa: a short history of the continent with the longest human history in the world. But history is not only about the past; it also informs our present and shapes our future. And it matters to Africans, as I witnessed throughout my journeys. During a visit to the campus of the University of Lagos in Nigeria in 2019, I was both taken aback and relieved by my conversations with students. When I asked several of them what they knew about their country's history, they replied: 'Slavery, colonialism and the creation of Nigeria as a country in 1914.' Fortunately, they also wanted to know much more about their more distant past as well as that of the whole continent.

Young Africans inhabit a world that is very different from the one I was educated in. The teaching and study of history are becoming more responsive to the views of Africans themselves. In 2015, the movement to 'decolonise' history curriculums was given a new lease of life by the eye-catching 'Rhodes Must Fall' protests by students in South Africa. They wanted courses that better reflected African perspectives, and acknowledged the wrongs of slavery and colonialism. Similar calls spread across the world, including in the United Kingdom's universities and its cultural sector. I hope this book has helped to furnish readers both with the means to indulge their curiosity and with a starting point for further exploration.

Africa has the youngest population in the world, with an average age of 19. By contrast, the average age in Japan is 49, and 41 in the UK. Far from being a curse, Africa's burgeoning numbers should be seen as a boon. Its population has grown from 140 million in 1900 to more than 1.4 billion – from 8 to 18 per cent of the global population. It is projected to double by 2050, and by then nearly a quarter of the world's workers, producers and consumers will be African. By the turn of the century, that figure could rise to 40 per cent. The young generation will create a new Africa. They are less attached to ethnic affiliations than their elders, and they did not experience first-hand the humiliations of the colonial era. Many move around the world as confident, global citizens.

They bring the enthusiasm of a digitally savvy population. Much is made of the impact of technology and artificial intelligence on the way we lead our lives, and its relevance for Africa is probably greater than anywhere else in the world. On a trip in 2022 to Kenya I met a young man, George, at a technology hub in a residential part of Nairobi. In a light and airy office, with sleek modern furniture, state-of-the-art computers and an espresso coffee machine whirring in the background, he told me about the e-commerce and food-delivery service he had set up during the Covid-19 pandemic.

Young entrepreneurs like George are perpetually coming up with innovative ideas across all sectors, including digital health and education services. The creative industries are thriving. Billions of dollars are being raised for start-ups in Africa. Fintech – the use of technology in finance – is booming. More than 95 per cent of households in Kenya (by far the biggest proportion of any nation in the world) use some kind of mobile banking service, most notably M-PESA, a money transfer service launched in 2007. Africa accounts for 70 per cent of the world's mobile money market. According to the African Development Bank, the size of Africa's digital economy is projected to rise by more than 6 per cent a year from $115 billion today to $712 billion by 2050. Since agriculture is still the bedrock of most African economies, imaginative and sustainable ways are being found to boost production. Some farmers are already using AI to obtain information on soil diagnoses, pests and market prices, as well as to 'climate proof' their crops.

As mature economies in the Global North grapple with updating old systems of transport and infrastructure, African cities are being built and developed in a greener and more sustainable way. In Kenya, 92 per cent of electricity is already generated from renewable sources, and rapid electric buses run up and down Nairobi. Around 600 million Africans, however, still lack access to electricity, and the continent needs time and investment to develop a diverse energy mix. Nevertheless, African communities are showing the world the way forward, and there is immense potential for geothermal energy in Africa.

Young Africans are under no illusion about the myriad challenges they confront but they approach them with determination and a deep well of optimism. Many reject any characterisation of Africa as a hopeless continent just as resolutely as they seek answers to the problems.

We are all too familiar with the doom-and-gloom narrative that pervades discussions about Africa. As we have seen, colonial and post-colonial economic realities have consigned Africa to the status of a junior partner in the international order. It is an exporter of raw materials and commodities – and a net importer of expensive, value-added finished goods and products, which leads to severe budgetary imbalances. There are more people living in poverty in Africa than in the rest of the world put together, and decades of economic mismanagement and lack of good governance have held the continent back. African leaders must provide all their people with the peace and prosperity they deserve.

Yet the continent cannot be defined by its difficulties alone. These must not obscure the vibrancy that I have seen across Africa, from coast to coast, cape to cape. I saw a hunger for progress in the eyes and endeavours of the young people I spoke to. The green shoots of a new Africa *are* emerging. Elections, however imperfect, have become the norm on the continent. Sixteen are due to be held in 2024. Presidents who change the rules to run for a third term attract widespread criticism. Leaders trying to rig results are confronted by a citizenry armed with mobile phones who record voter intimidation, violence and poll irregularities. They disseminate information and mobilise through social media. Even the re-emergence of coups in many countries in the early 2020s in West and Central Africa is unlikely in the long term to deflect the continent from the path of democracy. Unlike in the past, putschists now face condemnation from their peers in the African Union, which votes to suspend their membership.

Africans are demanding a better and brighter future, including quality education and jobs. They are protesting across the continent against authoritarianism and conservative social mores. Mass demonstrations in Africa have increased sevenfold in the previous decade and these have been predominantly youth led. In 2019 in Sudan, the peaceful revolution to topple President Omar al-Bashir, after 30 years in power, was bravely initiated by young people – with many women in the vanguard. There, as elsewhere, even the murderous crackdowns by the armed services did not extinguish the fight for freedom.

And although Africans suffer disproportionately from the impact of global warming, the picture is not one of unrelenting pessimism. According to Our World in Data, Africa's contribution to global carbon emissions from 1751 to 2017 was just 3 per cent; south of the Sahara that share falls to a mere half a percentage point. By way of comparison, the US accounted for nearly 25 per cent in the same period. Africa needs billions or even trillions of dollars in investment for energy, climate adaptation and early warning systems for climate disasters. But far from being the worst victim of global warming, Africa could become a world superpower in providing global solutions to tackle carbon emissions. Indeed, it is hard to see a way forward without the continent! Africa is home to nearly a third of the world's mineral reserves, including lithium, graphite, cobalt, bauxite, platinum and other materials that are crucial for low-carbon technologies – the continent holds an ace in its hand.

African leaders and people are taking control of their own natural resources and are saying 'enough, no more'. Africa is still predominantly an exporter of relatively unprocessed agricultural or mineral products to a limited number of markets. However, there are clear signs that the continent is industrialising. The nexus of conflict, rebels, minerals and foreign backers that has bedevilled the Democratic Republic of the Congo for so much of its history is beginning to change. The DRC has been reviewing all of its mining joint ventures with foreign investors to ensure that contracts create real value for the nation. (Whether any additional revenues are deployed transparently is, of course, another matter.) In 2022, Namibia banned exports of raw lithium as it sought to gain more of the mineral's value by processing it domestically, taking a step up the value chain. African governments are beginning to understand that they must deliver strong regulatory frameworks and stability for investors to allow the foreign and domestic private sectors to flourish.

Africans are also arguing for a pathway to development that is uniquely African. The diversity, creativity and inventiveness already evident will shape a future that builds on Africa's history and heritage, 'rooted in its Africanness', as Nelson Mandela said. For example, the pursuit for justice, reconciliation and healing in Rwanda after the 1994 genocide drew on 'Gacaca courts', a system of community justice that has endured for centuries. Africans are implementing their own blueprints for their future, pursuing greater economic integration such as through the landmark 2018 African Continental Free Trade Area Agreement (AfCFTA), the biggest common market in the world. Initiatives to promote greater understanding of such pan-African projects exist across the continent.

Many African economies have advanced in leaps and bounds over the last two decades. Despite severe setbacks during and after the Covid pandemic, the International Monetary Fund projects that Africa's growth rate will exceed the global average. It is expected to become the fastest growing region in the world by 2027.

The Covid outbreak brought home the need to prioritise self-reliance. Africans found themselves at the bottom of the pile for obtaining vaccines. Western countries hoarded them and rushed to double or triple vaccinate their own people, buying up limited supplies, when only a small fraction of Africans had even received their first jab. Rarely have I heard Africans so angry. For a leading African scientist, the Cameroonian-born Professor Christian Happi, who abandoned his laboratory at Harvard University and headed to Nigeria to become director at the African Centre of Excellence for Genomics of Infectious Diseases, the vaccine inequity represents a real opportunity for Africa to further its own science and develop its own vaccines. Professor Happi argues that Covid-19 exposed how easily international cooperation and multilateral agreements can dissolve: Africa has no choice but to guarantee its own health security. He believes that, with the right investments, Africa can position itself as a world leader in science – the natural home for a global centre of knowledge about infectious diseases. Africa may constitute less than a fifth of the global population, yet it is where 70 per cent of pathogens with pandemic potential emerge. African genomes are the oldest and most diverse. Yet only 2 per cent of the sequenced analysed human genome is African. With greater funding of research on the continent we could learn more from this diversity, helping to lead to breakthroughs in gene-based therapies to cure cancer, infectious diseases and many other illnesses.

Africa, a loose-limbed giant with 54 countries – the most of any continent – has come of age. It is asserting itself on the world stage with powerful advocates demanding fairer terms of trade and more equitable financial architecture that does not forever condemn its nations to spiralling debt repayments. These advocates include countless civil society activists and Africans who lead major international organisations, such as Dr Ngozi Okonjo-Iweala, director-general of the World Trade Organisation, Amina Mohammed, the deputy secretary-general of the United Nations, and Gilbert Houngbo, who heads the International Labour Organization.

Africans are seeking and gaining better representation at the top table. Otherwise, they know they will be on the menu! In one significant shift in 2023, the African Union became a member of the G20 club of nations – the world's premier economic coordination body. In August 2023, the president of South Africa Cyril Ramaphosa stood behind China's president Xi Jinping ahead of the BRICS (made up of Brazil, Russia, India, China and South Africa) summit in Pretoria and carefully placed around his neck the Order of South Africa, a gold medallion hanging from a blue and white ribbon. It is the highest honour he could bestow on a foreign dignitary. The days when Africans had to choose between the West and the rest are long gone. In 2024, Ethiopia and Egypt become full members of

BRICS. We live in a multipolar world. Africans enjoy multilateral partnerships with countries in the Global South such as Brazil, India and China as well as other emerging economies and middle powers, including Türkiye, the UAE and Malaysia. All are increasingly involved in Africa.

As a member of an ever more interconnected global African diaspora, I am realistic rather than starry-eyed about the continent of my birth, and the path forward for each country will be different. But we should celebrate what is right with the continent just as we condemn what is wrong. I believe the future belongs to Africa and its youth. Their history, as we have seen, is full of inspirational figures who have shaped the world: there are many more yet to come.

Dr Kenneth Ombongi of the University of Nairobi finished our conversation with this thought: 'We Africans have survived slavery and colonialism. We are surviving the post-colonial tendencies that subjugate us more than support the development of our continent. It is a history that gives us hope, that speaks to the resilience of the Africans. We have made it in the past and the young people on the continent need to know that we have what it takes to meet future challenges and create an Africa better than it is today.'

Young Africans are inventing the present and future for the continent. This book, I hope, has shown them, and the world, that they should do so with their heads held high and their hearts full of pride in their magnificent past.

Notes

Chapter 1: Our Family and Other Hominins

1 Interview with Richard Leakey conducted in October 2015.

2 Many linguists divide African languages into three major categories: Niger–Congo, Afro–Asiatic and Nilo–Saharan. Afro–Asiatic languages are mostly associated with North African inhabitants such as the Berbers and include Arabic, which of course comes from Arabia; Nilo–Saharan languages differ greatly within the group, extending across areas as diverse as the Niger River, the Nile Valley and Tanzania. One early language in this category, Nsibidi, was written down, and the earliest example of such writing, dating about 5000 BCE, was found by the Kharga Oasis in the southern part of the western desert of Egypt. Niger–Congo languages are spoken by huge numbers of people stretching across West and Central Africa.

3 John S. Mbiti, *African Religions and Philosophy* [1969] (Heinemann, first published 1969, second edition 1990), pp. 14–13.

4 Mbiti, *African Religions and Philosophy*, particularly chapter 2.

Chapter 2: Gift of the Nile

1 Quoted by the Smithsonian National Museum of African American History & Culture in the online commentary for Fuller's *Ethiopia* (1921), https://nmaahc.si.edu/meta-vaux-warrick-fuller-ethiopia-1921.

Chapter 3: The Kingdom of Kush

1 In a bulletin for Boston's Museum of Fine Arts, October 1918, quoted in Isma'il Kushkush, 'In the Land of Kush', *Smithsonian Magazine*, September 2020.
2 Robert G. Morkot, *The Black Pharoahs: Egypt's Nubian Rulers* (The Rubicon Press, 2000) p. 215.
3 'Sudan Temples shed light on "secrets of Africa"', France 24, 10 February 2017.

Chapter 4: Ezana of Aksum and the Rise of a Christian Kingdom

1 Information on the churches and the hymns is courtesy of Tekletsadik Belachew of the Christian History Institute.

Chapter 5: The Cross and the Crescent

1 Miguel de Castanhoso, *The Portuguese Expedition to Abyssinia in 1541–1543 as narrated by Castanhoso*, ed. and trans. R.S. Whiteway (Hakluyt Society, 1902), p. 41.
2 Castanhoso, *The Portuguese Expedition*, p. 51.

Chapter 7: Islam and the Dynasties of North Africa

1 St Augustine, *Confessions* (397–400), 6:15, trans. Henry Chadwick [1991] (Oxford University Press, 2008).
2 Ahya, 'Khalifa Uthman bin Affan – Recall and re-deposition of 'Amr b Al 'Aas', https://world.ahya.net/konu-786-ga6.html.

3 The remaining quotes in this section are also drawn from Books 6 and 7 of Ibn Khaldun's fourteenth-century *Kitāb al-'Ibar*.

Chapter 8: Mansa Musa and the Kingdoms of West Africa

1 Quoted in J.S. Trimingham, *A History of Islam in West Africa* [1962] (Oxford University Press, 1970), p. 55.
2 D.T. Niane (ed.), *General History of Africa IV: Africa from the Twelfth to the Sixteenth Century* (Heinemann/UNESCO, 1984), p. 52. Volume IV of the *GHA* was a useful source for much of this chapter.
3 Trimingham, *A History of Islam in West Africa*, p. 79.
4 See Niane, *General History of Africa IV*, p. 59, for Ibn Khaldun's timeline.
5 Leo Africanus, *The History and Description of Africa*, ed. Robert Brown (Hakluyt Society, 1896).
6 From the *Tarikh al-fattash*, the seventeenth-century chronicle by Mahmud Kati. Translation from Omer Abdel Raziq El-Nagar, *West Africa and the Muslim Pilgrimage: An Historical Study with Special Reference to the Nineteenth Century*, PhD thesis, SOAS University of London (1969), p. 91.

Chapter 9: Tippu Tib and the First Enslavers

1 Information from Sylvia Serbin, *Reines d'Afrique et héroïnes de la diaspora noire* (Éditions Sépia, 2004).
2 Quotes from Tippu Tib's autobiography are from Stuart Laing, *Tippu Tip: Ivory, Slavery and Discovery in the Scramble for Africa* (Medina Publishing, 2017).

3 Quote sourced from Laing, *Tippu Tip*, p. 153. Originally from Henry Morton Stanley, *Through the Dark Continent* (Harper and Brothers, 1879).

4 Quote sourced from Laing, *Tippu Tip*, p. 279. Originally by A.J. Swann for the London Missionary Society.

5 Quote sourced from Laing, *Tippu Tip*, p. 276. Originally by Richard Meinertzhagen in 1957.

Chapter 10: Cast in Bronze

1 Michael Mosbacher, 'Who really owns the Benin bronzes?', *The Spectator*, 1 August 2021.

2 Osarhieme Benson Osadolor and Leo Enahoro Otoide, 'The Benin Kingdom in British Imperial Historiography', *History in Africa*, 35 (2008), pp. 401–18.

3 Mawuna Koutonin, 'Story of cities #5: Benin City, the mighty medieval capital now lost without trace', *Guardian*, 18 March 2016.

4 Translation from Thomas Hodgkin, *Nigerian Perspectives: An Historical Anthology* (Oxford University Press, 1960).

5 Flora Edouwaye S. Kaplan, 'Images of the Queen Mother in Benin Court', *African Arts* 26(3) (July 1993).

6 Adam Jones, ed., *German Sources for West African History, 1599–1669.* (Steiner, 1983).

7 Smithsonian National Museum of African Art, 'Chief S.O. Alonge – History of Benin', https://africa.si.edu/exhibitions/past-exhibitions/alonge/history-of-benin.

8 Mawuna Koutonin, 'Stories of cities #5: Benin City, the mighty medieval capital now lost without trace', *Guardian*, 18 March 2016.

9 Dan Hicks, *The Brutish Museums: The Benin Bronzes, Colonial Violence and Cultural Restitution* (Pluto Press, 2020).

10 Osarhieme Benson Osadolor, 'The Benin Royalist Movement and Its Political Opponents: Controversy over Restoration of the Monarchy, 1897–1914', *The International Journal of African Historical Studies*, 44 (1), (2011).

11 Aindrea Emelife, 'West Africa's art scene: uncovering a long legacy of creativity', *Financial Times*, 11 March 2023.

Chapter 11: Southern Kingdoms

1 James Theodore Bent published his views in James Theodore Bent, *The Ruined Cities of Mashonaland: Being a record of excavation and exploration in 1891* (Longmans, Green & Co., 1892) and later editions.

2 Webber Ndoro, 'Great Zimbabwe', *Scientific American*, Special Editions 15 (January 2005): 74–9.

3 Quote cited by Preben Kaarsholm in 'The Past as Battlefield in Rhodesia and Zimbabwe, collected seminar papers of Institute of Commonwealth Studies, 42 (1992): 156–70. Original source Peter S. Garlake, *Great Zimbabwe* (Thames & Hudson Ltd, 1973), p. 204.

4 Quote cited by Kaarsholm in 'The Past as Battlefield in Rhodesia and Zimbabwe'. Original source Helmut K. Silberberg, 'Zimbabwe Ruins – A Mystery Solved', *Arts Rhodesia*, No. 1, p. 53.

5 Vicente Pegado's reports were quoted by João de Barros, in *Década da Ásia* (Lisbon, 1552). See https://zimfieldguide.com/masvingo/great-zimbabwe-%E2%80%93-early-written-descriptions-and-photographs.

6 Quoted by David Chanaiwa, 'Politics and Long-Distance Trade in the Mwene Mutapa Empire during the Sixteenth Century', *International Journal of African Historical Studies* 5(3) (1972): 424–35.

7 A.M. de Mello e Castro to M. de Mello e Castro, 1785, quoted in S.I. Mudenge, 'The Role of Foreign Trade in the Rozvi Empire: A Reappraisal', *The Journal of African History* 15(3) (1974): 373–91.

8 Mudenge, 'The Role of Foreign Trade'.

9 António da Conceição, *Treatise on the Rivers of Cuama (Tratado dos Rios de Cuama)*, ed. and trans. Malyn Newitt (Oxford University Press for the British Academy, 2009).

10 Ndoro, 'Great Zimbabwe'.

11 T.R. Batten, *Tropical Africa in World History* (Oxford University Press, 1956), vol. 1, p. 39.

Chapter 12: Asante Ascent

1 Quoted in Joseph K. Adjaye, 'Asantehene Agyeman Prempe I, Asante History, and the Historian', *History in Africa* 17 (1990): 1–29.

2 George P. Hagan, 'The Golden Stool and the Oaths to the King of Ashanti', Michigan State University paper, 1968, p. 2.

3 Kwame Arhin, 'The Asante Praise Poems: The Ideology of Patrimonialism', *Paideuma: Mitteilungen zur Kulturkunde*, 32 (1986), pp. 163-197.

4 T.C. McCaskie, *Asante, Kingdom of Gold: Essays in the History of an African Culture* (Columbia University Press, 2015).

5 Thomas Edward Bowdich, *Mission from Cape Coast Castle to Ashantee* (John Murray, 1819), pp. 84–9.

6 Quoted in Sharon F. Patton, 'The Asante Umbrella', *African Arts* 17(4) (August 1984), pp. 64–94.

7 Bowdich, *Mission from Cape Coast Castle to Ashantee*, pp. 34–5.

Chapter 13: Asante Courage

1 Winwood Reade, *The Story of the Ashantee Campaign* (Smith, Elder & Co., 1874), pp. 357–8.

2 Quoted in Wilhelmina Joseline Donkoh, 'Kumase: Ambience of Urbanity, Tradition and Modernity', *Transactions of the Historical Society of Ghana*, New Series 8 (2004), pp. 167–83.

3 Quotes from Prempeh I drawn from Adjaye, 'Asantehene Agyeman Prempe I, Asante History, and the Historian', *History in Africa*, pp. 1–29.

4 Quoted in W. Tordoff, 'The Exile and Repatriation of Nana Prempeh I of Ashanti (1896–1924)', *Transactions of the Historical Society of Ghana* 4(2) (1960): 33–58.

5 Quoted in Tordoff, 'The Exile and Repatriation of Nana Prempeh I of Ashanti'.

6 *The Times*, 27 January 1896.

7 Quoted in Edwin W. Smith, *The Golden Stool: Some Aspects of the Conflict of Cultures in Modern Africa* (Afro-Am Press, 1969), p. 6.

8 Smith, *The Golden Stool*, p. 7.

9 R.S. Rattray, *Ashanti* (Clarendon Press, 1923), p. 293.

10 *Gold Coast Leader*, July 1923.

11 *Gold Coast Leader*, February 1924.

12 *Gold Coast Leader*, 29 November 1924.

13 For more details, see 'Afrobarometer Dispatch No. 461' by Lionel Ossé, published 1 July 2021. https://www.afrobarometer.org/wp-content/uploads/2022/02/ad461-ghanaians_united_and_tolerant_-_except_toward_same-sex_relationships-afrobarometer_dispatch-29june21.pdf

Chapter 14: Slavery and Salvation

1 Gomes Eannes de Azurara, *The Chronicle of the Discovery and Conquest of Guinea*, eds Charles R. Beazley and Edgar Prestage (Hakluyt Society, 1896).

2 Adaobi Tricia Nwaubani, 'My Great-Grandfather, the Nigerian Slave-Trader', *New Yorker*, 15 July 2018.

3 'The life of Omar ben Saeed, called Morro, a Fullah Slave in Fayetteville, N.C. Owned by Governor Owen', 1831, Protestant missionary Isaac Bird's undated translation between 1860–64, Omar Ibn Said Collection, US Library of Congress, transcription provided by Dr Adam Rothman.

4 Quotes are from Olaudah Equiano, *The Interesting Narrative of the Life of Olaudah Equiano, or Gustavus Vassa, the African*, first published in London, 1789. The full text of the 1794 edition is available at https://en.wikisource.org/wiki/The_Interesting_Narrative_of_the_Life_of_Olaudah_Equiano,_or_Gustavus_Vassa,_the_African.

5 Wenda Parkinson, *'This Gilded African': Toussaint L'Ouverture* (Quartet Books, 1978), p. 37.

Chapter 15: Land, Gold and Greed

1 As relayed to me by Professor Nigel Penn.

2 Sameer Naik, 'The story of legendary King Shaka Zulu makes it on to Netflix as film earns international accolades', *Saturday Star*, 13 August 2022.

3 Quotes from Shaka and others are taken from the poet Mazisi Kunene's version of *Emperor Shaka the Great: A Zulu Epic* [1979] (Heinemann, 1986), an epic Zulu poem based on oral tradition; quoted in Mbongeni Z. Malaba, 'Super-Shaka: Mazisi

Kunene's "Emperor Shaka the Great"', *Research in African Literatures* 19(4) (Winter 1988): 477–88.

4 Nathaniel Isaacs, *Travels and Adventures in Eastern Africa* (E. Churton, 1836); letter quoted by Dan Wylie, *Myth of Iron: Shaka in History* (University of KwaZulu-Natal Press, 2006).

5 Isaacs, *Travels and Adventures.*

6 Letter to Governor Sir Benjamin Pine, quoted in Richard Lidbrook Cope, 'The Origins of the Anglo–Zulu War of 1879', PhD thesis, University of the Witwatersrand, 1995, p. 52.

7 Paul Williams, *Custer and the Sioux, Durnford and the Zulus: Parallels in the American and British Defeats at the Little Bighorn (1876) and Isandlwana (1879)* (McFarland and Co., 2015), p. 27.

8 Diary of the 1st Division, 15 May 1879, WO 32/7740; telegram from General Crealoc to Chelmsford, 16 May 1879; quoted by J.P.C. Laband, 'Humbugging the General? King Cetshwayo's Peace Overtures During the Anglo–Zulu War', *Theoria: A Journal of Social and Political Theory* 67 (October 1986): 1–20.

Chapter 16: The Kingdom of Kongo and the Scramble for Africa

1 The phrase 'Scramble for Africa' is used with reference to the definition in the *New Palgrave Dictionary of Economics*, eds Steven N. Durlauf and Lawrence E. Blume (Palgrave Macmillan, 2016 online edition).

2 Joseph Conrad's journal, Stanley Falls, September 1890; in Joseph Conrad, *Last Essays* (J.M. Dent & Sons, 1926), p.10.

3 Excerpt of letter from Nzinga Mbemba (Alfonso I) to Portuguese King João III, 18 October 1526, in World History Commons, https://worldhistorycommons.org/excerpt-letter-nzinga-mbemba-portuguese-king-joao-iii.

4 Linda M. Heywood, *Njinga of Angola: Africa's Warrior Queen* (Harvard University Press, 2019).

5 John K. Thornton, *The Kongolese Saint Anthony: Dona Beatriz Kimpa Vita and the Antonian Movement, 1684–1706* (Cambridge University Press, 1998).

6 Elias Papaioannou and Stelios Michalopoulos, 'The Long-Run Effects of the Scramble for Africa', *American Economic Review* 106(7) (July 2016): 1802–48.

7 Thomas Pakenham, *The Scramble for Africa: The White Man's Conquest of the Dark Continent from 1876 to 1912* (Weidenfeld & Nicolson, 1991).

8 Hilaire Belloc and Basil Temple Blackwood, *The Modern Traveller* (E. Arnold & Co., 1898), p. 40.

9 'Koning Filip betuigt "diepste spijt" voor Belgische wandaden in Congo', *VRT News*, 30 June 2020. Translation as rendered on the Wikipedia page 'Belgian apologies to the Congo', https://en.wikipedia.org/wiki/Belgian_apologies_to_the_Congo.

10 The full name of the report I contributed to was 'Report of a Commission of Inquiry Established by Oriel College, Oxford into Issues Associated with Memorials to Cecil Rhodes', published in April 2021.

11 United States Institute of Peace. 'Certificate Course in Conflict Analysis', 30 January 2008. https://www.usip.org/sites/default/files/academy/OnlineCourses/Conflict_Analysis_1-30-08.pdf.

12 'Outreach Programme on the 1994 Genocide Against the Tutsi in Rwanda and the United Nations', United Nations, undated, https://www.un.org/en/preventgenocide/rwanda/historical-background.shtml.

13 Robinson, Amanda Lea. 'National versus Ethnic Identity in Africa: State, Group, and Individual Level Correlates of National Identification', Working Paper No. 112, Afrobarometer, September 2009. https://www.afrobarometer.org/

wp-content/uploads/migrated/files/publications/
Working%20paper/AfropaperNo112.pdf.

Chapter 17: Africa's Resistance and Liberation

1 Joseph Ki-Zerbo, *General History of Africa I: Methodology and African Prehistory* (Heinemann/UNESCO, 1981), pp. 46–7.

2 Omar García-Ponce and Leonard Wantchekon, 'Critical Junctures: Independence Movements and Democracy in Africa', *American Journal of Political Science* (August 2023).

3 Siavash Saffari, Roxana Akhbari, Kara Adbolmaleki and Evelyn Hamdon (eds), *Unsettling Colonial Modernity in Islamicate Contexts* (Cambridge Scholars, 2017), p. 135.

4 All Babikr Bedri quotes are from Babikr Bedri, *The Memoirs of Babikr Bedri*, trans. Yousef Bedri and George Scott (Oxford University Press, 1969), p. 19 ff.

5 Winston Churchill, *The River War: An Account of the Reconquest of the Sudan* (Longmans & Co., 1902), p. 31.

6 From *The Memoirs of Babikr Bedri*, trans. Yousef Bedri and George Scott, p. 128.

7 Babikr Bedri, from whose memoirs I have quoted, died two years earlier in 1954, when he was well into his nineties. He was my great-grandfather and was the pioneer of female education in Sudan, setting up schools for girls. Later, a university for women, called Ahfad (meaning grandchildren), was established in the capital in his honour by his son, Yousef Bedri.

8 Abukar Elmi, 'The Somali Ornament: How it ended its journey at the British Museum in London', British Museum (undated), https://objectjourneys.britishmuseum.org/the-somali-ornament/.

9 The quotes here are from al-Sayyid's poems, sourced from Said S. Samatar, *Oral Poetry and Somali Nationalism: The Case of*

Sayyid Mahammad 'Abdille Hasan, African Studies Series, No. 32 (Cambridge University Press, 1982).

10 Kwame Nkrumah, *Class Struggle in Africa* (Panaf Books Limited, 1970), p. 88.

11 Ben Macintyre and Paul Orengoh, 'Beatings and abuse made Barack Obama's grandfather loathe the British', *The Times*, 3 December 2008.

12 Valentine Low and Jane Flanagan, 'King Charles expresses "reget" for Kenya colonial violence', *The Times*, 31 October 2023.

13 Patrice Lumumba, 'Speech at the Ceremony of the Proclamation of the Congo's Independence', 30 June 1960; Patrice Lumumba, *The Truth about a Monstrous Crime of the Colonialists* (Foreign Languages Publishing House, 1961), pp. 44–7, transcribed by Thomas Schmidt.

14 Jason Burke, 'Belgium returns Patrice Lumumba's tooth to family 61 years after his murder', *Guardian*, 20 June 2022.

15 *Taking Root: The Vision of Wangari Maathai*, directed by Lisa Merton and Alan Dater (2008).

Sources

All interviews in this list were conducted by the author and were recorded for the TV series *The History of Africa with Zeinab Badawi* (BBC World News, 2017–2020). The entire series is available to stream on the YouTube channel for BBC News Africa. Where possible, individuals' titles have been updated to their most current at the time of writing; otherwise they reflect the person's position at the time the interview was conducted.

Chapter 1: Our Family and Other Hominins

Books and articles

Chaudhary, Nikhil and Annie Swanepoel. 'Editorial Perspective: What can we learn from hunter-gatherers about children's mental health? An evolutionary perspective', *Journal of Child Psychology and Psychiatry*, 64 (10), (2023): 1522–5.

Crittenden, Alyssa N. and Frank W. Marlowe. 'Allomaternal Care among the Hadza of Tanzania', *Human Nature*, 19 (3), (2008): 249–62.

Mokhtar, Gamal (editor). *UNESCO General History of Africa II: Ancient Civilizations of Africa* (James Currey/UNESCO, 1990).

Moussa Iye, Ali. *The Verdict of the Tree. The Xeer Issa: An Essay on an African Endogenous Democracy* (2014).

Shillington, Kevin. *History of Africa* (Bloomsbury Academic, 2018).

Interviews

Adeboye, Olufunke. Head of the Department of History and Strategic Studies, University of Lagos, Nigeria (November 2018).

Adekanmbi, Olusola H. Associate Professor of Palynology and Environmental Botany, University of Lagos, Nigeria (November 2018).

Bhebe, Ngwabi M. Professor Emeritus, Midlands State University, Zimbabwe (February 2017).

Bocoum, Hamady. Director General at the Fundamental Institute of Black Africa (IFAN), Museum of Black Civilizations, Senegal (August 2015).

Chami, Felix. Professor of Archaeology, University of Dar es Salaam, Tanzania (September 2016).

Dipio, Sister Dominica. Professor of Literature and Film, Makerere University, Uganda (May 2019).

Dungeni, Musa. Retired Zimbabwean headteacher and oral tradition practitioner (February 2017).

Hachi, Slimane, Former Director, National Centre for Prehistoric, Anthropological and Historical Research (CNRPAH), Algeria (March 2016).

Hadzabe Community (in particular Nobako and Haaono), Lake Eyasi, Tanzania. Aided by David Maragu, interpreter for the Hadzabe Community (September 2016).

Haile-Selassie, Yohannes. Director and Virginia M. Ullman Professor of Natural History and the Environment, Institute of Human Origins, Arizona State University, US. Interview at Addis Ababa Museum (January 2016).

Holl, Augustin. President of the International Scientific Committee of UNESCO's General History of Africa. Interviewed in Luanda (September 2019) and London (December 2019).

Kukhanya, Charles and Dube, Sibongile. Zimbabwean farmers (February 2017).

Leakey, Richard. Former Chair, Turkana Basin Institute (October 2015).

Mabulla, Audax. Associate Professor in Archaeology and Heritage Studies, University of Dar es Salaam, Tanzania (December 2015 and September 2016).

Mahlangu, Lindiwe. Tourist Guides Supervisor, Maropeng and Sterkfontein Caves Visitor Centre, South Africa (November 2014).

Mallen, Lara. Former curator of the Origins Centre, University of the Witwatersrand, South Africa (November 2014).

Marite, Kinama. Former Discovery Centre Interpretive Guide. Discovery Centre, The Serengeti National Park, Tanzania (September 2016).

Mwawara, Daniel. Community elder, Rabai, Kenya (May 2019).

Nyathi, Pathisa. Executive Chairman of Amagugu International Heritage Centre, Zimbabwe (February 2017).

Thackeray, Francis, Professor of Paleontology and Kibii, Job, Archaeologist, University of the Witwatersrand, South Africa (March and November 2014).

Virunga National Park (Rwanda team, in particular our guide, Patience), Virunga National Park, Democratic Republic of Congo (March 2016).

Personal correspondence

Shillington, Kevin. Historian and author. Email correspondence with the author (2019–2023).

Wrangham, Richard W. Research Professor of Biological Anthropology, Harvard University, US. Email briefing (January 2017).

Yaï, Olabiyi B. J. Former Chair of the Executive Board of UNESCO. Email briefing (July 2017).

Chapter 2: Gift of the Nile

Books and articles

Mokhtar, Gamal (editor). *UNESCO General History of Africa II: Ancient Civilizations of Africa* (James Currey/UNESCO, 1990).

Samaan, Magdy. 'Mummies found fitted with golden tongues inside a network of tombs near Cairo', *The Times*, 28 November 2022.

Lectures

Hinson, Benjamin. Curator in the Middle East Section, Victoria & Albert Museum. 'Egyptomania!' [online lecture] (26 January 2023).

Interviews

Abdelrazik, Yasser. Archaeologist and guide at the Valley of the Kings, Egyptian Ministry of Tourism and Antiquities, Egypt (April 2016).

Boubaker, Diop. Professor of Egyptology, Cheikh Anta Diop University of Dakar, Senegal (August 2015).

Hawass, Zahi. Archaeologist and Egyptologist, Former Minister of State for Antiquities Affairs of Egypt (February 2017).

Mahmoud, Mahmoud Mohammed. Farmer, Aswan, Egypt (April 2016).

Samir, Ahmed. Curator, The Egyptian Museum in Cairo, Egypt (April 2016).

Shaheen, Bahia. Professor of Greek and Roman Studies, Alexandria University, Egypt (April 2016).

Sobhy, Fatima Mohammed. Culture expert, local freelance guide in Aswan (April 2016).

Personal correspondence

Mojsov, Bojana. Egyptologist, historian, archaeologist and writer. Email correspondence with the author (January 2022).

Chapter 3: The Kingdom of Kush

Books

Breasted, James Henry. *Ancient Records of Egypt: Vol. 1: The First to the Seventeenth Dynasties* (University of Illinois Press, 2001 [first published 1906]).

Mokhtar, Gamal (editor). *UNESCO General History of Africa II: Ancient Civilizations of Africa* (James Currey/UNESCO, 1990).

Morkot, Robert G. *The Black Pharaohs: Egypt's Nubian Rulers* (The Rubicon Press, 2000).

Redford, Donald B. *From Slave to Pharaoh: The Black Experience of Ancient Egypt* (John Hopkins University, 2006).

Welsby, Derek A. *The Kingdom of Kush* (British Museum Press, 1996).

Interviews

Ali, Abdelrahman. General Director of the Sudanese National Corporation for Antiquities and Museums (NCAM) (May 2015).

Fadl Hassan, Yusuf. Professor of History, University of Khartoum, Sudan (May 2015).

Taha, Shadia. Archaeologist, University of Cambridge, United Kingdom (February 2017).

Welsby, Derek A. Curator, Department of Ancient Egypt and Sudan, British Museum, London (April 2017).

Chapter 4: Ezana of Aksum and the Rise of a Christian Kingdom

Books and articles

Belachew, Tekletsadik. 'From Abba Salama to King Lalibela', *Christian History Magazine*, issue 105 (Christian History Institute, 2013).

Shillington, Kevin. *History of Africa* (Bloomsbury Academic, 2018).

Welsby, Derek A. and Phillipson, David W. *Empires of the Nile* (The Folio Society, 2008).

Interviews

Gebreselassie, Teclehaimanot. Assistant Professor, Addis Ababa University, Ethiopia (January 2016).

Libseqal, Yosief. Director of National Museum of Eritrea (April 2016).

Sena, Princess Mariam. Granddaughter of Emperor Haile Selassie, Addis Ababa, Ethiopia (January 2016).

Sulayman, Omar. Archaeological site guide at Qohaito, Eritrea (April 2016).

Tesfay, Yalem. Archaeologist, Aksum, Ethiopia (January 2016).

Chapter 5: The Cross and the Crescent

Articles

Pankhurst, Richard and Rita Pankhurst. 'Ethiopian figurines from Mugar monastery in Shawa', *African Arts*, 37 (3), (2004).

SOURCES

Interviews

Gebreselassie, Teclehaimanot. Assistant Professor, Addis Ababa University, Ethiopia (January 2016).

Ibrahim, Sheikh Maftuh Abubaker. Descendant of Emir of Harar, Harar, Ethiopia (January 2016).

Idris, Saleh. Community leader, Dahlak Islands, Eritrea (November 2016).

al-Karamani, Abdul Ahmed. Community leader, Dahlak Islands, Eritrea (November 2016).

Mathias, His Holiness Abune. Patriarch of the Ethiopian Orthodox Church (January 2016).

al-Nour, Hadj Mohammed. Secretary of Islamic Community Asmara, Eritrea (November 2016).

Redwan, Amir. Guide at the tomb of Sheikh Abadir, Harar, Ethiopia (January 2016).

Weber, Hawera. Civil servant, Harar, Ethiopia (January 2016).

Woldegiorgis, Fikru. Lalibela cultural expert and tour operator, Lalibela, Ethiopia (January 2016).

Zekaria, Ahmed. Historian and Chief Curator, Institute of Ethiopian Studies Museum, Addis Ababa, Ethiopia (January 2016).

Chapter 6: Ifrikiya and the Amazigh

Books

Livy, *History of Rome, Volume 2: Books 22–22*; trans. B.O. Foster (Loeb Classical Library/Harvard University Press, 1929)

Miles, Richard. *Carthage Must Be Destroyed: The Rise and Fall of an Ancient Civilization* (Penguin, 2011).

Scullard, H. H. *A History of the Roman World: 753 to 146 BC* (Routledge, 2012). Polybius. *The Histories, Volume 1: Books 1–2*; trans. W.R. Paton (Loeb Classical Library, 2012).

Interviews

Atki, Mustafa. Archaeologist and historian, Volubilis, Morocco (December 2016).

Atout, Mohammed. Berber merchant, Jemaa el-Fnaa, Marrakesh (December 2016).

Boussoffara, Ridha. Professor at the National Heritage Institute, Tunisia (May 2016).

Chantit, Abdelahi. Independent Marrakesh heritage guide, Morocco (December 2016).

Elfekair, Redha. Archaeologist at the Archaeological Museum of Cherchell, Algeria (March 2016).

Hachi, Slimane, Former Director, National Centre for Prehistoric, Anthropological and Historical Research (CNRPAH), Algeria (March 2016).

Hakim, Redha. Archaeologist and Directorate of Culture, Tipasa, Algeria (March 2016).

Jamaledine, Mohammed. Resident of Ait-Ben-Haddou, Morocco, interviewed with the assistance of Professor Nouhi al-Ouafi (December 2016).

Kitouni Daho, Keltoum. Historian and Director of Cirta Museum, Constantine, Algeria (March 2016).

Ladjimi-Sebaï, Leïla. Archaeologist and President of the Friends of Carthage Society (May 2016).

Mohib, Abderrahim. Co-director of Prehistory of Casablanca scientific mission and archaeologist for Ministry of Culture, Morocco (December 2016).

al-Ouafi, Nouhi. Historian, Royal Institute of Amazigh Culture, Morocco (December 2016).

Razzak, Bensalem Abdu. Archaeologist, Regional Cultural Office, Algeria (March 2016).

Toufik, Abdelkaoui. Independent Timgad guide, Algeria (March 2016).

SOURCES

Chapter 7: Islam and the Dynasties of North Africa

Books

Ki-Zerbo, J. and Niane, D.T. (editors). *UNESCO General History of Africa IV: Africa from the Twelfth to the Sixteenth Century* (James Currey/UNESCO, 1997).

Shillington, Kevin. *History of Africa* (Bloomsbury Academic, 2018).

Interviews

Assouline, Rabbi Henri. Vice President of the Community of Jews in Marrakesh and Essaouira, Morocco (December 2016).

Bennison, Amira K. Professor in the History and Culture of the Maghrib, University of Cambridge, UK (July 2018).

Boussoffara, Ridha. Professor at the National Heritage Institute, Tunisia (May 2016).

Essaied, Haythem. Local businessman and horse owner, Hippodrome de Ksar Saïd, Den Den, Tunisia (May 2016).

Fadl Hassan, Yusuf. Professor Emeritus, University of Khartoum, Sudan (May 2015).

Ka, Thierno. Director, Islamic Institute of the Grand Mosque of Dakar, Senegal (August 2015).

Kbiri Alaoui, Mohammed. Professor and lecturer at the Institut National des Sciences de l'Archéologie et du Patrimoine (INSAP, the National Institute of Archaeology and Heritage), Rabat, Morocco (December 2016).

Kenbib, Mohammed. Professor and lecturer in History, Mohammed V University, Rabat, Morocco (December 2016).

Ohana, Michel. Member of the Moroccan Jewish community and local businessman (December 2016).

al-Saied, Abdelbaki. Islamic scholar, Al Azhar Mosque, Cairo, Egypt (April 2016).

Siraj, Ahmed. Professor of History, Hassan II University of Casablanca, Morocco (December 2016).

Tshibandu, Father Ambrose. Formerly of St Augustine Basilica, Hippo, Algeria (March 2016).

Chapter 8: Mansa Musa and the Kingdoms of West Africa

Books and articles

Brians, Paul et al. (eds.). Translation of Leo Africanus, *Reading About the World, Volume 2* (Harcourt College Publishers, 1999).

El-Nagar, Omer Abdel Raziq. 'West Africa and the Muslim Pilgrimage: An Historical Study with Special Reference to the Nineteenth Century', PhD thesis, School of Oriental and African Studies, London, UK, January 1969.

Ki-Zerbo, J. and Niane, D.T (editors). *UNESCO General History of Africa IV: Africa from the Twelfth to the Sixteenth Century* (James Currey/UNESCO, 1997).

Interviews

Abdallah, Abdelwadoud. Professor of History, University of Nouakchott, Mauritania (January 2019).

Amara, Mohamed. Mayor of Chinguetti, Mauritania (January 2019).

Bagayoko, Amadou and Doumbia, Mariam. Malian musicians, Mali (January 2019).

Bello, Sule. Professor of History, Ahmadu Bello University. Interviewed in Kano, Nigeria (November 2018).

Deyah, Mohammed, Chinguetti resident, Chinguetti, Mauritania (January 2019).

Diabaté, Toumani. Musician, Mali (January 2019).

El Hadj, Salem Ould. Culture and heritage expert, Timbuktu, Mali (January 2019).

El Islam, Sayf. Retired teacher, Foundation Al Ahmed Mahmoud, Chinguetti, Mauritania (January 2019).

Ka, Thierno. Director, Islamic Institute of the Grand Mosque of Dakar, Senegal (August 2015).

Kane, Mamadou. Director, National Museum of Mauritania, Nouakchott, Mauritania (January 2019).

Konaté, Abdoulaye, Artist, Balla Fasséké Kouyaté Conservatory, Bamako, Mali (January 2019).

Konaté, Doulaye. Historian, University of Bamako, Mali (January 2019).

Maiga, Fatimata and Tandina, Marian. Gao residents, Mali (January 2019).

Sanusi II, Muhammadu. Former Emir of Kano, Nigeria (November 2018).

Seeka, Simakha. Storyteller and praise singer, Nouakchott, Mauritania (January 2019).

Traore, Ladje. General Secretary, Soninke Association, Nouakchott, Mauritania (January 2019).

Chapter 9: Tippu Tib and the First Enslavers

Books and articles

Adu Boahen, A. (editor). *UNESCO General History of Africa VII: Africa under Colonial Domination 1880-1935* (James Currey/ UNESCO, 1997).

Downing, Angela. 'The autobiography of Hamed bin Muhamed el Murjebi, 'Tippu tip', *Bells: Barcelona English language and literature studies*, 1, (1989): 61–70.

Laing, Stuart. *Tippu Tip: Ivory, Slavery and Discovery in the Scramble for Africa* (Medina Publishing, 2017).

Trabelsi, Salah and Leservoisier, Olivier. *Résistances et Mémoires des Esclavages: Espaces Arabo–Musulmans et Transatlantiques* (Karthala, 2014).

Uzoigwe, G. N. 'The Slave Trade and African Societies', *Transactions of the Historical Society of Ghana*, 14 (2), (1973): 187–212.

Documentaries

Mazrui, Ali (dir.). *The Africans: A Triple Heritage.* BBC/PBS/Nigerian Television Authority (1986).

Interviews

Abdulkadir, Mohamed. Lamu resident, Kenya (May 2019).

Chami, Felix. Professor of Archaeology, University of Dar es Salaam, Tanzania (September 2016).

Gates Jun., Henry Louis. Alphonse Fletcher University Professor and Director of the Hutchins Center for African and American Research, Harvard University, US (October 2023).

Katama, Father William. Priest, St Paul's Church, Rabai, Kenya (May 2019).

Momade, Fatima. Mozambique resident (August 2018).

Moussa-Elkadhum, Djaffar. UNESCO official, Luanda (September 2019).

Mwenje, Mohammed. Curator of Lamu Museums, Sites and Monuments, National Museums of Kenya (May 2019).

Regulo, Mauricio. Professor and lecturer in History, Lúrio University, Mozambique (August 2018).

Said Msellem, Amira. Guest lecturer at Moi University, Kenya (May 2019).

Santana, Eugénio Pinto. Doctoral student in Anthropology, Eduardo Mondlane University, Mozambique (August 2018).

Twahir, Fatma, Principal Curator, Fort Jesus, Mombasa Island, Kenya (May 2019).

Chapter 10: Cast in Bronze

Books and articles

Adebowale, Oludamola. 'Creatures of the Benin Kingdom: A Tale of Mystic, Magic and the Supernatural', *Guardian Nigeria News*, 17 May 2020.

Kaplan, Flora Edouwaye S. 'Images of the Queen Mother in Benin Court Art', *African Arts* 26 (3), (1993).

Ogot, B.A (editor). *UNESCO General History of Africa V: Africa from the Sixteenth to the Eighteenth Century* (James Currey/UNESCO, 1999).

Otoide, Leo E. and Osadolor, Osarhieme B. 'The Benin Kingdom in British Imperial Historiography', *History in Africa*, 35 (2008): 401–18.

Plankensteiner, Barbara (Ed.). *Benin Kings and Rituals: Court Arts from Nigeria* (Snoeck, 2007).

Pan-Atlantic University, School of Media and Communication. 'Remarkable Historical Figures of Ancient Benin Kingdom', Centenary Project, https://artsandculture.google.com/story/remarkable-historical-figures-of-ancient-benin-kingdom-pan-atlantic-university/fwXBiUQgLcccIw?hl=en.

Interviews

Docemo, Erelu Abiola. Erelu Kuti (Queen Mother) of the Yoruba people of Lagos, Lagos Island, Nigeria (November 2018).

Falaiye, Muyiwa. Professor of African Socio-Political Philosophy, University of Lagos, Nigeria (November 2018).

Ikwubuzo, Iwu. Professor of Igbo Studies, University of Lagos, Nigeria (November 2018).

Oduwobi, Tunde. Professor and lecturer in the department of History and Strategic Studies, University of Lagos, Nigeria (November 2018).

Osadolor, Osarhieme. Professor of History and International Studies and Diplomacy, University of Benin, Benin (November 2018).

Umogbai, Theophilus. Director and Curator of Benin National Museum, Benin City, Nigeria (November 2018).

Chapter 11: Southern Kingdoms

Books and articles

Chirikure, Shadreck. 'Unearthing the Truth', the *Economist*, 18 December 2021.

Kaarsholm, Preben, 'The Past as Battlefield in Rhodesia and Zimbabwe', Collected seminar papers of Institute of Commonwealth Studies, 42 (1992): 156–70.

Ki-Zerbo, J. and Niane, D.T (editors). *UNESCO General History of Africa IV: Africa from the Twelfth to the Sixteenth Century* (James Currey/UNESCO, 1997).

McIntosh, Roderick J. and Coulson, David, 'Riddle of Great Zimbabwe', *Archaeology*, 51 (4), (1998): 44–9.

Pikirayi, Innocent. 'Great Zimbabwe in Historical Archaeology: Reconceptualizing Decline, Abandonment, and Reoccupation of an Ancient Polity, AD 1450–1900', *Historical Archaeology,* 47 (1), (2013): 26–37.

Shillington, Kevin. *History of Africa* (Bloomsbury Academic, 2018).

Interviews

Bhebe, Ngwabi M. Professor Emeritus, Midlands State University, Zimbabwe (February 2017).

Chitungu, Victoria. Director, Lusaka National Museum (August 2018).

Karekwaivanane, George H. Senior Lecturer in African Studies, University of Edinburgh, Scotland (September 2019).

Nyathi, Pathisa. Executive Chairman of Amagugu International Heritage Centre, Zimbabwe (February 2017).

Phiri, Bizeck J. Professor of History, University of Zambia (August 2018).

Regulo, Mauricio. Professor of History, Lúrio University, Mozambique (August 2018).

Setlhako, Cedric. Guide, Mapungubwe Interpretation Centre, South Africa (interview conducted by Lucy Doggett, March 2019).

Timba, Moises. Curator of Maputo Fortress, Mozambique (August 2018).

Chapter 12: Asante Ascent: Osei Tutu and Abena Pokou

Books and articles

Adjaye, Joseph K. 'Asantehene Agyeman Prempe I, Asante History, and the Historian', *History in Africa*, 17 (1990): 1–29.

Akyeampong, Emmanuel K. *Independent Africa* (Indiana University Press, 2023).

Adu Boahen, A (editor). *UNESCO General History of Africa VII: Africa under Colonial Domination 1880-1935* (James Currey/ UNESCO, 1997).

Adu Boahen, A. *Yaa Asantewaa and the Asante–British War of 1900–1* (James Currey Publishers, 2003).

Bowdich, Thomas E. *Mission from Cape Coast Castle to Ashantee* (John Murray, 1819).

Fuller, Harcourt. 'Building a Nation: Symbolic Nationalism During the Kwame Nkrumah era in the Gold Coast/Ghana', PhD thesis, LSE, London, UK, August 2010.

Fuller, Harcourt. 'Commemorating an African Queen: Ghanaian Nationalism, the African Diaspora, and the Public Memory of Nana Yaa Asantewaa, 1952–2009', *African Arts*, 47 (4), (2014): 58–71.

Hess, Janet B. 'Imagining Architecture: The Structure of Nationalism in Accra, Ghana', *Africa Today*, 47 (2), (2000): 35–58.

Ogot, B.A (editor). *UNESCO General History of Africa V: Africa from the Sixteenth to the Eighteenth Century* (James Currey/ UNESCO, 1999).

Tordoff, W. 'The Exile and Repatriation of Nana Prempeh I of Ashanti (1896–1924)', *Transactions of the Historical Society of Ghana*, 4 (2), (1960): 33–58.

Interviews

Ampah, Linda. Fashion designer and CEO of Cadling Fashions/ KAD Manufacturing Ltd, Ghana (November 2018).

Amtwi, Fred. Kumasi community leader, Kumasi, Ghana (November 2018).

Asokore, Nana Boakye-Ansah. Asante Chief, Kumasi, Ghana (November 2018).

Ayesu, Ebenezer. Senior Lecturer, Institute of African Studies, University of Ghana (November 2018).

Brobbey, Justice. Curator, Manhyia Palace Museum, Kumasi, Ghana (November 2018).

Gyimah-Boadi, E. Professor Emeritus at University of Ghana, and Co-Founder and Chair of Afrobarometer (April and August 2023).

Rawlings, Nana. Former First Lady of Ghana (November 2018).

Safo-Kantanka, Osei-Bonsu. Historian and Asante Culture and Heritage Guide, Manhyia Palace, Kumasi, Ghana (November 2018).

Tagro, Francis. Curator, Museum of Civilizations of Côte d'Ivoire, Abidjan, Côte d'Ivoire (April 2019).

Chapter 13: Asante Courage: Prempeh and Yaa Asantewaa

Books and articles

Adjaye, Joseph K. 'Asantehene Agyeman Prempe I, Asante History, and the Historian', *History in Africa*, 17 (1990): 1–29.

Akyeampong, Emmanuel K. *Independent Africa* (Indiana University Press, 2023).

Adu Boahen, A (editor). *UNESCO General History of Africa VII: Africa under Colonial Domination 1880-1935* (James Currey/UNESCO, 1997).

Adu Boahen, A. *Yaa Asantewaa and the Asante–British War of 1900–1* (James Currey Publishers, 2003).

Bowdich, Thomas E. *Mission from Cape Coast Castle to Ashantee* (John Murray, 1819).

Fuller, Harcourt. 'Building a Nation: Symbolic Nationalism During the Kwame Nkrumah era in the Gold Coast/Ghana', PhD thesis, LSE, London, UK, August 2010.

Fuller, Harcourt. 'Commemorating an African Queen: Ghanaian Nationalism, the African Diaspora, and the Public Memory of Nana Yaa Asantewaa, 1952–2009', *African Arts*, 47 (4), (2014): 58–71.

Hess, Janet B. 'Imagining Architecture: The Structure of Nationalism in Accra, Ghana', *Africa Today*, 47 (2), (2000): 35–58.

Ogot, B.A (editor). *UNESCO General History of Africa V: Africa from the Sixteenth to the Eighteenth Century* (James Currey/ UNESCO, 1999).

Tordoff, W. 'The Exile and Repatriation of Nana Prempeh I of Ashanti (1896–1924)', *Transactions of the Historical Society of Ghana*, 4 (2), (1960): 33–58.

Interviews

Ayesu, Ebenezer. Senior Lecturer, Institute of African Studies, University of Ghana (November 2018).

Brobbey, Justice. Curator, Manhyia Palace Museum, Kumasi, Ghana (November 2018).

Gavua, Kodzo. Archaeologist and Associate Professor of Archaeology and Heritage Studies, University of Ghana (November 2018).

Gyimah-Boadi, E. Professor Emeritus at University of Ghana, and Co-Founder and Chair of Afrobarometer (April and August 2023).

Ouattara, Alassane. President of Côte d'Ivoire (April 2019).

Chapter 14: Slavery and Salvation

Books and articles

Beckles, Hilary McDonald. *How Britain Underdeveloped the Caribbean: A Reparation Response to Europe's Legacy of Plunder and Poverty* (University of the West Indies Press, 2021).

Ogot, B.A (editor). *UNESCO General History of Africa V: Africa from the Sixteenth to the Eighteenth Century* (James Currey/ UNESCO, 1999).

Rodney, Walter. *How Europe Underdeveloped Africa* (Verso, 2018).

Interviews

Akyea, Nkunu, Local historian and guide, Cape Coast Castle, Ghana (November 2018).

Allen, William E. Professor of History, University of Liberia, Monrovia, Liberia (April 2019).

Beckles, Hilary McDonald. Vice-Chancellor, University of the West Indies, Barbados (July 2021).

Broh, Susan. Water seller, Liberia (April 2019).

Burrowes, Carl P. Historian and Vice President for Academic Affairs, Cuttington University, Liberia (April 2019).

Coly, Eloi. Chief Curator of The House of Slaves, Gorée, Senegal (August 2015).

Correia, António. Professor of History, University of Cabo Verde, Praia, Cabo Verde (March 2019).

Domingos, Ziva. Director of National Museums in Angola (September 2019).

Dias, Adilson. Director of Museums, Cultural Heritage Institute, Praia, Cabo Verde (March 2019).

Endee, Juli. Musician and Cultural Ambassador, Liberia (April 2019).

Gates Jun., Henry Louis. Alphonse Fletcher University Professor and Director of the Hutchins Center for African and American Research, Harvard University, US (October 2023).

Jouga, Anne. Former Deputy Mayor of Gorée, Senegal (August 2015).

Holl, Augustin. President of the International Scientific Committee of UNESCO's General History of Africa. Interviewed in Luanda (September 2019) and London (December 2019).

Ikwubuzo, Iwu. Professor of Igbo Studies, University of Lagos, Nigeria (November 2018).

Perbi, Akosua A. Professor of History, University of Ghana, Accra, Ghana (November 2018).

Phiri, Bizeck J. Professor of History, University of Zambia (August 2018).

Tagro, Francis. Curator, Museum of Civilizations of Côte d'Ivoire, Abidjan, Côte d'Ivoire (April 2019).

Toe, Henry 'Amaze'. Musician and activist, Liberia (April 2019).

Personal correspondence

Lovejoy, Paul. Distinguished Research Professor and Canada Research Chair at York University. Email correspondence with the author (November 2017).

Chapter 15: Land, Gold and Greed

Books and articles

Ade Ajayi, J. F (editor). *UNESCO General History of Africa VI: Africa in the Nineteenth Century until the 1880s* (James Currey/ UNESCO, 1998).

Baskaran, Gracelin. 'Could Africa replace China as the world's source of rare earth elements?', Brookings Institution, 29 December 2022.

Chanaiwa, David S. 'The Zulu Revolution: State Formation in a Pastoralist Society', *African Studies Review*, 23 (3), (1980): 1–20.

Golan, Daphna. 'The Life Story of King Shaka and Gender Tensions in the Zulu State', *History in Africa*, 17 (1990): 95–111.

Joyce, Peter. *A Concise Dictionary of South African Biography* (Francolin Publishers, 1999).

Malaba, Mbongeni Z. 'Super-Shaka: Mazisi Kunene's "Emperor Shaka the Great", *Research in African Literatures*, 19 (4), (1988): 477–88.

Meredith, Martin. *The Fortunes of Africa: A 5,000 Year History of Wealth, Greed and Endeavour* (Simon & Schuster, 2014).

Ogot, B.A (editor). *UNESCO General History of Africa V: Africa from the Sixteenth to the Eighteenth Century* (James Currey/ UNESCO, 1999).

Shillington, Kevin. *History of Africa* (Bloomsbury Academic, 2018).

Interviews

Buthelezi, Prince Mangosuthu. Prince, Former Chief Minister of the KwaZulu government and great great-nephew of Shaka Zulu, South Africa (August 2018).

Penn, Nigel. Professor of History, University of Cape Town, South Africa (February 2020).

Simpson, Thula. Associate Professor of History, University of Pretoria, South Africa (August 2018).

Thabede, Bongi. Zulu cultural expert, South Africa (August 2018).

Chapter 16: The Kingdom of Kongo and the Scramble for Africa

Books, articles and reports

Adu Boahen, A (editor). *UNESCO General History of Africa VII: Africa under Colonial Domination 1880-1935* (James Currey/ UNESCO, 1997).

Akyeampong, Emmanuel K. *Independent Africa* (Indiana University Press, 2023).

Brockman, Norman C. *An African Biographical Dictionary* (Grey House Publishing, 2006).

Commonwealth Observer Group, 'Kenya General Election: 9 August 2022' (Commonwealth Secretariat, 2023).

Heywood, Linda M. *Njinga of Angola: Africa's Warrior Queen* (Harvard University Press, 2017).

Ki-Zerbo, J. and Niane, D.T (editors). *UNESCO General History of Africa IV: Africa from the Twelfth to the Sixteenth Century* (James Currey/UNESCO, 1997).

Michalopoulos, Stelios and Papaioannou, Elias. 'The Long-Run Effects of the Scramble for Africa', *American Economic Review*, 106 (7), (2016): 1802–48.

Thornton, John K. *The Kingdom of Kongo: Civil War and Transition 1641–1718* (The University of Wisconsin, 1983).

Interviews

Dianzinga, Scholastique. Professor of History, Marien Ngouabi University, Brazzaville, Republic of the Congo (July 2019).

Domingos, Ziva. Director, National Museums of Angola (September 2019).

Inamizi, Dominique M. Politician and member of the Bayeke royal family, Katanga (July 2019).

Khanakwa, Pamela. Historian, Makerere University, Uganda (May 2019).

Mukanda-Bantu, Kalasa. Member of the Bayeke royal family, Katanga (July 2019).

Kashoka, Ignitius Mawala. Chief Ngabwe of the Ngabwe District, Zambia (August 2018).

Nyaga, James. Research Scientist – History, National Museums of Kenya (May 2019).

Santana, Eugénio Pinto. Doctoral student in Anthropology, Eduardo Mondlane University, Mozambique (August 2018).

Zidi, Joseph. Professor of History, Marien Ngouabi University, Brazzaville, Republic of the Congo (July 2019).

Chapter 17: Africa's Resistance and Liberation

Books and articles

Adebowale, Oludamola. 'The Labour of Our Heroes' Past Must Never Be in Vain', *Guardian Nigeria News*, 2 October 2022.

Adu Boahen, A (editor). *UNESCO General History of Africa VII: Africa under Colonial Domination 1880-1935* (James Currey/ UNESCO, 1997).

Akyeampong, Emmanuel K. *Independent Africa* (Indiana University Press, 2023).

de Haas, Michiel and Emmanuel K. Akyeampong. 'Interview: Emmanuel Akyeampong', African Economic History Network, 12 February 2018.

Mazrui, Ali A (editor). *UNESCO General History of Africa VIII: Africa since 1935* (James Currey/UNESCO, 1999).

Samatar, Said S. *Oral Poetry and Somali Nationalism: The Case of Sayyid Mahammad 'Abdille Hasan*, African Studies Series no. 32 (Cambridge University Press, 1982).

Interviews

Al Mahdi, Sadiq. Former Prime Minister of Sudan (April 2019).

Boudir, Haj Zubeir. Veteran of the Algerian War of Independence. Algiers (March 2016).

Chifita, Henru Sibbaba. Chief, Kabwata, Zambia (August 2018).

wa Kahengeri, Shujaa Gitu. Secretary General, Mau Mau War Veterans Association, Kenya (May 2019).

Khanakwa, Pamela. Historian, Makerere University, Uganda (May 2019).

Kimongi, Rachel. Kenyan farmer, Nairobi (May 2019).

Kuti, Seun. Nigerian musician (April 2019).

Lumumba, François. Businessman and son of Patrice Lumumba, Kinshasa, Democratic Republic of Congo (July 2019).

Mpyangu, Christine M. Lecturer in Religion and Peace Studies, Makerere University, Uganda (May 2019).

Ndaywel è Nziem, Isidore. Historian and Professor, University of Kinshasa, Democratic Republic of the Congo (July 2019).

Nkrumah, Samia. Politician and daughter of Kwame Nkrumah, the first President of Ghana (November 2018).

Nyaga, James. Research Scientist – History, National Museums of Kenya (May 2019).

Ombongi, Kenneth S. Senior Lecturer and Chairman, Department of History and Archaeology, University of Nairobi, Kenya (May 2019).

Senghor, Racine. Chairman, Museum of Black Civilizations, Dakar, Senegal (August 2015).

Epilogue: A New Africa

Books and articles

Adebowale, Oludamola. 'Nigeria60: Reflections on "Then and Now"', Horniman Museum & Gardens, 24 September 2020, https://www.horniman.ac.uk/story/nigeria60-reflections-on-then-and-now/.

Africa-Europe Foundation. 'The Africa-Europe Foundation Report 2022', October 2022, https://back.africaeuropefoundation.org/uploads/AEF_High_Level_Group_Report_2022_dbf2bbfd35.pdf.

Commonwealth Observer Group. 'Kenya General Election: 9 August 2022' (Commonwealth Secretariat, 2023).

Africa-Europe Foundation. 'Transforming Dialogue into Action', Impact Report, April 2023, https://back.africaeuropefoundation.org/uploads/Impact_2022_82250106b7.pdf.

Lopes, Carlos. 'Africa must pursue industrialisation sustainably', LSE Blog, 3 August 2023, https://blogs.lse.ac.uk/africaatlse/2023/08/03/africa-must-pursue-industrialisation-sustainably/.

Mo Ibrahim Foundation. 'Africa's Youth: Jobs or Migration?', Forum Report, April 2019, https://mo.ibrahim.foundation/sites/default/files/2020-05/2019-forum-report_0.pdf.

Mo Ibrahim Foundation. 'Global Africa: Africa in the world and the world in Africa', April 2023, https://mo.ibrahim.foundation/sites/default/files/2023-04/2023-facts-figures-global-africa.pdf.

Ossé, Lionel. 'Afrobarometer Dispatch No. 461', 1 July 2021, https://www.afrobarometer.org/wp-content/uploads/2022/02/ad461-ghanaians_united_and_tolerant_-_except_toward_same-sex_relationships-afrobarometer_dispatch-29june21.pdf.

Townsend, Robert; Ronchi, Loraine; Brett, Chris; Moses, Gene. 'Future of Food: Maximizing Finance for Development in Agricultural Value Chains', World Bank, 16 April 2018.

Speeches

Adesina, Akinwumi A., President, African Development Bank Group. Speech at the official launch of the Investment in Digital and Creative Industries, State House Conference Center, Abuja, Nigeria, 14 March 2023, https://www.afdb.org/en/news-and-events/multimedia/video/dr-akinwumi-adesinas-keynote-statement-launch-investment-digital-and-creative-enterprises-program-idice-abuja-14-march-2023-59788.

Okonjo-Iweala, Ngozi. Director-General, World Trade Organization. Speech at Global Economy Prize 2023, The Kiel Institute for the World Economy, Germany, 19 June 2023. Written transcript received in private correspondence.

Illustration Credits

The publisher and author have made serious efforts to trace the copyright owners of some of the images in this book and have been unable to do so. The publisher and author are willing to acknowledge any rightful copyright owner on substantive proof of ownership and would be grateful for any information as to their identity.

p. 12 'The bone fragments belonging to Lucy' © Bloomberg / Contributor / Getty; **p. 40** 'The Narmer Palette' © Heritage Image Partnership Ltd / Alamy Stock Photo; **p. 50** 'Sphinx of Hatshepsut' © Tomas Abad / Alamy Stock Photo; **p. 55** 'Statue of Ramesses II', 8 October 2010, uploaded by Pbuergler, Wikimedia Commons under Creative Commons Attribution-Share Alike 3.0 Unported license; **p. 68** 'Western Deffufa' © Design Pics Inc / Alamy Stock Photo; **p. 69** 'Kerma grave' © Matthias Gehricke; **p. 87** 'Granite statues of the Kushite kings', courtesy of Charles Bonnet; **p. 90** 'Pyramids of Meroe, Sudan' © Maurice Brand / Alamy Stock Photo; **p. 101** 'Sphinx' courtesy of the Eritrean embassy; **p. 104** 'Coin, Endubis, Aksumite Kingdom' © The Trustees of the British Museum; **p. 111** 'AXUM. Ezanas. Circa 330-360', 8 February 2022, published by Classical Numismatic Group (CNG) Coins on Wikimedia under Creative Commons Attribution-Share Alike 3.0 Unported license and GNU Free Documentation License; **p. 112** '4th century King Ezana's Stela at the Northern Stelae Park in Axum' © Arterra Picture Library / Alamy Stock Photo; **p. 126** 'Rock-Hewn Churches' © UNESCO / Francesco Bandarin, published under Creative Commons Attribution-Share Alike 3.0 IGO license; **p. 143** 'Massinissa, circa 240-148

Empire' © The History Collection / Alamy Stock Photo; **p. 332** 'Stowage of the British slave ship *Brookes* under the regulated slave trade act of 1788', December 1788, Plymouth Chapter of the Society for Effecting the Abolition of the Slave Trade, Wikimedia Commons, public domain; **p. 341** 'The interesting Narrative of the Life of Olaudah Equiano' © Abu Castor / Alamy Stock Photo; **p. 367** 'Sketch of King Shaka', illustration by James King, 1824, featured in *Travels and Adventures in Eastern Africa* by Nathaniel Isaacs (1836), Wikimedia Commons, public domain; **p. 382** 'King Lobengula' © Hulton Archive / Stringer / Getty; **p. 389** Queen Njinga statue courtesy of Zeinab Badawi; **p. 395** Cavazzi, Giovanni Antonio. Relation historique de l'Ethiopie occidentale: contenant la description des royaumes de Congo, Angelle, & Matamba. A Paris: Chez C.J.B. Delespine le fils, 1732. v.4, Harvard University; **p. 408** 'Amputation' © Universal History Archive / Contributor / Getty; **p. 424** 'The Mahdi' © Rischgitz / Stringer / Getty; **p. 441** Nkrumah and family courtesy of Samia Nkrumah, Nkrumah family collection; photographer unknown; **p. 444** Gitu wa Kahengeri courtesy of Zeinab Badawi; **p. 451** 'Deposed Congo Prime Minister Patrice Lumumba' © Associated Press / Alamy Stock Photo; photograph by Horst Faas, taken 2 December 1960

Acknowledgements

I have many people to thank for their advice, encouragement and expertise. First, Professor Augustin Holl, Dr Ali Moussa Iye and Lamine Diagne were instrumental in the success of UNESCO's *General History of Africa* project; they and many other wonderful African academics and contributors inspired me and made this book possible. I have received ideas, facts and phrases from so many sources and conversations, informal and formal, that I cannot acknowledge every single one in this book, but please know I am so grateful to you all. Thank you to UNESCO's Director General during the period of my research, Irina Bokova, along with her deputy Getachew Engida and Assistant Director General Francesco Bandarin, for their unwavering support for this project. I am grateful to the eminent historians Professor Sir David Cannadine and Dr Kevin Shillington, who read early drafts of the book and gave me substantial support and confidence, as well as Professors William Beinart, Emmanual Gyimah-Boadi, Christian Happi and Dr Nicholas Westcott, who imparted insights for the epliogue and some of the chapters. My gratitude goes to the team from the *History of Africa* television series: James Hickmann, Bridget Osborne, Dina Selim and especially Lucy Doggett. My deepest thanks go to Bertrand Facon, who with his painstaking forensic skills combed through every detail demanding ever greater clarity of thought, as well as to James Facon for his invaluable assistance in sourcing maps and images. An enormous thank you to Tom Killingbeck, my literary agent at A.M. Heath who started this journey with me and provided a bottomless well of encouragement, and to my editors at Penguin Random House, Jamie Joseph and Amanda Waters, who guided me with enthusiasm and verve every step of the way, along with all the publishing team. Thank you to Leah Jacobs-Gordon for her stunning jacket design. Above all, I express my deepest gratitude to my son Joseph Badawi-Crook, who with his intellectual brilliance and erudition read every draft of this book and gave invaluable feedback on content, made corrections and injected zing and style; I owe him an immense debt for his time, diligence and commitment. Finally, thanks to all my loved ones for their patience! It has been a long and amazing journey of discovery and learning for me, and I hope you found that it was for you too.

Index